CLUTTER Be Gone!

Cleaning Your House
the Easy Way

DON ASLETT

BETTERWAY BOOKS
CINCINNATI, OHIO

Other fine Betterway Books are available from your local bookstore or direct from the publisher.

10 09 08 07 06   8 7 6 5 4

ISBN-13:   978-1-55870-538-8
ISBN-10:   1-55870-538-4

Table of Contents

The Ultimate Self-Improvement Book

This book will make you happier, freer, neater, richer, and smarter. With a little help from you, it will solve more home, family, marriage, career, and economic problems than any book you've ever read. De-junking your life will cost nothing and will pay 100 percent returns.

" *You'll immediately lose 100 pounds without dieting* "

INTRODUCTION

It *is* a pretty good life, isn't it? We might have a few stresses and strains, but as a whole, we're safe and well fed and sheltered, surrounded with plenty, comfort, luxury, convenience, and freedom. We can, one way or another, attain the pleasures, places, and things we want—when and where we want them. Most of us do just that—attain, accumulate, collect—but plenty always seems to require more. Enough is never enough.

Then the big hitch comes—when we realize that all that comfort, convenience, and *stuff* really costs. We have to pay for it, keep track of it, protect it, clean it, store it, insure it, and worry about it. This takes energy and effort (in fact, a great part of your life). Later we have to move it, hide it, apologize for it, argue over it.

It stifles us and robs us of freedom because it requires so much of our time to tend. We have no time to have fun, to do the things we really want to do. Not only are our houses, drawers, closets, and vehicles so crowded we can't breathe, but our minds, emotions, and relationships, too, are crowded into dullness and immobility. We're so surrounded with stuff, we don't even have time for the people who mean the most to us.

Finally—often too late—we realize that most of that which has surrounded us, choking out good living, squeezing the physical and emotional life out of us, is just junk—*clutter.*

Millions of us are here, with feelings and sensitivity gone. Our life not only seems to be but *is* swallowed up. We don't own ourselves any more; we feel smothered and depressed.

Getting the clutter out of your life can and will rid you of more discouragement. tiredness, and boredom than anything else you can do.

There really is a solution

In this book I will try to help you:

1. Learn to identify junk and clutter, since *you* are the one who ultimately has to do it.

2. Realize what clutter is doing to you personally.

3. Give you some practical direction on de-junking.

Start now

I promise you no recipe, remedy, reorganization, or rebuilding plan will renew you like the simple, easy, inexpensive process of de-junking. I hope you'll find this book the catalyst to get the job done.

Junkee Entrance Exam

DIRECTIONS: Read the question, then rate yourself. . . .
Circle your answer and transfer the number to the "score" column.

	MORE THAN I'LL EVER ADMIT TO	MORE THAN I'D LIKE	ONLY A FEW THINGS	NONE	SCORE
1. If I had to move to Hawaii suddenly, how much stuff would end up in the alley?	1	2	3	5	
2. If my closets and drawers were searched right now, how much junk would be found?	1	2	3	5	
3. I have more-than-a-year-old magazines stored/lying around.	1	2	3	5	
4. I am carrying around excess pounds.	1	2	3	5	
5. I own clothes that won't fit or are ugly or hopelessly out of style.	1	2	3	5	
6. I have shoes I don't like or don't wear.	1	2	3	5	
7. I have old games/puzzles/patterns with pieces missing.	1	2	3	5	
8. I have photos I seldom look at because they're stashed away and hard to find.	1	2	3	5	
9. I watch junk shows on TV and junk movies.	1	2	3	5	
10. I have keepsakes that I can't remember what sake they were kept for.	1	2	3	5	
11. I keep toys (adult or juvenile) that are broken, outgrown, or not used.	1	2	3	5	
12. I save old uniforms or maternity/baby clothes I don't need any more.	1	2	3	5	
13. I use drugs, medicines, seltzers, salves, and treatments (prescribed and unprescribed).	1	2	3	5	
14. If I held a garage sale, how much stuff would my customers get to paw through?	1	2	3	5	

	MORE THAN I'LL EVER ADMIT TO	MORE THAN I'D LIKE	ONLY A FEW THINGS	NONE	SCORE
15. I have paraphernalia from hobbies, projects, and classes I started and "may someday" re-activate.	1	2	3	5	
16. When someone visits my home, how many excuses does my junk seem to call for?	1	2	3	5	
17. How many unused recipe cards/cookbooks/do-it-yourself manuals do I have?	1	2	3	5	
18. I consume colas, coffee, and other stimulants to revive me and keep me going.	1	2	3	5	
19. I have machinery and appliances that don't work or have parts missing.	1	2	3	5	
20. I store old paint (half-cans or less), stiff brushes, and matted rollers.	1	2	3	5	
21. I hang onto broken or never-used hair gadgets (dryers, stylers, hot combs, electric curlers, etc.).	1	2	3	5	
22. I have empty no-return or other honestly useless bottles inhabiting my house.	1	2	3	5	
23. I have old wedding announcements, greeting, or Christmas cards squirreled away from acquaintances I scarcely recall.	1	2	3	5	
24. I keep unread junk mail and lapsed driver's licenses and expired policies.	1	2	3	5	
25. My medicine chest holds bottles of ancient vitamins and antique prescriptions.	1	2	3	5	
26. I have furniture or other items I am going to fix, sell, or refinish some day.	1	2	3	5	
27. I have souvenirs or knickknacks that I dust, clean, store, and abhor.	1	2	3	5	
28. I use toppings, dressings, spices, and sauces on my food.	1	2	3	5	
29. I keep plain old ordinary empty boxes.	1	2	3	5	
30. I save leftover scraps of Christmas wrap or rumpled gift wrap that I never use.	1	2	3	5	
31. I have bad habits that really mess up my life.	1	2	3	5	
32. I've kept books and paperbacks I couldn't force myself to finish.	1	2	3	5	
33. I clip out coupons and special offers on products that I never buy.	1	2	3	5	
34. I save colognes and after-shaves I can't stand the smell of, or makeup I tried and didn't like.	1	2	3	5	

	MORE THAN I'LL EVER ADMIT TO	MORE THAN I'D LIKE	ONLY A FEW THINGS	NONE	SCORE
35. I save notes, clippings, ideas, and plans that haven't been filed or acted on.	1	2	3	5	
36. I eat sweet, salty, or greasy snacks or other junk food.	1	2	3	5	
37. I have old curtains or blinds stashed away that I've dragged from past residences.	1	2	3	5	
38. I keep old plans, patterns, and scraps of any kind that are probably destined never to be used.	1	2	3	5	
39. I spend time in places that I don't really enjoy.	1	2	3	5	
40. I save every drawing my children ever made, and all their school papers since the year one.	1	2	3	5	
41. I keep ballpoint pens that skip or dried-out felt-tip markers.	1	2	3	5	
42. I hoard odd socks or pantyhose with one ruined leg.	1	2	3	5	
43. I own costume jewelry, pins, badges, brooches that I never wear (for good reason).	1	2	3	5	
44. I don't throw out tools and gadgets I know are worthless.	1	2	3	5	
45. I have wristwatches or clocks that aren't working.	1	2	3	5	
46. The trunk, floor, and glove compartment of my car are filled with old torn maps, inoperative flashlights, and fast-food debris.	1	2	3	5	
47. I put up with people who hang on me and waste my time.	1	2	3	5	
48. If someone gave me $10 for every piece of junk I have, how much money would I get?	1	2	3	5	
				TOTAL	

0-100	100-150	150-175
A TERMINAL CASE . . . Therapy or a massive transplant might help, but maybe you should just give up.	THE END IS NEAR . . . You're in trouble. Read *Clutter Be Gone!* three times, gird your loins and start de-junking ruthlessly. You might possibly survive your junk.	YOU'RE ON THE BRINK . . . If you start to de-junk today, you can make it. Read *Clutter Be Gone!* and commit yourself to do it.

175-225	225-240	
THERE IS HOPE . . . If you can clean up/come to terms with those few problem areas, clutter won't have a chance to spread.	YOU ARE PURE. Read *Clutter Be Gone!* to perfect yourself and then pass it on to a junkee friend or relative.	

The biggest reason clutter piles up on us and chokes us out of living is because we know and use all manner of excuses to justify keeping it—which, if repeated in a reverent enough tone, no one will question.

We've heard ourselves and others spout these rationalizations so long that we think they're Scripture. But they're not; this is why I've taken the time to assemble some of the most common of the thousands of excuses I've collected from junkees over the years.

Breeze through this condensed list of invalid excuses—excuses you'll not be allowed to use when you begin to de-junk your life.

Let's start with a few of the classics:

Bent rolls of leftover Christmas wrap: *"I can always iron it."*

Correspondence and birthday cards from long-ago acquaintances you scarcely knew then (they probably moved to Chugwater, Wyoming): *"I need to copy these addresses off the envelopes."*

Abandoned do-it-yourself projects you found you *couldn't* **do yourself:** *"I'm going to write the company and tell them their instructions are lousy."*

A broken watch: *"It may never tell time but I can use the crystal for a magnifying glass in a survival situation."*

Ugly $8.99 wind chimes: *"I only bought them to change a twenty."*

Puzzles with pieces missing: *"Oh well, we never put them completely together anyway."*

Dresses and pants you haven't been able to zip for years: *"They're a good incentive to lose weight."*

Partly used bottles of the wrong color makeup: *"Who knows, maybe I'll get a tan next summer."*

Stacks of expired coupons for products you never buy: *"These are still some really good buys."*

Three-quarters-full notebooks from past classes: *"I may want to brush up on that someday."*

Recipes that bombed: *"I ought to give them one more chance."*

Dishpans and buckets that leak: *"These might be cute outside somewhere with petunias planted in them."*

Cheap ballpoint pen that mostly skips or won't write: *"Maybe I can pick up some cheap refills."*

Bottles of expired vitamins: *"Well, we'll just have to take twice as many of them now."*

Old piled-up blankets with frayed bindings: *"These can be used in a pinch for quilt bats."*

Faded bedspreads and curtains from former homes: *"Maybe I could dye them."*

Stacks of empty adding machine and aluminum foil and freezer paper rolls: *"I'm saving these for when I have grandchildren."*

Leftover roll-ends and scraps of wallpaper: *"Someday I'll build a doll house."*

A plumple: *"The poor kids in India are starving; I can't let this banana split go to waste."*

A chain smoker: *"It takes a lot more guts to face up to cancer than to quit smoking."*

Never-used gadgets and fancy attachments for now-defunct equipment: *"This is still a perfectly good automatic toenail polisher."*

Long outdated packets of garden seeds: *"Those expiration dates are just gimmicks to get you to buy new seeds."*

Favorite parlor games with half the pieces missing: *"If we buy a new one, we can use these as spare parts."*

Assortment of four-inch-wide neckties: *"You never know when these will come back in style."*

Pantyhose with a two-inch runner up one leg: *"I can always wear them with slacks."*

Owner of a world-class junk collection: *"It runs in my blood—show me a Dane [Pole, Italian, Scot, German, etc.] and I'll show you a clutter collector."*

Cheap bargain-store tools you've found to be worthless: *"I'll save these to loan to the neighbors."*

The dresses you used to wear with go-go boots: *"I can always convert these to tunics."*

Tangled wads of leftover yarn and embroidery floss: *"These will give me something to do on a rainy day."*

Three extra cars: *"I'm the victim of a materialistic society."*

Hand-knitted slippers with the bottom nearly gone: *"The top is just fine; I can always wear socks with them."*

Half-read books you couldn't force yourself to finish: *"If I get jailed, snowed in, or hospitalized, these will be my salvation."*

1901-1958 sewing patterns: *"I'm waiting till I have a chance to go through them."*

The circa 1940 refrigerator: *"It doesn't work too well, but it has beautiful lines."*

Lone earring: *"I can always make it into a pendant."*

The float you made for the Fourth of July parade six years ago: *"I still have plenty of room for it."*

Old chamber pot: *"I'm saving it for a white elephant party."*

Can of apple filling that went down the Colorado River with you: *"But we went through a lot together."*

Stuck-together stamp collection: *"One man's junk is another man's treasure."*

Pots from all the plants that died: *"If I'm de-junked, I'll be too sterile a person."*

Lidless cookie jar: *"Throwing innocent objects into the garbage seems merely a step away from murder!"*

Fabric scraps your mother, sisters, cousins, and friends were delighted to get rid of: *"I'm a natural scavenger."*

The stained and sagging couch that's perfect for the family room you don't have: *"I'm saving this in case I have to furnish another house."*

The great horned owl head your Uncle Otto left you: *"It would cost too much to replace."*

"It's a conversation piece."
It gives people who come to my home something to talk about: "What's that?" "What does it do?" "How old is it?" "Amazing." (Does this mean you're too boring to get by without it?)

"Someday I intend to fix it."
See pages 31-51. *"I'll have more time later."* This is sometimes expressed as—to fix it . . . to finish it . . . start it . . . look further into it. . . . Another variation on this is *"When I retire I'm going to. . . . "*
Who would dare doubt a senior citizen's dream? I don't really need to comment on this, do I? Who ever has more time later? Have you gotten any less busy as you've grown older?

"It's been in the family for years!"
"I might want to look at it for old time's sake."
"I'm saving it for posterity."
"I'm sentimental."

See pages 88-111 for some guidance through this quagmire of guilt and good intentions.

"I paid good money for this."
See pages 196-202

"I'm married to the head pack rat."
See pages 204-221

"**W**hy do I keep it? Because of 'someday'. Someday I'll quit doing PTA business, diaper business, my husband's business, and I'll have time to try out 597 recipes, file a few thousand magazine articles, and leisurely reread all my old *Reader's Digest*s. Someday there'll be a bread sack shortage and I'll need 1,300 bread sacks. Someday they'll pay me for my old telephone pole insulators. But someday is like tomorrow—it never comes."

Stacks of Christmas cards you got in years gone by: *"I'm going to take up decoupage when I retire."*

Half-finished sewing project that you ended up hating: *"Maybe when my daughter gets this size she'll finish it."*

Twenty-three-year-old shorthand book: *"I bought it to learn shorthand as a spare-time project. I know I'll never get around to it, but if I throw the book away it means I've given up. As long as I have it, there's hope."*

Tons of clutter can trace its ancestry to a worthwhile enterprise. The excuse for keeping it is: I'm saving it for a (Scout, 4-H, church, school, hobby, club, class) project. This might have been true ten years or even ten months ago, but if an undertaking is dead—I mean its interest or its value lost to age, geography, or a change of friends and interests—*don't keep it*, even if it has cash value. Give it away or sell it before it drains all the energy it once gave you. *Decide!* (whether you want to learn shorthand, want to finish that dust ruffle or not). The unresolved is probably unnecessary.

Aftershave and cologne you never liked the smell of, a wallet you wouldn't be caught dead carrying, knock-'em-dead earrings that will indeed, a tie not even Dick Tracy would wear, a crewel covered bridge that does *NOT* belong in your living room: *"I hate to hurt Aunt Annie's feelings."*

Yes, it's worthless, but it was a *gift*—you'd have to be a heartless wretch to throw out any gift. You have to keep it and maybe even display it, don't you?

See pages 88-111 for some guidance on this sticky subject. And remember: Why did someone give a gift to you in the first place? As a *token* of feeling and appreciation. Love isn't a tangible thing, so whether you keep the gift or not it has no effect on that all-important relationship between you and the giver. Many of us junk gift keepers are insecure or egotistical—we have to keep and display the "evidence" to assure ourselves that we're loved.

Those Wonderful Second-Bests

Is second-best clutter or "just-in-case?" Add up all your second-bests and tell me what you're doing with them now. I'll give you a few minutes.................

Can't think of much but "spares," eh? I'll help you. You've just bought a new watch, work boots, briefcase, gloves, blender, fishing pole, tennis racket, butcher knife, tea kettle, sewing machine, bike, salad bowl. Where are the second-bests?

OK, a little more help. Why did you obtain a best? That's easy: because you were unhappy with the old one—it was worn, old, getting ugly, not working right any more, or you were simply tired of it. Why do we keep things we're not happy with? No answer, except that we're clutter collectors. It's just like an old piece of chewing gum: we hate to pitch it because it still works (has no flavor but plenty of flex!). Sure, there's some glimmer of hope for those old worn watches, stiff work boots, leaky air mattresses, the bike with the bent frame, the too-small briefcase, that battered and shabby purse, that balding dress coat, the nicked butcher knife with the cracked handle, your no-longer-favorite rifle—but once you have the new in hand, those seconds (like the gum) have lost their flavor. Once you get your ego snuggled up to the new one you'll never want to be seen with the old one again—don't keep it around to disflavor your life!

Here's an example: everyone I know has a suitcase with a broken latch. After it pops open on the airport carrousel or in the cheerleaders' bus, they're shamed into the purchase of a nice new "best." But the old one is never pitched; it's a "spare" or "extra" that to justify its retired status is filled with junk and stored.

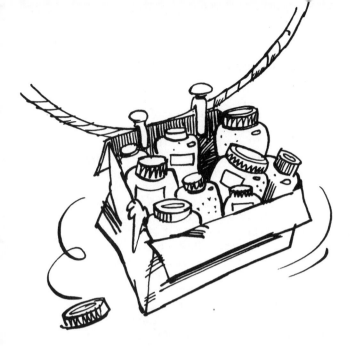

"It may come in handy someday."
"I may need it someday."

You may be right, *if you can find it*.

"Button, button, who's got the button" isn't just a funny game for the family, but a frustrating reality for all those who strip and save old buttons. A few spares are wisdom; a few jars full are runamuck junk you'll spend hours pawing through (once you find the jars).

Most people can't find it or forget where they put something when they do "need it someday"—so they usually end up buying another one.

Another version of this old favorite is: "I'll always be ready for _____." The only thing clutter collectors are always ready for is to rummage to try and find something they think is there. People free of unnecessary "stuff" are really the only ones who are prepared for action.

"This _____ is still perfectly good."
"I'm saving it for spare parts."

Ever notice that when someone throws out an old shoe, the leather is probably still worth almost what it cost when the shoe was new? Nobody has trouble pitching the shoe, but everyone takes out the old lace and keeps it forever. I've hardly met a person who doesn't do that, and haven't met anybody who ever uses the lace!

If there's anything resembling a good part on something worn or broken, we want to strip it off and save it, whether we need it or not: buttons, buckles, belts, the feathers and bands from old hats, doorknobs, shades that will never look good on another lamp, any old wheel or tire.

Watch it, or strip or "rescue" junk will strap you. What was once an important instinct is in this modern day (when time and space are more valuable than most manufactured items or materials) a mighty questionable venture. Do you really have room to keep it, or time to inventory it *in case* you can ever use it again? If you're honest with yourself, you'll realize you probably don't.

> "*S*omeday I'm gonna need it! When the Lord comes in the Millennium, He may ask me for that ice-cream scoop with the broken handle, those boxes of baby food jars, the bottoms of all my cut-off Levis, or the pile of paper bags (all folded neatly)."

"As soon as I get rid of it, I'll need it."

This is one of the feeblest of all feeble excuses. The truth is, the day after we get rid of it (*if* we ever do) the guilt of feeling like we murdered it mounts up, so for the next two years we unconsciously search for a use and always find some weak application to feed the feeling that we prematurely disposed of it. It's like the light fixture we took out of the living room during a remodeling job six years ago. It was junk then, but keeping it made us feel better. Several months after we chuck it, one of our new ginger jars goes on the blink—and our junking soul instantly activates the old "I knew I should have kept it." If we did have it, *we wouldn't use it anyway.* Only the fact that it's gone gives us the courage to consider it.

Evidence Junk

Dumping our raw, glaring, worthless junk is easy, but on the second go-round I found, undumped:

1. Three boxes of original edited manuscript and rough art from my first published book.

2. A drawerful of worn-out work gloves.

3. My first wristwatch I bought in 1949.

4. My college textbooks.

None of this stuff was of any use to me—and certainly not to anyone else, so why did I keep it? For *evidence.* Because it seems that nothing can beat hard cold evidence as a souvenir of our maiden voyages through life.

Junk proves that I was there: that I once had a 26-inch waist, that I once did score 31 points in that game against Inkom, that I once had curly blond hair. . . .

I wanted to have my "original" manuscript to show off in writer's speeches, to show my kids or clients what I went through to write a book. I wore out all those gloves in three weeks building a large masonry shop in my spare time; I showed off the gloves and they made a striking impression, but less and less of one every year. The fact that the building stands there or that the book is still in print is surely evidence enough, far more impressive than any of this "evidence junk." Evidence junk is among the most difficult to dispose of; the best solution is probably to spread it out and photograph it—dive down in the middle of it if you must, and have someone take a snapshot of you embracing it (with a look of convincing reverence on your face). Take slides; then you can project your evidence on a wall, or get a color print made so you can flaunt it easier.

"But they aren't making it any more."
"They aren't making these the way they used to."
"Someday you won't be able to buy one of these."

Those may indeed be true statements, but why do you suppose they quit making them in the first place? Simple—there was no market, there was no longer enough demand for it to produce it. It was out of date, out of style, or something else now does what it did better or easier. You can bet that if a thing is valuable from *any* angle, someone in our competitive economy will make it available for the market.

Stored in remote corners of buildings you'll find, under the dust and cobwebs, 900-pound woodstoves, retired mangles, old treadle sewing machines, 40-pound frying pans, ghastly huge (and warped) pieces of furniture, massive electric roasters, 12-foot clocks with chimes so loud you can only turn them on for

exhibition, etc. Their era is gone; they've been replaced by lighter, quicker, safer things—but because they're thick, heavy, and have put in service time, we keep and coddle them. It's amazing the tools we keep for things we don't need to do any more—from bucksaws, cranks, and butter churns to fire bellows and buggy-whip winders. I love these old things, and marvel at the sentiment they can stir, but we can't keep the whole farm. If we keep too many of them for "atmosphere," we won't be able to breathe.

How many of us want to hunt with a 19-pound smoking flintlock shotgun when we can use a sleek 7-pound self-loading automatic? Who wants to lug a 70-pound hinged hardwood trunk through airports when a 5-pound nonsagging fiberglass suitcase will do the job better? Sturdiness alone is not a reason to keep the old; if so we would still use covered wagons, wooden shoes, and serge stockings. If you're unwilling to *use* something (do you really want to fuss with an icebox?), if you hardly ever *look* at it, if it doesn't delight your soul or stir memories every time you look at it, if it's just rotting out in the shed—do it (and yourself) justice by getting rid of it.

Selling Your Junk . . .
Some False Hope

"It may be worth something someday."
"It will be an antique someday."
"It will be valuable someday."

The glittering illusion of the possibility that someday you might be able to sell that piece of junk for a phenomenal sum creates an excuse to cling to even the most worthless items. All sorts of appetite-whetting success stories appear in the media, telling how some lucky soul wandered into his attic and found a rare old coin, kettle, or credenza that made him rich. Don't let that hope get you out of perspective—only a few pieces of junk in tens of thousands are rare and valuable, and if you averaged the value of all the hours spent to sort and clean it up to sell it, your wages would probably be about 7¢ an hour. There isn't much cash in your closet, mostly clutter. I've seen many people spend $100 on gas, signs, and advertising for a garage sale to take in $50—and that isn't profitable either in terms of the pocketbook or of your life's time taken.

If you have doubts in your bouts of deciding what to keep, don't waste time listening to friends (fellow junkers). Take a few minutes and call an expert and ask, "How much is a 1917 corn husker worth?" You'll know instantly—and can then make a decision to keep or sell. Many a clutter keeper has gone to a lot of trouble to keep worthless stuff because he "imagined" its worth. Remember, since the onset of mass production and the craze for antiques and collectibles, fewer and fewer items are scarce enough to become valuable. (Yes, that does cast suspicion on your set of commemorative moon landing glasses and Bicentennial bell jars.)

The Ubiquitous *They*

"They left it . . .," *"They* gave it . . .," *"They* bought it . . .," *"They* insisted . . . ."

This excuse was eloquently demonstrated by a fellow passenger at the airport who walked ahead of me to the baggage-claim area. It was apparent he had been gone awhile from the way his family swarmed him; after all the hugging his wife cast a quick glance at him and said in a disappointed voice, "Looks like you ate well." He patted his protruding middle: "Yes, I must have gained ten pounds—*they* fed us to death, *they* served too much, *they* should have eased up, but *they* didn't, *they* put lots of pounds on all of us." One of the kids piped up: "Those people just don't care how you look," and they all left, the blame for the weight squarely on the feeder, not the feedee.

A cruel fact of clutter is that there is no one to blame—it is mostly *our* fault. Yet we often feel abused—the "world" (our parents, our mate, the government, the company, our society) has inflicted it on us, we were innocent bystanders, seduced and left wounded.

My favorite wall motto:
"Your situation is exactly what you make it, or what you allow it to be."

No one guides your quivering hand in a junk shop but you, no one holds your face in junk reading, viewing, and listening, no one but you says yes or no, keep it or throw it. Your present clutter quotient is where *you* put it, where *you* allow it to be. None of the excuses listed in this chapter (or any new ones you might think up) can excuse clutter or the damage it will do.

For Hard Times' Sake

"I was raised during the Depression and we were taught to save everything. . . ."

"I'm saving it for hard times." We've all heard this one, and I've saved it till now because it's a real heartbreaker. It would be downright reckless to stop saving for hard times—or would it?

Horror stories of the Great Depression have planted fear in all of us and if such a dire event should roll around again, we want to be somehow prepared. Hair-raising stories from our folks and grandfolks of no food, fuel, tools, toys, or blankets give us a compassionate view of all of the clutter they're stashing away. Believe it or not, there are lots of "depression savers," who survived the last one and are saving *everything*—rewearable, restorable, reusable, or not—to have on hand during a coming downswing.

There is good news and bad news for you depression savers.

The good news is that your junk *will* have a use during the next depression—as fuel for your fire to keep you warm. The bad news is that the last thing of value will be junk. No one will have cash to buy your clutter except the filthy rich, who will already have too much of their own junk to guard. Stash food, friends, talent—those might save you. When things get tough, the less you have to tote, store, keep warm, and watch out for, the better off you'll be.

Hard times were put well in perspective by a clutter confession I received in the mail:

All my life I've been told to save for hard times. So all my life I've saved for harder times to come. But no matter how hard times got, it has never been hard enough to use or re-use all the worn-out, broken junk I've saved. I finally realized that the hard times come when you try to clean around it, keep track of it, or move to another house. Please help me to not want to save everything that passes before me.

Don't Let Clutter Make a Monkey Out of You

We've all heard the story of monkey traps. When hunters discovered how greedy and possessive monkeys are, instead of running them down with nets and spears, they took coconuts, made a hole in each of them, tied them to a tree, and went home. The next morning they'd return to find dozens of wild monkeys, unharmed, with their little hands stuck in the coconuts. How did this work? Simple: the hole in the coconut was cut just big enough for a monkey's hand to squeeze through; inside the coconut were placed some tasty goodies (maybe monkey M&Ms). The monkeys would creep up on the trap, smell the bait, reach in and grab a fistful of whatever—and when they tried to bring their hand out, the fist of course wouldn't pass through the hole. The monkeys all jumped and screamed and struggled to get free, but unwilling to release the bait, they were caught.

Now being smart humans, we instantly reason: "Why didn't the stupid monkeys

let go of the stuff, pull their hands out, and run away?" Well, they didn't because they are, in that respect, human. They refused to let go of something they had. To hang on meant the stewpot, but the thrill of possession overruled all risk and reason.

We could all entertain a crowd of monkeys for hours with our "junk traps"—all of us have clamped onto things and even though they have us trapped, immobilized, stripped and strapped, we hang on, refusing to release and run away to better, safer things. The monkeys at least have the excuse of being hungry; for much less good reasons we want our goodies so much that our minds, like the monkey's fist, close up and there's no giving up. Like the monkeys, we jump and scream to go and do and are denied because we refuse to turn loose our loot.

Too often we confuse ownership with companionship, not realizing that certain things, even good things, change and lose their value and we don't need them any more. We've outgrown, outlasted them, or something new and better has come along. We have to release them, but in our greed and possessiveness and "loyalty" outdo the monkey and hang on, even at the peril of our physical and spiritual lives.

I've seen fine farmers who refused to let go of horse machinery lose everything. I've seen families refuse to sell and move off a beloved but unproductive old homesite—and deteriorate in poverty. I've watched merchants who hung onto old styles and procedures be forced out of

existence. I've seen companies who refuse to change communication systems and sales methods corner themselves into bankruptcy. I've seen owners of old, outgrown buildings who refuse to let go and consider new construction concepts lose their life savings. I've seen hundreds of people refuse to let go of deadly health habits suffer serious (and unnecessary) medical problems. I've watched mothers, fathers, and grandparents miss trips and other life-enhancing experiences because they wouldn't loose their death grip on their junk. I know people who hang onto old lost loves so tight that no new love can squeeze in, and they wilt and die miserably. Our refusal to surrender worthless harmful worn-out things keeps us from growing and maturing.

Odd, isn't it, that the junk itself has to initiate action. We actually have to be injured by an old quack remedy or medicine before we quit it (then after we stop using it, we store it just in case aging it a little might improve its potency).

We actually have to reach the point where our junk inflicts pain or inconvenience on our physical and emotional selves—that it interferes with our lives—before we're smart enough to think of shedding it. Most of the time it just lies there, dormant and useless and often out of sight—until one day we have to move it for the carpet layer, or move to another house, or we stumble over it, or somebody makes us account for or insure it—before we consider releasing it. It has to affect our appearance, our strength, our speed, finally offend our *vanity* enough that we realize it would have been wise to let go. *Hanging on will hang you.*

The Air Force has it in perspective: my brother-in-law, a lieutenant colonel, told me once that when his transport was delivering a $7 million piece of complicated scientific equipment they lost power in two engines and immediately dumped the equipment. I was impressed at the quick decision to release all the expensive machinery. "When we take off," my brother-in-law said, "we're told that the nine human beings in that plane are the only things that will not become obsolete, that are not expendable." *You*, your loves and life and relationships are all that count.

Face it: there is a wisdom in letting go of things that clutter and choke your life. There is nothing more stimulating and noble than change and growth. Most of us never taste the new, the fresh, the zestful because we have our heads and hearts gripped clear to the quick in clutter.

Committing Junkicide

Junkicide is a slow, painful strangulation and dying of the senses. Although our brains are still intact, we've simply replaced *thinking* with *things*. We've crowded out creativity with accumulation. We've frozen flexibility with profusion. We've snapped up so much free stuff and bought so many things to keep, store, clean, polish, and protect that we don't have any freedom.

Junkees are destined to commit junkicide. They are the ones of us (all of us) with a tendency to load up plates, places, vaults, homes, and conversations with more than is needed.

Junkees are afflicted with the endless urge to have more. Enough is never enough. The have-notters want some, the have-enoughers want more, even the have-too-muchers want more. Ever wonder why most frauds, schemes, cons, embezzlements, etc., aren't committed by the have-nothing desperate but by the nice well-to-do citizen? People with plenty, position, and more things than they can already use are often the people who defraud to get more. Jails are filled with people who never could get enough.

Junk is insidious because it's so gradual. Like those extra pounds of flesh, it silently, sneakily mounds in and around, on top of and under us until we're surrounded. It's all so slow and subtle we don't realize how much is there.

Clutter Will Cramp Your Style

In 1979 I took ten Boy Scouts on a two-week trip to Philmont, the 30,000-acre Scout camp in the rugged New Mexico mountains. Sprinkled in the vast wilderness were twenty base camps, each designed to educate Scouts in a different subject—gold mines, archaeology, lumbering, mountain climbing, etc. We were to spend eleven days on foot with a pack, hiking from camp to camp. We were cautioned before we started out about footwear, bears and snakes, getting lost, etc. Then, sensing our junkee tendencies, the ranger put us through a pack shakedown (which would be a neat idea for all of us). We had to spread a blanket in front of our tent and dump our packs out on it, showing everything we were going to take on the eleven-day hike. (It shamefully revealed everything from toothpicks to love notes.) Then the ranger walked through and de-junked everyone's treasures, giving reasons such as, "You won't use this," "This is silly," "This is too heavy," "This attracts bears." Out went the smuggled radios, bulky binoculars, blow dryers, cast iron kettles, comic books, and all that was junk on the trail. The ranger said, "We have a tendency on our journeys to take more than we want to end up carrying." I nodded agreement and saw to it that my boys had lightened loads. Then I spotted the fold-up fishing rod and other things the ranger had booted out of *my* spill of goodies. I repacked my Jansport, and when the ranger wasn't looking threw in some books (a taboo), a couple of sharpening stones, two wood rasps, and a few other extras in case I had spare time. This made my pack a firm, compact fifty-five pounds. For ten days and nights, in 50°-to-98° weather, going up and down 10,000-foot peaks, fording slippery streams, I sagged under my pack and stumbled over my dragging feet, groaning, promising myself that never again would I take more than I could carry. My junk was such a burden I could scarcely savor the fun of the trip.

Clutter is doing the same thing to your journey through life—your job, raising your family, going to school. Junk will dilute the quality of our life, not add to it as we thought when we packed it in.

As a personal demobilizer, clutter rates right in there with crippling diseases, being bedridden, unable to drive, or trapped in a prison cell. Our junk ties us down—away from adventure, affection, and accomplishment—and we can't go when and where we want to.

I had a mild case of junkitis, as most of us do. How can *you* tell if you're a candidate for committing junkicide? Check the list on the opposite page.

Junk seldom gets the blame for life's problems, but it's one of the biggest contributors (if not *the* biggest). There is probably more violence—arguments, fights, and killings—over worthless junk than over anything else.

Marriage and family failures are often the result of selfishness—someone is spending too much time surrounding and securing him- or herself with junk. Often couples have so insulated themselves with clutter in the form of excess clothing, jewelry, hobby gear, housing, transportation, etc., that they can't get to each other to love. When we're extending our feelings to junk, we're exhausting emotions that could be generating affection. It's like our house—if we fill it with junk, clutter, and things, there's no room to keep or exercise anything of value. Junk uses *all* our space. When loving people come our way they can't find us or our feelings. And this dulling of our sensitivity and compassion by junk and clutter is so gradual that few of us realize it's happening.

If you wander through shops and garage sales when you don't need anything in particular, you're infected. Aches and pains will soon develop—the aching tendency to weigh a good thing down with too many extras, the pain of wondering why you don't have as much fun as you used to.

There's no escape from the toll clutter takes of our life. The most valuable "someday useful" junk will stymie our

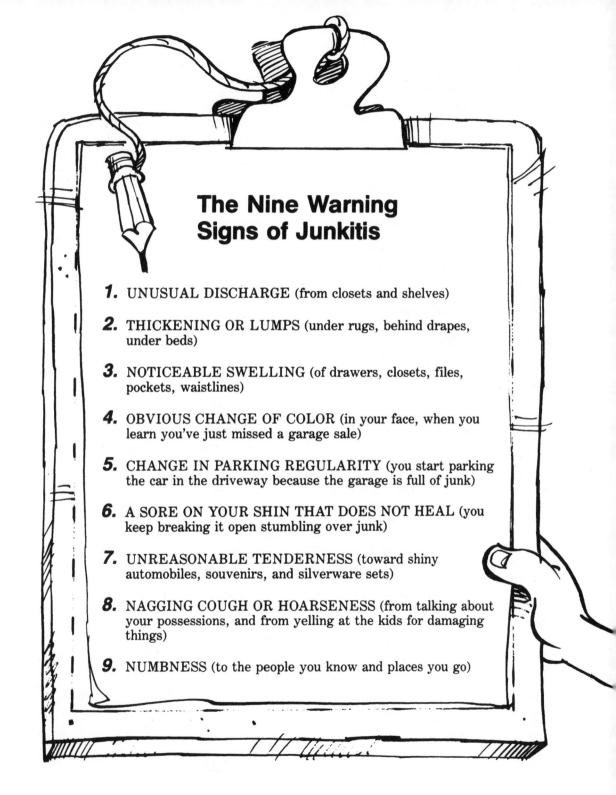

The Nine Warning Signs of Junkitis

1. UNUSUAL DISCHARGE (from closets and shelves)

2. THICKENING OR LUMPS (under rugs, behind drapes, under beds)

3. NOTICEABLE SWELLING (of drawers, closets, files, pockets, waistlines)

4. OBVIOUS CHANGE OF COLOR (in your face, when you learn you've just missed a garage sale)

5. CHANGE IN PARKING REGULARITY (you start parking the car in the driveway because the garage is full of junk)

6. A SORE ON YOUR SHIN THAT DOES NOT HEAL (you keep breaking it open stumbling over junk)

7. UNREASONABLE TENDERNESS (toward shiny automobiles, souvenirs, and silverware sets)

8. NAGGING COUGH OR HOARSENESS (from talking about your possessions, and from yelling at the kids for damaging things)

9. NUMBNESS (to the people you know and places you go)

emotional freedom if we let it pile up on us. Everything stashed away or hidden, discreetly or indiscreetly, is also stashed away in our mind and is draining our mental energy. We can't hide our junk in a deep enough hole or in obscure enough corners to keep it out of our mind. Once physically discarded, it's also discarded from our mind, and we're free from keeping mental tabs on it. But as long as we own it, we'll mentally tend it. We feel obligated to use our junk, whether we need it or not. If we don't or can't use it, then we worry about why we have it at all! Junk will get you—don't sit there and argue that it won't.

The guilt of junk possession is overwhelming. Just get someone talking about their junk and stand back and listen: they'll release the most incredible personal information you've ever heard. It's kind of like a public confession of sin. Feeling guilty and frustrated about our piles of clutter, knowing we have to deal with the problem but not knowing where—or really wanting—to start is pre-junkicide depression. Watch out!

A stately German woman who survived the war considered herself wise, but wasn't wise at all. Recalling her past the day we met, she said, "We lasted through the war, we held on to our things, preserved all that was valuable to us. Then it all ended one day, late in the war: a big bomb hit our house and we lost everything; my whole life was gone with the blast. With all I'd accomplished, everything gone, I felt it no use to go on."

She had clearly committed junkicide. Her pots, pans, sofas, mantelpieces, and dwelling place were destroyed, but all that is replaceable. She didn't stop to realize that she still had perfect health and sight, youth, ingenuity, and her family (as well as her land and the freedom to build again). But all her blessings were of little consequence, because clutter had preoccupied her for years.

Junkitis is generally the real culprit when people cave in or fall apart in despair and discouragement. Junk pushes our thoughts, time, budget, space, and physical energies to the edge. Then, when the *real* crises of death, sadness, or separation come along, we haven't the capacity to cope with them. When the big emergencies or strains come and we have to rally our total self to hold up, we just aren't able to do it. We can't handle it; we can't love and serve and endure because we're so absorbed in worrying, watching, weighing, waiting on, and wishing for junk. We just don't have anything left to give: we've burned so much fuel preserving our junk that we have little or none to burn the torch of strength when it's needed. A big strain on an already strained capacity usually results in failure, if not disaster. But demand on a person who isn't worrying about clutter just causes him or her to work harder and get through the crisis.

Bottom Line: Junk

"Loss of productivity" and unrealized ambitions, if dissected, will often be from junk. That's what inefficiency is—clutter in one form or another getting in the way of achievement and inspiration. Businesses and businesspeople can commit junkicide, and I've watched people with brilliant talents of every kind (athletic, artistic, musical) not be able to use an ounce of it because the clutter in their lives smothered and hid their ability.

Are You Indisposed?

The sure sign of evolution from a mild to a chronic junkee is when we save (or even have the *urge* to save) disposables. Many things are made just well enough to serve once, then be discarded. With great imagination or dexterity they might squeak by another trick, but all in all a disposable, for health and wealth, should be disposed of.

Before you think of pointing the finger at all your friends who are saving no-return bottles, examine your own behavior.

Are you:
- Saving lids from long-gone jars?
- And the little plastic hangers from new pairs of socks?
- Occasionally reclaiming used plastic wrap?
- Tempted to reuse a tea bag?
- Graduating "throwaway" plastic tumblers to the china closet?
- Keeping and using foil pie tins until they're wrinkled beyond recognition?
- Slow to throw away dull disposable razors?
- Salting away fast-food containers and used Styrofoam cups?

(If you checked three or more, keep reading.)

- Always fishing parts of saved plastic forks out of the base of the dishwasher?
- Hoarding those cute little film canisters?
- Saving the boxes from every piece of jewelry you've ever bought or been given?
- Keeping appliance package padding (in case you reship)?
- Stockpiling empty whiskey decanters and cologne bottles?
- Sometimes trying to straighten out old straws?

"*I* watched her spend $95 on drawer organizers so her 2,700 used twist-ties wouldn't get mixed in with her 4,500 reusable coffee stirrers."

Cathy comic strip

Do you want to spend your life in junk games?

JUSTIFICATION

JUNK

Form a circle—the leader in the middle, who walks around suspiciously and suddenly stops and names a junk item (tangible or intangible) and points to a person, who says "Guilty" or "Not guilty." If not guilty, leader repeats the procedure with another item. If the person yells "Guilty," then he has to justify it to the group on the spot, in one sentence. If he fails, the group yells "Junkee" and the person is out of the game. "Save it" means he stays. Last one out is the winner.

JUMPING

JUNK

A game of real ingenuity in using one piece of junk to vault your whole pile of junk in one leap. Can be played outside or inside, depending on how big a stack you have and your running room.

JUGGLING

A game that takes all your physical and emotional concentration to keep all your junk in view/exhibited. The object of the game is to get so engrossed with keeping your clutter circulating that you completely forget the people and other things in your life.

JAMMING

This is seeing how much junk you can get in the smallest spaces (like seventeen sweaters in one drawer). Only fists and feet can be used for stuffing. Can be played with drawers, closets, shelves, rooms, and trunks.

JOSTING

Consciously or unconsciously prodding each other with your clutter. This is where you choose a partner and try to cruelly knock him or her around and off balance with your junk.

Junk Shows on You

No matter how sharp you are, what you own, how famous you are—if you eat, wear, live, and love junk it will cause ugly bulges somewhere on your person or your psyche.

So many of us worry about cancer and accidents, we can't imagine how anyone could commit suicide, yet with our junk we're slowly, daily doing that very thing.

A junkee works more and more hours to get more money that is almost all spent on excess—*junk*—that he never has or takes the time to enjoy. We run in this circle of nothingness until we drop—or just wear out—watching, chasing, and weighing junk.

Junkees gain little sympathy from friends or loved ones. People feel compassion for the sick or handicapped, but where sickness is self-induced (cirrhosis of the liver, insomnia) and is essentially self-abuse, people feel that somehow we got what we deserved. Nobody these days at work or home or play has time to dig us out of a pile of junk places and nonproductive habits.

We've become so conditioned to clutter's call that we look out for "things" often *before our own lives.* Once, years ago, native American and white men were working on a big reservoir construction project. One of the levels above where they were working had a flaw in it and about mid-day, when the water pressure mounted, the levee gate broke and a flash flood descended on the workers just a short way down the valley. Although all the workers were together in the same area, when the casualty report was finished, all the twenty-five white workers had drowned—and not one Indian.

"That's incredible," said the investigator. "How could that happen?"

One of the Indians had the answer: "When the dam broke and the big water came, we Indians saw, we ran for our lives, we reached high ground. The white man ran for his money, and he drowned."

Why wait until clutter has choked you to death before thrusting it off?

YOU KNOW YOU'RE A JUNKEE WHEN . . .

- Strangers say your house is "interesting."
- You send a search party into your basement—and they never return.
- You entertain dinner guests by showing them your odd sock collection.
- You'd like to change the channel—but you can't find the pliers.
- The Welcome Wagon comes and leaves you travel brochures.
- You dust off the picture of the President proudly hanging in your library—and it's Herbert Hoover!
- You have to tear yourself away from those little piles of sample squares outside carpet shops.
- You call an accumulation a collection.
- The fortune on the scales says, "Come alone next time."
- Throwing out an empty jar takes an enormous effort of the will.
- You have stacks of plant pots in the garage with mice nesting in them.
- Only *you* know what the tangled masses of rusted iron in the shed once were.
- You win an all-expense-paid trip to Hollywood and a date with a star—and you choose Sanford and Son.
- You've still got your 1961 Student Activity card in your wallet—right behind your Howdy Doody Club membership.
- The cat has a pile of plates of his own.
- You still have the aftershave your kids gave you last Christmas. And the one before. And the one before that. And you've kept the wrapping. And the ribbon.
- You set your handbag down to write out a check and passersby chuck trash into it.

The Economy of Clutter

The well-known 80/20 rule of business says: If all of a given category of items are sorted in order of value, 80 percent of the value will come from only 20 percent of the items. Think about that in terms of clutter. Eighty percent of the space on our shelves (and in our mind) is occupied by stuff we never need. Eighty percent of our beauty and hygiene routine makes use of only 20 percent of the cosmetics and potions we have stacked around. (How much of the remaining 80 percent is junk?) Eighty percent of our family fun comes from 20 percent of the games and equipment and puzzles we've got jammed into our closets. (How much of the remaining 80 percent could be junked without it ever being missed?) Eighty percent of our reading enjoyment and information comes from 20 percent of the material in our bookcases and magazine racks. (How much of the unopened 80 percent would we ever miss?) Eighty percent of our home maintenance and upkeep is done with 20 percent of the accumulated paraphernalia in our cellars and garages. (How much of the remaining 80 percent is unnecessary clutter?) Eighty percent of the outfits we wear come from 20 percent of the clothes cramming our closets and drawers. (How much of the remaining 80 percent could Goodwill get more use from than we do?) Is this all just fancy business theory? Not on your life! If you got rid of the 80 percent that's clutter you'd be more than 20 percent more efficient.

Clutter Makes Every Job Take Longer

Clutter is one of the greatest enemies of efficiency and stealers of time—and that includes yours.

For every chore he tackles, the average person spends more time getting ready—hunting for a place, the tools, a reason to do it, etc.—than actually doing it. It takes only six seconds to drive a nail, often ten minutes to find the nails and hammer. But the nailing is all that counts and brings the benefit; the fumbling and finding doesn't. If a job is buried in junk we never get started—we just thrash.

I'm often asked, "How do you get so much done?" The answer is that I (and anyone else "successful") hit the ground in the morning running and doing, and plan so I don't get hung up hunting for information, tools, and help. There is a great frustration in having to (or waiting for someone else to) sort through piles of junk to get to the *action*. We end up unfulfilled and unsatisfied, bogged in the nonrewarding junk preliminaries.

Clutter makes every job harder and makes cleaning take forever. Any project we tackle, from building to disassembling, will be slowed, dampened, and diluted if we constantly have to fight our way to it in the midst of clutter. As a professional rug cleaner, paid by the square foot, I noticed that sometimes my crew would clean a large living room in one hour; sometimes the exact same size room and type of carpet took three or four hours. First I figured some workers were just plain slower than others—but closer scrutiny proved I was wrong. In the first house, for example, it took 15 minutes to move stuff, 45 to shampoo, and 15 to move the stuff back; in the second it took 1½ hours to move stuff, 45 minutes to shampoo, and 1½ hours to move the stuff back. There was so much stuff you could barely find the floors.

If junk is taking up your good storage room it means you have to reach further and dig deeper to get the tool, book, suitcase, shirt, etc., you need. "Getting something out," instead of being a few-second job, often ends up a twenty-minute search-and-rescue mission. I've watched bedlam occur in homes when $2.50 in change is needed to pay the paperboy or a roll of tape is needed to repair something. We can't progress when we spend all our time pausing and pawing to find the "good" in among all that clutter.

Take the stuffed shelves of the average kitchen pantry. You're making soup one day and decide to toss in a can of tomatoes. You have to rummage past the celery soup bought by mistake, the canned lotus root for the Indian dinner you've never gotten around to fixing, the aged pinto beans you ought to throw away, and the rum extract you use only at Christmas. You find a can of tomatoes and pitch them into the soup—whoops, they're the elegant plum tomatoes you were saving for sauce, not the grade Bs you wanted, but they're tomatoes. Later, putting the leftover soup away, you poke

through the orphaned canisters, that incredible assortment of glass jars you've saved, and all that Tupperware, and finally find a whipped topping container that's just the right size. But where's the lid? You try lid after lid from the pile. None fit. You push the containers aside on the shelf thinking the lid must have rolled to the back—and you knock over a jar, which falls to the pantry floor, shattering and spraying shrapnel over half the kitchen. You now have to sweep or vacuum the whole kitchen and empty the whole bottom of the pantry (the toolbox, the garden sprayer, those flattened slippers and bags of rags, the fan, the space heater, the cat litter) to be sure you've eliminated all those deadly shards.

The junk in your pantry has just cost you an extra half hour in one day. An unnecessary half hour of shuffling clutter around every day adds up to an entire week each year. (And how many of us repeat this sad scenario in one form or another *more* than once a day? We have to dump out and claw through a shoebox or sewing-box full of unwinding spools to find the navy blue thread we need to put the blazer button back on, run an arm up into sixty pairs of wadded (washed or unwashed?) pantyhose to find three runless pairs to throw in the suitcase.)

*T*ime is
part of
your LIFE

Clutter Makes Cleaning Take Longer

As a maintenance design consultant, I've become super-conscious of the tendency to clutter up even construction. We seem to take quality items (even beautiful, expensive building materials), then pile, I mean almost *cram*, them onto a structure—trying to give it life or looks or "atmosphere." While sitting in a lecture hall of a fine university, I took note of the fact that in the interior of that one room there were nine different types of material making up the walls: glass, wood, paneling, carpet, stainless steel, tile, paint, fabric wall covering, brick facing, and Formica—all fine materials. But to take care of all the variations in surface material and texture took an extra janitor and a cleaning cart the size of a foreign car (which skinned up the facilities as it moved around). Whenever we try to crowd in too much, we pay a toll in "taking care of"—and the bottom line is less time for living.

This goes back to the first value of de-junking: it creates simplicity. The amount of time saved by simplicity is phenomenal.

Don't Let Clutter Call the Tune

Have you noticed that as we grow older our time to do things is more condensed? At the age of ten we had all day to play, make a project, or get a chore done; at eighteen, only part of the day; at thirty, only hours; then, years later, we often have only minutes. We simply have so many more people, places, and things crowded into our lives that we *have* to condense or become more efficient if we intend to make good use of the little spare time we have.

I found this the case with my music. I get a lot of pleasure out of strumming and honking around with guitar and harmonica, so over the years, like the rest of you into any kind of music, I've collected lots of songbooks and sheet music. Like you, I often bought an entire songbook for the two or three songs I wanted inside and, of course, kept the entire score of that special once-in-a-lifetime performance. My shelves and drawers were bulging and the piano bench wouldn't close.

Recently I had fifteen minutes free to play a number or two, and attacked my music pile—it took ten minutes of sorting and digging to find "Blue Tail Fly," "Lara's Theme" from *Doctor Zhivago,* and "Aunt Rhody," so I ended up with only five minutes to play. I suddenly realized that 90 percent of my pile of music was never used—and it was actually keeping me from enjoying the 10 percent of it I loved.

The day I decided to de-junk my music was the day I began again to have time to use and enjoy it. I piled it all up in a giant heap and, in a few hours, pulled and ripped out all the music I really used and wanted and for $3 copied and bound it into a ring binder. When I went through my little mountain of music, I threw out all the ruined sheets, the songs I never liked and the ones I'd fallen out of love with, and songs like "Malaguena," which

LESS IS MORE Here's some simple math to prove it. Good Stuff + Clutter = Junk.

has chords and keys I couldn't play (and after keeping it around for twenty-nine years hoping to absorb it by osmosis, I finally was willing to admit I never would).

While I was at it, I took back the four hymnbooks I'd accidentally carried home from church, and cast off the choral music that called for 600 people to sing with me. I ended up with all my music in one neat file drawer.

Man, what a change—no more sorting and searching and thrashing—I use *all* the time now just to play.

Caring for It Costs

On a special contract assignment at a Sun Valley resort one year, my company furnished decorated Christmas trees to the guests. The company that provided this service the year before lost $5,000 on the job, because they hired carpenters and highly paid laborers to put up, adorn, and take down the trees.

Hoping to improve efficiency, we enlisted local college kids and bought the decorations and trees wholesale. When the holiday season was over, our crew picked up the trees, took off the lights and metal stands, and packed and stored them for the next year's use. When it was totaled up, we lost only $900—an improvement, but still a deficit.

Then we did some "de-junking" thinking, and the following year made over $2,000 clear profit with half the headaches. Our secret? We just followed the basic rule of de-cluttering economy: when the Christmas holiday was over, instead of picking the trees up, undecorating them, accounting for all stands, and sorting and packing, hauling the decorations to the storage warehouse, etc., we just pitched the trees—decorations and all—into the trash. The feeling of "waste" kept me awake for a while until I weighed it against the reality of the rewards. The savings on storage, light, heat, energy, fuel, and labor were far more than we paid for the decorations!

But these things are valuable, you say? What about the value of the life and time to store, to clean, to insure, to transport, to protect—what does that cost? More than money: "afford" is not simply a question of money, it's also an emotional and physical appraisal—what is the effect on your job, your physical being, your peace of mind? "Afford" is the capacity to absorb into your being, not your bank balance.

Have you ever talked to people who've lost all their physical possessions to flood or fire or hurricane? Have you noticed how rapidly they seem to adjust—and are often whistling, singing, and humming a few days later? If they lose their loved ones, their reputation, health, or position they often *never* recover. Yet the majority of their time and effort is spent acquiring, protecting, and caring for physical possessions instead of the loved ones. It doesn't make sense, does it?

The Value Is in the Using

Rich people, poor people—when it comes to junk, one is as bad as the other; one's junk may just be a little more expensive. Rich people are notorious collectors of things they always wanted when they were growing up. There are people who all their lives dream about the ranch or restaurant or yacht or whatever they want above all, and as their life nears its

No matter how you look at it, clutter takes your time.

end they finally accumulate the cash to have the big dream come true. Even if they can't use it much, they go buy it—thinking that the having is the ultimate. But it all comes to little because they can't smell and feel and share in the glory of production. The value is in the using and building and growing, not simply the *having*. They have to hire someone else to run the operation for them; they only get the woes and financial drain; maybe once a year they visit and look over their kingdom—it generally becomes just another piece of junk to them.

Deadbeat Junk: Doesn't Pay Its Way

Thinking about fire extinguishers and spare tires might cause us to ask: How often do you have to use something to justify owning it? What about those hand-thrown pottery apple bakers—is the annual meal of apples worth it? How about cherry pitters and melon ballers and butter molds, pasta machines, fondue assemblies, and cheesecake pans? That's a lot of stuff to shuffle, store, and maintain.

Don't be awed by ownership. "I own it" is a ridiculous statement to make about anything, when you think about it. *Use* is the only value a thing has. War, fire, flood, famine, robbery, or death can undo and devalue ownership instantly. Don't get too attached to "mine"—*my land, my house, my lake, my plane, my book . . .* might be my undoing.

Like you, I hate to rent, I'd rather not borrow, I like to own—but don't be too proud to change. People buy $700 worth of ski stuff to ski once a year, or a 30-foot ladder to reach the eaves of the house once every four or five years. In either case they could rent the right equipment and not only save money but the lugging, storing, selecting, insuring, and general complication of their lives. *Use* should be the deciding factor—and not just *will*, but *how often* will you use it. And do you really like (or need) what it will do for you? Maybe you could just eliminate the activity or area it's "needed" for right out of your life.

Storing It Costs

Out of sight, out of mind might apply to lovers, but not to junk. We pay money and emotion for it, no matter where it is.

Storage—(or, more specifically, lack of it) is one of the most frequently asked questions in the "house care" world. There never seems to be enough. When you point out to the average American that they have on the average 50-75 cubic feet of storage per person they look at you perplexedly and say, "Well, then, what's wrong?" It never crosses our mind that it's what we have too much of—not too little of—that causes the problem.

Remember that storage costs money: Storage space rents for 10¢-13¢ a square foot (or as much as $10 a square foot, if you're using house space for storage). Clutter also serves as an enticement for burglary and fodder for accidents, and it makes nice fuel for fires.

Not only is up to 25 percent of our homes devoted to storage, but we have to seek ways and means beyond our own walls to store the overflow. And once we discover how easy it is to damage something by packing it too tightly or packing a heavy item atop it, we take the reverse approach and pack inefficiently, wasting the space we do have. But no matter *how* we store, we expand. We butt it under beds, under stairs, in wall units, in attics, basements, furnace

rooms, "spare" rooms, fill the garage and the garage attic with it, then migrate to the yard and get little sheds . . . they fill and then we head for the local rental unit.

I had a friend who bought a wrecked car for $25 to get $125 worth of parts, a smart move—but then he had to obtain a $30-a-month rental storage unit to stash it for a year until he got to it. And how smart would you say a person is who'll rent a $300-a-year storage unit to store $150 worth of junk? Millions do it. A "self-storage center" in a town of only 40,000 near me has 600 storage units, and there's a six-month waiting list.

Storage units are the ghost towns of clutter, a testimony of shame. Why do people store things in another place? Because *they aren't using them!*

If we could peer behind those sliding tin doors and into all those locked vaults and cubicles (and many of us junk voyeurs would like to), we'd be disappointed; we'd see all the same worn and broken-down stuff about to overflow our own home—they're simply ahead of us in the progression. Most of it is non- or never-again-used stuff. A rental unit is a kind of oversized Emotional Withdrawal box (see pages 204-221).

Storing is in most cases a hypocritical practice—when we decide to store it away in a rental unit, or Grandpa's old barn, or the extra room at home, we're usually acknowledging that we don't need it any more. It served well and enriched our life—but when that time of our life is past, we should release the old junk so we can have the freedom to greet a new season and grow again. Paying ransom in money, time, or emotion for bygone clutter is pathetic.

Most buildings and houses don't burn easily; it's the *contents*. Fire inspections always reveal burnable storage as the greatest hazard (you just can't win storing junk).

STORAGE—

THE EXPENSIVE WAY TO DELAY THROWING OUT

SHUFFLE

DISPLAY

USE

BUY

WANT

"*I* finally found a place for it—I put it in my unused camper!"

Guarding It Costs

If your junk is valuable enough that you're willing to take the time to move it and the money to store it, it may also be attractive to predators—both the two-legged and six-legged variety. And then you have to protect it.

You can either take the fortress approach—energy-eating floodlights, an intruder-eating Doberman, and an expensive sophisticated alarm system—or stash your smaller valuables in those costly and inconvenient little safe-deposit boxes—or cold storage. No matter how you choose to guard the mink, the emeralds, the home computer, or your super-good sound system, it takes time, money, and mental effort. And of course, it all has to be insured.

Insurance is simple, you say? Just pay the premium. However, other "premiums" are paid, in the case, for example, of elaborate alarm systems. I've been in homes where the anti-burglar devices are so complicated it's hard for the owner to get out unshackled (let's not even discuss the complexities of getting in). And every night the alarms have to be set, just before the four hours of sleep you might

get before the cops roust you out to check out the false alarm.

Only you can decide whether it's worth it to de-mothball and re-mothball your wool opera cape every time you wear it, or to remember to switch off the car's burglar alarm before the parking lot guard comes at you with handcuffs, or to pick up your great-aunt Wilma's sterling from the bank every Thanksgiving and take it back the Monday after. But you at least ought to *think* about whether it's worth it—instead of automatically going to all that trouble.

Moving It Costs

The average American moves fourteen times in a lifetime. If a third of your stuff is clutter, you could save eight moving van loads if you de-junked! People spend literally millions moving junk.

A couple of my acquaintance, promoted to a new assignment, was amazed at the boxes that had to be put away after the van unloaded and pulled away. Three of the first eleven boxes were boxes of trash and garbage to be thrown in the alley, but the movers, apparently unable to see much difference, had packed and

The Evolution of Moving

B.C. (Before Clutter)   1720s   1820s

1920s   1940s

Today

transported them across the entire U.S.

We all haul junk around at great expense and effort—at moving time, not to mention all that moving of things from room to room, to and from all our storage areas, our briefcases, and even pockets!

It's an unnecessary load; dump it before you move on—it's a lot easier to cope with *before* than after. You'll *never* have the time to "go back through."

All our stuff-shuffling even has a (loony) life cycle of its own:

People with apartments collect and store tons of extra things they don't need in preparation for the time "when they get a house." Finally, after suffering years of crowded inconvenience, they *get* a house and spread stuff all over to fill it up—just in time to retire and move back into an apartment, and there is all that stuff that must be disposed of. Is the short span worth it? Think ahead when you're gathering (and saving) "treasures!"

Any move—to college, camp, a new job, a new home—is a trauma in itself, but add 4,000 pounds of excess to the transition and it's a nightmare. If you have any hint you're going to move, de-junk three months prior and you'll bless yourself for it.

Even Owning It Costs

If we really hated taxes, we wouldn't be junkers. All that extra that we don't really need doesn't just slip by uncounted. I had a few office machines, some scaffolding, some old worthless desks, some extra property, and old lawn equipment not being used, just sitting around, fully paid for, so it seemed to be harmless, not costing me anything. WRONG. Taxes don't retire when you retire clutter. I received my tax bill and a list of the taxable items—there was lots of junk on that list! I was shocked to discover that "extras" aren't only a pain to look at, shift around, and protect, but I have to pay for them, not once, but year after year after year, until I get rid of them. Great de-junking incentive, eh?

Tragedy . . . Clutter's Ultimate Cost

Beholding the fresh beauty of a baby or small child can affect most of us more than any other experience. And so no matter what state of exhilaration I might be in, when I read or hear of a tiny boy or girl being drowned, run over, or hurt, I'm upset for days; I find it almost unbearable when such a needless tragedy occurs to a friend or family. The hours following these happenings often kindle anger when the cause of the loss is known: hundreds of cheerful playing children smother to death each year in carelessly discarded junk appliances and containers; thousands die painfully from old poisons and cleaners piled in junk stacks: thousands die in fires from non-used flammables, carelessly stored solvents and fuels, or from negligent smoking habits. Junk!

When you hear of a death or serious injury, notice how often it results from some kind of junk we were too lazy or too sentimental to get rid of. Junk on vacant lots and in storage yards takes a heavy toll. Many an adult is laid low by clutter in the home: What did they stumble over, what was on the stairs? What did they try to lift? What did they bump into? Too many times it's clutter. Many a car accident happens because of objects in cars that impede or distract the operator—junk!

A medical lecturer told me once that over half the illnesses in the United States are mentally or emotionally induced—have nothing to do at first with physical impairment. If you were a betting person, what percentage of that half would you say was caused by worry and stress over junk—or a junk habit? If clutter doesn't inflict some physical damage on you, it'll take its toll of your psyche—you can count on it.

No Matter How You Look At It, Clutter Is A Poor Investment

It's a poor investment indeed when we put so much of our life and our money into compiling a collection of treasures that suddenly it begins to dictate our schedule and make our decisions. We can't or don't dare leave it for a trip. We yell at the kids whenever they get near it, worry about the babysitter or our mother-in-law somehow messing it up.

When we find ourselves in this situation we have two choices:

1. Spend more money and time (life!) to earn more so we can protect and keep our junk.

2. Have less junk to maintain.

A profit and loss statement is basic accounting. Figure a balance sheet before you invest in more junk.

Item: Genuine handmade Laplander doll dressed in real reindeer hide

ASSETS

1. Cute souvenir to prove we've been to Lapland.
2. People back home could see what real reindeer hide looks and feels like.
3. Has genuine hand-painted narwhal ivory eyes.
4. Grandkids would think it's cute.

LIABILITIES

1. Who needs proof we've been to Lapland?
2. I'll have to protect it from moths and silverfish.
3. Would cost me $65 plus duty.
4. Too expensive for the grandkids to play with.
5. Doesn't fit in with my decor at home.
6. Where would I put it?
7. Would be hard to keep dusted and clean.

(Conclusion: If I really think it's that cute, take a snapshot or slide of it for less than a buck, save $65 plus duty, and still have proof to show people back home, if I need it.)

Item: Red silk blouse with electric blue flowers

ASSETS

1. It's on *sale*—I'd save 30 percent.
2. Silk blouses are really in right now.
3. It's my size.
4. It's got a designer neck label.

LIABILITIES

1. I don't have anything to wear it with. It would cost me more than the 30 percent I'd save to buy something to wear with it.
2. I'll have to be super-careful washing it—or dry clean it.
3. Puffy-sleeved blouses don't do much for me.
4. Who's going to see the neck label?
5. I like red, but I don't really care that much for the electric blue flowers.
6. I've got sixteen blouses already.

(Conclusion: Take the 30 percent I would have saved, and save it until I find something I *really* like—then I'll probably be able to afford it!)

Item: Night out on the town

ASSETS

1. They have a great floor show.
2. I can mention that I went there. It will make me sound like a swinger.
3. I can drink away a few pressures.

LIABILITIES

1. The whole thing cost me $131.50.
2. I can't remember how much fun they told me I had.
3. I've got a terrible hangover.
4. I lost my leather gloves.
5. I don't remember having that scrape on the right front fender.
6. I insulted my friend.
7. I have to apologize to the boss for a bad joke.

TOTAL...................... ____   TOTAL .... ____

Make a ledger sheet on some of your junk. If the liabilities outweigh the assets (be honest), it's time to de-junk.

Age—Don't Fight It

If old Ponce de Leon had truly found a fountain of youth, many of us would enthusiastically immerse some of our clutter before ourselves. Aging is a natural life process in ourselves *and* in the things we use—accept it! We junk up our quality of living by trying to retard aging, cosmetically or otherwise. When an era, an item, a vehicle, a system grows old, let it go. We can't stop aging, but we can start new things and grow and enjoy again instead of letting dying junk take some of our strength with it.

Time after time I've watched an ancient backyard tree start to wither away. The owner goes crazy vaccinating it, wiring it, propping it, performing limb surgery on it. The twisted stump still sprouts a single leaf-yielding limb, so restorative repairs are continued. All for what? It's unsightly, costs a terrible amount of time and money, and gives no benefit in looks or shade.

Had the owner dug it up, used it for a cheerful Christmas fire, and planted a new tree, he would have been stirring some new growth in his own life, too. Metal, mortar, wood, glass, places all get old in time and change is needed. Don't cling—you'll be cluttered if you do!

We've been taught we're bad if we waste—"waste not, want not." But we waste more valuable time and energy working over and trying to save worthless junk than many an object was ever worth originally.

Why spend (waste) an afternoon (or a week) restoring and finishing a slivering old wicker chair that you never *have* used and never will? Or get a hernia moving a 250-pound roll of worn-out carpet we're saving for some place that hasn't popped into our mind yet? Why spend three hours every couple of months reapplying naval jelly and porcelain patch to an ancient sink that's going to keep rusting no matter what?

Like you, I'd never think of throwing away anything I like that's still good. But why not be a little more realistic about the almost-gone gizmos? We often foolishly risk our financial (and physical) necks trying to squeeze 5 percent more use out of an item that has served its honorable time.

One summer a surge to save $5 cost me over $400. There was a worn tire on the back of our Trans Van: it had served long and well, but on examining it before a trip to San Francisco, I had to see if I could squeeze 2,000 more miles out of it. In the middle of the loneliest stretch of Nevada desert it gave up its life, causing the other (good) dual to go. Then there was the $175 tow to the Desert Automotive Service and the cost of two tires at premium price, not to mention the six hours lost and the accident involving my family that I had risked.

"I'll Fix It!"

About 2 percent of broken junk is ever fixed. Mass-produced molded or stamped objects of this era are difficult to repair. (Forget the miracle glue ads, because few things will stick together as permanently as your fingers.) Few people have the time or facilities to fix things, and most of us don't like to use or display patched stuff anyway. Do you or your kids wear fixed clothes? Rarely! Do you know how many heels broken off high-heeled shoes are waiting somewhere to be fixed? Well, they can't, and won't be.

Most things wear out first, then break or cease to operate—but a few things *do* break while they are in the prime of life, and it's uneconomical to "bury" them. They can and should be fixed, and the act of fixing them can contribute triumphantly to your emotional well-being. But don't try to get this elative creative charge tinkering on undeserving gizmos.

While in New York once my wife and I were roving downtown streets when a

"Fix-It" Tally Sheet

Answer honestly—how many of these broken items have you fixed lately?

- [ ] shredded cassette tapes
- [ ] hair dryers/hot combs
- [ ] pot or pan handles
- [ ] broken chains
- [ ] torn upholstery
- [ ] toasters or waffle irons that burn
- [ ] leaky teapots
- [ ] Christmas tree lights that don't
- [ ] chaise longues with rotted webbing
- [ ] dead flashlights
- [ ] loose-headed hammers
- [ ] defective clocks/watches
- [ ] inaccurate thermometers
- [ ] broken strollers
- [ ] socks or sweaters with a hole in them
- [ ] umbrellas with one cracked rib

- [ ] sprung scissors
- [ ] sagging screens
- [ ] shaky card tables
- [ ] ruined electrical cords
- [ ] frozen lawn mowers
- [ ] TV with a bad tube
- [ ] eyeglasses with broken frames
- [ ] broken mobiles
- [ ] dismantled lamps
- [ ] chipped teacups
- [ ] broken antennas
- [ ] broken zippers
- [ ] dismembered dolls
- [ ] injured musical instruments
- [ ] cracked dishes
- [ ] unstrung rackets
- [ ] suitcases that won't latch
- [ ] wobbly chair legs/arms

IF YOUR SCORE WAS:

15-34	You must own a repair shop.
10-15	You must be part Scottish.
5-10	Your TV must be broken.
2-5	You deserve applause.
0-1	You're normal (and honest).

Now de-junk the other items and sigh a great sigh of relief.

guy jumped out of an alley, flipped open his coat, and gave us a "want to buy a (hot) digital watch" pitch. Wanting a real "con" experience, we bought two, mainly as conversation pieces. They were cheapos, but what the heck, a bargain! We gave one to our son and one to our son-in-law. In a few months, my son's flickered into timelessness and with no regrets he chucked it. But our son-in-law's was a brute—he managed a concrete/brick plant, worked as a mechanic, welder, loader, and that watch ran and ran. It told better time than my or my wife's expensive quartz models. He beat it, jarred it, drowned it, but it ran and ran, keeping absolutely perfect time. We all began building a certain loyalty and respect for that watch—it's still running today, two years later. But I know someday soon it will twitch and quit. And when it does, do you think we're going to chuck it? Not on your life. Amazing how we forge a relationship to a thing; we actually think we owe it something—surgery, even a life-support system if necessary.

We don't owe it and you don't owe it anything. It isn't worth fixing; don't let love affairs with things junk up your life. They have a way of ticking their way into your heart, but be objective: if fixing isn't worth it, dump it (without a wake or mourning).

Give Broken Things a Break—Make Fixing Easy (Accessible!)

The biggest reason fixable things never get fixed isn't lack of mechanical ability, time, or even industriousness. It's lack of *availability*. For example, I find a split in the seam inside my suit jacket. I know my wife can fix it in seconds, but it never gets fixed, and every time I wear it I get irritated because she hasn't performed her seamstress act on it. Of course, each time I wear the jacket I hang it in the closet; how could she know the bad seam is there? She can't—she's no mind reader!

The kitchen towel drawer sticks and is miserable to open and close—the rollers need adjusting. Every time my wife opens the drawer she's irritated with me for not doing my mechanical fixing number. I never use the drawer, I never know—so I never fix it! My coat gradually rips and ruins (it's her neglectful fault, of course). The drawer deteriorates from kicking, beating, and prying—that's my fault!

Nonfixing is generally caused by such lack of awareness and refusal to surrender the item in question out of activity. So set up a Fix-It box—

TO BE FIXED

throw your genuinely fixable items in, and you'll be amazed how sensitive everyone at home, work, etc., will become. The box will be the perfect cure for "broken communication." Things *will* get fixed, and the backlog of repairables will be a great "what-to-do-in-spare-time" provider and inducement to industry for everyone. Try it—you'll fix it!

Twelve Hands Are Better Than Two

When I was on the "People Are Talking" show in Philadelphia last spring, to demonstrate the cost of clutter/litter I handed six members of the audience each a slice of bread, and had them tear the bread in pieces and throw it on the floor in front of them. Then, with one TV camera on the clock and one on the host, I had him pick up everyone's discarded bread as fast as he could. It took 25 seconds. I then gave each of the same people another slice and had them tear up and throw down the bread again. But this time I had each one who threw the bread pick up his own mess—or in essence, take care of his own clutter. It took *less than 5 seconds.*

But the art of comparison is often our enemy—just because 5 seconds is less than 25 doesn't mean it's smart to handle junk at all. Less clutter-handling is better but *no* clutter-handling is best. No junk is efficient or economical to care for, because it uses up time, energy, and emotion—in other words, *life.*

The picking up of *other* people's junk (as in the example above) is the most inefficient and expensive clutter cost of all—like the mother who spends all her time picking up after a cluttering husband and careless kids. Women all over the world are wasting their youth and high spirits and creativity playing janitor to their families. If your family habitually leaves clutter around they're going to keep doing it—are you going to keep

picking up? Do you think tolerating that kind of thoughtlessness in them is really doing them a favor? Have a house meeting and put everyone over two years old on notice—hubby included—that mess is picked up/cleaned up by whoever makes it. They'll be better people for it!

Littering

At 7:00 one fresh spring morning I was standing in front of one of America's most stately hotels. The place was immaculate—the brass outside polished, the flower beds manicured, the mats "living room" clean. Then the litterer arrived. He walked through the door and stood waiting to be picked up. After he flipped his mangled toothpick in the flowers, he ripped open a pack of cigarettes—dropping the cellophane at his feet and following it with one, two, three cigarette butts. He blew tar stains on the glass, dropped ashes and gum wrappers in the flower bed, and clipped his fingernails on the carpet before someone finally hauled him away.

You might try to classify litterers as mild, medium, or chronic, but maybe they should fall under one classification—*slob.* Harsh, perhaps, but litter results are harsh, too. The litterer is an inconsiderate clutter strewer who thinks nothing of harming his fellow humans or the environment.

In many buildings more is spent to clean and police the cigarette butts, bottle caps, gum, etc., out of the entranceway and exterior than to maintain all of the landscaping outside. *Clutter—our own or others'—doesn't come cheap in our lives; we pay for it.* I don't want to be guilty of foisting my junk on others, do you?

Any residue we leave in life should be contained. If we are old enough to mess up, we are old enough to pick up after ourselves.

Nothing exists in and of itself. Everything has a cost to acquire and to maintain. And *all* the costs of clutter add up to one mighty bad investment.

Home Sweet Home . . .

(Full of Junk!)

Do you need a double garage . . . maybe a triple? . . . or a commitment to de-clutter?

While cleaning a large, plush home during my junior year in college, I managed to wade through and clean a luxurious, treasure-laden bedroom and embarked on cleaning the closet. In addition to the expected arsenal of pricey wearing apparel, I had to move five exquisite cigarette lighters, forty-seven pairs of women's shoes (I kid you not), a case of 1920s *National Geographics*, several tennis racquets, fourteen boxes of Christmas cards, a side-saddle, six poodle collars, and numerous other items. It was a neat but completely stuffed closet, in harmony with the style of the woman who lived there. She was fifty-five years old, and possessed a handsome home filled with elaborate art and delicate tapestries, carved furniture and exotic lamps that she had spent part of her life collecting and the rest of her life cleaning and dusting and keeping track of. This project of shuffling treasures around had taken

her over half a lifetime; she had been committing junkicide for thirty-five years.

Sound a little like someone you know? Well, I can beat that. Some friends of mine helped a family move into a new home. They piled all their stuff in several downstairs rooms, lived there a while, and like most of us, never got through all the junk they dragged with them. They decided to have a fireplace put in the family room downstairs and called a local mason. When they gave him the address he thought a minute and said, "I put a fireplace in there two years ago." They ran downstairs, moved the junk, and there it was—a fireplace!

Another friend told me his mother was a "collector." Since her health was no longer robust, she had to move from her home of fifty years to an apartment. When her son and a helper went to move her belongings (she'd told them to only bother with the good stuff), they backed a 16-foot-long, 4-foot deep, 2½-ton grain truck up to the side of the house and started in the attic. They filled the truck to level, then heaping—and were still on the upstairs. The son, an avid junk collector himself, only managed to salvage a couple of boxes of "good stuff" for his mom and one small box for himself; the rest was pure, unadulterated clutter. The woman never missed the three truckloads her son took to the dump, and found her de-junked life a happy one.

I'm sure we could fill several books with this kind of junk story, and that you could add a few fascinating chapters of your own (about your friends and relatives and they about you).

Most of us are in the same (junked) condition as the owner of forty-seven pairs of shoes. We can find our fireplace, but not our matches, and our junk could strain a semi instead of a grain truck. Our house treasures may not be as expensive, but we have as many cubbyholes for them—that we shuffle through, sort and re-sort, climb over, worry about, and maintain for hours on end.

Not only can we not take it with us when that final departure date arrives, but keeping it with us under the same roof is creating more conflict than we imagine. We really can't win with clutter. Sooner or later we're sick of it, tired of being a slave to it. It doesn't matter if it's valuable or not: if it's unused, in the way, and takes emotional and mental energy away from us, we feel guilty about it—in fact, deep in our heart, we hate it. Every time we come home from the shopping mall with more pictures, trinkets, and goodies for the walls, shelves, drawers, and sideboards, we're more frustrated

The difference between man's junk and woman's junk: he builds a $3,000 shop around his and calls it "tools."

because there's no place to put anything. We're tormented by the thought that we may have to throw out some old junk so there will be room for the new—in a house that already looks like a department store or a rummage sale. There are rarities hanging all over, we want to show everything off—but are, as of late, having difficulty getting through the house, not only to check on things and clean but just to stroll. We hesitate to de-junk that house; we want to be able to wander through to show off our treasures—maybe even build a museum and charge for it. But sad to say, few people are interested in our holdings. We toil to accumulate things that will impress others, but when it comes to house junk, nice or elaborate, little kids don't care, teenagers think our obsession with inanimate objects is obscene, rich friends hate us for our cheap junk, poor friends hate us for rich junk, medium friends think we're showing off because our junk matches theirs. The truth is all of these— plus the fact that the house is using *us* instead of our using and enjoying *it*.

Clutter Is Alarming, Not Charming

Most junk is overkill; that's exactly what makes it junk. I read in the *Wall Street Journal* about some people outfitting their bathrooms to "flush plush," spending millions of dollars on gold-plated faucets and other elaborate accessories:

mother-of-pearl sink stoppers, heated towel racks, and mink toilet seats. Around the same time, I saw an article in a family home magazine, titled "Put Charm in Your Bathroom." It took a nice functional easy-to-clean bathroom and added ungodly apparatus to every surface and fixture—wall hangings, inlaid shelves, decorative cabinets, elaborate lights and accessories that made it a grotesque spectacle as well as a nightmare to clean.

It's hard to do much living in a living room these days. There's so much stuff on the end tables, coffee tables, bookcases, and magazine racks that a rail has to be installed so none of it will fall off. Lamps are lucky to find a place to roost these days and even spots to *sit* are at a premium. The floor, too, is taken up with ceramic wolfhounds, ivy-planted spittoons, and colonial cat doorstops

tailor-made for tripping over. Aside from it being difficult to move around in, it's tough to dust and vacuum and straighten up a cluttered living room—and that's the room we always want to look nice for company.

We do much the same thing with clothes, jewelry, food, automobiles—often until the clutter almost totally obscures function, i.e., the doorlatch to the bathroom is so fancy, we can't figure out how to get in.

A workshop is a place to work, relax, create, and fix. A kitchen is a place to conveniently cook. Look at what we have done and are doing to both these areas. Kitchens are getting so overdesigned with accessories, decorations, gadgets, and "storage" that we're afraid to cook in them because we'll mess them up, or they'll take too long to clean afterward.

Every other issue of the home

> **"I** have supplies and racks of spices like you wouldn't believe, 95 percent of which I've never used. But someday I'll come across a recipe that calls for one of those exotic spices. Meanwhile, I rummage through them daily to get the cinnamon, salt, and pepper!"

magazines has an article on "beautifying your kitchen": the pictures show a room rife with aspic molds and giant stirring spoons, and so many colors and textures it looks like the inside of an Easter basket. There are enough ovens and cooking apparatus to feed a whole barracks of soldiers. There are racks, holders, clamps, and even art objects so thick on the walls and shelves that the average person would do $50 worth of damage just trying to have a bowl of cornflakes. Too much is junk. Don't let those who don't *use* kitchens talk you into one of these gorgeous galleys of gimmicks and gadgets. It will only clutter and complicate your life.

A hammer, saw, and bench was a workshop when we started out and we actually produced. Now we spend most of our time mounting and storing all our new progressive tools and producing nothing. Did you know the average guy with a workshop buys his shelves premade?

There's a Little Pack Rat in All of Us

As a little fellow, I remember helping install a freezer on the back porch of our farmhouse. A floorboard was lifted up—and Mom uttered a shriek and took to higher ground, mumbling something about a "rat's nest." I peered into the gap where the floorboard had been and there was an intriguing sight—a total inventory of all the items we'd lost, cushioned in cotton, rags, and a little straw. To me it looked just like my hobby drawer (or one of my aunts' sewing boxes). "Stay away from there," my mom yelled, "it's a pack rat's den!" She then explained that the "no-good rat" scurries around and picks up things and takes them to his home and stuffs them in every available spot, then curls up in the middle and lives there. He has no reason to take the stuff—doesn't use it or even know what it is—but just

can't stand not to have it. That didn't sound too strange to me. I'd watched my parents, uncles, aunts, friends, and teachers doing the very same thing for a long time.

Every one of us has pack rat inclinations and expresses them by stashing clutter in unviewable areas (attics, cellars, closets, under the beds, under the eaves and rafters, by the footings, under the steps). Look in, around, and under your house and in your private nesting areas. I'll bet if you sprinkled a little cotton, rags, and grass on it, pack rats would want to hold a convention there. Get rid of the junk and clutter before someone lifts *your* board and shrieks.

It's not enough to de-junk the visible eyesores—"out of sight, out of mind" doesn't apply here. Your hidden "rat's nest" will clutter your mind as well as your premises. A life spent collecting and storing debris you don't need (regardless of its value) is a waste of time. *Only a rat would do it!*

Room Spells Doom

Too often we judge our capacity to own by the room we have available, not our actual need. Did you know that the average American dwelling has at least forty drawers, twenty-four cupboards, six closets, three bookshelves, two medicine cabinets, and one file cabinet? Some homes have more than a hundred places deliberately designed to harbor junk (mine has over three hundred!). Now add to that the additional possibilities of a pantry, assorted knickknack and curio shelves, various nooks and crannies, an attic and/or basement (with all the attendant boxes and trunks), a garage, a rental unit, a friend's (or relative's) spare room, and you're looking at well over 150 places!

With over a hundred junk hangouts, is it any wonder we get migraines just finding something or when we think about cupboard-cleaning day, or getting ready to invite guests?

The amount of room or places available in your home for "stuff" can have either a disciplinary or a devastating effect on you. If you start thinking it's wasteful to leave space unfilled, you're dead. Wide open spaces are American! Walls don't have to be peppered with pictures, attics don't have to be insulated with magazines and old clothes. Basements don't have to resemble clutter-aging cellars. Just because a shelf exists doesn't mean that it has to be filled; ripping it down or leaving it stark and simple are choices, too. Drawers are for the convenience of keeping active everyday usables out of sight and unsoiled by dust—they aren't archival vaults for junk. Room is reasonable and relaxing. When you clutter your closets and drawers with things, you're cluttering your feelings and thinking—freedom in your dwelling allows freedom to dwell in *you*.

> *T*he "junk room" is an accepted, even honorable, convention in our society—like the fruit cellar, the guest room, or the recreation room. Are you surrendering a full quarter, fifth, or even tenth of your hard-won home space to an idle collection of clutter? The true name for your junk room or area is "The Indecision Room."

You Can't Stow Home Again

Many of us not only have our homes and bins and carports filled but have junk out to pasture yet farther afield. We have a boat in our brother-in-law's yard, a snowmobile in the shed out at Grandpa's. And the most convenient place of all (once the junk stashes under our own roof are exhausted) is the parents' house! I've had many a conversation with people who, when their possessions are being reviewed, will say enthusiastically, "Boy,

you haven't seen anything yet. I have more stored at my parents'!"

Only a low-down cur would inflict clutter on his or her parents. When you leave home it's only moral, decent, and merciful to extract your junk. Parents have enough of their own; how can you put them in a position of gate-keeping—guarding yours too? You may choose to inflict clutter on yourself for various reasons, but forcing, because of bloodlines, your trash on someone else (who feels *obliged* to store it) is unforgivable. Go get it *right now*—they need the room!

De-Junk or Perish

With all that we have to worry about in our busy lives, it's not necessarily our fault that things accumulate so fast (and in so many places!). But rationalizing worthlessness after we discover it *is* our fault. Most of us will go to all kinds of creative measures in order to avoid that inevitable showdown with our home junk.

We'll go so far as to:
- buy and build accessory storage sheds
- claim that "We're just getting that room ready to repaint"
- wait till after dark to put the car in the garage
- train our children to decoy company away from the entry closet while we hang up their coats
- threaten bodily harm to anyone who opens a drawer in front of company
- hang an "Out of Order" sign on the bathroom whenever the Avon lady comes
- claim that our basement is the drop-off point for the local charity drive
- and so on, and so on

But, as you know, this mad deception can go on only so long (maybe five or ten years). Eventually we all must come to the same point—de-junk or perish!

Free Yourself from Household Imprisonment

One woman, never able to get all her cleaning done, had to move—but not to a permanent place at first, so she packed all the family's belongings in boxes and sealed them, holding out just what they needed to use. They stayed at different spots from month to month, leaving the sealed boxes in the basement, and strangely enough, the packed-up belongings never were missed. And the woman noticed that by some miracle she had a clean house. At last! It had been the clutter that broke her back. Her case of junkitis was dormant in the basement; she was temporarily cured.

Think about the storage problem in your home: a lot of the stuff you're storing is useless; it's a constant source of worry. Much of it is unsafe, outdated, and ugly, so why keep it? Why spend a valuable part of yourself polishing, washing, dusting, and thinking about it? *You can't afford clutter.* It will rob you physically, emotionally, and spiritually. Freeing yourself from junk will automatically free you from housework (and it won't take any soap and water either). If you'll just de-junk your home, you'll have the time to take that course, write that book, run that marathon, or make that visit.

It's unbelievable the effort some people go to to have an immaculate germ-free house when even platoons of germs and layers of dirt can't hurt the quality of our life like clutter can. A germ might give us a sniffle or two, but junk around the house can create a monster in our basement that will dissipate our energy, thwart our values, misdirect our emotions, and steal our money.

"Well, you've got to be able to live," claim most junkees whenever their beloved clutter is questioned or threatened by a mate, a friend (or this book). But *live*—in the sense of the things that you most enjoy, that most turn you on—is exactly what junk prevents you from doing.

The big question is whether it is *active* or *inactive*. Even an unsightly pile of stuff is not junk if it's stimulating some personal or group improvement. I've seen fathers who never teach their sons to build anything because they don't want any sawdust around the house or to dull up any of the tools. I've seen mothers who wouldn't teach their daughters to sew because the patterns and the snippings would be clutter. Not so! It's not making a mess—but leaving one and living with it forever that is harmful. "Growth projects," such as finishing a room or remodeling, create temporary junk or mess, but it's going to a good end.

The unfinished house is exciting: it's a living lesson and visual aid. The family learns to do without, build, appreciate—which they never would in a fully finished house and grounds. The clutter of construction is something positive and is not junk.

Too Much Is Junk . . . So Is Too Nice

Something that is "too nice to use" is undoubtedly about the most ridiculous kind of junk one can own. Yet our homes in America are crammed with "too good to use" things, or things put up until later because they are too nice to use at this time in our lives or in *this* house. I knew a woman who had a living room she was saving for the Queen's or President's visit; her kids were only allowed in there if their shoes were off and their Sunday clothes on. It held an array of beautiful furnishings, of which the crowning feature was the plush velvet chairs and couch. The problem was, every time someone visited and sat in those chairs or on the couch, a big fat imprint would be left, so vivid one could tell exactly where Uncle Jim, little Heidi, or cousin Donna had sat. The minute the company left, the woman had to get a pan of water and a little brush and brush all of these prints out and stand the nap up so her room would look good again. Can you imagine spending your valuable time and life getting out *rump prints?*

You can't? Well, before any of us get too self-righteous on this matter, let's sit down and take a little inventory of the things we have now that are put up, hidden, stored, still in the box, etc.— because they're "too good to use." Austere as I like to think of myself, I notice I have a couple of expensive (gift) wallets stored in my drawer that I push aside every day to get to my socks and hankies. I've had them for years: my old calfskin wallet seems to last forever, and besides, if I did use them, I'd get paint on them, get them wet, or nick them with my putty chisel. I've also got a sweater I'm hoarding to wear when I'm an old retired author. I'll probably end up retiring to Tahiti; meanwhile, it's in the way every day of present living.

You'll be surprised how many "too good to use" things you have—lots of it is clutter! Use it or lose it.

Racked, Stacked, Packed Away

On a beautiful fall afternoon, a fourteen-year-old neighbor boy spotted me home from a European trip and walked half a mile across the meadow to visit. We worked together a while, and since the last of my six children had recently left the nest, he was a welcome and refreshing experience (plus I was getting some great project help out of him). "I can stay until Grandma comes," he told

me. "Do you have a pair of binoculars I could use to watch for her?" I have two pair but . . . you guessed it, they were so well packed and hidden away I didn't use them—and in fact, until he reminded me, I'd forgotten I had them. I dug them out and they made a much longer visit possible.

After he left, I stood with the binoculars looking out over the beautiful valley and marsh dotted with cattle and migratory geese, muskrats scurrying down the creek banks. I took the first real look in a long time at the craggy snow-capped peaks fingering down into rugged ravines, the ancient eroded lava flow bristling with stubby junipers, the old abandoned narrow-gauge railbed and the overgrown traces of the storied Oregon trail. . . . I'd been missing lots. One very good reason to de-clutter is to allow you to find and use all that "good stuff" you've almost forgotten you have.

I Know I Have It Here . . . Somewhere

You know you have it: Is it in the pantry cupboard, or the hall closet, or . . .? How embarrassing to have so much clutter you don't even remember where it all is! Having extra vacuum cleaner bags, spare fuses, candles, a cake decorating set, a chimney cleaner, a hiking compass has no merit when you can't find them. When you don't know where something is, you'll dig like a hungry dog for a bone trying to unearth it and tear up every storage area in the whole house.

Having useful or even valuable things and not being able to find them is no better than not having them! Basically, de-cluttering your home involves getting rid of the things you don't use, that you don't enjoy, that aren't necessary. This leaves plenty of room for the things you really need, because *where* you put the things that will be used is important.

Make sure you have a place to put everything you really do use that's close to where you use it. That's why most of us keep toothpaste in the bathroom or the spice rack over the kitchen counter. But we don't always carry out this principle in the way we arrange our drawers, closets, and other storage areas.

Think about the way you live and the things you use most often; this is the stuff that should go at the front of drawers or on the most accessible shelves. (You can also use this principle to encourage good habits—maybe the dental floss should go right out on the vanity.)

Refills should be stored as near as possible to where you'll run out. Remember not to pack objects in so tightly that you can't shut the drawer again unless everything is just so; you should be able to reach into a cupboard or drawer and grab a commonly used item without disarranging everything else. And while you're at it, set up a loose classification system to help you remember where things are—medicines at the top of the bathroom cabinet, for instance, toiletries at the bottom.

Converting Clutter by Relocating It

Some things we like and use are clutter only because of where they're located. We had some of the best fruits and fresh potatoes and carrots and all sorts of good things from our farm. However, they were in the root cellar, fifty yards across the snow and ice from our kitchen. That fifty yards caused lots of good food to rot, because when we wanted something it meant coats, hats, boots, and shoveling the snow off the cellar door. Most of the time we decided we didn't want it that bad and so didn't go. Had they been in the next room, we would have consumed and enjoyed them all.

Another such case for me was my safety goggles. I kept them in my briefcase (to be ready for consulting jobs) or in my toolbox. Trouble was, whenever I worked with metal or my big electrical grinders, the goggles weren't there. They were junk to me simply because I wasn't using them. A piece of steel finally got me in the eye, and so I hung the goggles right on the side of the grinder—so simple but I hadn't thought of it before.

We all have lots of good things that are junk simply because we haven't located them for easy use. What good is a pocket knife in the top dresser drawer? Why do we put towels in the hall closet—why not in the bathroom? Most of us end up using one towel to death while a dozen sit unused in the hall closet . . . why? . . . location. Where is your flashlight right now? I bet if the main breaker blew in the basement, a real search would begin in the dark. The flashlight (at least one) should be by the breaker box. Your umbrella: how many of the people you see wilting in the rain have umbrellas at home—almost all of them! Why are those people getting wet? They couldn't find an umbrella, or it was on a top shelf in an upstairs room—not worth the effort to retrieve. Fly swatters, too, are a piece of junk if they aren't handy when the pesky fly appears. Garbage cans are worthless if they're too far from the source of the garbage. When you can't find, can't reach, or it's too unhandy to use, what good is it? And much clutter comes from things that are too inconvenient to return or replace.

Do me and yourself a favor. When going through your junk and all that good stuff you buy and never use, ask the big question about location. You'll be surprised at what you can activate and not have to store or throw away. I don't need to outline the exact process for you because your places and purposes are different from mine. It will be easy.

Do You Really Need More Than One?

Of some items it seems logical to own more than one: these are usually little things that contribute to big important end results, like a measuring tape. I own at least eight of these wonderful tools, but never have one in hand when I start a construction job. Light jackets, scissors, address books, screwdrivers, sponges, can openers, and rolls of tape are also charter members of the "got-more-than-one-but-I-can't-find-any" club. And these are high-use items. Knowing you have more than one of something around has a way of making you more careless ("I'm bound to stumble across one of them")—and all that extra clutter compounds your problems.

I struggled with this for twenty-nine years, and finally figured it out. One is easier to keep track of than eight. Then I did three things that helped:

1. Put my name on it (big!).

2. Decided on an exact place to put it.

3. Always *returned* it to that spot the minute I was done with it.

Knowing where everything is is important, but I'm the last to direct anyone to a tidy/perfect/set way to put, hang, or box everything. More and more bags, hangers, racks, and trunks aren't an asset; they just help turn de-junking into re-junking—just help you compact and hide a little more clutter for a little longer. They're *junk bunkers!*

Junk Bunkers

We finally reach the day when our clutter is so overwhelming that there's not a single place left to put anything: even the walls are full. It is then that we're most vulnerable to the hidden persuasion of a *junk bunker.* That, simply, is an item we

can use to store more junk, stacked higher and packed tighter. Junk bunkers come in various models, called desk organizers, closet racks, shadow boxes, shoe organizers, gun racks, pen-pencil holders, trophy cases, entertainment centers, china cabinets, jewelry boxes and ring holders, pegboard organizers—and magnets (so what you can't hang on walls, you can stick on your refrigerator).

Once we get that handy-dandy "holder," we're psychologically primed for paraphernalia. It irresistibly beckons us to fill it up:

- There's that **seven-story tool box** that encourages us to buy piles of handsome exotic hardware to fill it.
- The **solid oak knife block** with four empty slots—which leaves us no choice but to buy four more knives we don't need.
- The **utensil holder** that beckons us to buy more utensils to balance the set.

- The **new shelves** we feel
  compelled to fill with vases and
  other bric-a-brac.
- Those **two extra rooms** we built
  for just-in-case have to be filled
  with furniture.

Have you ever noticed that most of the
books and articles on how to more
efficiently organize a house really show
how to hang up, hide, file, tolerate, and
make decorative use of junk? I paged
through a pile of top-selling books,
magazines, and catalogs that had one
page after another of slick hangers you
can buy (or make) to hang up coats you
never use (coats that should be given or
thrown away), racks for hats you never
wear, see-through boxes for sweaters
you've outgrown, drawer organizers that
take up a good 10 percent of the drawer's
total space, and tiny trinket shelves with
which you can clutter your walls with
utter abandon.

Consider those vegetable bins to handle
refrigerator greenery; they end up taking
twice the space and only provide a place
for vegetables to rot organized and
unseen.

Then there is the big pouch shoe holder
that attaches to the back of our closet
door: the perfect place to put all the shoes
we were going to have to throw out. Now
and forever they can swing and bounce on
the door, nestled down like baby
kangaroos. And let's not forget the one-
or two-story desk-top organizer that
stacks and divides and stands up all the
papers that were all over our desk. Our
desk will be just as messy as ever—but
the clutter will be vertical instead of
horizontal. (And probably forgotten—
because having put it in the organizer, we
feel something's been done about it.)

Some of the sneakiest junk bunkers are
the vinyl slipcovers or handsome leather
binders for magazines. Timed almost
perfectly to the moment our stack of
magazines has left us no alternative but
to throw the ugly old things out, the
publisher will offer an impressive slipcase
or "volume binder." Wherein those
outdated, stained, dog-eared periodicals
can be clasped together in a coat that
makes them blend right in with the
classics on our shelf. What an excuse to
keep a bunch of stuff that we'll never look

at again. (The cardboard coffins available at stationery stores for old letters fall right in here, too.)

For floors, walls, and furniture saturated with clutter the junk bunker tycoons sell devices to hang clutter from the walls or ceiling. There are even instant junk bunkers everywhere in kits, just snap them together and presto—a clever rack for the back of the toilet, the top of the TV, or under the sink—you can stash three times the junk.

Junk bunkers are like a shot of morphine: they ease the pain, take care of the problem for a short time—and then back it comes. Most of them can accommodate only a *little* junk, and as they become overstuffed, they also become saggy and ugly and dangerous. They don't sort our stuff in quite the way that would be most useful, or they have too many or too few drawers for what we have/need. Or they tempt us to over-organize things in a way that isn't really functional or realistic—so we don't keep it up. And they collect dust and are hard to clean.

There is no redeeming way to better organize and store clutter! Throw it out or give it to someone for whom it won't be junk. The Lord will bless you for giving, and you'll bless yourself for getting rid of it.

If you've stooped to buying organizers for junk, you're swinging on rusty hinges. Once you get all that junk neatly placed in or on the organizer, pick it up and heave it, bunker and all!

Where did all that junk in the bunkers come from? Well, a lot of it is home gadgets.

Gadgets . . . Make Life Easier?

Americans are bombarded with clever, handy gadgets that are not really needed but are too tempting to turn down. Going for a gadget, depending on artifice or automation instead of our own ingenuity, is an accelerated way to collect and own clutter. Just because something works faster and neater than we might doesn't necessarily mean it saves time or makes life easier. It all depends on when and how often we use it, how much time and effort it takes to care for it, and how well it really does the job at hand.

Take corn-on-the-cob holders, for example: those couth little pins with handles you stick on an ear of corn so you can eat more graciously. But you only eat corn on the cob a few times a year—and then you can't find the gadgets. Unless company is there, you never do use them (you forget); and even if you do, they're hard to stick in the cob, and hard to hold onto. Your company has never used them either, and feel as stupid as you do when all of you try to use them. To top it off, they're hard and dangerous to clean, and they have to be stored. You have corn on the cob three weeks of the year and have to shuffle those sharp piles of holders around for the other forty-nine. Are they worth it?

High on the list of useless gadgets/tools is the TV or bargain store do-it-yourself spray gun. The sucker bait on this gadget is, "Just press a button (or pull a trigger) and presto, the work is done." But they don't work half the time (they clog so easily), they're tricky to adjust, they aren't fast (if you count all the times you have to start over and redo), they're messy, and unless you've had a lot of practice you'll end up with a terrible job (you should have stuck with the brush or aerosol). You can't get a good spray gun for $19.95, $49.95, or $99.95—and even the $3,000 ones I've used professionally are a headache; without great skill you'll get misses and runs and bubbles (and ants and bugs stuck in the three square inches of the job that did come out right). Plus the overspray will texturize your

neighbor's picture window. Anything sold
with promises to rid your life of all work
is a strong hint that you're getting some
junk.

Then we have special nozzles for the
garden hose (that we'd use once or twice
a year, and a thumb over the end of the
hose would probably work as well—then
the nozzle becomes junk to store). Pipe
holders for the workshop, so we don't
have to set our new briar down on the
sawhorse, gads! Special spears and grips
to get olives out of the bottle without
using our fingers (just how often do we
have to get olives out of a bottle?).
Hamburger patty molders, spatula
resters (while the hamburger cooks),
special shish kebab grills, grape draining
dishes, taco holding racks, radish rose
cutters, garden seed spacers—and on and
on and on. Junk gadgets may provide us
with the glory of the moment, the
convenience of the hour, but can end up
being the plague of the day. Bigger—
fancier—flashier is not always better.

Most of the miracle gadgets we end up
hating because we got taken—but we
refuse to get rid of them because we paid
good cash for them. We've been duped
into believing that *convenience* is
invariably desirable, even if it clutters

our lives. Convenience is often junk
hypnosis: if it's a gadget, shiny,
attractive, easy to reach for, easy to pay
for, we buy, accumulate, and then shuffle
it from cupboard to cupboard.

I'll bet every family has one or more
exercise gizmos—springy exercisers,
collapsible bikes, rowers, pulley ropes,
gadgets that work in motels, in doorways,
on fire escapes, in prison cells, boats,
trains, and compact cars. Exercise
equipment for the most part—for old and
young, flab and fat—is found in a drawer
or on a closet shelf. The most exercise
anyone ends up getting from it is moving
it from one junk storage area to the
next.

Shocking Junk

The word "electric" offers security and
sanctification to many clutter
accumulators. We presume that if
anything is electric it must automatically
be better and faster than manual. Don't
you believe it! In the time we take to find
and plug in the electric charcoal lighter
(bun warmer, single hamburger maker,
hot dog roaster) we could have done it
easier and faster by hand—even the
mosquitoes have given up. A lot of these

things are a waste of good electric cords and not worth owning for their infrequent use. How many people actually use their electric scissors, electric card shufflers, electric sifters, electric carving knives, electric bottle warmers, or electric toothbrushes? Ninety-five percent of fishermen never catch enough fish to need an electric fish scaler; the other five percent use an old pocket knife. At every garage sale you find an electric warming tray—why? It didn't justify the bother and space. Why was it bought in the first place? Because it had an electric cord sticking out of it. I'll bet if you stuck an electric cord on a pair of chopsticks or knitting needles, there'd be a stampede for them.

"Electronic," and "solar," too, share the same mystique. Suddenly stores announce: "This is going to be an electronic Christmas." Suddenly everything—scales, temperature gauges, light switches, doorbells, dog whistles—

has to be electronic or it's passé. Electronics are superb to have and have made life much easier, but electronic isn't automatically better. High tech is a degree of technology—not an assurance of efficient function. How comfortable you feel with things also has something to do with how useful they are to you. I still use an old manual typewriter. Beating hard on the keys releases my tensions and I can roll out reams of writing (more than many of my colleagues who insist I'm an idiot for not using an electronic processor). Of the thirty friends and associates I've questioned closely about their high-tech home computers, I've found most of them just have an expensive way to play Pac-Man.

One hour of power junk Snow blowers are an extremely useful tool, when there's enough snow to justify them. In many areas of the northern U.S., the home use for a snowblower is about one major snow every three years, or a couple of hours' work for the blower. The other 1,000 days it sits in the way of other things. It's far from being a piece of junk, yet owning one to only be used in the occasional heavy storm clutters your life (besides, a couple of hours on the old shovel, provided we go about it sensibly, wouldn't hurt most of us out-of-condition folks)— and a shovel is cheaper and stores a lot easier.

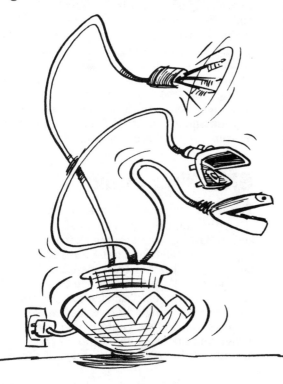

Have You Got Money to Burn?

The argument we hear for some of our latest and proudest junk is that it's "a vast saving on energy"—and who in this energy-tense day would dare question any installation or acquisition that has the potential to save energy? Take the national rage (in any place in this country even remotely northern) for the good old wood stove. Holes have been ripped in many a house and thousands of rock wall protectors installed so those "money-saving" wood stoves can be installed, and once in, it's easy to identify the owner: "I haven't turned my furnace on yet this year." Yes, wood stoves are efficient in a well-insulated home, but so is an electric or gas furnace (and the fuel for them is usually more accessible—and often cheaper). I saw the following in a newspaper; it beautifully (and quite accurately) sums up the economics of some money-saving items.

Remember, it's not just "Is it faster or neater?" but "How often will I use it?" (vs. having to buy it, store it, remember to bring it out and use it, service it) that's the issue: you might want to think twice about that automatic stamp licker, hydraulic pillow fluffer-upper, self-starting orange peeler, or electric ice cream scoop.

How You Can Save with a Wood Stove

Stove and pipe installation	$ 458.00
Chainsaw	149.95
Gas and maintenance of chainsaw	44.60
4-wheel-drive pickup (used)	8,297.04
4-wheel-drive pickup (maintenance)	538.00
Replace window of pickup (twice)	310.00
Fine for cutting unmarked tree in state forest	500.00
14 cases beer	126.00
Littering fine	50.00
Tow charge from creek	50.00
Fee for removing splinter from eye	45.00
Safety glasses	29.50
Chimney brush and rods	45.00
Log splitter	150.00
Emergency room treatment (broken toe from dropped log)	125.00
Safety shoes	49.95
New living room carpet	800.00
Paint walls and ceiling	110.00
15-acre woodlot	9,000.00
Taxes on woodlot	310.00
Divorce settlement	33,678.22
Total first-year costs	**$54,941.26**
Savings in fuel: first year	62.37
Cost of year's wood burning	**$54,878.89**

—author unknown

Junk Multiplies Junk

Bear in mind too that clutter amazingly multiplies itself. I once leafed through a pre-Christmas gift newspaper and a full 50 percent of the things in it weren't needed, but luxury, "convenience" items that when brought into your life would draw other junk items. Among other gems, there was a cookbook holder, a giant ugly thing of wood and clear plastic, maybe useful—if you'd remember to use it—but it would be hard to clean and take a place to store (and your favorite cookbook probably wouldn't fit in it).

Junk multiplication is so subtle, and so easily justified: as you get something, you need a rack for it, a place for it, and then some more junk so you can use it better—and so on.

Accessories to the Crime

I think the original intent of most accessories was to make a thing neater and easier to handle—is it working? Look at asparagus; it grew wild on the ditch banks and a few people picked it and ate it, no big deal. Then someone started inventing things to properly handle asparagus . . . like special asparagus steamers, asparagus knives, asparagus ladles, asparagus racks, special string to tie up the stalks, special dishes to serve it in. The more gizmos to handle the wild weed of the ditch bank, the more prestige it gained—and the more expensive it got (up to $5 a pound, when you can get it). Now did you know the accessory entrepreneurs are trying this same approach on the good old egg: we have egg prickers, egg peelers, egg slicers, egg poachers, egg timers, egg turners, egg tongs, egg cozies, egg holders, egg slicers, egg separators, egg platters, and deviled egg rests. They're trying with accessories to do the same thing they did to asparagus: take it out of the hand of the common man by creating a whole special set of equipment for it.

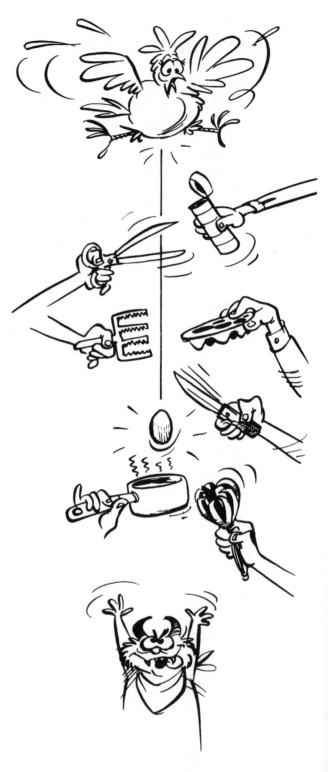

Just about any food or beverage these days sprouts accessories like fungus on a fallen log. Look at all the special coffee brewers, bean grinders, milk heaters, mugs, cups, and freezer jars to keep the beans fresh (how did people drink coffee all those centuries before freezers?). It's much the same way with wine—there are clay coolers for white wine, cooling buckets for sparkling wine, dozens of corkscrew designs—and woe to the host gauche enough to serve sherry in the wrong kind of glass. . . .

Whether we're hooking a fish or making a waffle, popping a bit of popcorn or trying our hand at homemade bread—there's a sea of gadgetry and special equipment we can easily sink in.

Unreasonable Attachments

As foods and gadgets sprout accessories, so do appliances. Most of us, for instance, have a love/hate relationship with our vacuum cleaners. Mostly, we love the cleaner, we hate the attachments. The cleaner does 98 percent of the work; the miracle attachments (which we fell for after a salesman's fast talking) we seldom need or use—so they're shuffled around from closet to closet in their clever display box until the bottom rots out—then the attachments are thrown in a drawer, never to emerge again (except maybe as "guess-whats" in a parlor game).

Nothing is more of a disgrace than owning attachments with nothing to attach them to. I'm sure *you* wouldn't be so stupid, so let's point out a few things for your attachment-laden friends. In the backs of closets you find table leaves—the table they fit was worn, warped, and whisked away to the junkyard five or ten years ago. Because the leaves were seldom used they remained like new—and who could throw out beautiful new solid wood or shiny Formica leaves? Maybe we figured we'd buy or build a table to fit, so we kept them. That's almost as bad as

keeping someone's new false teeth when he's died—you'll never find a fit! Same with the old 16-inch tires, the sheaths of those knives you've lost, those brand-new special bulbs for a light fixture you pitched years ago, the saddle and tack you've had since the horse keeled over and you moved to the city seventeen years ago.

The attachment problem is compounded by the fact that machines today have so *many* attachments available. Besides a menacing array of shiny attachments for vacuums, there is a galaxy of glamorous sewing machine attachments—little bobbin adjusters, ruffle grabbers, seam stretchers, needle straighteners. My wife, who is an excellent seamstress, has often commented that it's the accessories to a sewing machine that make everyone want one. Yet in producing the average dress or shirt or bathrobe, hardly a one of these accessories is brought into play. (By the time we find and hook one into the machine, we could have done it faster and better with a needle and thimble.)

Remember when the can opener was a handy little thing—inexpensive, easy to tuck away with the knives and forks. Of course with electricity, we did improve it and make it faster, but now just opening cans isn't enough. Hung on that once-simple opener is a knife sharpener, scissors sharpener, bottle opener, magnet, light, and top cupboard or bottom counter mounts (to make it as difficult to clean as it now is to use). Then of course we have beauty kits with motorized callous sanders, elbow creamers, eyebrow stencils, pore massagers, wrinkle relaxers. Even the kitchen mixer has all sorts of squeezers, slicers, kneaders, manglers, and juicers—next thing you know, they'll launder pantyhose. (After twenty-eight years my aunt's old mixer finally gave up the ghost; it went, but not the juicer. After all, it was brand new, had never been used—she still has it in the top cupboard today!)

House Junk Hall of Fame

PATHETIC PLASTIC

There is no "plastic surgery" for junk, yet kitchens and cupboards and cellars are full of plastics bent and bowed by heat or weight or both—plastic containers, lids, utensils. Even records get warped and are generally worthless, but notice they don't go. We have secret thoughts of restoring them to functionability—but there's no hope, and even if there were, it'd be cheaper to buy a new one. You haven't used that half-melted plastic container, that fried plastic spatula, or warped plastic lid for years and you *won't*—dump it!

BROWN PAPER BAGS

Are the mice in your home starving to death because those extra paper bags are compressed so thick and tight between the fridge and the counter that they can't get through, let alone eat anything? We save bags because we do use them occasionally—but for most of us the rate at which they accumulate far outstrips the rate at which we can use them up. There aren't enough turkeys to be baked or Sunday school projects to be made to ever exhaust your supply. De-junk before bugs breed in them or your compressor overheats and sets them on fire. And do you have sixty crumpled shopping bags stashed, though when you need one, you'll spring for a fresh crisp new one at the store, as usual? And what about bread wrappers and the little plastic bags that come on the newspaper . . .?

We're really hard up for clutter when we buy and display handcarved decorative soap. I never found any thrill rubbing Donald Ducks over my back, and less interest in showing my soap off to a friend: "Look, after four baths, it still has the head on it." Everyone's afraid to actually use the things, so they stay around forever, turning floury in their plastic wrappers. And even if some brave soul *did* use them, a plain old bar of soap would have worked much better anyway.

Some of us stoop to taking something we don't want and no one will eat and putting it into indefinite suspension in the freezer, so it won't ruin while we're dodging the question of what to do with it. Eventually it gets freezer burn, or becomes so unrecognizable in its frost coating that we have to thaw it out to identify it. And then, at last, the show-down—we can't freeze it again so we have to throw it out (we should have just chucked it in the first place).

Leftovers can be junk, too, if we never did want to eat them and are just refrigerating them as a way of delaying throwing them out. Keep a sharp eye out, too, for aging refrigerator odds and ends: just because it's full of preservatives doesn't mean it'll last forever. De-junk those year-old dregs of salad dressing, that ancient bottle of seafood sauce, those maraschino cherries that are a fixture in the door shelf, the six containers of rock cornish hen giblets you keep meaning to make gravy with. . . . Patrol your refrigerator regularly for condiments and relishes moving past their prime and eat 'em or throw them out.

UNIDENTIFIED KEYS

I'll wager you have at least twenty old worthless keys, between your house and workplace. Identify (some hard thinking and detective work may be called for here) and mark every key in your possession or throw it away. Keys are clutter, if you don't know what they're to!

SEEDY SAMPLES

What is it about free samples given to us or left on our doorstep? I've watched cleaning samples sit for years and years in houses. They won't be used, but won't be thrown out, because they were free. Even after they get mashed and beat up and dented and weevily and the labels are gone we cling to them tenaciously.

If no one in the household is enthusiastic enough about a packet of shampoo/cream rinse or hand lotion to use it within a couple of weeks of its appearance at the door, chances are no one will use it ever. But do we throw the packet away? No—it sits in the bathroom drawer with seventeen other shriveling packets, awaiting the fateful day when you might run out of the stuff you usually use.

Lots of gifts and free samples arrive over the holidays to litter our homes—like calendars too big or too small, those terrible telephone chin holders with someone's company name printed all over them, skimpy wall notepads with a skipping ball point pen that won't write uphill—junk!

FAKE FRUIT

Won't rot when it gets old and will sit around in that display dish forever. Not only do you feel obligated to keep it once you put it out, because it psychologically suggests that it's *food* you won't ever pitch it (who could bring himself to waste good food?). Truthfully now, have you ever seen artificial fruit you could generate any real enthusiasm for? So why buy it and let it hang around catching dust while the *real* fruit is in the fridge, where you won't think to eat it? Melt those ugly apples, pears, and bananas down, or throw them at a junk performer.

YOU MAY HAVE A SERIOUS JUNK PROBLEM IF YOU:

- hide when the doorbell rings
- wear your coat when you answer the door so your caller will think you were just leaving
- wait till after dark to pull the car into the garage
- live in fear that someone you respect may someday open one of your closets
- have to think about how to cross a room
- finally find the Christmas tree lights while hunting for the Easter baskets
- finally replace a badly worn or broken part—then keep that broken part
- fear lifting the lid on some of the Tupperware in your refrigerator
- hide the tangled contents of a messy drawer by laying a couple of neatly folded things over the top
- drag a 22-cubic-foot chest freezer into the yard to keep the repairman from coming into the house
- have an unquenchable desire to paw through a moving neighbor's garbage before the trash truck comes

Knickknacks

Humankind, deep in its secret heart, has always wanted to create and control its own world. To do so on a big scale like the Lord did is a little out of reach, so we mortals settled on a lesser but representative approach. We created little wood, plastic, china, metal, and paper models, miniatures, and duplicates of every creature and structure ever devised, rounded them up, and put them on a shelf so we could rule over them. And we named our scaled-down universe *knickknacks*.

Creation was easy, and surprisingly enough, so was reproduction. Once they were in our possession, they multiplied and peopled the shelves many times over. Do those little suckers breed at night? No—they don't need to, with us around. As soon as we get an object, no one in the house or family rests until it has a match, mate, or companion. A pair is nice, but not as nice as a trio, because you can place three of anything in an interesting arrangement—though four would be more symmetrical—and five can be lined up in some kind of order and a set would be more impressive. . . . So

grows our world of knickknacks. A few are true treasures; the rest of those hundreds of others, those tiny porcelain people, fanciful fowls, and morose mammals just sit there with insipid looks on their faces. Some of those little Alpine yodelers we've had so long we don't remember whether they're Bavarian Burghermeisters or extras out of *The Sound of Music*.

Many of us don't look at, use, or even like our knickknacks. Then why do we keep them? Because when visitors come, that's the only thing they know how to comment on; they will always gaze intently and finally say, "Cute." That benediction, sincere or not, is sanction to save—and so lives on that shelf full, wall full, cabinet full, room full of dust and grease collectors. The only time our interest is aroused much is when one of them gets knocked off and broken; then we wail and sob like a wounded pack rat (we'd glue it back together but can't remember if it was a Mayan warrior or Pluto the dog).

Although life was never officially breathed into our knickknacks, nor did we teach them, they themselves became clutter collectors, demanding more and

more shelves, stands, racks, and cases to migrate to.

Knickknacks may be smaller than Frankenstein's monster, but they have a much better chance of doing us in. Save your "sacred" figurines or knickknacks and somewhere, somehow, someplace—dump the rest! One fell swoop of arm isn't hard to do, but plucking the marked ones singly is awfully painful. Donate them en masse to a museum so the whole county can admire them; besides, in a museum they'll be class ("culture," not "cute").

Before you throw one of your copper horses or ceramic chickens at me for suggesting genocide of your knickknack kingdom, I realize there might be some emotional value to your collection. Do you think I'd pitch my bust of Beethoven, or even my Bell System fishing lure? No way. Some knickknacks, as worthless as they might be, have real ritual value. One of our most fulfilling and relaxing pastimes is dusting, washing, and caring for them every so often. If they soothe you, regenerate you, quicken your heartbeat at every touch, keep them. (But pitch the other 182 that don't.)

Behind Closed Doors (Closets!)

The old "skeleton in the closet" didn't originate in fiction. Closets hide more ugly, embarrassing, frightening "dead" junk than any other home environment. If your closet were three times the size it is now, it would still be full, and most of us would have to rummage and burrow to retrieve the object we know "is in there somewhere." My description of closet chaos in *Do I Dust or Vacuum First?* triggered thousands of letters and comments (most of them apologies for cluttered closets).

A closet is really the most logical place in the house to put the things we need to have handy. Closets are our most functional and critical storage area, but they are also the perfect convenient place to stash useless unneeded items out of sight. Closet junk is the most emotionally devastating because we see it many times a day. I wouldn't want to go picking through your closet—it's none of my business—but if I could get you to make it one of the main events of your de-

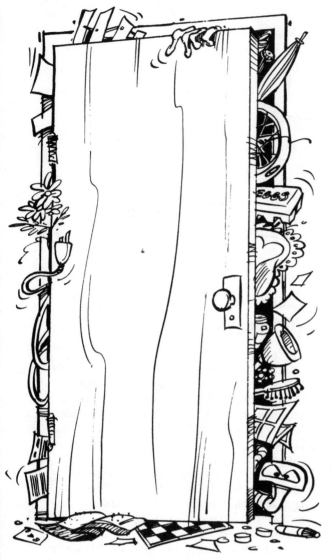

1. You start in a closet by de-cluttering it. That is the simple (and often heart-rending) process of getting rid of everything you don't use or need. We all know what is junk and what isn't. Dresses, pants, shirts, and shoes that haven't fit or pleased you for the last twelve years won't ever—pitch them! Those hand-painted ties and leopardskin clutch bags aren't coming back in style; pitch them. Those boxes of Christmas cards from 1978, 1979, 1980, 1981, complete with address list: face the fact that you'll never write them. Give them away or dump them.

2. Move the useful but used-once-or-twice-a-year (or every two to five years) stuff to a less critical (inactive) storage area. Remember, closets are your most accessible (active) storage area. Attics, under the basement steps, or basement storage rooms are not, so transfer the worthwhile but not-frequently-used stuff (like camping gear, out-of-season clothes, scuba-diving masks, suitcases, etc.) to other areas.

3. Get stuff off the floor. Floor mess is about the most psychologically devastating of all messes. Most closets have a lot of unused upper room—a few dollars worth of material and a spare hour or two and you can install (or barter with a friend to install) a second or third shelf above the one over the hanger rod. This makes more room for worthwhile keepables.

4. Wall-hang everything you can. Remember, nothing—absolutely nothing—goes on the floor. If you are a person who rotates shoes or clothes, there are wall and other organizers you may find useful. Just use your

junking marathon, it would delight me!

How can you shape yours up? If the situation is really bad you could buy an insert closet liner (like a garbage can liner) and yank the entire insert out every year and drag it to the junk pile. Seriously, though, I'd like to suggest here some junk-inhibiting practices from the Clean Closet Set:

head in choosing—and installing— storage accessories or "closet organizers." Some are real helps; others, just another kind of clutter.

5. Remember, *before* you stash is the best time to exercise control. (You'll never have the time to "go back through it.") Do you really *want* it? Do you *need* it? Does it have to go *there?* I realize most of us don't have enough closet space—but try, really try, not to pack too much into your closets. You'll defeat the purpose. No matter how cleverly you pack it all in and organize it—if a system won't stand up to quick, convenient use, it's ultimately doomed and will aggravate the mess. Overcrowding makes it a lot tougher both to get things out and to put them away. And you'll end up with a lot of re-ironing and re-pressing that shouldn't have been necessary.

6. Use hard-finish, light-colored enamel or gloss latex when you paint the closet interior, and hanger marks can be cleaned off easily.

Be careful of those clever holders and organizers that drape on the backsides of doors and doorknobs. Most of them are only places to store junk you should have tossed. And those glue-on, snap-on, stick-on "space expanders" can ruin good functional structures. The classic one of these is the over-door hanger for the extra unworn clothes you should have thrown out. Many a door, handsomely designed and carefully stained and finished (to open and close—not be a mobile mannequin) is mutilated by these poorly thought-out things. Inside most of today's (hollow-core) doors are cardboard reinforcing strips; hanging forty pounds of shabby sheepskin vests and velour outfits on the door will crush them and buckle

the door. The average new door, hung in place, costs as much as $250. Think of that when you see one of those nifty $2.49 accessories.

Spin the Bottle/Jar/Box/Tube

The perfect miniature of the clutter-filled closet is the bathroom medicine cabinet . . . such a simple, innocent, and shining thing on the outside. The medicine cabinet was placed above the sink so it would be easy to reach . . . it's easy to stash things in also. Let's just open the door and look in. . . .

Who convinced you to buy all this, anyway? It's unsafe, unsightly, and uneconomical—and most of it is just dead weight; it doesn't really do anything for you. The real name for this is "clutter chest."

Life isn't that complicated. Some of the healthiest, happiest, handsomest people in the world survive without any of this. Starting and ending every day looking into this collection of clutter has to affect your daily outlook, your dreams.

Coping with Kiddie Clutter

Most kids, if given a chance, will de-clutter themselves. Little kids, in particular, are great de-junkers; they play with or wear something until it falls apart or they lose interest (then they wisely break it, lose it, or give it to a friend). But if we really work at it, we can teach our kids to be clutter collectors too. All it takes is intense examples from us grown-ups, constantly bombarding them with junk gifts and junkee ideas.

For instance, we come unglued when we find out that our kid did away with his old plastic tricycle with the wobbly back wheels. It's gone, no good—but that night the junk-prone parents have him under the light: "Think now, Junior, where did you leave it? Did the neighbor boy touch it?" The kid wouldn't have received half the attention if he'd broken an arm or burned down the local school.

We owe kids better than this. If we let junk, litter, and clutter become a constant condition in their lives, they'll get accustomed to it, feel comfortable around it—and later will duplicate the situation in their own cluttered lives and homes.

Here are some kiddie clutter cutters:

1. Much of kids' clutter is excess we've given them—get rid of (or store and rotate) those excess toys, clothes, games, scooters; they won't miss them!

2. Give kids a place for their stuff. Growing people have their own inventory, but most of the storage space in the home is taken by adult junk. If there's a place to put it, the chances are 60 percent better that it will get put away.

3. Lower dresser and closet hanger rods so kids can hang things up easily.

4. Put casters on the toy box so the kids can pull it around to their disaster areas—it makes a pickup a lot easier and more likely.

The Nerve
of Some Junkees
(Exterior Junk)

Hoarding, hiding, and shifting your junk in private is at least good manners. There are those among us, however, who are natural exhibitionists. When not busy adorning their bodies, decorating their cars, or showing off their offices, they impose their clutter on others on the outside of their houses and in their yards. We all hate junky yards—even someone whose yard looks like the city dump will, when viewing another sloppy junk-plastered yard, squint his eyes and say, "What a disgrace, just look at all that trash, they must be real slobs."

You feel the same way, don't you? But how is *your* yard? Is it an All-American avalanche of "antiques"?

Right out the back door junk starts with rusted or broken wind chimes, deceased weather instruments, bent-back awnings covered with sagging lattice, a slum birdhouse or two in condemned condition, a lean-to shed bulging with sun-cracked hoses, handleless tools, and rotting stakes and bushel baskets.

YOU ARE NOW ENTERING THE COMBAT ZONE

Against the fence is an abandoned rabbit cage, car parts, decaying barrels. Then there is a coy cherub fountain, unhung hanging baskets, some broken aluminum lounge chairs, a mound of salvaged bricks and blocks, a peeling Paul Revere lamppost and a couple of faded plastic squirrels. And oh, yes—that pile of boards scrounged out of a junk pile, worn not from age, but from ten years of being moved around to more inconspicuous places. Let's not overlook those twirling plastic sunflowers, tire tulip beds, miniature white plastic picket fences, rusted swingsets, chipped and yellowed drinking fountains, abandoned outgrown swimming pools, rusted grills from the past three seasons, and the TV antenna that toppled during the worst storm of the '70s. Not to mention last year's Christmas tree saved for kindling, outdoor Christmas lights standing fast in July, and overgrown and untrimmed, dying, dead shrubbery.

Dangerous When Junked

The first time I saw an Army obstacle course I was impressed, because it took real eptness and agility to complete it—not to mention the ingenuity and planning that must have gone into its construction. But it's a shame so much time and money must be wasted by those obstacle course designers and constructors when in our very own town, our very own neighborhood (maybe even our very own little acre), we have back yards that without design or intention could beat anything those colonels could ever dream up. Moving through some people's yards, dodging all the junk piles, traps, castellations, blockades just to get from the back door to the garage, is a maneuver to match topping the highest battlement. If a sharp rake or slung hose doesn't get you, you can count on being garrotted by a low antenna or clothesline wire, or stepping into a barbecue burial pit. The injuries possible from a junky

yard are scary, but still not as pitiful as the fact so much of your fine expensive green yard is so covered with junk that it can't be *used*. Imagine that cruddy clutter cheating you out of a fast cartwheel on the grass or even forbidding you to invite the Henrys into the yard for a look at your lilacs.

Seedy junky yards truly do lose us respect and friends (as well as property value). Exterior junk costs us a lot of lawsuits and injuries to children and adults as well as sheer shame.

Scout your yard, and surprise the worms, bugs, and beetles building colonies under your exterior inventory.

De-Garbage Your Garage

Once we can make our way through the yard in a straight line, it's time to stride over to the garage and take a hard de-junking look at it. The garage to most of us is our enclosed junkyard—kind of a giant seasoning cellar for our debatable belongings. Yet believe it or not, the garage is the first, most, and last used location in a home. We leave from it to work or town or the yard, and return through it from work or town or the yard, often with arms full of stuff, both coming and going. A garage is a very logical place to be kept in clean and useful condition.

It doesn't cost much (in fact *less*) to be de-cluttered. For example—three 8-foot 2x12s and a few cinder blocks can offer order, safety, and convenience in the form of instant garage storage shelves for items that get a lot of use. But that's only the beginning. Here are a few ideas that will help:

1. Store anything light by hanging it as high as reachably possible. This keeps it out of the stumbling-over path, yet readily accessible.

2. Find, buy, or make a wall-hung cabinet (six feet tall if possible) to store small hand tools, paint, lawn chemicals, etc. Concealing stuff that must be stored in the garage has emotional as well as physical advantages.

3. If you wish to mount or hang frequently used hand tools (or display them for friends who borrow) the smart, practical, and economical way is to install a 4x8-foot piece of quarter-inch pegboard on the wall (just like you see in store displays)—you can do it easily and a variety of peg hardware is available.

4. Make sure you can see! Most garages are inadequately lighted, which makes them feel like a mine shaft instead of part of a home. The wiring is usually adequate; just convert the incandescent fixtures to fluorescent tube lights. It will make the garage look better and will be safer and cheaper.

5. Paint the garage walls—90 percent of garages are unfinished, and thus look naked and shabby. Two coats of a good enamel (new or left over from another job) can be applied for a few dollars and reward you for years. (If the walls are bare studs, put up sheet rock first.)

6. Prepare and seal the floor, if it's concrete, and has been down for at least thirty days. This will make it fast and easy to maintain and improve the looks and feel of the garage.

Here's how:
Remove all possible furniture, tools, etc., from the floor; sweep up all the surface dirt. Mop on a solution of strong alkaline cleaner (TSP), or better yet, etching acid diluted in water. (Your janitorial supply house or paint store has these—be sure to follow the specific instructions on the label.) Let it soak in awhile; if the floor is old and marked, you might want to scrub it with a floor scrubbing maching. Flush the solution off, preferably using a floor squeegee, and rinse with a hose. Allow the floor to dry for at least five hours, then apply transparent concrete seal or an all-purpose seal, either of which can be obtained at a paint or janitorial supply store. Apply the seal, according to directions, with any applicator that will distribute it in a nice even coat, and let it dry. I'd advise a second coat to ensure good coverage.

Blue Ribbon Junkees

I don't like to single out any specific class or social order of junkee for dishonorable mention, but you farmers deserve it (men and women both, so don't any of you try to sneak off). Everything written in this book about clutter can be applied "double strength" to most farm people. Few city or suburban junkees can touch your bumper crop of good old clutter. Don't think I'm judging you harshly or unfairly—you know you're guilty. As I write this, I look out the window at my 100-foot-long, 30-foot-deep farm shop that contained not some, not a lot, but *tons* of junk.

Farmers have one distinct advantage over town junkers: they have more room to spread it out. They can distribute it eloquently from the north forty to "out behind the barn." They have silos, barns, sheds, cellars, extra houses, feeders, and granaries all available to store junk—and they do.

Farm men are almost twice as bad as farm women (who are twice as bad as a normal uptowner); they can blame everything on making a living and throw in a couple of big words they learned from the Extension Service agent and nothing will be questioned! Farmers keep *everything* because room is no problem— old tractors, machines, and vehicles they just park farther out in the field each time. They keep them for parts, of course, and the ancient 1880 junk they keep to snare a dumb city slicker who'll come along and pay $500 for a rusty milk can or a warped wagon wheel. Most farmers keep their old work boots so long that they can walk off by themselves— and the old gloves, hats, jackets, and coveralls they keep, alone, could stuff a silo. They have enough bolts buried somewhere to bolt the cover down on an MX missile, and as for tools, most have a $70,000 inventory. Yet they keep the wire and string from every bale of hay, and every bucket, can, barrel, sack, and container that ever ambled onto the place. (We'd *all* like to do that so we all envy them.) They never throw away a worn or broken part, because if the new one breaks, they can recycle the old one even twenty rusting years later. But the absolute clincher is: once a farmer owns a welder and a blowtorch (which most do) *nothing* is junk. Everything—even a license plate frame broken in four places—is kept because with a torch and welder you can make or repair anything and must have scrap metal around. I've seen hundreds of farmers cut some good metal off an old truck bed and then keep the old flaking skeleton for years, secure in the thought that they'd be able to pry a 10¢ lock washer off someday . . . if they need it. . . .

Brethren of the soil, I've struggled with this myself through two generations of farms and ranches and most of it is clutter! Haul it off and plant something—you'll reduce the rattlesnake breeding grounds and help prevent injuries and divorces, as well as the profanities you utter every time you're looking through it for a part.

I love farm women—they're the real class and beauty of the world's womanhood, so I won't mention the fact that they are also the champion bottle collectors of the world, the garden junk accumulators of all time, the sewing scrap savers supreme, queens of the recipe collectors, and of course the cellar shelf fillers without equal. Farm folk, de-junk—and the junkyard won't know what hit it!

By Their Junk Shall Ye Know Them

All the rest of you now chuckling at those junk-collecting farmers, don't feel too smug (or slighted that you aren't in first place) because there are other groups that are right in there. If we had a "Profession Possession Printout," you'd probably find *artists* crowding the top. They can and do keep anything and everything, even old stiff and battered brushes, because after all, everything has art form. Some of their old paints are harder than a new cook's pie crust; their half-finished canvases could ruin your appetite. They have drawers full of rusted lettering pens, colored pencil stubs, grubby bits of crayon, globs of kneaded eraser, petrified poster paint, solid oils, cracked linoleum, scratched scraper board, tea-stained drawing board, powdered charcoal, empty glue tubes, and a secret horde of half-joined-up dot-to-dot books. Their "To Do Someday" file fills two portfolios—and they keep it all, in the name of art!

Schoolteachers, too, are right in the running for the Junk World Series. Teachers have to contend with sample books, programs, and a half-century of yearbooks—not to mention the inevitable gifts from students. They pick up information (and things) enthusiastically and have the perfect excuse . . . they always need background material and visual aids.

For geologists anything on or in the earth's crust is fair game for keeping—the result often being a fine collection of fossil junk. Engineers save every broken machine and appliance and length of pipe in hope of rebuilding or salvaging or devising something useful. And book editors save every snippet.

At least professional junkees have the excuse of making a living. Junking hobbyists clutter for the sheer fun of it—and once they've filled their own homes to bursting with ceramic owls, macramé plant hangers, paint-by-number portraits, sequined light switches, and decoupaged desk accessories, they start in on their friends' and relatives' houses and fill those. By the time they've saturated their entire acquaintance list, they've become not only proficient, but *fast*—so they have no alternative but to move on to church and school craft bazaars, hobby fairs, and flea markets. They are then classifiable as professional craftspeople, and their garages and basements and spare rooms swell with stock, supplies, display materials, and equipment to match—not to mention a conglomeration of clutter in various stages of completion, because they've moved on to assembly-line production!

Those Personal Treasures

. . . Might Some Be Clutter?

Don't think you're the only one who has a heart wrapped around treasures you'll never use, that are doing no good, but are unique, valuable, and impress others with your good judgment for possessing them. As I write this, I only have to look about to spot four of my favorites. One is a perfect replica of the first Bell telephone, handmade, only ten like it in the world, a fine and beautiful thing worthy of any Bell System consultant like me. There's not really any place to put it, so I use it for a bookend so I can rationalize keeping it. (The books it tries to hold tumble it over easily.) Next I have a pair of genuine Mexican mariachis; they won't stand up, and roll off any flat surface I set them on. I did put them in the speaker of the genuine 1876 Bell phone for weight, and of course then when I got out a book, both the phone and the mariachis toppled over. Then there is my brass bugle, my finest treasure—I can't play a lick on it, but I've wanted a bugle since I was eight

years old. One of my managers gave me one for Christmas when I was forty-five, gads, I love it, it just hangs there waiting for a battle or revival. I put it in the telephone speaker in another attempt to improve my "bookend," but it looked bad so I rehung it.

Then there is my beloved collection of toilet miniatures, including toilet pencil sharpeners, toilet erasers, toilet soup mugs, toilet squirt guns, toilet salt and pepper shakers, toilet keychains, toilet clocks, toilet charms, toilet pendants, toilet neckerchief slides, etc. Although I am a professional toilet cleaner, these beauties have cost me numerous hours of dusting, cleaning, arranging, and protecting. I can't bring myself to de-junk them, so I made a $180 recessed glass display case and now they rest safely in undisturbed beauty. That's what I did in one attempt to contain the "personal treasures" problem.

Can Jewels Become Junk?

In Hawaii at age twenty-one, I was fascinated by a little ship made out of seashells with thread rigging. I bought it because to me at the time it was a masterpiece to behold. I brought it home and moved it, dusted it, cleaned it, repaired it; it sat on my shelf for twenty-seven years and had without doubt the finest physique to capture cobwebs of any object ever invented. As the years went on, I said, "Boy, that's ugly, but I've had it twenty years, it would be a shame to break the record," so I kept it another five. It looked more hideous every day and finally became so barnacled with grime and flyspecks that a self-respecting fly wouldn't even land on it, so I pitched it. The first five years I owned the thing I enjoyed it. The last twenty years were misery—it took something from me. Clutter of many kinds evolves in our life: without changing appearance it can quietly shift from a plus to a minus.

We are free agents unto ourselves

when it comes to junking up our lives—we investigate, accumulate, and then suddenly discover much of our lives is spent regulating the clutter we have accumulated. It grows old fast, and our junk around us, on us, in us begins to irritate. Most people, when they reach the state of irritation, do the wrong things, go the wrong way; they accumulate more gadgets to help organize the junk and that only leads to more junk and more irritation.

Highbrow Junk

Cost and *class* are not always partners. The word "expensive" has whitewashed junk for far too long. We snigger aloofly at the ugly dimestore vase, while an elaborate engraved urn that does the very same thing (stands a flower up so we can smell it) gets the stamp of approval. The difference between porcelain and plaster of Paris here is piddly; both are often obnoxious, seldom used, and not as attractive as a clean simple container would be. Highbrow junk, we can call it. Those elegant gifts or purchases of lion claw candlesticks, silver cigarette lighters, unspeakable opera glasses, chic little bowls, exotic lamps, $200 beer steins, and copper or brass kitchen extras cost a lot more but are still right in there with the five-and-dime stuff.

Many of these inexpressibly elegant things don't actually *do* anything—they are pure decoration, exquisite objects that just *sit* in a house. They don't perform any function—which is fine if you really enjoy them, take real *pleasure* in looking at them and rearranging their display. But junk is junk if you don't take much notice of it, and it has no real useful purpose.

Sold as Brass

"Brass" and "copper" are important words in the highbrow junk vocabulary. A woman I overheard commented that every time her husband came back from a foreign country, he brought her something—it didn't really matter what, as long as it was *brass*. She complained, said that she could start a metal recycling foundry in her living room, but he continued bringing things home because they were not only a bargain, they were *brass!*

Brass and copper *are* durable, but not necessarily better for every purpose and they are high-maintenance materials. They cost a small fortune to buy and a bigger fortune in time to keep looking good. (The owners of brass beds often complain they spend more time polishing than using them.) I helped clean King Charles II's 350-year-old brass candleholders in England's Winchester Cathedral—those massive, elegant things are worn thin and frail from being polished once a week for all those years. Even the solder is wearing out from cleaning. How many lifetimes have been polished away in that time? Do any personal treasures take precedence over human life—especially yours?

Elaborate, overdone furniture is a must in the highbrow clutter collector's inventory. These things are designed, built, and sold to be looked at. I can enjoy the love and association of eating at a nice big handsome table—but I have a hard time understanding how and why people will stand in line and pay to look at a table. "It's a Chippendale," someone gasps. I'll wager you nine out of ten of us would enjoy the other Chip & Dale (those two cartoon chipmunks) more.

Another fixture of highbrow junk is the twinkling crystal chandelier. As a professional cleaner, I hate those things. Light is light, and rarely can a person tell the difference between polished plastic and crystal in a light fixture, yet there the crystal must hang to hang you and your pocketbook—and impress other neck-craning clutter collectors. Crystal, like china, seems to be bought mainly to lend an elegance to the household that the dwellers seem to lack.

You could easily argue that highbrow junk is *more* immoral than lowbrow junk

because it's more expensive both to buy and own. It's more squandrous of our life's substance—or the lives of others. We could have spent that money to feed a starving child or help a struggling student, to fund a cause, friend, family—something alive! We can saturate our junking impulse in a big spree at Woolworth's and not feel too bad—we may have a pile of awful things but we're only out fifty bucks or less. Highbrow junk is hundreds or thousands of dollars and we can *still* have a pile of awful stuff.

Highbrow junk consumes a lot of our life force, especially when we have to part with it. That's the reason many people dread dying so much—they have to leave all their junk. If it were worth nothing, they'd feel they had nothing to lose and leave this planet more peacefully.

Our walls and yards sport some grotesque images we call art. But because it was expensive, original, highbrow merchandise we grin and bear it.

How many of us, deep in our hearts, would like to tear down and shred to bits some "artistic" monstrosity we've had to courteously acknowledge for years? Cheap junk is easier to chuck. Highbrow is sacred? Don't you believe it.

China and Silverware Displays

Some clutter seems to be used to resolve a family identity hangup. The classic is china and silverware. To accumulate that one special set of china and sterling (right down to the embossed liver ladle) is a lifetime dream of many. When they finally get it all, there's no way they'll risk breaking, scratching, or losing any of it. So a nightmare of a china closet is secured and therein—behind glass—is the treasure. The silver is velvet-draped in an oak casket, double-locked in the bottom drawer of the same cabinet.

Who in the right mind would really take all this space, time, trouble, and insurance money to display a bunch of *dishes?* Think about it—a bunch of eating tools—so people can gaze and say, "Oh, your saucer is so captivating. Is it Haviland or Royal Doulton?" If we're going to mount some house tool we use this much, why not something with more character—like the can opener, potato masher, even the garden spray nozzle? Most "good" china is used once or twice a

year; silverware less. It takes tons of energy to keep it. After you die someone will probably end up feeding their mangy hound dog out of it anyway. Those place settings would pay for a trip or an education that would nourish you much more than any food eaten off them ever will!

Hobbies and Collections

Some of the most worthwhile and inspiring achievements in the world come from people who gathered, preserved, restored, and displayed things and appreciated their greatness. But the value of this whole undertaking is in *sharing* it—displayed (or otherwise used) hobbies and collections stimulate our fellow humans and prod them to accomplishment.

As long as a collection produces those effects, it's probably a plus, but think of how many "collections" end up out of bounds and perspective. The model train that took a space on the floor . . . then the room . . . then the adjoining room . . . then a choo-choo rolls out of every cupboard and the dog and the kids get kicked for fiddling or playing with it. Our stained glass or jewel collection often gets too valuable to be used or left in sight and we wouldn't think of selling it—then what value is it? A time, space, and energy robber!

Locked or hidden away, collections can be a mental drain to their owner, because they generate no love and appreciation, yet the owner has to store, insure, clean, and protect them. But it can't be denied that some of us get a (perhaps not admirable) thrill out of simply acquiring, hoarding, counting, running our fingers over, polishing—all by our own personal selves—our *collections*. If it really adds to our life, then it is of unquestionable value; this again is why "junk or not" is a judgment only you can make.

Hobbies and collections can help us develop great discipline and organization,

but too often, as time passes we've outgrown them—yet the skeleton remains to haunt us in the form of clutter. Use it (to show, etc.) or lose it. Make sure it rewards you and others.

Antiques

We all cherish the history, character, and spirit that antiques convey. They are great on display in museums or mounted in galleries or put to use in homes, but when our whole house becomes a "no touch" antique asylum, we may want to reassess our "valuable" merchandise. Is it just for show, status, an "I got it first" ego object? If so, it will junk your life— donate it and have them engrave your name on a plate and fasten it to the case. That way you'll get full credit, thousands will see it, and it will last many of your lifetimes (that's more than you were accomplishing with it around the house).

One of the biggest problems with antiques is that we all have a friend or have read an article that tells us we have a fortune under those cobwebs; we are often naive enough to elevate that careless inexpert opinion to a bona fide art appraisal, an endorsement to save clutter, if not an agony of unfulfilled expectations. When I worked with teams of horses as a youth, old worn-out horse collars were of zero value, and we junked them. So when in Jackson Hole, Wyoming, I saw a collar with a mirror mounted in it, price-tagged at $200— gads, I was sick; I'd thrown away at least $2,000 worth of horse collars! I resolved henceforth to save all old farm stuff in case another such opportunity arose. After six sheds filled up and seventeen dealers were craftily detoured through them and still no one was knocking at my door, I realized I was deceiving myself. Don't horse around with imagined antiques—and as for the real ones, use them or lose them.

It's amazing how an aged, broken, chipped, scarred, worn-out object dug out of storage or the trash becomes valuable—what is it that accounts for this sudden worth?

Why do people have a fascination and longing for the old, the quaint, the antique? They want to retreat to, be reminded of, be projected back to a simpler day of greater freedom and integrity—they secretly want to be *de-junked!*

Junk Doesn't Generate Self-Esteem

During an evening discussion of clutter (which one often has when writing a book about it), three sharp professional home consultants brought up an interesting concept. They visit many homes helping people straighten up their lives (and dwellings), and had observed that people (rich and poor) who have themselves and their homes overloaded with things often have extremely low self-esteem. After that conversation I began to pay close attention to those who should be de-junking. Many are professional people, astute community leaders, etc., but they don't seem to measure up to what they're trying to be. They have tons of "in" or "proper" things but seldom ever *use* them—the stuff is just displayed like banners or flags, a kind of testament of intention. These people have jogging suits but they don't jog, exercise bikes that are rusting out, how-to-discipline-children books but unruly kids, and tons of hunting or fishing or camping gear but they never hunt or fish or camp. They buy cookbooks to assuage their guilt for never cooking. By owning and surrounding themselves with the trappings, they somehow satisfy the need to be what people expect them to be.

Often the best-equipped, best-prepared person is the one who does the least—he'll buy a Whole Hog Industrial Power Pack III when a nice home-model Black & Decker would do just fine. A friend of mine once bought a 790-piece tool set from Sears in a rolling tool chest; he never turned a bolt, but it made him feel he was *equipped* to do anything that might come up.

Junk doesn't generate self-esteem or fulfill our ambitions—only *we* can do that. "Owning" is like theory, totally worthless if not put to use. Sitting there in idle beauty, clutter can in fact *undermine* our self-esteem—all those "I ought, but I don'ts" will get you every time they're brought to sight or mind.

No Strings Attached

Why do we keep old musical instruments (Grandma's organ) indefinitely?

Anything that has strummed our heartstrings like an old guitar (even two of them) is difficult to pitch. I never could part with the first guitar I had, an old flatbox folk guitar. It wouldn't stay in tune and finally was impossible to play, but I'd learned a lot of chords on it, and it was so "purty" I couldn't throw it away. I hung it on our western-styled kitchen wall for decoration, and there it stayed, collecting grease, for five years, until one day our house was robbed and the guitar went with the burglar (I'll bet he cusses me every time he tries to tune it).

My second guitar was a cutway electric I'd had since 1953 (through high school, college, and many performances), a premium model—but the treble switch was staticky and the strings finally shorted out—even people who borrowed it for free, never did so again. But yesterday, when I came home with a brand new electric guitar, throwing that old one out seemed like cutting off an arm—it was all those memories. I finally gathered up my resolve and in last ceremony played "The Cowboy's Lament," took it to the valley, laid the sod o'er it and amazingly, it didn't hurt a bit!

When four reeds are plugged on the old harmonica, when the piano ivories are headed for the elephant's graveyard, all the knobs are gone on the radio, and the stereo speakers are cracked and rattley—when you're shuffling through those warped and skipping records and the tapes you never play—do like the song says, "Please release them."

While we're tuned to the channel of freeing ourselves, let's not forget those delightful and intriguing music boxes. Though they rarely are used as the jewelry box or beer mug they pretended to be, their sound justifies their possession—and so our dresser tops boast them over time until the love theme from *Rocky XII* or "A Tisket a Tasket" no longer tinkles forth. The twirling ballerinas lapse into spasms and the latches are sagged or broken from showing it off. It's now mute and ugly but we'd sooner part with our season symphony tickets than discard that broken music box. De-junk it at its demise—thank it and cast it forth!

Lettered Litter

Anyone who thinks of starting his own business or ranch will, even before important financial and logistical considerations are weighed, immediately determine how his name or brand will appear. There is some understandable ambition in wanting to see our name in lights, and since there's no way we can drag a 3,000-watt marquee or a 12-pound branding iron around with us, having our name on smaller things—well, it hypnotizes us. If someone engraved our name on a steel manhole cover, we'd find a way to roll it home and store it. If we could, we'd carry home *all* the stuff we've ever name-branded—every beech tree, cliff, school desk, and restroom wall. Our name, even our initials, emblazoned on anything seems to be the official stamp of

discard immunity. A 35¢ hanky, once stained and stinky, can be junked easily; a 35¢ monogrammed hanky in similar condition merits full-scale restoration. People keep nonfunctional suitcases with their initials on them far longer than they keep the same non-initialed type. Same with belts, shirts, shorts, bracelets, and tools. The mystique of a monogram protects tons of junk—silly, and impractical, too. Many such things are designed more to show off a monogram than for function, and you can't even loan things!

The only thing sillier than being obsessed with wearing your own initials is being obsessed with wearing someone else's. Celebrity monograms (about ½¢ worth of thread) have about a 10,000 percent markup. I bought a suit in Miami, and because my color-matching leaves a lot to be desired, I had the salesman pick a tie out for me. A few days later when I was wearing it in Chicago on business, a man said to me, "Anyone who wears a _____ can pay the price." It turned out my tie had a designer monogram on it, which no doubt was why it cost $32.50. Why should I pay extra to flaunt someone else's advertising around? I gave the tie away! Don't waste good money and good taste flexing your monograms.

Is Nothing Sacred?

Because many people are interested in but few understand religion, with its many confusing denominations and approaches, they want to make sure they are spiritually secure. So they think owning something "religious" or "God-related" will help—the more they have, the thicker the spirit will be. And it's hard to get rid of religious junk because we're afraid dumping it might be an unholy action.

I know I'm treading on hallowed ground now, so I'll only suggest you cast an eye over all the stuff you've saved to "save" you and handle it appropriately (pamphlets, replicas, wall hangings, plaques, bottled Holy Land dust, even the magnetic cross for your refrigerator door that glows in the dark). Let me just point out something to get you going. I'm not without religious conviction—I served two years in the mission field teaching Scriptures, I speak regularly at religious events and gatherings, and try to enact Christian principles in my life and business—but haven't you noticed our hangup with *owning* Bibles instead of reading them? In the course of an average life you could accumulate, without ever buying one, a whole library of Bibles. Dusting the Bible is no joke—it could be a three-acre undertaking.

I've seen all of these Bibles in one person's possession. Check the list—how many do *you* have?

- family Bible
- his-and-her Bibles
- storybook Bible (for the kids)
- large print Bible
- red letter Bible
- Grandpa's old Bible
- school Bible
- Army Bible
- Bible you won
- pocket travel Bible
- Bible on tape
- computer chip Bible
- postage stamp Bible
- leather-bound Bible
- Gideon Bible (swiped from the motel, just in case)

Thirty-three Bibles crammed in drawers and glove compartments won't impress anyone—surely not the Lord, who said:

Not everyone who sayest "Lord, Lord," shall enter the Kingdom, but he that doth the will of my Father in Heaven. . . .

Conduct is the only criterion for blessing. Holiness is in the application of the message—not ownership of it. "God Bless Our Home"—no matter how charmingly cast in plaster or stitched on linen—won't do the trick. Wandering through a perplex of pious paraphernalia is a waste of time. Leave some space for Him in your life, the space all that junk is taking up. . . . Amen, brother.

HOW DO YOU JUDGE VALUE?

Judgments on the worth or worthlessness of things are, in the end, your business, not mine as a writer or celebrated toilet cleaner. I'll be satisfied if I manage to make you stop and think about, weigh the worth of some of the "valuables" you hoard, guard, polish, worship, and display.

Don't be like the father who had four antique guns—not one-of-a-kind collector's items, but respectable pieces worth about $5,000 each. When his daughter reached college age, the family was pinched for cash and could see no way to pay $5,000 per year to see their vibrant and musically talented daughter fulfill her education and her dream. She never did, and the father kept those old guns around in a rack until he died. Then the kids divided them up, sold them, bought cars and couches, and partied. His daughter could have been a living inspiration for all his posterity; his guns ended up valueless. I know people who buy silver saddles and snowmobiles before putting braces on their children's crooked teeth. Fascination with trinkets passes, but a self-conscious child is cheated for fifty years.

Capital Clutter

Money was once a medium of exchange; somehow it has gotten to be a measure of personal value. Of course money is needed for sustenance and some convenience, but the time and energy we spend on its handling and possession can easily be the most catastrophic clutter in our life. Let me share some things I did at home and in my business that freed me to find the time and life and production I lost when buried in "finances."

Watching the financial "geniuses," reading the financial books and papers, and paying close attention to the classy ads and articles, I spread my money around, dealt with several banks, and had a dab of money in this investment and a dab in that investment and some in different savings accounts. Really a meager amount, but it felt so up-to-the-moment and impressive (like reading the whole stock page because you own three shares of stock in some firm).

I had three drawers full of checkbooks and deposit slips and six separate files for different statements and transactions. Some accounts only had $35 in them, but took as much room and mail as if it were $35,000. For fifteen years I kept a separate savings account for some leftover escrow money—less than a hundred dollars—yet every time a statement came (expensive for me and the bank) I had to file it, and every time tax time rolled around all those times, places, and amounts—no matter how paltry—had to be added in and around. When my accounting bill got to $3,000 I realized how stupid all these little things were—some $25 insurance dividend funds cost over $45 in legal and accounting fees yearly (not counting my own time and effort).

The balancing and paperwork to keep up these financial appearances ("image") wasn't worth it. All those accounts and investments junked my life; it was a total waste of time and space. *All* financial institutions offer the same product—*money.* Who you deal with and how they deal with you is the only important variable. I finally found one banker I liked and got rid of my numerous accounts. At tax time or any other time I need anything there is only one summary sheet, one person to deal with.

Like magic, my mail and accounting costs and "personal finance time" shrank when I consolidated things and got rid of all the twinky and squirrelly financial involvements. Every day I get calls for "deals" where I only have to put in a little each day or week or month and. . . . The trouble with these, no matter how legitimate they may be, is that you forget how much of yourself will also be invested there.

People who make percentages off you are experts—when they know you can't afford something, financially or emotionally, they work out a payment deal so you can get it. Fifteen percent return on something that strains a relationship, a marriage, or your health is a poor investment.

My life blossomed when I de-junked my financial clutter. The week I used to spend rounding up all the deals, the week of the accountant's time to check and calculate, I now use for a week in Hawaii or with my grandkids. The fewer window envelopes that arrive at the first of the month, the more I can see and feel the refinements of living.

The Polite Man's Burden: Gifts

Most of us manage to obtain ample (excessive) junk through our own efforts; we don't really need the help of friends contributing to our stack, but they do. Christmas, Hanukkah, birthdays, Valentine's Day, goodbyes, hellos always inspire a gift, of cash or sentimental value. It's the thought that counts, of course, but once the thought is registered, we still have the item hanging around. We all get gifts that are junk, but it isn't couth to throw out a gift. "What if I throw it out and they find it in the trash," or "What if they come to my home and don't see it in use, won't their feelings be hurt?" Well, they probably will be, but getting rid of the stuff would help eliminate daily irritation in *your* life.

Someone gave my mother-in-law a beautiful thick hand-knitted wool Kleenex box cover, the sole purpose of which was to make a Kleenex box pleasing to look at. It also made the box bulky and hard to carry around, and pulling tissue through the slit in the top was not undifficult by any means. Her husband became a raging bull each time the knitted cover was reinstalled, but my mother-in-law refused to part with this hard-to-clean, non-matching, totally unuseful piece of clutter—because it was a *gift*.

It is "ill-mannered" to give or throw a gift away—no matter how worthless it may be—so we keep it. Most of this is or becomes junk. (Have you ever noticed how just about everything in a "gift shop" you could get along very well without?) So those dreadful bookends and fancy pen sets, overdone ashtrays, busts, plaques, and plates accumulate, collect dust, and in general complicate life. Who needs them? Paperweights, for instance—has anyone ever established what, when, and why paper has to be weighed down? Any paper on a desk long enough to be weighed down should have been acted on or thrown out. Give a paperweight long enough and it will get scratched or stolen, broken or back-drawered, all testifying it is junk. But again, it's a "gift"—which seems to sanctify it and earn it a right to plague us the rest of our lives. The Board, the kids, the Scouts, the team gave it to us, or our sweet caring mother (and in this case, it's probably a hand-hooked rug with a decided resemblance to the Washington Monument). We'll drag it around from house to house like an old buffalo hide, never used—but *Mother* gave it to us. Or it's a razor-sharp seashell-encrusted purse that matches nothing, and holds less—but our son brought it back from the South Pacific. So our lives are "gifted" to the point of strangulation; this is when people plan fires, escape to Tahiti, or contemplate suicide. They can't face the junk any more, but can't face the donor if they dump it.

What Is the Value of a Gift?

A gift, regardless of its value, if given sincerely has a certain sacredness. It is a concise message of love and appreciation, a nod of acknowledgment for something felt. But we should always remember not to confuse the *meaning* of a gift with the gift itself. The actual gift is only a vessel to express; once it does that, it generally has fulfilled its function. Its message will live with us, be part of us—forever, possibly—but should we drag around the vessel after it has served its purpose? That's like leaving the scaffolding up after a building is finished—take it down!

An incident that sheds some light on the question of gift values occurred on the way home from a two-week consulting job. I bought my wife a dozen long-stemmed red roses and presented them to her as I stepped off the plane. She was thrilled. The roses said I was thinking of her, the velvety petals were a delight to look at and touch, the scent stimulated old memories and some reflection on our future—all in all, it showed that I cared, that she was important to me. After she displayed them for a few days and basked a little in the jealousy of her friends, the roses withered and drooped and were thrown out with no regrets. They had accomplished their job; it was $27.50 well spent.

En route to the airport in Atlanta on Valentine's Day a couple of months later, I spotted a tailgate sale on the side of the road. There was a gigantic display of oversized stuffed animals—I mean some

were five feet high—tigers, skunks, pandas, bears, deer, etc. I stopped and selected a big yellow dog with a bright red tongue; it was impressive if I say so myself. Wanting to get rid of every toy, the guy sold it to me for $27.50. It was a bear to get home on the plane, but I managed and presented it to my wife at the airport. As before, she was thrilled, the giant fuzzy doggie with the big eyes said I was thinking of her, its enthusiastic expression caused some old memories to come back and some reflection on our future—all in all, exactly like the roses, it showed that I cared, that she was important. After she displayed it a few days, stroked and cuddled it, and her friends saw it, the doggie drooped a little, one eye loosened and fell off, but no way was she going to throw the ailing animal out. It stayed around, fell over, got torn and dirty, the stuffing straggled out. It was a real pain, but it was *tangible*. The minute I gave it to her we got our $27.50 out of it, just like the roses—them you can pitch, but the mutt stayed to make life miserable.

One day we finally decided that dingy dog went or else—we'd enjoyed it, why not let it work again for someone else? A little neighbor got more mileage out of it, and again it thrilled someone (almost as much as me).

Think of the things you have received or given that cost even less than meals, roses, perfumes, etc., that are long gone, but that you got your money's worth and more out of even though you have nothing physical left to show for it. Many of the things that bring fun or enjoyment to our lives, promote good will, give us a good thrill, or carry a caring message are not *objects*. So why keep every trinket? You don't have to keep them to prove anything. The memories and feelings don't reside in the gift, but in *you*, and a tangible gift can actually become a junk millstone around your neck.

> *Give gifts that dissipate—*
> *like perfume! But clutter*
> *collectors could foul that up,*
> *they'd keep the bottle. . . .*
> *Give a basketful of fruit,*
> *they'd love it, eat it, and it*
> *would be gone—except*
> *they'll keep the basket!*
>
> *A $5 ticket—a smile/a*
> *message—gone*
> *A $5 trinket—a smile/a*
> *message—keep*

Dare to Be Really Different

We all like to be unique in our personality and possessions, and this "individualism" contributes mightily to clutter accumulation. We'll search unrelentingly for something "different"—for us, or for a gift. Giving the unusual is the highest standard of gift giving. The harder to find, the rarer, the odder, the greater the mystique, the greater our point score and (regardless of its worth) the more greatly it is valued. An object's actual use or contribution is no consideration here—only the fact that "no one else has one." This is why those catalogs crammed with monogrammed toilet paper, electric bookmarks, talking lamps, and walking false teeth are so compelling.

What happens to such things after the giddy moment of presentation is generally ignored. The "different" thing is among the most eligible to become junk. To really be different, let's not waste each other's time and money on them. I won't dump any on you if you won't on me, because we'll both have trouble discarding them.

Can Charity Be Uncharitable?

We've all fallen once or twice for the tempestuous acquisition of a gift for no one in particular. We spot something we want, we don't really *need* it, we can't really afford it, it doesn't 100 percent suit us—but it's lovely: we want it. Our conscience sides with dejunking and tells us no!—but it's so *nice* (it could be a simple clay pot or a slab of salmon). We finally resort to Scripture, which tells us charity is the most honorable of human acts, so we get it "to give, to someone." Now that we have bought it without guilt, one of three things will happen:

1. We will never give it to anyone.

2. If we *do* give it to someone we hold dear, we'll have to give them another gift on top of it (because we know *they* don't really want it).

3. We'll end up giving it to someone we had no intention of giving anything to. We really aren't being kind—we're making *ourselves* feel better.

Listen to your conscience—IT KNOWS!

When giving gifts, don't saddle your giftee with junk. Ralph Waldo Emerson gave some good guidelines for a gift:

> The only gift is a portion of thyself. Thou must bleed for me. Therefore the poet brings his poem; the shepherd, his lamb; the farmer, corn; the miner, a gem; the sailor, coral and shells; the painter, his picture; the girl, a handkerchief of her own sewing. This is right and pleasing, for it restores society in so far to its primary basis, when a man's biography is conveyed in his gift, and every man's wealth is an index of his merit. But it is a cold, lifeless business when you go to the shops to buy me something which does not represent your life and talent, but a goldsmith's.

How to Dispose of Junk Gifts

You are not obligated to prolong the misery of a possession someone (however sincerely) had the poor judgment to lay on you. We love people for the *thought* of the gift, not the gift. Once they present it and we've accepted it, the relationship is strengthened and made richer (which is the value of any gift). If the item happens to be a loser, make it a winner by chucking it.

But as sure as we finally take it to the thrift or secondhand shop, the owner will wander in the establishment the next day and weep over our heartless gesture. If we store it, it won't be visible when they visit, and they will quiver and pout. My wife always sicced the kids on unwanted gifts and they got broken and thrown out pronto. But the kids had a way of blabbing to the donor in detail how their mama begged them to play hockey with it. And the time-honored tactic of re-wrapping and re-giving (preferably to someone you don't care all that much about) is risky business in this small world of ours.

If a Gift Is Good or Valuable

Give it to someone else down the line in the family who might actually need it. "Passed for posterity" is usually accepted *within* a family.

You can take a color picture of the gift—then forget where you put it. The picture is evidence that you must have appreciated it—after all, who would photograph junk?

You can leave it in your car, on the back seat (gift-wrapped if necessary), and park your car, unlocked, in a rough section of town. If it doesn't disappear quickly, leave the window down a little. When you tell the giver the gift was literally swiped from your car, they will be flattered that (1) you were carrying it around, and (2) someone wanted it enough to steal it. That's double value—triple if you count your relief.

My brother pulled off a useful variation on this approach. He had two unwanted bucket seats so he left them on the front lawn while the family went on a trip. Sure enough, upon their return, the seats were gone. Before their next move they did it even more easily: "We just left the garage door open, old sofa in front, and as the song goes, 'Phtt—she was gone.'"

You can put your name on a gift and donate it to a museum—that really turns the giver on: they'll love you as much as you love getting rid of the junk. Or if you can, donate it to an auction (just make sure it's in another town).

If you let the word out that you don't like expensive gifts, or that it is against company or personal policy to accept gifts, it's amazing how quickly gifts stop.

As a last resort, go join a religious order, make a pilgrimage, take on a mission! Anything you rid yourself of in the name of the Lord will never be questioned.

Or you can write a book on clutter—it's amazing how fast people quit giving you trinkets. My last birthday found me in the middle of editing this book; at supper my two daughters and wife confessed they had no present for me; they'd looked for four hours and found nothing I hadn't attacked in this volume. The fact that they had spent four hours flattered me—what a gift—I loved it! We all came out ahead! My mother sent me a cassette on which she'd taped my favorite violin music, another daughter called from Ottawa, my son-in-law baked a mess of trout he'd caught, my granddaughter gave me a card she'd crayolaed on construction paper, and my oldest daughter canned me fourteen quarts of fresh raspberries. I've treasured that birthday as my all-time best!

Homemade . . . Makes It Hard

Homemade, with their own hands, from the heart—even the most heartless de-junker flinches when trying to dispose of that 400-pound solid chipboard bedstand or that pink and purple Mother's Day apron the kids made in camp or at the school shop. Show me a daddy, mommy, grandpa, or grandma who can easily part with even the most obnoxiously misspelled handicraft. Besides being hard to lift, those precious handmade shoeshine boxes, plaster hand casts, end tables, and jewelry boxes are durable as granite and will survive six generations. Once made, you're stuck: since you usually don't want to be seen with them, they don't have a chance to wear out or get broken. Deep in my heart I have a solid respect for what those schools and camps produce through a bunch of kids. They embalm a pile of popsicle sticks with white glue and those babies are indestructible. Earthquake, flood, or fire—they will survive it all, so don't consider any arsonistic approaches. And of course, no one in the right mind would steal them.

What's the solution? I'm stumped, and I have a two-pound tooled leather keychain, a three-inch-thick wooden soap holder, a painted rock, and a pine-cone panther mounted on a slab of barnwood staring me in the face right now. If there are unusually tender feelings involved, it's probably worth the sacrifice to use it—it's no worse than telling someone how great his or her cooking is when it really requires a Rolaid encore. If not, try to have it disappear on a transfer from home to office (everyone will understand).

Sneakiest of all is feigning a real act of love—give it back to them as a cherished memento of *you* to appreciate (they'll trash it, instantly, without a qualm).

What about Trophies and Awards?

Helping others, winning, succeeding, participating, playing, working, attending, or entering just about anything is likely to earn you a trophy or award. These come in the form of certificates, cards, pins, badges, plates, plaques, figurines, bookends, and desk sets.

Trophies and awards, like gifts, are basically a "thank you," a tangible affirmation of success or excellence. It's a thrill to get one, no doubt about it. But if you are really good and get better, you'll get more and more and more—and evolve from an end table to a mantel, to a shelf, to a wall, to an entire room to hold and display them all.

Every year I donate to the Scouts they give me an oak wall plaque. Every time I raise the ante they enlarge the plaque; I'll have to quit donating now after fifteen years because my wall is full.

At a seminar in Bridgeport they gave us the board that came under the eight-inch sandwich we had for lunch. Because I shared the forest on my ranch with a church group, they presented me with a plowshare on which was engraved their thank-you. At my numerous "Life After Housework" seminars I receive all kinds of gifts, from groups and individuals, ranging from miniature flowers to bronzed toilet brushes. Like all of you I appreciate these things, but at some point what do you do with all this? Too many awards can bother rather than build your life. Besides, I'm a little leery of people who have to line their walls with certificates and awards. If you've got it or had it, it should show in your personality and production. Glory is air—but the strength of character and body you developed on your way to earning the award is yours. It's not junk, but a life-giving resource.

Don't take old trophies and awards too seriously. Most of them look like they were carved or cast out of one of the same three molds anyway, and they tarnish, tear, tip over, and provide a

landing strip for flies; you end up spending most of the athletic or creative skill you earned them with now manipulating them.

Cull out the dead ones and keep the living; when the living ones are no longer giving, dump them! Build a trophy room or case if you must, but if you don't get them out from underfoot, they'll become snares instead of signatures of accomplishment.

Consider *giving* them away—let your kids, grandchildren, and your neighbors' children thrill again to them as toys or rewards for chores or heroics. Kids are smart enough to wear it out or lose it. This is also a good place to make use of the photograph technique: take a good sharp photo of it for your album or scrapbook, and you may be able to part with it at last. You can even group all your trophies in one picture. The memory won't go—only the memorabilia.

And if you're *giving* an award, try to remember that trophies are basically useless. An ax can chop and serve; a trophy with a golden ax on top is good for nothing. Give a living award—films, tapes, equipment, clothing, cash, trips—not a shrine that must be tended.

What to Keep of the Keepsakes

Memories are our most valuable possessions, and collected tokens of them can stimulate those memories to be relived again and again. Some tokens and keepsakes are valuable: they enrich life, and we should keep and take care of those. But in the lives of even the most sentimental of us a time arrives, often during a basement- or attic-sorting surge, when memories and junk have to be separated. On a thing as personal as a keepsake, that can only be *your* decision. I offer just one guideline before you start:

Don't love what can't love you back

"I am so sentimental"—aren't we all! But you don't have to *own* something to experience it. A memory, a look, a word,

a touch can generate greater good feelings than a box of "stuff."

We all want to cherish a good memory or experience forever, but preoccupation with physical reminders can lead us to live in the past. One of the toughest and most necessary things in the world for growth and happiness is to release our hold on things, places, and people we've outgrown. Too many people never grow and gain expanding new experiences because they can't see the wisdom of releasing old ones. Junk squeezes out new life. It's more fun being a present or future hero or heroine than a past one.

Consider my high school graduation tassel, a nylon witness of four long and eventful years. It was blue and white, but age turned it yellow and black (our competitor school's colors); it began to fray and shrink, and even the " '53" rusted.

Everyone knew I had graduated, and now all my kids were graduating from college. I lived those days, it fulfilled its purpose, and after twenty-five years, I finally pitched it, wondering why I untangled and worried about it for all those years.

Aftermath junk Be sure you distinguish keepsakes from aftermath junk—which has got to be about the sickest junk of all. This consists of keeping something to remind you of a terrible experience, like the knife that cut the tendon in your hand, that old cast, your kidney stones, your ex-boyfriend's insulting letter and even his frayed jacket, the tennis shoes you were wearing when you scored the goal for the other team and lost the national tournament. Some people can't stand a mate—so they de-junk, get rid of him or her—but then they keep all the little things that remind them of that person. With all the new life and love out there, constantly resurrecting old suffering memories is really straining for something to do in our spare time.

What we hold dear we become Should we choose to spend our lives collecting, preserving, and storing artifacts and inactive possessions we will find ourselves, as we wander through them taking inventory, wandering past the precious moment of life at hand. Holding fast to the unneeded and unused—no matter how valuable it once was—will crowd out the capacity for new and greater honors and accomplishments. As a reminder, record, or instructor, our "past things" have value, but the secret is to not let charm turn into chains, sentiment become a sentence.

This is one of the most important judgments you'll ever make—only *you* know the moment when collectibles have become clutter in your life, and only you have the responsibility to put it right. De-junking will fertilize the soil of your future and make room for more living.

When you stop dragging the skeletons of the past, the once-was or once-did with you, you'll have more freedom to love and be loved. Free yourself from clutter at the critical moment when what you are giving *to* it outweighs what you are gaining *from* it. De-junking is the easiest and most rewarding way to change a plain life to a plus life.

When it comes to keepsakes, ask only one question: *For whom are you keeping it?* Who is the documentation for—you? *You* don't need proof—you *experienced* it. Meaning isn't kept in things, but in memory.

There is no possession finer than a good memory of something. You can use it over and over again, it can make your pulse quicken, your heart sigh, bring tears of joy to your eyes or a laugh to your day—and a good memory of something costs nothing to keep.

Keep It in Your Heart, Not Your Closet

Two weeks after my father's death, Mother brought me his hunting boots (we wore the same size). As I went to place my foot in one, I hit an obstruction—and pulled out a piece of 2x4 carved into a crude but effective block to keep the shape. Those blocks were Dad all over—his ability to get a job done well and inexpensively. I could have cast them away there and then, but I kept them a day or two to absorb their image and feeling—and then was able to pitch them and still feel good about it.

We can't hang onto everything our loved ones ever owned or gave to us, or even to all the things of theirs we find meaningful. But don't hurry to dispose of their belongings; keep them awhile, meditate on them, store up the memories—then save a few most-cherished items and give or throw away the rest.

MINIATURIZE

Miniaturize It

It's perhaps a compromise, but miniaturizing is a solution especially suited to keepsakes and sentimental items—sort of a "reduce-it-if-you-*must*-keep-it" strategy. You might call it "tons to tokens!"

Miniaturizing is the art of taking a big piece of junk that has to go and reducing it to a little piece of junk that can discreetly stay around. It takes little skill and even less imagination to pluck just a button off that shaggy dog sweater, snip a swatch of the wedding dress, press a rosebud instead of the bouquet, salvage the hood ornament instead of the whole car, save the emblem instead of the entire jersey, keep the elk's tooth instead of the elk's head. When the pangs of reluctance tug at you to keep what must go, sit back a second, look at it, and find a way to reduce it to miniature. For stirring memories a piece, symbol, or sample is as effective as the whole.

A woman in Texas was de-junking her house, and had a special problem. Her nineteen-year-old son had died a year earlier; disposing of his belongings was difficult. She had faced the fact that he was gone, but wanted his memory to stay alive and active. He had been a pencil collector, and had accumulated a fine array of them—of no real use to anyone in the family, but a precious reminder of their son's interest. "Should I let them go, or what?" the mother asked me. I agreed that the memory of the pencil collection was important, but to cart a roomful around for the next forty years would benefit no one. I suggested that she select seven or eight that represented the collection and mount them handsomely with a picture of the boy. As for the rest, I suggested taking a couple of nice photographs of them and putting the photos in an album where others could admire and remember, then giving the remaining pencils to a special boy who might have an interest in continuing the collection.

Miniaturizing works on many kinds of clutter, and not just physical objects. If you must use abusive language, for instance, instead of two sentences of ranting and raving uncouthness—reduce it all to one little snarl or arf. It's really the most effective, impressive, and efficient way to swear.

Those headhunters had the right idea for their trophies—*shrink those babies!* Still clutter but less cumbersome.

Consider a Scrapbook—the De-Junker's Bible

I love scrapbooks! They are one of the finest ways of de-junking life and abode. A good scrapbook is interesting and inspiring even to a stranger. Experiences, awards, friends, and accomplishments can all be dramatized and summarized in the pages, where they can be easily shared or enjoyed to our secret heart's content. Well-put-together scrapbooks and photo albums have warmed more hearts, aroused more loyalty, and advanced more personal relationships than any bound book because it's *your* life and feelings between those covers. The secret is to assemble the most meaningful documents and materials, prune them down to the important parts, and display them attractively in a sequence that's logical and easy to follow. Without a good scrapbook much that's memorable in life is forgotten or damaged or lost. If you don't have one, start one today—whether you're nine or ninety—and watch the responses of others. They can now enjoy what you enjoy, feel what you feel—and what could be greater than that!

Can Posterity . . .
Be Preposterous?

Preserve for posterity, but don't become a posterity pervert. Too often our efforts to record an event for posterity end up reducing its significance. Preservation should be a by-product of an event, not dominate it. Take weddings, for example—a serious spiritual time of commitment between two people. We can't simply and quietly allow the couple to have full feeling for the occasion; too often, the whole ceremony has to be scheduled and conducted around the formalities of pictures, flower girls, souvenir-saving, and speeches. The photographers seldom stand aside and take a real action photo of the occasion; they halt the ceremony and move people around according to height, relationship, seniority, and what-have-you. They make the bride and groom stand, sit, kneel, calf-eye with every (even distant) member of the family. No one can gather around the cake at its cutting because the photographer has to be in front to get a clear shot for posterity. The rings have to be placed on the fingers two or three or four times, the cake cut and re-cut to get

the "right" things for posterity—everyone is so bent on preserving they never savor the actual rapture of the moment. Sports events, graduations, showers, baptisms, too, are often so shaped around formality and documentation that the participants are too preoccupied and harassed to feel much going through the motions—they have to look at the pictures to actually experience the event.

At a Scout Jamboree we had 3,000 youngsters to a church service, a great speaker, a great morning to remember—but the media and the posterity perverts ruined it all by trying to preserve it. My most vivid memories are of whirring tape recorders, camera/video technicians crowding their rumps in our faces, and then a helicopter (large Army model) hovering and passing over us ("whop, whop, whop")—such that we all missed most of the service.

Experiences are meant to be just that—an actual live experience. They shouldn't be prerecorded to be "aired" later in life. I've watched people at Yellowstone so bent on collecting "records" to enjoy later, they missed the beauty of the park. They were so buried in junk food, so busy shooting pictures, buying souvenirs, T-shirts, and maps to the next sight that they never took a minute to stand and soak in the actual experience of that spectacular place. We can't prerecord our life for replay, because at the replay we're only spectators. The joy comes from the participation. Laying up treasures of the event to enjoy or for posterity to enjoy is not even in the same league with experiencing the event itself, letting all preservation be an optional by-product. Preoccupation with preservation doesn't heighten an experience; it diminishes it.

Your Last Gift: Don't Junk from the Grave

We all die, but life is eternal; our spirit, legacy, legend, and influence live on! So leaving and giving junk to your family is not only unnecessary but unkind. The "gift" obligation is a hundred times stronger when the giver is deceased—they'll never be able to dump your junk or rid themselves of guilt if they do. Get rid of your clutter and collections before you cash in—don't give junk a chance to be resurrected in someone else's life.

Everyone over fifty spends too much time and emotion worrying about what they'll leave to their family; everyone under fifty spends too much time and emotion worrying about what they're going to inherit. It's downright dumb. Leaving junk to a family is often more an act of revenge than of love. It's pathetic how families are broken apart, divided into a mass of quarreling maniacs squabbling and suing over dead people's junk. Oddly enough, it's usually not the normal inheritances of land or money that everyone gets most uptight about—it's the junk, the stuff only valuable to the person who previously owned and treasured it. After deaths and divorces I've seen families split apart, people quit speaking and do ugly, ugly acts trying to get their fair share of somebody else's

junk—a $3.95 pocket knife, a monogrammed hanky, a broken arrowhead collection, a rifle that hasn't fired straight in thirty years, an old ax, a worthless sewing machine, Grandma's rhinestone brooch, a disintegrating quilt.

Inheriting the Hoard

Think a minute—what will happen to all of *your* belongings, those stashed sentimental personal items, when you pass away? Someone, someday, will have to come and unappreciatively wade through it. To you, most of it is treasure; to them, it's trash—except the particular items they most associate with you. Unfortunately, it's trash they'll feel guilty disposing of because it's *yours*—the dear departed one's. Who were you saving all this for? For *you*. That's pretty ironic, because you never seem to use it or even take the time to look at it. I know we all imagine a miniature elf version of ourselves reverently handling all our leftovers. Not so—only *you* hold reverence for your own junk. So *use* it or, if others would, give it to them now, or sell it, so you can have the living thrill of benefit, instead of nagging regrets.

Don't burden someone else with your junk. Spend it, give it away, sell it—don't leave for heaven without it. Cash in your clutter before *you* cash in—start at age forty-five just to be safe.

How would you like your obituary to read like this:

She is survived by: a ceramic Elvis decanter; six bags of lint from the dryer; a corset puller; a purple fur-flower arrangement; three pairs of bronze booties; seven hundred copies of *Good Housekeeping*; an assortment of old campaign buttons; fifty-six lid-less cottage cheese cartons; fourteen half-finished needlepoint projects; eleven matted teddy bears; two cartons of unfiled recipes; a dried-up china-painting kit; seventy-three empty cigar boxes; a jug of pennies; a Ping-Pong paddle; a box of fortune cookie fortunes; and every birthday card she ever got.

Taming the Paper Tiger

and Other De-Junking Adventures

Touring the impressive S. Rosenthal printing plant in Cincinnati one evening, we saw massive 23-foot high machines and other astounding production mechanisms that would rattle anyone's imagination—but the grandest daddy of all, the sight that awed us out by the railroad dock, was a 1,000-pound bale of paper. Why was that colossal bale so captivating? Because both my editor and I were thinking the same thing (as you would be also)—"I wonder, if all my paper junk at home were baled, I could match this massive bundle!"

Sad to say, most of us *could* match the print shop's impressive packet if we baled up all our worthless paper.

We are inundated daily with displays of reading matter—signs, menus, magazines, maps, papers, programs, brochures, labels, newsletters, books. We don't have to ask for it or buy it—it comes spontaneously, generously, regularly, much of it free. Seventy-five percent of it is or will quickly become clutter, and will smother the life out of us if we don't exercise some kind of control over it.

Go ahead and blush over your dead magazines and newspapers, but there's plenty of other incidental papery you need to start feeding the baler. Ever notice how most people keep expired life-insurance policies? Just in case reincarnation might occur in reverse, we'd better keep it. It looks so "legal." We paid so much for it.

The other faithful piece of paper junk never thrown out is the old raffle ticket; the fact that we keep it, though the drawing date was 1965, indicates that human hope truly never dies (as long as we keep junk around to remind us of it). Deep in our heart, we feel there may yet be a telegram from heaven telling us that we won after all. It'll never come; throw the ticket out. If you can't pass up the hope for a delayed win, microfilm the stub.

How much unopened junk mail, how many outdated brochures and newsletters, obsolete schedules, old lists, worn slogan stickers, wrinkled posters and old greeting cards and calendars, half-filled-out questionnaires, old contest entry blanks and magazine subscription offers, outdated résumés, box tops, expired coupons, and unidentifiable envelopes of stuff do you have stashed somewhere? (Probably under all your old hunting, fishing, and driver's licenses, or those eighteen never-used datebooks and diaries.) What about ancient books of addresses and names of associates—met once, long ago? Will you ever use them, or will they pile up and crowd out new friends and opportunities? All those handwritten notes awaiting translation might be memoir-excusables—but not the mounds of catalogs bulging out of every nook. (I know a well-educated woman who has over 600 assorted catalogs.)

The "paper weight" on our lives from keeping all this undiscarded print is a psychological ton. We can't shake the conviction that we are morally obligated to read, or at least scan, it before the trash truck totes it away forever. But remember, 75 percent of it is obsolete hours after it's printed, and after ten years under your wing of "gonnas," I think the other 25 percent has given up the ghost. Dump it! Don't give the old "I'm waiting for the Boy Scout drive" alibi—rip into that paper. If you get over a thousand pounds, call me—I've got to see it!

What Percentage of Mail and Magazines Is Junk?

When living on a remote farm in the '40s, my dream was to have a full mailbox—that was about the only outside contact besides radio that we had. I would send for Henry Field seeds, Lone Ranger bullets, Jack Armstrong treasure maps—anything to get mail. Today my dreams, like yours, have been fulfilled beyond my wildest imagining. My personal, company, and post office mailboxes are stuffed with tons of junk mail in the course of a year—contests, real estate offers and condo deals, catalogs, sale brochures and flyers, box holder's notices, solicitations, address stickers, name-imprinted pens and pencils—plus, of course, my regular mail. I often have to pick up my mail in crates. This happens daily (except Sunday), so unless it is processed promptly, a pyramid of junk will form that I have to fight through to get to the serious business.

How many of you have old magazines or unprocessed mail lying around?

When I ask this question of my seminar or TV audiences, I get downcast eyes and a deep moan of guilt. Junk mail—or even "good mail" that ends up junk—is one of the most universal junk problems. It is stuffed, hidden, spread, stacked, piled, stored, filed, boxed, and even carried around in such abundance in most homes and offices (dorm rooms, cars, school lockers, too) that it's actually physical labor to handle, as well as an emotional drain to keep track of. Desk tops can't be found, bulging boxes are piled in closets, drawers are so clogged with junk mail they can't be opened. Most of this aged mail is worthless and is silently destroying some of your finest nerve fiber, and taking up some of your most valuable home space.

The "ostrich approach" to the mailstream can and does hurt employment, relationships, and the pocketbook. It can represent you as a trasher and thrasher, unable to handle your personal responsibilities. Dealing with mail and magazines is one of the most shamefully procrastinated acts of all. Instead of feeling bad or casting down your eyes any longer, take care of it.

You Can Handle Junk Mail in Minutes

Let me help you sort. You don't have to do it like I do—you can adjust the process to suit yourself—but here are some guidelines to expedite the task:

First, I never throw anything away before I look at it. It is only American to advertise, sell, and offer, and you should give *some* consideration—however brief— to what is sent or said to you. I once ripped up and threw away an envelope that appeared to be an insurance advertisement, only to find out later that it was a $1,300 check I'd been waiting for. Some "junk" mail is legitimate, so give it a look.

Magazines are fun to read and the stories and ads keep you aware of what's new, but remember a couple of things. Number 1: In most magazines, nothing is printed that is too profound or controversial or they would lose advertisers; most magazine material, while perhaps enjoyable, is not fantastically edifying to the mind. Number 2: Up to 70 percent of a magazine is advertisements and they are updated every month, so you don't need to keep them. You can go through a trade journal or newsletter in minutes, scanning the headlines. If there happens to be an article you want to read or save, tear it

out and read or file it, and throw the rest away—it's pure junk. Yet people store tons of magazines. What value is a ninety-pound box of 1968-72 *Better Biscuits and Garters?* Seventy percent is out-of-date ads; most of the rest is obsolete or out-of-style ideas.

When it comes to magazines, a little hard thinking while you're poised over the order blank can save a lot of guilt and accumulation later. Are you *really* going to read it? Or do you just want it to be seen in your mailbox?

And because you paid for it doesn't mean you have to read it. If you miss something, there's a good bet you'll be able to read it a year later in the doctor's office, because he keeps his even longer than you do.

Bills The most dreaded. In almost every home I cleaned in twenty-five years as a professional, there was a little den or pile of unpaid (and unopened) bills. Always open every bill immediately—never pitch or file one because you haven't the money to pay. Many of us have suffered for this. I had one for six months; I didn't open it 'cause I didn't want to know how much, and when I did it was worse than I thought. In fact, it was a ripoff on some construction work done for me. I yelled my head off about the $250 they had overbilled, but to no avail because six months had gone by—wheat had grown over the proof. I "hid" another bill from myself for months when cash was desperately tight; I worried, sweated, and finally opened it—to find it was a credit of $200, asking how I'd like it, cash or a check. If you can't take care of all your bills, at least be aware of to whom, how much, and when. Instant adjustment to the shock is less damaging than long-unknowing suspenseful agony. Don't keep bill stuffers; they're bulky and usually irrelevant—all you need is the statement or invoices, and if you insist, the envelope.

P.S. Unless you're into calligraphy, writing out return addresses on each bill envelope by hand is a junk pastime, so keep your eyes open for some tasteful means of "automating" it (a stamp or stickers).

Contest mailers Ahhh, just rub off the plastic cover, peel to reveal the hidden code, or simply match the numbers. And what do we win . . . a drawer full of false hope . . . junk paper. We keep the labels, cards, and coupons, peck out the jingles, and peek out the window to see if the mailman is bringing our $50,000 jackpot. He isn't, but he does bring us more and more and ever more junk mail, as our name is computer-plucked from contest rolls for future junk bombardment. When a real opportunity for fame and fortune comes to our door,

we miss it because we can't see over the pile of entries on the kitchen counter.

Sorry I'm so opinionated on this, but I think mail contests are almost immoral. Giving nothing and getting lots just doesn't work and never will. Hoping for something for nothing, which most contests encourage, will junk up your life. We waste a lot of valuable time and emotion dreaming and hoping—and even if we were the .000001 percent that won, our troubles would just begin. Many of the prizes are junk we don't want or need, and winning a vacation (or a lifetime) with nothing to do would ruin most of us. Complete the following sentence in twenty-five words or less:

Junk mail abounds in my abode because _____

_____

_____.

Deals and Offers

When people have to solicit us for a deal, it is definitely not as neat a deal as we could go after on our own. There are plenty of deals in the mail, good and bad ones among them.

Have we got a deal for you: *COME TO LONE PINE CONDO* and be the first to get in on this time-sharing opportunity, for a tiny down payment, you'll have part ownership, horses, pine trees, privacy, swimming, friends, and quiet . . . all for $5,000. You'll get a FREE prize, free dinner just to come and look.

The best land deals and investment opportunities seldom come announced in bulk mailers. Most of them you can pitch, especially if they start: "You have been selected. . . ."

There seems to be magic in the word "investment," especially when we read rags-to-riches stories, how-I-gained-power tales, and "how by investing five minutes a week I made a million dollars, a master touch on the piano, this bustline or that bicep."

In this frame of mind we're set up for a plunge into the pool of gimmicks, not investments. Our world has fast become one big sphere of promise. Almost every person, company, group, organization, or government is constantly, twenty-four hours a day, trying to get us to invest in something. In the course of an average week in our life we'll be exposed to three hundred opportunities to improve life, gain a friend, see the world, master our emotions, or make money. All we have to do is say "Yes," then pay up, and wait for our ship to come in. . . . A great opportunity? No! On many of these investments there isn't even a ship sailing—you can be swindled. It happens fast; it happens often.

Make-money-at-home junk mail is awesome. There are hundreds of such schemes. When someone promises to make you a Rolls Royce-driving millionaire with no work, no investment, no selling, no risk, for a $10 formula, you are being insulted, not approached. If small fortunes were being made quietly at home raising earthworms, knitting nosewarmers, or stuffing envelopes, it wouldn't be a secret long.

A U.S. Postal Services expert testified in a TV interview that he had not seen even one of the hundreds of mail-advertised "make money at home easy" deals that he'd investigated work. Yet thousands of people respond in hope of financial solutions and send in some of the little money they do have, as the ad asks them to. Be careful—a dotted line can make a junk transfer in seconds.

Many of those direct-sales, "pyramid" fortune-building outfits promising something for nothing are among the biggest junk concepts in the world. Few ever make it. But homes and offices are littered with glorious brochures showing smiling families posed in front of their big shiny car and landscaped yard, proof that by using others you, too, can build a fortune.

Welcome to the (Clutter) Club

The most exhausted moment of my life was an evening I staggered to the bunkhouse after rounding up, on foot, a big herd of our cattle from a 640-acre pasture. The agony and fruitlessness of the whole job could all be traced to a single pin I had carelessly left unlatched on the gate. All was well, the stock were mooing and grazing where they belonged—until one cow leaned against the unlatched gate and it swung open. One started, they all followed, and then they all had to be rounded up. I thought I'd learned my lesson, but no—a pen the same size as the pin opened another gate . . . to a "Book-of-the-Century Club."

I read the coaxing, colorful ads for years and finally one book popped up that I wanted. It was free just for joining. I signed the coupon and the gate swung open and those paper dogies didn't stop. I'd read the bulletin buildup and find nothing I wanted so they'd send me *their* choice (*The History of Masking Tape*). I'd get so irritated that on the next offer, before they could just send me *A Rudder Study of the Great Sailboats*, I'd order it. I tried to get rid of my book club inventory as Christmas gifts, but others were doing the same and I ended up with gift copies of the same books I'd gleefully given away.

I stuck it out with the club for five years—do you realize how many months there are in five years? The books and extras were pretty, but seldom really edifying (or read). It was hard to get out because I still felt guilty about getting that free book up front, but finally, after being thoroughly junked, I withdrew.

Feeling relieved, de-junked, unburdened from that monthly pressure,

I still hadn't learned my lesson. A business book library offer came (what a clever way to disguise the *real* name—book club) and I fell for it. These were different, however—they cost $39.95 instead of $9.95 each and my corporate name was peddled to every mailing list and merchant in America. I really opened the gate this time—I had catalogs arriving hourly selling surplus Army jeeps, sexual aids, pewter paraphernalia, electronic dominoes, desert land, and ocean bottom. I never did read any of the big complicated business books, but the catalogs usually each had one item I might buy someday, so I kept them. In two years I could have opened my own publishers' clearing house—90 percent of the material, no matter how beautifully printed and presented, was junk.

Catalogs Allowing sleek, slick catalogs, large and small, to steadily enter your dwelling is like touring the bakery to start a diet, or opening the gate for a stampede of junk to follow. Remember the run on the L.L. Bean Company? L.L. Bean, known for years as a supplier of quality outdoor gear, was spoofed in a takeoff of their popular catalog that featured a bunch of adorable little items like doggie brassieres, a steal at $7.75 . . . sheepskin-lined cases for

canned tuna, $5 . . . even genuine edible moccasins for $41.75. The response was overwhelming, orders poured in, the phone lines were clogged.

Our fascination with the glossy anthologies of clutter called catalogs knows no bounds. The new ones pile up and take time we don't have to go through and discover new things we wouldn't have needed or wanted if we hadn't seen them there in all their full-color and backdropped glory. The old ones pile up because we never get around to wading back through them to weed out. And the clever companies who send the same catalog with a bright new cover four or six times a year (how can we throw it out—there might be *something* different in it) really thicken the stack. Catalogs not only add to our *paper* clutter, they have (in those innocent-looking little order blanks) the incredible potential to multiply every other kind of clutter on our premises astronomically.

Men who criticize their families or friends for having old papers or magazines around will have literally hundreds of pounds of old parts or equipment catalogs—you know, the looseleaf kind the parts guys thumb through on the counter. Every salesperson in the world must get a commission for the amount of ring-binder catalogs he or she unloads. Most are obsolete in a year or two. Once I bought an old bankrupt lumber store and found two pickup loads of binder catalogs dating back to 1947. I kept half a pickup full of the binders for four years to hold all my papers—and finally ended up dumping them. You'll never be reincarnated as a purchasing agent, so dump those old catalogs right now.

I haven't missed those books or catalogs since I de-junked them, and I sure love the space in my life I have left to pick what I want to read when I want to, and the space in my home to store the things I really want to keep.

Letters Open immediately, and if the address and date are on the letter, pitch the envelope. Read the letter, and if it doesn't call for a response, pitch or file it or save the address or make out a check or whatever and move it out. If it needs an answer, carry it with you until you answer it. That will be the best disciplined and most efficient way to be sure you do.

One of the most valuable skills of time management is learning to use time fragments—the ten minutes waiting in line, the twenty minutes waiting for a meal, the thirty minutes riding somewhere, etc. Letter-answering is an excellent way to do so. An unanswered letter is a prime candidate for mental debt—free yourself and your life!

Old letters aren't always clutter, neither are special cards and notes and postcards—they are human history. The letters that bring tears to our eyes and a flood of memory and love may be old and yellow, but never junk. Meaningful writings are easy to store and the amount of feeling they hold is well worth the space. If necessary, trim them down to get rid of the bulk.

I cut out the most meaningful parts of my favorite letters, laminate them, and insert them in books as markers. When I open the book—monthly, yearly, or every five years—there the letter is, in perfect condition, to remind me.

Calendars You only need a couple of calendars in a house, yet after Christmas we have one for each month. Because of the friends who gave them, or the fact that they came in the mail, or were given to us *free*, we feel obligated to keep all calendars and they end up being clutter. Our digital watches, TV, and newspaper remind us almost hourly what day and year it is; don't take or keep calendars if you don't need them—they cost the distributor a bundle and you'll never be able to throw them away because of all those pretty pictures.

Calendars—The Bigger the Better

The "big calendar" concept used by home efficiency expert Gladys Allen and others is a wonderful way to eliminate junk mail, unnecessary phone calls, and clutter.

A big calendar is one with the days marked off in squares big enough to write notes inside. Purchase the one with the largest squares you can find. Hang it on the wall next to your telephone and bulletin board (if your bulletin board isn't next to the telephone, move it!), near the heaviest flow of communication. Mount a pen or pencil on a string or in a slot beside your calendar. From now on, as soon as invitations and announcements arrive in the mail or are brought home, instead of hanging onto them (but never being able to find them when you need the information), simply transfer the data (address, time, etc.) onto the appropriate square of your big calendar, then toss the card or mailer out before it can clutter your house—and clutter your mind trying to keep track of it!

Place a wastebasket on the floor beneath your big calendar and watch the basket fill up with that flurry of junk you formerly had been saving, shuffling, hunting for, and worrying about. Things like wedding and party invitations, notifications of events, schedules, appointment cards and reminders, loose addresses of places you're going, assignments, instructions, letters containing specific information, etc., etc.—often we have our desk drawers stuffed full of this junk. We cram these things in our wallets or purses or stack them on the refrigerator to "remind" us of things we need to do. It's so messy and confusing—and so unnecessary—to keep it all around.

A great feeling of power comes from feeling in control of your life's events, from knowing what's coming up and where you've been. Big calendars can help you achieve that control at a quick glance.

If your mechanic tells you the brakes should be checked again in six months, flip ahead on your calendar and write in the checkup date. If your insurance comes due twice a year, don't always be caught unawares. Page ahead and calendar in reminders to yourself so you can budget ahead and have the money available.

Calendar in important birthdays and dates a year ahead, then mark reminders to yourself a week before so you can get the greeting card off on time.

Hang onto your big calendars and file them. They're a concise record of family history. They tell you everything you and your family did all year and exactly when you did it. Take the time at the end of the year to review your calendar month by month and write up a brief recap of your life for that year. It's easy with all the data right there to remind you.

File It Doesn't Mean Pile It. . . .

Files are one of the greatest repositories of "invisible" clutter going—just because it's alphabetized and tucked away in a drawer doesn't mean it isn't junk.

My values and needs change, as yours do, as the years pass and the thrust of my life changes, but seldom do I (or you) go back into my files and throw out the clutter and stuff that no longer applies. because "it would take forever." And besides, you say, you can throw it out when you happen to run across it going through for something else.

Well, it won't happen, and your files will grow into a Pentagon paper storage bank that makes retrieving anything (*if* you can find it) slow and costly. Yet it takes only minutes, while you're watching

a TV show or when you can't get to sleep some evening or your ball game is rained out—to sit down and riffle through some of your files. This is fun, educational, and reminds you how clever you are for saving all this stuff. If you chuck the clutter periodically, your files will stay healthy, and when you need something you won't have to mount an expedition or perform an excavation to get it. Office or home, *you* have to do it: if someone else cleans out your files, that is exactly what they might do—clean them out, and there goes the picture of you forty eons or so ago, the masterful letter that proved you weren't speeding, your grandfather's letter from Teddy Roosevelt. Sift your files yourself about once every three years—it's fun, and emotionally stabilizing.

Without a functional filing system, finding and using can be a maddening and disappointing quest. But there is such a thing as over-organizing—when you have to use a separate set of files to find where something was filed or otherwise put away, that's one step too many.

File to fit your personality and needs—don't try to follow the Dewey system invented for the American University Library. Surprisingly few folders or notebooks can organize almost anything you need and do it well. Don't stuff things in a drawer—that simple file folder, with a title or topic written across the top, will only take a minute to make and cost only twenty cents. When you need it, you'll be able to find it.

"I Know I Kept That . . . ."

1. We see or hear something interesting.

It's so great we want to save it, savor it, share it: a good joke/cartoon, an excellent article, a great idea, an exciting job, an important address or date, an intelligent quote, a tempting recipe, a solution.

2. We start to record it.

Because of the unpredictability of the moment, we often end up with our valuable bit of information written on the back of a used envelope, a napkin, the corner of a program, a candy wrapper, a hanky or shirt cuff, a piece of board, a boxtop, the back of a business card (or if we're lucky, a notebook or phone pad or calendar square).

3. We search in despair.

"I know I kept that . . . it would be just perfect for what I need if I could find it. . . . Where did I put it?"

If we do find it, we can't decipher it— too much time has passed!

4. Or use and share. . . .

This valuable material enhances our lives and others'. (If you are here you can skip the next page.)

Losing track of something we liked and saved is almost as sad as losing a cherished memory of a loved one: snatching gems of thought out of the torrent of life is one of our great pleasures. Develop your own system to be sure you save and *use* them. Your method will have to fit *you*, but it can help to get with someone who's a good "saver" and ask them to share their secrets (99 percent will be flattered to do so).

My system isn't sophisticated, but it works, and here is all I do: I save everything that impresses me (five to fifty tidbits a day). I carry a leather notebook shaped like an outhouse (you can be sure that no one wants to steal it). It has a pouch and a pad—everything I collect or jot down goes in one of these.

My notes I write out on the spot in my notebook on a sheet titled "Write & Record." I write each separate thought out in complete sentences under a key word or topic heading. I don't go into full detail or describe it completely, just enough that if I *do* want to go back to expand on it I'll know clearly what I meant. Writing down the notes only takes a minute, if done right at the moment the thought strikes.

When I get home I drop all my Write & Record notes (snipped into their separate topics) into a box labeled "Write & Record," and drop all the printed materials, programs, photos, documents, forms, booklets, etc., I've picked up into the "Important Paper" basket on my

desk. This way I have all my notes and gleanings in one of two places—not in pockets, bags, boxes, books. . . .

I don't use prime/highly productive/all-cylinders time—such as morning hours—to file the material in these two boxes; this can be done in time fragments, on semi-sick days, while watching TV or tending kids, while waiting for someone, right before and after meals, on sleepless nights, etc.

My files are arranged so that I have a drawer for each of my important interests and one alphabetized "general" file drawer. My immediate-interest projects/current enthusiasms I keep in ring binders—such topics, for me, for example, as The Life Story I Will Write Some Day, Salable Article Ideas (I've accumulated over 8,000 without any special effort to do so), Janitorial Humor, etc.

Ring-binder notebooks are cheap (most of my binders are scrounged "recycles") and simple to use, and you can assemble a useful library of your very own just in your spare time and odd moments.

I use an inexpensive rubber stamp to stamp my name on all my file materials—and I don't loan files! In seconds I can find anything I have and use it.

School Papers and Projects

After investing $2,000 each to bring our babies into the world, then another $10,000 to $15,000 to get them six years old and in school (plus an incalculable amount of love, effort, and emotion along the way), we seek evidence to assure ourselves they are going to be productive people. The first trickle of assurance comes in the form of some scribbled art done in kindergarten, and we snatch it into scrapbook storage. By first grade we actually see intelligent words (even if the letters are a little out of alignment);

every sheet is collected. By the second grade sentences overcrowd the scrapbook and stuff the drawer. By the eighth grade, we have mountains and foothills of evidence that our offspring indeed are literate. Once *we're* satisfied our kids have made it, we still can't dump the stuff because surely our kids' kids will want to see how their parents did—so we keep those school papers for the grandkids!

Kids' or your own, don't try to keep them all—just enough to be a decent sampling—and store the ones you save in a folder. Four Dick and Jane workbooks for every grade will end up flunking you (junking you). A few representative "works" for each grade really should suffice to soothe any pangs for fleeting childhood.

As for your own excess school papers, here is a definite solution. Throw away Cs down through Fs, so if your kids take after you (are just as dumb) you'll be safe. If your kids are smarties like you, you have lots of evidence of their inherited super-intelligence and don't need papers for proof.

Newspapers

A newspaper is an important tool of communication in our lives; it is also one of the most common forms of litter and clutter in our homes, offices, streets, and public buildings. As soon as a newspaper is read (and maybe an article or two torn out), it is obsolete; it's junk. Yet the average person keeps a week's (or a month's or . . .) papers around in case he might want to go back and reread. Who has ever read a newspaper twice? But once you set one down or tuck it away, the chances of discarding it are infinitesimal.

The bad news is that there is no magic formula for keeping newspapers from becoming one of your biggest, most consistent clutter headaches. Newspapers are as dependable as the dawn. If you fall behind in reading them, they will be there in an enormous pile waiting; when you finish, they will be there in an enormous pile waiting to be disposed of. The uses for which old newspapers work *best* are almost nil—counting all the bird-cage bottoms, paint jobs, moving or packing stuffers, window shining (ugh), dog training, and newspaper fireplace logs on this continent—only about .001 percent of newspapers are used after reading.

There is only one way (aside from a faithful paper drive or recycling box in the garage) to handle newspapers and that is *instant* disposal—the instant you are finished reading it. Don't ever lay a read paper down for "later"—the last guy to read it should be the last person to see it alive. If you miss a few days, don't try to catch up; much of what is in a daily paper will be recapped later somewhere else (radio, TV, weekly magazine, conversation) and not much really new or important (except Doonesbury or Ann Landers) happens in a few days of a daily newspaper.

Office Clutter

The words "shop," "industrial," and "office" offer a great (but invalid) sanctuary for junk. Somehow we feel we can get by with piles of garbage if it is hidden away "at work." But don't kid yourself: offices, for example, offer some prime dejunking inventory. Hidden away in desks and credenzas, gathering dust in file cabinets and coat and janitor closets, are massive amounts of clutter.

In twenty-five years of cleaning and inspecting some of our country's largest and most elite office complexes, I've found that a high percentage of cleaning, breakage, fire, and injury costs result from plain unnecessary clutter. Boxes of outdated files and discontinued printing are everywhere, stacked to dangerous heights, inviting toppling and lifting injuries. Extra pencils, pads, pens, clips, and handy-dandy trays are generally overdone at least 50 percent. On tops of desks and cabinets you'll find department store displays of ungodly excess: ashtrays, trophies, commemorative paperweights, cartoons, centerfolds, candy dishes, elaborate nameplates and pen sets, ceremonial letter openers, moldy coffee cups, and outdated paperwork. Though fancy pen sets come in every design and material imaginable, I've never found any that write much better than a 69¢ Bic. Few of us like to carry good pens because the carried pen/pencil mortality rate is about 60 percent. If we don't lose them, some absentminded guy like me innocently rips it off you. So I have many gold gift sets that I shuffle and dust, waiting for the day that I'll write a book in public view. Meanwhile, they're crammed away, jamming my drawers every time I open or close them.

Office junk includes unnecessary furniture, too, because of the unwritten office rule that you never surrender any item of furniture once you get it—whether you need it or not.

Most office storages are blessed with rolls or boxes of fresh new labels (business cards, or stationery) with outdated or misspelled or slightly misprinted addresses. Everything else is perfect—the paper, the stickum, the color, but they are utterly worthless. Keeping them in hope of having a $1-an-hour kid go through and revise them with a rubber stamp will never happen—and if they stay around, someday new office help will find and use them, with some resulting very sad situations.

And why can't we throw out obsolete or disintegrating rubber stamps? It seems that once a name or message is engraved in rubber on the bottom of a wood block, it's engraved in our very souls. I found thirty of those in an old desk I bought, and kept them for years because they cost $5 each now and after all they *did* print. Finally, realizing I'd never use them (I couldn't update their 1940s message to the 1980s), I tossed them! Then at home in my desk I found two others I had made up for a job I held as a representative—no place or way I'll ever use them again. Today as I write this, they went.

Every office has its catacombs of clutter, even a professional cleaning firm like mine (here comes another confession). As our business grew, we kept up with the needed new furniture, forms, and equipment. About twelve years ago, to expedite matters further, we made what we considered a wise purchase and bought two large full-key electric adding machines. You could punch in anything, hit the total button, and those things would snort, whirl, and click out the most impressive rhythms of taps and grinds you ever heard, finally spitting out a tape of the transaction—we thought we had Einstein encased in plastic!

Two months later I was in a friend's office, and he showed me this newfangled electronic calculator, a tiny thing that did twice as much as mine in less than half the time and cost a fourth as much. I thought it was a hoax, and of course you know it wasn't—those amazing, accurate, efficient, and low-priced midgets have since taken over.

And today my two big ugly electric adding machines, still brand-new, sit under the dust and cobwebs in our stationery storage room, poised for the day the cunning calculator might fail and they can be reenlisted. That day will never come. Those adding machines are as worthless as the four chairs with armrests and two casters missing, those balding blotters, the original 1953 carbon dip copiers, the hole-puncher we used three times in five years, the stapler that jammed as often as it stapled, the green typewriter ribbon somebody thought would be a nice change, and the 1979 calendar note pads waiting to be made into scratch paper. I'll cast my clutter out, if you'll cast out yours. Gadfrey, we hate to admit mistakes, especially we businesspeople!

Business Before Treasure

Fancy offices are for ego (or for a cushy prelude to over-billing!), not production. In some offices there are more swords, bits of armor, helmets, sheepskins, ships, tapestries, carvings, and extra cushions than a Viking could carry out on a good day. Others are so loaded with oriental rugs, glowering old oil portraits, and antique English furniture that you're waiting for the hounds and huntsmen to come thundering down the hall. Atmosphere comes more from people than from props—"image"-strewn offices generally house a person with more than the average share of insecurities. (Check out your psychiatrist's office—you might be able to help him or her with a de-junking problem.)

All of this costs money to buy, time to clean, and worry to protect. Office junk costs us a small fortune because we professional cleaners learned that it's just a matter of time until those excess decorations will be destroyed or damaged, or will disappear.

And when you have to wrestle daily with an elegant unwieldy phone, carefully remove a special envelope from a special holder, or come to terms with the fact that your snazzy revolving address file has spilled its guts all over your desk top, *production* is impaired. When arranging the accessories or debating the decor won't allow you to focus on the problem at hand, *function* is suffering.

Walk into any office and inventory the visible junk honestly. Now inspect the bottom desk drawers and cabinet storage areas (careful that the old exit signs, empty boxes, used mailing tubes, retired notebooks and briefcases don't crush you). I'll bet you'll average 50 percent junk. If you don't want to go through this clutter inventory now, just wait until you move.

You'll see! If you are the junkee, repent. If the employer of the junkee, command and demand de-junking. It'll save a fortune in time—and be a lot safer and better-looking, too.

In Brief, Junk

Hope chests, vaults, safes, fruit and wine cellars, and portfolios can all house clutter and few will dare question it. But the most sanctified of all official clutter containers is the briefcase. To carry, or even own one, seems to be a milestone in many lives. You can tell the executive stature by the size and style of the case—the slimmer and more refined it is, the more important the character carrying it. Briefcases and all their brethren are now being designed into junk; we have teak and zebrawood attaché cases and elegant leather ones costing up to $800, not to mention snakeskin, sharkskin, stainless steel, brushed aluminum, plastic, wicker, cow fur and coyote hide—and to carry what? If you looked in most of them, the only briefs you'd find are some worn shorts.

Briefcases are generally full of things people don't use but are supposed to carry—or things they're *not* supposed to carry. I just looked in mine—I am a corporate president, chairman of the board, sit on several other boards, own and run several businesses—I'm lugging around three Hyatt Regency pads and two pens that don't work (I must have kept them to clean my ears), a $400 dictaphone I've used once in five years (though I did entertain my grandkids with it once), Idaho potato pins, toilet keychains, squeegee tie tacks, a harmonica, guitar pick, my Boy Scout merit badges, three procrastination projects, and . . . well, never mind, it's too embarrassing.

No clutter is excused by its container!

No Book Is Junk . . . or Is It?

Finally inspired to de-junk my large library, I was at the garbage barrel casting a dilapidated book into a blazing fire. My wife and my mother-in-law, returning from the store, jumped out of the car and headed for the burning barrel on the run. "Don't burn that book!" (They didn't even know what book I was burning.)

We all have a certain awe for a book, almost regardless of the contents. A book seems to be an entity or institution in its own right. Maybe because we remember the difficulty of checking out a book past a stern-faced librarian; maybe because our parents or grandparents had only a few books and kept them forever. Or maybe because we associate books with the positives of education, knowledge, and wisdom. Once that mass of paper, regardless of what it says or shows, is bound and titled we feel it's sacred.

My wife pulled on my arm—"Oh, don't burn those books, give them to the Salvation Army, or a friend, or something." Then I showed her the books. They were books I had kept in my library, moved, tended, protected, and cleaned for twenty years (and books are among the heaviest of items to carry or store!).

The first was a 1929 typewriting book,

yellow and brittle with age; you should have seen the whalebone shoes and long dresses on the typists. Then there was *Modern Taxation Moves for a Small Business* (1951), a 1928 book of modern classroom accounting, a guide to gear ratio adjustment on the modern tractor (1934), a turn-of-the-century guide to irrigation systems, a 1947 almanac, *Current Used Car Prices 1963*, a 1971 college catalog, campground guides from the late '50s (I knew these were useless when I ended up camping in a shopping mall), a road atlas from the Pleistocene era, a *Political Geography of the World 1937*, and eleven boxes of other beautiful books that had absolutely zero value to me or anyone else. They contained outdated, incomplete, or inaccurate information, but they were books!

Honesty and My Library

Do you know why I had eleven boxes of no-good books to burn—why I had kept them, bought them, sent for them, pulled them out of others' junk piles? It was for ego and show. Most people dream of and plan a family room or den—and true to decorational demand, an impressive wall of books must be there. Those books are seldom opened; they just sit and gleam and multiply and give an intellectual air to the room they adorn, or serve as a reminder to the kids, visitors, and relatives that we have scholastic and educational wisdom in our home. Oh, and we should also have several prestige books worthlessly sunning themselves on a coffee or reception table: their titles—*Early Prints of Andrew Dauber, Great Midwestern Castle Architecture, Lampshades Through the Ages*—are a dead giveaway of their purpose—show! The most handling they get is when they're dusted.

When I ran out of room, when my home office wall was full, did I throw out the worthless books? Nope, like you I bought or built more shelves or boxed and kept them in case I got another office and had to have *two* displays. As a professional, was I backed by layers of deep knowledge in my tax and business-planning books? Nope, because in the fast-moving business climate and fluctuations of the economy, those books are almost worthless a year after I get them. When I need an answer, I can get it current and accurate in four minutes from my banker or accountant.

The Epitome of Book Vanity

I was in a board of directors' meeting in elite Scottsdale, Arizona. The meeting room decor reeked of power, authority, and the deep knowledge of bygone masterminds. The stately bound classic books on the walnut mantel cast an almost oracular spell over the room. During the boring parts of the meeting my eyes scanned the books and rested on one beauty familiar from my teaching days. When break came, I vaulted to the mantel and reached for the treasured book. It wouldn't budge! I pulled hard and it moved, but so did all the others. I jerked, and the whole row of books came teetering down—they weren't for reading, they were for show—all the covers were glued together!

How are the pages of *your* books? Maybe not physically glued, but if you never crack them they might as well be. Showing costs your life. Most of it is clutter!

De-Junk Your Bookshelf

There is no sacredness to books any more: TV, radio, and other media present "live" material we once had to read. Books are available now everywhere, not just in schools and libraries. There are more than 40,000 new books published every year.

Books today are cheaply produced from cheap materials, and printed on large presses that can roll out 10,000 books in a few hours. Most books today are not beautiful and they're not made to last as they once were; even the paper in them deteriorates in an amazingly short number of years.

Many books today are not painstakingly compiled wisdom or information but essentially entertainment. Once the majority of books were educational, uplifting, edifying; now many are strictly for profit—anything that will sell will be written and published. Books, in short, are not the special repositories of distilled knowledge they once were.

Yes, there are still books today that are sturdy, beneficial, and better than the old. I can't and don't want to pass judgment on your books because you can do it perfectly well if you'll be 100 percent honest with yourself: you wouldn't read many of the books on your shelves if you were trapped with them on a desert island.

Yes, Even Cookbooks Can Be Clutter

Two of the biggest-selling types of book on the market today are cookbooks and diet/exercise books. Guess how many are kept: all of them. How many are used? Few. If and when a cookbook comes off the back burner, it is usually just for a few recipes in the entire book. And though a book might be worth buying for one or two items, the other 372 pages of exotic dishes in the large binding are junk. Most home cooks use a handful of recipe cards (or the recipe on the box or package) for their favorite standbys, but *all* keep drawers or cupboards full of cookbooks. (The average home has thirteen; real junkers have twenty, thirty, forty; the record is probably 184).

Cast out your unused cookbooks! But before all of you gourmet cooks baste me at the stake, remember I told you to be objective when de-junking. Cookbooks may make you *feel* domestic, but do you ever use them for cooking? When (honestly) was the last time you used a cookbook? I've posed this question to many a group—silence usually follows, no one can remember. I suggested to one woman, "Have you used yours in the last six months?" Silence. Everybody laughs—someone finally chirps, "I made gingersnaps once." Another says, "When I have lots of friends over." Clip the few recipes you need and meet me at the burning barrel.

When you throw out, give away, or sell those books that have no value, you'll spell relief F-E-W-E-R B-O-O-K-S. Good books that nestle in you when you nestle with them are one of the finest of all gifts, and worth keeping and giving and loving; just don't try to become the city library. (You might try *using* it though—it's one of the best ways to avoid buying the books you'd only read once or only need once in a great while.)

Good reference books, and books, adult or juvenile, that you'll read over and over and enjoy, are worth buying and keeping in fine editions. The one-timers like *Watergate Witchery Volume XIV* or *200 Uses for a Stiff Opossum* are one-time shots not worth $14.95 to clutter a shelf.

132

Get a $4 paperback and once you've read it, pitch it or pass it on to someone else.

P.S. When de-cluttering, don't forget to check out your "mini-books," too: for outdated government publications and old maps and guidebooks and pamphlets and brochures, instruction booklets to appliances you no longer have, old phone books, instructions for crafts you've given up, etc. And don't be so eager to *add* booklets to your shelves (and suitcases). Are you really ever going to want to read the guidebook to Howe Caverns again?

Shutterbug Clutter

Let's zoom for a minute to the classic picture-sorting situation: one member of the family holds up a picture for the others to see.

"Who is this?"

There is silence, no one knows, but because they have the picture, it must be someone. . . . Finally. . . .

"Durned if I know."

"Seems like I've met them . . . once."

"We'd better keep it; it might be someone we know."

You could drive clutter collectors crazy by slipping a photo of a Brazilian countess into their family album. I bet they'd keep it forever!

Even good and worthwhile things can evolve into junk and clutter your life and environment. A prime example is photographs. What a priceless property our own pictures can be—they allow us to relive precious moments, stimulate memories and feelings, bring laughter and warmth to our families, friends, and co-workers. But if you're like most people, probably 75 percent of your pictures are piled, boxed, buried, bent, or unfindable. *The only value a photo has is in being seen.* If that isn't possible, what good is it?

Slides, even those that will never win a photo contest, can be exciting to family and associates, but most slides are

jumbled and bunched in the box and for the most part we don't even remember we have them. Prints are the same story—if you have to sort, hunt, and dust before viewing them, you'll seldom or never see them. Hence these expensive, potentially stimulating, heart-warming items are junk, litter, clutter to you. For years this has been the case, yet we continue to take more pictures and slides, show them for a while when they're fresh, then throw them in a drawer, box, or pile, thinking, "Someday I'll. . . ."

Photos aren't junk; don't let them become so. Transform them into a treasure that will bring joy into your life and others'. In a few spare evenings or Sunday afternoons, you can de-junk a lifetime of pictures.

My father-in-law, Jerry Reed, is a mobile portrait studio and darkroom. He carries a 35mm SLR, a 16mm movie camera, a Polaroid, and a video camera.

He uses his pictures to change lives and entertain; we love him for it—his pictures have enriched our families' lives and built worth and confidence in our children, neighbors, and relatives. It took me a long time to realize why he and his pictures do so much good, since everyone has tons of slides and photos. Jerry simply makes his pictures *accessible* to family, friends—even strangers. In his car or house, even standing in the doorway visiting, you can always see one or more of his pictures. They're on the walls, in handy slide trays, in neat folders, or in his well-organized video library. In a flash you're enjoying new or vintage photographs. I learned much from Jerry and converted my photographs from stored junk to meaningful, enjoyable displays.

Let me pass on what I learned to you. First I had, with my family, a day of "Sort."

Create some categories that fit *you*, such as:

Family Your immediate family, old and new, group and solo shots. Maybe include here also your home(s), pets, vehicles, and all "family feeling" things.

Friends All the friends and places of your wider life—high school and college, colleagues, buddies from service or single days, friends of the family, neighbors.

Vacations That California, Nova Scotia, or Mexico trip, the grand excursion to China or Israel. Keep the pictures from each trip separate within this category. You might want to make a category for:

Special occasions or *one-time events* Special ceremonies, weddings, bar mitzvahs, milestone birthdays or anniversaries, special celebrations or parties.

Other categories Could be business- or career-related, a group or organization you are involved with, your hobbies, sports, certain types of shots you like to take just for the fun of it. Fit the categories to *your* life, because you'll be using them.

2 Eliminate bad or unwanted pictures.

Discard ruined shots, blurred and cut-off shots, too dark, too light, slips, bad photos (except maybe for your only picture of Cousin Lula, hazy as it may be), and *those totally black slides and prints!* You'll never use them and besides, they insult your photo prowess.

Give away You may have lots of pictures (good) that have little or no value to you, but may be of interest to subjects in the shots. Give or mail them to people who might want them. This will give joy to others and make you friends for life!

3 Sort all the remaining

pictures into the categories they fit—you'll probably find yourself adding or changing a few categories as you sort through. You might want to identify all faces and places while you remember who they are.

FAMILY
FRIENDS
VACATION
OTHER

Now decide on the medium to best display your pictures. Remember, a picture's only value is to be *seen*. You want yours to be protected, but easily located and displayed and organized so new pictures can be added easily.

Prints can be mounted in sturdy, durable albums—you have hundreds of choices of types. If your albums are composed well, they'll be looked at and enjoyed often.

I like the ring-binder albums with looseleaf plastic pocket pages. These are inviting to use and practically indestructible. The prints are nicely displayed (and the pages can be handled safely even by little children, who get the most out of pictures).

Mounted on the wall your pictures can be enjoyed more by you and others than any other kind, at any cost!

Mounting and displaying pictures doesn't have to be expensive or difficult. Frame shops will do it.

True, they charge, and if you can't hack it, there are frame-it-yourself centers that offer inexpensive guidance, and department stores—even nickel-and-dime stores—have a selection of frames and mats in which you can in minutes mount your pictures and hang them. As a cleaner, I really like things hung instead of placed (on pianos, etc.). If you have to move Grandpa every time you clean or dust, you grow to dislike him!

Store negatives in manila envelopes in a handy file so you can get at them easily to have copies made for the friends and family who want them.

Slide trays are neat, really worth the money. They simplify not only storage but use. I like the standard 140-slide tray; it's easy to store, use, and add to. In slide trays your pictures will be permanently organized to look at again and again. Label the tray with the category or identification. These slide boxes can be stored in, on, or under anything and still be usable in seconds.

You can even make your own cassette—voice or music—to go along with some of the trays.

Make Your Own Slide Show

With a little imagination and effort you can place the best action or most expressive slides in a tray in a sequence that tells a story. On a piece of paper write a caption or comment to go with each picture (funny or clever is usually the most interesting kind); this only takes a few minutes and adds a lot when you show the slides. I leave the "script" in the slide tray and read it as the projector rolls out the pictures. Recording the copy on a cassette is simple, too—clink a spoon or something for the slide-change signal. Anyone can use and enjoy a slide tray with a cassette, and will do so, over and over again!

A book library? Why not a "photo library" of photo albums or slide trays?

Video is a fun, clever way to keep, organize, and enjoy photographs. It's really quite simple. Use your own video camera, or rent or borrow one. Load it up with a cassette, lay your pictures out, and simply film these in sequence as you would scenes with a movie camera. You might even play some music with the filming. You can't go wrong. Your pictures are all stored in one small cartridge and the investment is small. In twenty minutes you can put literally hundreds of pictures on a video disc and play them over your TV. Most families will like them better than a losing football game or situation comedy reruns. Video players will be as common as stereos in the home in 1990, and many of us have them now.

Dress Less for Success

(So Your Clothes Don't Wear *You* Out)

Isn't it strange how some little scene in a play or a movie will stick with you forever? One of my "never let go" screen glimpses came in *A Connecticut Yankee in King Arthur's Court*, starring Bing Crosby. Toward the end of the movie, Bing was forced into a showdown with the most ferocious knight that ever rode. Bing was prepared for battle, fully suited in his armor; as he moved the armor swayed and creaked and his voice sounded like he was in a tunnel. Mounting his horse and riding to the battle station was practically impossible. And when he stepped backward off a step, of course, because of all those pounds of armor, he teetered, fell over, and jangled and clinked rhythmically down the stairs like 600 empty pop cans. Realizing that his dress was so heavy and restrictive that he could hardly move, he de-junked himself of the whole cumbersome outfit, leaped on his horse, and, armed with only a lariat, was able easily to out-ride, out-maneuver, out-dodge, and finally topple the nasty knight of the court.

Nothing better describes for me the futility and frustration, the drawbacks of overdressing than this memory of Bing rolling helplessly down the stairs and landing in a huge heap of scrap. All of us can relate to the feeling Bing had when he suddenly discovered that he had so much to wear it was in fact a liability instead of an advantage. In the Dark Ages this excess of wearing apparel was justified by the word *protection;* today our excess of wearing apparel is justified by the word *fashion.* That magic word keeps the factories and looms of the world rolling by making sure, with semi-annual changes of style, that things keep coming in and going out.

We make it through the "Twiggy" look, and go from "mini" to "maxi," then we layer minis *over* maxis, the next year leathers and silks are in, then tweeds and knits, then it's on to "Ivy League" or "Preppy." Suddenly we're back to 1940s "hot pants"—that is, until we jump to designer jeans. We buy it all—and if we manage to resist, our kids, cousins, and friends buy it for us. Somehow we gather and keep all these clothes, compacting them tighter and tighter in our ever larger (and then extra and portable) closets and wardrobes with no hope of ever wearing them out. How many neckties or scarves or, for that matter, suits have you heard of (or owned!) that ever wore out? Style has generated more waste than any single word, when it comes to wearing apparel.

Fashion seduces intelligent human beings into paying ridiculous prices for clothing that makes them all look the same. The word "wardrobe" convinces others that they need platoons of shoes, racks of dresses, squadrons of suits, shirts, and blouses.

If our good sense starts to take over and says, "Hey, I don't really dig these saddle oxfords and this slick silk shirt," we can rest assured that the media will quickly come to our rescue—and present a parade of skinny strutting turkeys whirling around on some big-city stage. We sigh and say, "Who am I to question?"

While most of us stand by like a bunch of mute mannequins, somebody out there is piling clothes on us unmercifully. They are piddling around with our hemline, neckline, bustline, waistline—and most of all, our credit line. They take straps away and we buy and keep; they add straps and we buy and keep; when they can't alter the style any more, they change the colors by the year, and then the season.

Our beautiful apparel . . . clutter? Not a chance—it's necessary for image, employment, affection. . . .

Did you know (a look at your apparel inventory will verify this) that *you*, all by yourself, have more clothes than the whole general store in an early western town? That could make you right proud, pardner—but it doesn't, because for months and years already you've known in your heart that your inventory's overstocked. It's worried you, caused agonies of selection, taken room you didn't have, been a pain to move and clean and protect—and you have a small fortune sunk in your wardrobe. You sincerely tried to dress for success and ended up with a closetful of clutter. Now let's try dressing *less* for success. Throw some of it out (you want to, anyway). Clothes clutter affects your life in more ways than how hard it is to fit another hanger in the closet.

I've known many a dignified, wise country gentleman who always looked clean, neat, and presentable—but who never owned a suit. Some tog-touting relative will always come on the scene and say, "What! Zeke doesn't have a suit? Why, *everybody* has to have a suit!" Zeke doesn't agree—he hates suits and places that require suits—but the relatives work on the wife and convince her and they both browbeat Zeke into getting a suit. He yields, gets a suit, satisfies his wardrobe antagonizers, but never wears it. This piece of junk in Zeke's life now is fresh bait for the neckties, hankies, suit socks, watch chains, cufflinks, and suit bags that pour in on birthdays and Christmas. Since Zeke never wears the suit, his family gets him a sport coat, though old country gentleman Zeke needs a sport coat about like he needs another ailment. The sport coat inspires a similar flood of holiday receivership and he receives more accessories and footwear to match. With no room in the closet now for his overalls and boots, Zeke up and dies. Of course for his funeral the suit is out of fashion and he needs a new one—but his family keeps the other one, because "after

all, it was never worn."

Apparel that is neat, attractive, comfortable, wears well, protects us, and helps us project our feelings and physical self is a worthy investment. It's the clothes that over-decorate us, strain our personality and our pocketbook, that are clutter.

Most of us don't need clothes to take over for us. When you consider the power of the eyes, facial expression, voice, and body movement in the sum total of what makes a person "attractive," anything else seems insignificant. Yet we hang incredible arrays of fabrics and leathers (and if we can afford it, precious metals and stones) on ourselves. Draped over or fastened onto our bodies, they take hours and hours of our lives, not only to pay for, but to wear and care for. (Not to mention to sort through and argue over.)

For everyday living these "overdone" fashions will hobble us. And how foolish we are to spend what we can't afford on too many, too-fancy garments.

> **W**hen the best dressers are dressed, no one even notices what they wore.

We've all known people who have so much to put on and take off every morning and night they spend hours of their life doing it. When they travel, their suitcases and ditty bags are bulging with garments, accessories, and personal appliances that they need for their daily assembly and disassembly.

I've seen people so hung with elaborate material they look more like the living room drapes than a living person. Others are in clothes so styled, tailored, and tight—like old Bing in his suit of armor—

they can't sit, run, or breathe deeply (though they can stand and rotate). They are literally wrapped in junk, and no matter what their trappings cost, they look like an overdecorated tree.

Why should we clog our closets with things we wear rarely or never, that don't keep us warm or cool or dry when we need to be, and don't permit any comfortable movement ever?

Unclutter Your Closet

I once cleaned a woman's closet that had ninety-four blouses; her husband wasn't far behind with fifty-five slacks. Most were out of style or didn't fit (that's why the others were bought). And I was astonished once to discover that people even keep sections of clothes by size in their closet; one woman had a span of five sizes so she'd have something to wear at any weight she might be found.

Most closets have enough garments to insulate the whole home; some take security in such inventory, but the opposite is usually true—it's a mark of insecurity and indecision. No amount of clothing and trimmings can substitute for real personal confidence and self-worth.

Before we know it, our life becomes as jammed as our closets and our dresser drawers. Much of it is of little value to us. Most of us only wear about 20 percent of the clothes in our closets. But we have to sort through it *all* (100 percent) every time we go to get dressed—hunt, ponder, weigh, decide, and worry about when, how, and what we should wear. Excess clothes clutter our life with unnecessary stress. Like other junk, their ownership obligates us to use them. And when there are so many to choose from, we're almost always troubled by the possibility that perhaps another choice would have been better, and so we don't enjoy the choice we've made.

grandkids' burps would ruin it and hugging babies feels better than any coat. And I'd have to keep it in a special place in the closet, have to put it in cold storage and insure it and mothproof it and even worry about looking ostentatious." It wouldn't be worth the things she'd have to sacrifice for it.

She brought the same principle to my attention when I returned from a business trip with some white cotton shirts. I could care less what kind of white shirt I wear, but as I was buying a new suit, the pencil-moustached clerk and my district manager informed me that cotton shirts were the "in" thing—that anyone with any class wore only cotton shirts. I went along with this, but when I unpacked those dudes, my wife questioned my sanity. She didn't care what the stylish salesman said; the labor and money (ironing, starching) it takes to keep a cotton shirt looking nice was ridiculous. "Look at the one you wore home." I took my coat off; the sleeves were so wrinkled, it looked like a calf had been sucking on them. She was right, and they didn't look a bit better than my old Dacrons, which could be maintained in minutes.

So many of us weigh ourselves down with apparel that does as much damage to our freedom as hanging a millstone around our neck. Take a good hard look at those suits and skirts and slacks that only look good for the first half hour you wear them, and then sag and wrinkle and crush and embarrass you for the rest of the day . . . at those blouses and shirts that will never look good without dampening and starching and a good twenty minutes bent over the ironing board (a twenty minutes you're never willing to spend) . . . at the filmy numbers and special fabrics that have to be run through the dry cleaner after *every* wearing (how many times the price of the garment will you end up paying in "maintenance" fees?).

Be Careful with Apparel You Have to Be Careful with

Many people praise my wife because no matter where, when, or what the call for her help, she can be out the door in a minute for any emergency or for a three-week trip. Some of us take hours, days— even weeks or a month to get ready to respond to a sick friend, a sudden move, or a family crisis. The secret of her quickness? I think it has a lot to do with her wardrobe. . . .

Out of ideas for a nice birthday gift a few years ago, I asked my wife how she would like a beautiful fur coat—she turned me down! Her logic for the decision was excellent: "A fur coat, I'd have to be very careful with. There aren't that many places I could really go in it and even then I couldn't sit in it because the back would wear out. Knowing it was so expensive, it'd be hard to relax in it and I'd have to worry about it being stolen. I'd have to avoid Sue and Mildred, two friends who are allergic to fur. The

Unadmitted "Obsoletes"

Most of us have a small universe of things inhabiting our closets that we've outgrown, physically and mentally, or that are just outright unusable, but we haven't gotten around to admitting it yet. These are among the prime contributors to closet crowding, and can actually be rather easily de-junked if we force a (one-sitting, or keep-it-up-till-we've-worked-our-way-entirely-through) showdown with them.

Rare is the closet that can't be de-junked of darling little dresses that were *very* becoming on us (fifteen years ago), formals that have sat in their plastic wrappers for the last ten years (and will for the *next* ten), ugly old coats and bedraggled beloved bathrobes, ties that are out of style (or in style but we don't like them anyway), clothes that shrank or got iron-melted (but we couldn't face throwing them away right at the moment of trauma), too-small belts (or belts so exotic we'll *never* find something to wear with them), stretched turtlenecks, broken necklaces, disintegrating bras, mateless gloves, more "shirts and pants to wear when I'm painting" than a lifetime of remodeling will ever require, pantyhose and tights in colors we'll *never* want our legs to be, jumpsuits and floats we always admire but we keep shuffling past when it comes time to pick something to actually wear.

Impulse Clothes

The clothes we wear the least are often the ones we bought the fastest. We really didn't need or want them, but the mood of the moment mesmerized us. We've all done it—a drive through Dallas and we emerge with some Western duds, a couple of evenings on Oahu and we own aloha shirts and muumuus, not to be worn again until the next trip twenty years later. We can't get out of Wales without four wool sweaters to take home to Phoenix, we couldn't exit Acapulco without an incredibly embroidered stiff canvas shirt. Let a World Series or major tournament come anywhere near our area and we have an instantly outdated T-shirt and matching warm-up jacket. One visit to *Raiders of the Lost Ark* and we'll unflinchingly spring for a smelly leather jacket.

An excellent example of passing-fancy apparel is the cowboy hat. Almost everyone has to have one, because they travel West, live there, or were turned on by Gene Autry or Clint Eastwood. Cowboy hats are a true white elephant for 96 percent of their owners—clumsy and obnoxious inside planes, buses, auditoriums. They get ruined easily and take up a lot of space and almost as much time to care for. Real cowboys (for whom they were designed) shielded themselves from the sun with the hat's wide brim, clamped it over their ears and neck in blizzards, and used it to beat off mosquitoes, kill horseflies, fan fires, and feed their horses. (They also didn't care if their hats got stained or smashed.) We shuffle and protect ours to wear once a year to the rodeo—is it really worth it? My father—and other real cowboys who live on large ranches with lots of mooing cattle and shedding horses—never owned a cowboy hat!

Clothes bought in a hurry—for a party, trip, or new sport enthusiasm—are often an impulse purchase and often end up junk (yes, even jogging suits and "outdoor outfitting").

Costumey/quaint/outrageous/gift clothing often falls into this category, too. Okay, it's arty-looking and it was a great buy, but is *your* husband going to wear that beret? (Maybe if you buy him a mask.) Your wife *might* look great in that red satin Chinese dress slit to the waist, those rainbow-striped harem pants, or rhinestone-studded boots—but would she be caught dead in them? It's sometimes a nice idea to give gifts your loved ones would never indulge themselves in, but don't let your impulses and fantasies override their self-image—you might end up making them feel uncomfortable and guilty, in addition to junking up their lives.

Lettered T-shirts "It's just a T-shirt," you think. "That's not so extravagant." But to be the bearer—on body or clothesline—of an offensive or just plain inane motto or message is the height of pure junk ownership and display. When people can't manage to attract attention with their words, looks, and manners, they resort to buying and wearing a billboard. It generates junk reactions and junk opinion of self, costs far more than it's worth, and crowds the drawer. (Just how often can you wear an I'M A VIRGIN or THIS IS AN OLD T-SHIRT T-shirt anyway?)

Unused impulse clothes are among our most conspicuous clutter. They cause family fights and are a waste of money (and make ridiculous spectacles of us if we do wear them). Go to your closet right now. . . .

Pick out all your impulse clothes. . . .

Don't ask yourself "Why did I do it?" We're all weak. Ask yourself, "Why do I *keep* it?" Then you know what to do. (Aloha.)

Whittle Down Your Wardrobe

No matter how rich you are, whether it was a gift or not, non-used clothes are clutter.

When you have so many clothes that they can't fit into the normal closets of a normal home—mobile, condo, dorm room, or apartment—you have too many! Remember, there's only one of you—and if you have to stash and box and truck clothes away to get room for the ones you're actually wearing, *you have too many.* I'm not in any danger of being elected to the ten best-dressed list, but I try to always be presentable. After I de-junked myself, all the clothes in my section of the closet took up only two feet in width. I do farm work, hundreds of TV and in-person appearances a year, attend church, play sports, and lead Scouts, and everything I need only fills up one-third of a normal closet, as do my wife's clothes. I've been a lot happier since I decided I had better things to do than sort through a dry-goods store inventory every morning just to get dressed.

Know yourself, and think use. . . .

1. If it's not flattering to you—the color or the cut is wrong—pull it out.

2. If it doesn't fit or it's not comfortable—you have to suck in your stomach, you can't bend over or move your arms, or it's itchy—pull it out.

3. If it's too complicated—if you have to wrap or tuck or tie it just so, or if you have to remember to straighten the sash or pull the bodice up every ten minutes, pull it out.

4. If it's too fragile—if you can only wear it where there won't be food or drink or animals or children, where it won't be too hot because you don't want to sweat in it or too cold because a coat or jacket will wrinkle it—pull it out.

5. If it's badly damaged or has an important part missing that you probably won't be able to replace—pull it out.

6. If it needs to be altered or repaired before you can wear it—pull it out.

7. If you wear it never or very rarely (because your lifestyle has changed or it just isn't called for more than once a half-century), or if you can only wear it with certain things (that you don't have or really don't like to wear)—pull it out!

Leave in the closet everything you wear consistently and feel good in; and make two piles of all the rest.

ONE

Needs to be cleaned or repaired—there's some practical reason you're not wearing it.

TWO

Is out of style or doesn't fit or you've decided you just don't want to fuss with it any more.

Take Pile 2 to your favorite charity, or if you're not tough enough, to the garage. In four weeks you'll get rid of it easily because it's been so nice having it out of your way in the closet. . . .
 Pile 1—clean or fix (several of these pieces, when you look at them closely, will join Pile 2). Arrange what's left in the closet according to color coordination and needs. (And when you see something on sale, think about how it will fit in with your basic wardrobe and how *often* you'll wear it—not just how much you'll save.)

Down at the Heels: Junk

No more astonishing proof of human devotion to style at the expense of utility exists than in the case of our footwear. Shoes way down there on the grubby ground house our far-from-delightful feet and are a necessity to protect them. People possess shoes by the piles, many never worn more than a few times. Shoe buyers stalk, parade, twist, rotate, and jig in front of shoestore mirrors for an unbelievable length of time—not concerned with comfort or durability, but with how they'll look to others.

The lowly shoe is responsible for a lot of physical torture, too. The vast majority of shoe styles—men's and women's—are somewhere between uncomfortable and painful to wear. Trying to figure out why a woman would willingly subject her feet to a 4-inch spike heel—so she can't walk, but must wobble and hobble and lurch around—would boggle the finest mind.

Even being a conservative in the shoe style parade, I slid around in sleek slip-ons for fifteen years, because they matched—not my feet, mind you, but the other ridiculous apparel some rich designer designed. Even so, it was hard to buy a shoe I didn't have to snip the bells, buckles, and beads off so I could wear it discreetly. Some near-falls onstage and during TV appearances inspired me to seek a sturdier, more practical shoe. I bought a pair of plain ole "mailman" shoes, and gadfrey—my feet thought they'd been resurrected. I de-junked all my "sophisticated" ones, realizing it was better to plop a little than flop a lot.

How you dress your feet is probably more important to your spirits and physical well-being than anything else you wear. If your feet hurt at the end of the day, or after the first hour, it's time to retread your shoe wardrobe. Comfortable shoes are available for every occasion; it's worth some time, money, and trouble now to invest in a few basic pairs of sensible shoes. And throw out (or give away) all those pairs you aren't using. You'll have more room in your closet—and you'll be able to stride down the street, skip up the stairs, and whistle right past the corn pad display.

And All the Trimmings

Just as the just-right color and just-right amount of trim can make a plain house come alive, too much and in the wrong place can make the same house leap off the lot at you.

So it is with clothing and accessories. Just right is beautiful. Too much is clutter. There are "trimmings" complementary and even necessary to human beings—and there is too much. "Best-dressed" seems to get confused with "best-decorated." Over-dressing, like other junk, detracts because it makes us forget that it's *us* we need to present, not what we're wearing.

I heard a jeweler remark once in a convention address that when some men achieve "success" they buy big cars and nice homes. After discovering, however, that today many people, rich or poor or middling, have nice cars or big houses, they find a different way to flaunt their money: they buy their wives a giant diamond. It's not for the benefit of the wife, you understand, but for *him*—he's just using her to advertise, so people will say, "Boy, Harry is certainly successful, look at that diamond his wife has." Precious stones can be a good investment, but there are better ones—especially if all you're doing is feeding your ego. Jewelry has to be guarded, insured, duplicated, matched, and serviced—it often puts more junk than joy into our life.

Think about your jewelry—your baubles, bangles, beads, and bands. If you have to take them off when you wash your hands or try to work on something, take them off every trip through airport security, take them off when you're in a big city, hide them before you leave home, hide them while you're traveling, and hide them in a bank box the rest of the time, maybe it isn't worth it. It's just another thing to worry about and take care of.

And besides—what woman or man really believes that a flashy object dangling from ears or neck enhances personal appeal? What is it that people want most from each other? Warmth, affection, love, and feeling. What does $30,000 worth of the goldsmith's and silversmith's art do for a cold blood-vesseled hand? People wear jewelry more to impress than to attract, in sober fact.

The most beautiful jewelry is usually utterly simple and expressive of something meaningful; a mass of gaudy stones draped in six strands of chains is a great place to start de-junking.

A lot of our unused jewelry clutter originates in the strange notion there are certain trinkets we can't live without. Looking back thirty-one years, when class-ring-buying time came around to our high school junior class, $28 was a small fortune to me, and working in grease, on machinery, etc., as I did made ring wearing questionable. My announcement that I didn't want one was met with a barrage of opposition: "How will you remember your school?" "How will you identify your steady girl?" "How will you remember the Class of '53?" When they finished, I felt like a traitor but refused to buy one—I bought instead a catcher's mitt that served me well (in fact, I still have it). I never miss the ring, nor do I miss having it cluttering up my "unworn jewelry" case, like all the rest of the Class of '53. Know yourself and please yourself—don't worry about satisfying society's "supposed to," "ought to" traditions, styles, and fads. Most of it will end up junk to you.

Your Crowning Clutter?

Amazingly enough, some of our clutter is literally "home grown."

Anything hairy has caught our fancy in recent years (King Kong was born thirty years too soon). Hair gets more attention, care, coddling, consulting (and chemicals) than any other part of the body. People will let their lungs, heart, stomach, eyes stand last in line for expenditure—hair rates the first slot of value. We spend millions of dollars and hours of time daily to tend it, display it, repair it, enhance it. We nurture face and head hair to the abundance and extent that we have to hire artists to groom it for us.

Yes, it's been called the "crowning glory," but like anything too complicated, hair can be clutter. Nice clean hair, flowing or curled, *is* attractive, but when it takes more from us than it gives, it begins to dictate our existence. It's sad indeed when fear for our hair keeps us from swimming, out of wind and breezes and sun and morning dew, robs us of sleep (those cursed curlers), rules out warm hats, determines what we will do when, causes constant compulsive mirror checking. Hair care for many has become so dominant that our daily schedule revolves around "hair time." (*When* it has

to be washed, conditioned, set, styled, and for how long, etc.) At least the "greasy kid stuff" allowed kids time to be kids! Work, errands, weekdays, and weekends are altered and arranged for hairy reasons—not to mention the actual time taken up setting and grooming.

In most of our lives hair has become a taskmaster, as we spend up to two hours a day curling, straightening, washing, conditioning, tinting, bleaching, blowing, brushing, massaging, teasing, ratting, or otherwise styling it. And that's just *head* hair. Chin, chest, lip, or skull, it takes its toll of our hours and affections. Many a sexy sideburn and macho moustache takes precedence over concern for others' needs. Incredible how the output of an epidermal gland has somehow become the ultimate expression of our masculinity or femininity. Do you *really* feel your hair's worth an hour of your time a day or $50 a month to maintain, not to mention storing and thrashing through all the tools to groom it (or the devastation all that fussing inflicts on once-healthy hair and scalp)? A sane and simple hair style is an easy way to de-junk.

Boot Your Baggage!

Once we've de-junked what we wear, we'll want to do the same for what we carry. Wallets, purses, and bags are stuffed with clutter, necessitating a sorting exercise every time we need something.

No wonder people fumble. You're in a line and the customer just ahead of you, completing his or her transaction, reaches into wallet, pocket, or purse for money, checkbook, credit card, I.D., keys . . . and can't find it. Out comes every imaginable piece of junk. The fumbler can't find the needed item and frantically begins to fling things and rummage through every pocket and personal carrying space while the other people in line begin to mutter at the line blocker.

At an all-day seminar once I asked the audience to gather just the junk they were carrying with them (pockets, purses, briefcases), offering a prize for the most unique collection of clutter. They initialed it for identification. My son passed around a large drawer and in minutes it overflowed. What did I get, you wonder? Used flashbulbs, a 1976 calendar, old speeding tickets, partly eaten chocolate-covered peanuts, a hacksaw blade, a roll of toilet paper, three-year-old food coupons, rocks and pebbles, expired membership cards, half a sock, antique Christmas lists, broken compacts and empty lipstick containers, plus some censored items—and I suspect they held back plenty on me! The woman who won had a whole bulging handbag full—and she was the best-dressed person there!

Do you really want to be muttered about? When you find yourself throwing an extra comb in your handbag because you know your chances of finding the other one in there are slim, that's a clear signal that it's time to streamline the stuff you carry.

Lugging too much around with you can actually be dangerous. A young woman from London told me she had carried an "assailant protection" whistle in her purse for years, and one dark night when she was pursued—you guessed it—there was so much clutter in her purse she couldn't find the whistle. Fortunately, the would-be rapist, intrigued with her junk thrashing, tapped his toes at a distance for a while, then left.

Portable Compacters (Wallets)

We're all wowed these days by demonstrations of how much information can be stored on a tiny computer chip. But far more impressive is something we've managed to do all by ourselves for years—how much we can store in a tiny wallet. I've seen wallets that are so crowded, they actually issue a sigh of relief whenever they're opened.

Once a friend at dinner entertained his guests by going through the small compact leather container. There were six-year-old business cards (from two jobs ago), stashed cigar bands, 1977-78 fishing licenses (this was '83), a YMCA pass from a state he no longer lived in, and of course a complete portable picture gallery.

The weight and bulk of all this is phenomenal . . . and most of it is packed so tight the wallet itself is bulging and distended like a colicky cow. The contents themselves are all bent and frayed and blurred. If you want to have fun at a party, have a wallet-stripping contest. I'll wager 75 percent of your entries are either clutter or something you clearly don't need to be packing around.

Clutter Is Not a Credit to You

Among the real prestige clutter is the credit card collection. People love to open their wallets and purses and fan out a cache of credit cards capable of purchasing anything from a shrimp cocktail to a whole cannery—department store cards, discount store cards, check-cashing cards, gas cards, charge-everything cards, card protection cards—twenty, thirty, even more cards. All this demonstrates, of course, that they have fabulous credit (or are poor managers and have to charge everything on installment). Extra or unnecessary cards are junk, *plastic junk*. You don't need all of them; if you lose your wallet or purse your risk is compounded twenty times, besides which they are awkward to carry around. When I decided my clutter was killing me, my boulevard of credit cards went; for ten years now I've carried only two—and I've traveled the world over, bought dinners, lodging, gas, tickets, supplies, gifts, and never (even once) needed any more. It was one of the most delightful de-junking moves I ever made—try it! Plus you'll pay fewer card fees and spend less money on junk that was easy to buy with all those cards that made you think you were rich.

Junk on Wheels

Some Junk . . .
Drives You Mad

Because we all spend so much time in the confines of an automobile, cars carry some of the finest, most concentrated, and damaging clutter collections in the world. Vehicles are a mecca for junk congregation because we secretly believe that once we're outside our homes, our garbage is someone else's responsibility. When we leave the car and go inside the house, we feel our junk is safe in a sealed vault. So we can ignore those diapers fermenting under the front seat, the empty bottles rolling on the floor, the pits and dried peels, decomposing apple cores, broken dimmers, thermostats, and mirrors, the map of Yellowstone Park stained with sour milk right on the bear's face ("We might go again, after all, it's been five years"). The key ring is so heavy it throws off the power steering— it's filled with the sacred collection of Grandma's house keys, the keys to the broken lock on the storage shed, the bicycle lock, the executive washroom key, the key to the car sold four months ago, a can of Mace, a miniature (nonworking) flashlight, a plastic toll coin holder, and a magnifying glass with a screwdriver in the handle. Some cars in their senior year of clutter accumulation are eligible to graduate to garbage trucks.

Cars were never meant to be four-wheeled files for old parking stubs and unpaid tickets, antique gas receipts, peanut shells, pop cans, crushed fast food containers and tissue boxes, candy, gum and film wrappers, directions to past parties, single-lensed sunglasses, flattened matchbooks, partly peeled flares, dried-out first-aid kits, and non-fitting fuses. They're junk—why carry them around? I recently heard two Catholics discussing the fall from grace of St. Christopher, whose statue once stood fast on every dash—I'll bet the real reason was, the clutter competition crowded the old saint out!

Any time you eat in an auto, 23.7 percent of it ends up on you and the car: you get 3.7 percent; the car interior, the rest. (You think I'm kidding?—think again. A few years ago the growth of the fast food market forced the auto industry to make a big adjustment in their upholstery fabrics.) If you scanned the interior of most cars with a moldy food detector, it would light up like a pinball machine: there's relish on the running board, ketchup on the keychain, mustard packets lubricating the power seat mechanism, rigormortised french fries and sesame seeds lodged in every crack, baby slobber down the front and back seat, all-day suckers stuck to the instrument panel—food of all kinds slung, dribbled, and embedded so long that selling the car is the only way to clean it.

The junk problem in vehicles escalated when motor homes/vans came out. Like homes in miniature they have all the same junk hazards, including the literal kitchen sink that attracts dozens of ditsy little accessories, from spice racks and scouring pad holders to elaborate utensil collections: bagel slicers, cheese cutters, garlic presses, pastry crimpers.

One car can generate more junk than forty kids rummaging through neighbors' junk piles. Every vehicle somehow manages to sprout a bumper crop of extra rims, hubcaps, jacks, and yes, even those bug-spattered and gravel-dented old license plates. You finally sell the beast or drag it off to the junkyard, but the shrapnel of its demise remains behind—dispersed into every corner of the garage, attic, basement, and tool box. Certain that no one else would properly value the treasure that decorates your trusted transportation, you take hours to strip it of the decals, stickers, waving hands, fuzzy dice, leggy deodorant strips, broken scrapers, monogrammed floor mats, back seat clothes hangers, and as a last act scoop up the oil change stickers on the doorframe. Then, in the middle of the

mysteriously, friends scavenge off parts, our teenaged son backs into it twice with the new car, our neighbor's kid smashes his tiny finger in the door, a mother cat converts the back seat to a maternity ward. The hood, wide open like a begging alligator, matches the sprung-latched trunk. The old car is totally shamed and demoralized, but illusions of antiquity now cloud our judgment—we keep it.

Our three-year-old is now sixteen, and, growing up in the shadow of our shrine to Detroit, has become a car jock. He needs a part off the bottom, so he and five friends roll the car over on its side—and leave it. The oil drains out and stains the sidewalk and kills four imported African droop lilies. Seeing how stoutly the undercarriage is built, we fall for the most hypnotic junk phrase in the world, "They don't make 'em like they used to," and we decide to rebuild and restore it. The divorce threat following our announcement steers us reluctantly, at last, to the local car crusher, who when he comes nods his head, muttering, "Poor sucker—what a mess." We step forward to ask him to please not insult our cherished deceased property when we suddenly realize he isn't talking about the car. . . .

night, at the sound of a police siren, you realize you forgot the play fireman's blinkers and the extra flashing built-in brake light.

The epitome of car junkdom is keeping the whole car when it expires—people often do this when it's too far gone to trade in. They feel they owe old Betsy a decent home or, eventually, burial. Now, when a hungry car dealer won't even give you a trade, that's a pretty strong hint that what you have has moved beyond clutter, to *menace*. But we tow the clunker home and park it. The tires go flat, birds use it for a target range, the sun bleaches the upholstery and cracks the dash, the windows get broken

If a car won't run or isn't used, why keep it? It's taking space and junking up your yard. Unless you're restoring an old classic for a hobby or using a clunker to teach your children car care and hard work (or plan to throw it in a gully to check a flash flood), it can only clutter your life.

What is *your* opinion of car jocks—of car worshippers, of car clutter collectors, of junked-up cars, glove compartments full of junk, trunks full of junk—repulsive, aren't they—aren't *we?*

Few things are more unimpressive than a cluttered car. When we see a messy mobile unit we have a tendency to treat the owner as slouchily as he treats the car. And a seedy front seat tends to be a tipoff to a junked-up home or apartment—have you noticed how copiously crudded cars and sadly junked-up dwellings seem to go hand in hand?

The (Wrong) Automobile in Every Garage

Most people make poor decisions on automobiles, both owning and buying. A three-bedroom motor home is impractical for the average retired couple, a velvet-seated Lincoln is not the right transportation for a shepherd with four dogs and a sick sheep forever in tow, a slick two-door sedan is not the smartest way to haul four kids to Little League and newspaper routes (though a nice tough station wagon might be). A convertible is not the car for the avid skier—there's no place for the rack and in high country those babies are cold!

When you get a vehicle for show or ego, it usually ends up junking up your life—it doesn't serve your needs and you don't get the full benefit of what it *does* have to offer. And affordability isn't only a question of economics—many rich people can't emotionally afford the vehicle junk they have.

The pleasure of driving a fine machine isn't the main reason most people own a glamorous gas guzzler—they often only want to own one so they can be seen parking it, sort of like a big metallic piece of chic outerwear.

How often have we seen a struggling family—a young wife with several kids, barely able to pay the bills and keep the kids clothed, while her husband has to be the overloaded macho man with a giant jacked-up nobby-tired pickup or an impractical sports car loaded with options (junk) strictly for ego.

Car sales (and prices) soar when the manufacturer adds "XY-3," "WHIZ," or "Fireball" on a strip of plastic chrome. The reason dealers display their "play" line in the showroom is to get men (who are far weaker than women when it comes to cars) to come in and look, and imagine themselves careening past crowds of admiring onlookers as they maneuver this magnificent powerful machine through life. Entire families' future health and education (and many other things) are suffering because of poor judgment when buying a mode of transportation.

Four-wheeled junk We tread in sacred mud puddles when we question the value of 4-wheel-drive. While there are a few important farm, sport, commercial, and military uses for 4-wheel-drive vehicles, for most of us they're a junk power symbol: the need for 4x4 drive in this country now (especially in downtown

L.A.) is almost zero. I have lived in both the desert and the highest, toughest mountains—7-foot snows in winter—and I've never needed a 4x4, and I've never been stranded for more than a few hours because of weather. Four-wheel-drive costs about $1,000 extra, gives you an extra drive train to tend, and uses more gas—for what?

Paying extra for safety or comfort—maybe even power—on your vehicle might make sense, but most "extras" sooner or later become junk to you.

Consider that classic of conspicuous consumption—fancy hubcaps. You buy an economy car, standard shift, with a smaller, more economical engine—then get $400 worth of wire, turbo, or mag wheels on it. These are absolutely no aid to travel, and are easy to lose, hard to clean, and expensive to insure (and as a Portland accountant pointed out, "I get no enjoyment out of them. I have to stand in the front yard and have someone drive my car by so I can even *see* them"). The fancier they are, the more mental and financial concern they cause. Who (besides other car junkees) really notices or cares about hubcaps anyway?

There is always a sickening feeling about overjunked car purchase and ownership. The newness wears off in a few weeks and the reality of thirty-six, forty-eight, or sixty months of payments sets in—just for something to take us places. Transportation.

It doesn't really matter how sexy or classic or convenient the vehicle is, we bought it to drive and now, for a long time, we *will* drive it. Many of us try to get even with the car that bought *us* by never washing it and leaving junk in and on it, but it's really only we who suffer.

The time, money, and emotion spent on an automobile—a piece of plastic and metal—is incredible.

A businessman noted for the accuracy of his financial analyses produced some interesting facts about the "average" person. The average person who has a $385,000 lifetime income spends $81,000 of this on his automobile (more than on food or shelter!). One transportation analyst claims that the typical American devotes more than 1,600 hours a year to his car: sitting in it, hunting for parts and parking for it, working to pay for it (about 28 percent of his income). True auto eroticism can be found in some exclusive sections of this country where the average car is owned for about eleven months (a bit longer than the average house is retained in the same areas). An automobile is merely a mode of transportation, yet it has been designed and marketed as a status symbol, personality outlet, aggression releaser, and pacifier. People spend almost twice as much as they need to for a car, and brag or talk about it more than about family, friends, or personal health.

People can easily find hours to wash, polish, and baby a car, yet can't find minutes to floss and brush their teeth. They can make a staggering payment on a car, or spend $5,000 more on a prestige model, yet not be able to afford a weekly long-distance call to Mother or Dad or a $2 donation to the Girl Scout cookie drive. They will know every engineering wonder and calibration of that special model and not even know their nieces' and nephews' birthdays, or what time to be at work. Do you want to spend all that emotional, spiritual, and physical strength to sustain a *possession?*

Maybe It's *Not* Time for a Trade

One day a friend of mine mentioned that since he'd been married (he has seven children, three of them now in college), he'd spent a total of only $13,000 on automobiles (and he's always driven a safe, handsome, fully-paid-for vehicle around). That didn't seem possible to me

because for some time now those nice autos have been costing $9,000-$15,000 each. His simple secret (and what I do now): he waits a year or two, watches the paper, and buys a nice clean sound $10,000 used car for $3,500 direct from a first owner or wholesale from a dealer—and then keeps it maintained and de-junked. It lasts many years and will usually be running well enough to pass on to his children, who drive it another five years. Impossible, you may say: "My car wears out." Not really—we just get anxious for something new and begin to look for excuses to trade the old car in. Once we *want* a new car (slick TV and magazine ads help us out here) the justifications come easily enough. We've only got 30 or 40,000 miles on her, we've just about paid 'er off, and we're ready to leave her behind.

How did I decide to overcome this expensive habit of mobile mothballing, like we all ought to?

During a 300,000-mile publicity tour for one of my books last year, I asked an Indianapolis cabby (driving a plain old 1979 Plymouth just like we drive), "Hey, buddy, how many miles on this thing?" "275,000," he says, "it's about broken in!" Wow, what a blowhard, I said to myself— I thought people only lied about gas mileage. When I got to St. Louis, I asked *that* cab driver, "This thing got a few miles on it?" "325,000," he said. "You're kidding," I said in the back, trying to keep the disbelief out of my voice. "Sure it does, we have two Novas with 225,000 and [some other ordinary cars like we own] get over 400,000 miles—some of our cabs in New York City get 600,000 and over." Positive that I'd met two truth-stretchers in a row, in the next four cities I asked all the cabbies about their cabs and got the same answer (some of them owned the cars they drove). Their secret, I found out, is taking care of things—not necessarily overhauling, but routine maintenance and fixing problems as soon as they come up—and, of course, keeping the engine warm and going helps a lot.

I went back and reviewed the autos (business and personal) I'd owned since 1957 (sixty of them), and almost every one, once I sold or traded it, was run for years by the next owner and more years by the next owner. I figured the new owners must have rebuilt them entirely, but not so—they just replaced a belt and gasket or two and cranked 'er up. Once I bought a '54 panel truck with 70,000 miles on it, beat it up hauling cleaning gear for five years, and put another 70,000 miles on it. I figured it must be dead (the battery was weakening) and sold it to my neighbor for $25. He replaced the battery, fixed the door handles, and drove it for five more years. It finally got so ugly he figured it was dead, and sold it to a high-school kid. One day three years later, when I was doing my Christmas shopping in a town many miles from here, I saw the old '54 Chevy, same dents, my faded Varsity Contractors logo still adorning the doors, parked right with the Cadillacs and luxury Jeeps. A kid came out of the mall, jumped in, and drove off, smooth as silk!

When I sat down and thought about it, the reason I got rid of cars was usually that a latch was broken, the clock stopped working, the glove box light went out, a window stuck, or there was a rip in the upholstery.

Don't do it! It's a poor investment. Sit down and calculate your vehicle purchase and operation costs for the last ten or twenty years. Now figure what you could have done with that amount of money if you'd followed a more practical course.

The adjustment to a whole new way of thinking about vehicles is a shocker, but it will pay you some amazing dividends. I wasn't at all sure I should keep driving a vehicle when it reached the 100,000 or 125,000 mark. I'd start getting nervous and say, "Surely I better get a new one." I could scarcely believe it was still

running well, and pictured myself driving somewhere and the whole motor or transmission suddenly disintegrating or dropping out on the highway—but that nightmare never comes true. I'm just being seduced by the new-car enchantress.

Yes, I do have a little fix-it problem once in awhile, but the glory of no payments, low insurance premiums, and all the other nice paid-for sensations more than make up for it. *All* my vehicles have over 100,000 miles. They are real luxury units—I can relax (even leave the keys in!) when I park them or when someone spills a milkshake, jump in and take off without a thought in my grubbiest work clothes—yet they run and do everything the $15,000 models do.

Since I kicked the expensive habit of mobile mothballing, I've been constantly reassured it was the best de-junking move I've made—cars don't wear out as fast as our resistance to new models. Cars don't drive me, I drive them, and I love it. Your car can go to 100,000 miles— oh yes it can!

When Adding Subtracts. . . .

Some of the best designers, engineers, and decorators in the world work for automobile manufacturers, expending great research and effort to make cars efficient and beautiful. They work for years to achieve precision and balance in a car model's power, mechanics, size, and weight for maximum durability and safety. Yet when ownership falls into our hands our impulse to clutter it up is surpassed only by our urge to redesign it. We think we can grossly improve the unit by adding extras (junk)—and we succeed! We modify pipes for more noise, rip off the hood so everyone knows there's a motor in there, jack up or weigh down the frame, reshape the grille, install miniature traffic lights in the rear window, add larger tires, bigger carburetors, giant plastic bug guards, racks, winches, and a horn that plays "Dixie." As a final touch we have to play police with whipping antennas that get ripped off by every car wash and kid in town.

Few of us are convinced the auto company's gearshift handle designer is as smart as our local hot rod parts salesman and so, before our $14,000 vehicle can operate, it needs a genuine gold-plated goosehead gearshift knob. The goosehead is a bit awkward to handle and too bland for some real mover with silver-studded driver's gloves. He's more likely to reach for a German Luger handle, a dagger, or a replica of Mae West's bosom. And of course in the *real* macho car you'll find a scented satin garter clasped around the sun visor.

While serving briefly in the state legislature, I rode home on weekends with a fellow legislator. The view out my window was somewhat obstructed by an obnoxious black box fastened to the dash—a radar detector. My colleague proceeded to drive 80 miles per hour, the detector of course functioning to intercept any police radar, at which he would slow down to the lawful 55 miles per hour. He apparently felt that it was his right to break the laws that he was, as a public officer, on his way to enact.

The ownership of such an instrument is an admission of intent to break traffic safety laws. The speedometer gave him all the information he needed; it's designed into every car free! It's a great example to friends and family, too: "This is Daddy's sneaker cheater lawbreaking helper." If a kid cheats on a test, lies a little, or dodges a household duty, that same father comes unglued.

Junker sticker An ugly 12x4-inch piece of glue-backed paper, generally containing some unimportant poetic or political message, plastered on automobiles and other conveyances to get attention or create a distraction. Bumper stickers are a hard-to-equal demonstration of bad manners (even more obnoxious than blaring exterior loudspeakers). What's worse, while you're driving, than having a message preached at you off the back of the car ahead? One car reads "Honk If You Love Jesus"; the next, "Honk If You're Horny." Be it political or moral persuasion or the crudest "Get Off My _____," bumper stickers are junk, in bad taste, and (with the possible exception of "I Brake for Animals") *impair passenger safety.*

Decor Can Be Dangerous

Somewhere in the process of junking a vehicle we forget its original purpose—transportation. A telephone or stereo in an auto is often useful, but once we start in making our car a home away from home we add a TV, a bar, an icebox, venetian blinds, clothes hangers, footbaths, extra clocks, makeup mirrors, compasses, cup holders, thermometers, and cassette sorters. The car looks and feels obese—becomes unwieldy to operate and maintain—and unsafe. The last three times I've run into something on or off the road, I was watching out for, fiddling around with, trying to eat, or adjust a piece of junk.

Our efforts to decorate our vehicle and give it all the comforts of home are often at the expense of important and necessary equipment like safety flares, flashlights, first-aid kit, chains, jumper cables (that *work*), blankets, a shovel, etc. The food-stiffened seat belts are tangled and unfindable amid the rubble. Visibility suffers, too—there are gaudy souvenir stickers on every window, dancing dice, miniature teddy bears, dubious deodorizers dangling in the driver's line of vision; bobbing-headed dolls and stuffed snakes bring up the rear (window).

The tissue holder on the dash ends up poked down a defroster vent (which makes it a lot less likely that we'll ever get the frost out of our faces). The FM radio and tape player may make staying awake on long trips easier, but the moment we're dawdling with the dial and fumbling with cartridges could be the fatal one.

For a clutter-free vehicle:

1. Keep a garbage can in the garage or driveway area. This will help keep clutter from infiltrating your car and make it easy and convenient to de-junk when you pack up or unpack.

2. Be sure you have any necessary tools, shovels, emergency flares, chains, etc., in a sturdy box in your trunk. Better still, roll them in a pad. This keeps tools compact, quiet, and provides a nice mat if you need to crawl under or over the car.

3. Keep some small (11x17-inch) plastic trash can liners handy and as bits of food and other refuse build up on a trip, put it in the bag immediately. Odors and stains that junk cars usually result from *left* food, not the act of eating itself.

4. Carry a Masslin® dustcloth (see *Is There Life After Housework?*) in the glove box. It will pick up the dust effectively. I also carry a spray bottle of alcohol-based window cleaner and a cloth in the trunk for spills, mud on lights, and other instant cleaning needs.

5. Don't screw, bolt, or glue cheap accessories and gadgets all over the vehicle.

6. Clean and wash the *inside* of the car occasionally, too. A wet/dry vacuum and a hand brush will clean seats and floor mats easily.

Modern transportation offers us tremendous advantages and conveniences. But a vehicle is not an extra house, room, shed, or a mobile dining car. It isn't a trophy wall, moving van, or a six-cylinder billboard. *It is transportation!* One of the biggest destroyers of human life today is the automobile used for things other than reasonable transportation.

DRIVE DE-JUNKED. The skin and sanity you save will be your own.

Junkee Safari

Maybe we saw too many Tarzan shows in our youth, felt excitement stir in our veins as the great heroes and hunters stalked the field for trophies. Now we imitate those events perfectly—alone, in twos, and in families. Father and mother are the great "white" hunters (there's no minority edge in cluttering). The kids are the caravan led into the distant wilds of amusement parks, national parks, ballparks, state fairs, toll road restaurants, and gift shops anywhere.

Suddenly we see it . . . through the trimmed hedge . . . the "Congo Curio Cache." Our pulse is pounding like drums as we peer at: a granite gazelle, a teak tribesman with a bone in his lip, a brass camel nutcracker, a genuine jade juice glass, a varnished driftwood thimble holder and—hold it—a 6-inch alligator of glued-together guava pits (tremendously valuable—even more valuable than the sunflower-seed owl we got in Phoenix). We carefully examine the base of each unit, which identifies the country it was "homemade" in and what machine it was "handmade" by. Our chest swells with pride as we boldly pass up a eucalyptus umbrella stand and a set of tusk toothpicks. Then we find "it"—an ivory unicorn with obsidian eyes. How could we have lived without one all these years? Into the bag it goes. What fun it will be finding a place to display it!

We are finally exhausted pawing through the fifty of each of these "one of a kind" items, but wait—look! Colorful carved candles. "Who do you think would like one of these?" mother hunter asks, running an appreciative eye over them.

Father hunter says, "There must be somebody!" Kid beams a "beats me" look. They all think, but can come up with no one immediately needful of an elegantly carved candle. "There must be someone . . . I've got it! . . . The Jones kid is getting married. What a lovely gift."

(They'll have to put a note with it, telling the Joneses never to take the cellophane wrapper off, to be careful not to dent it moving it from display area to display area (for surely it's too pretty to burn), to store it in a cool place so it won't melt, and to be sure to pack it up in a big padded box when they move. . . .)

Have you been on a junkee safari lately? Examine your trophies—maybe you should have stayed in camp.

Location Lurking

If it's a forbidden or dangerous place we all have to go there—call it curiosity, inquisitiveness, or exploration, it's all the same. My mother always warned me to "stay out of the sagebrush, or you'll get ticks on you and catch spotted fever." As play at home in the yard dulled, the brush brightened, and sometimes I would drift to the edge—no spots appeared and not a sign of a tick! Soon I was playing in the brush, enjoying the challenge and mystery of it all (and still no spots or ticks). I would return from the forbidden fascinating location thinking I'd gone undetected; I didn't realize the rule of location lurking: it always leaves its marks on mind, body, wallet, and suitcase. When I'd get within twenty feet of Mom, the tangy sage smell would give me away: "You've been in the sagebrush, haven't you?" Fearing her apparent omniscience, I'd 'fess up. And as she'd pull off my shirt there were those tiny ticks all over me; my record was thirteen!

You might not collect any fleas from a flea market, but you'll pick up a bargain or two while you're "just looking" and enjoying the atmosphere. You snicker at fools who bid their heads off at auctions— but if you hang around or attend many, you'll be one of them. At a garage sale your inquisitiveness will soon evolve to acquisitiveness and you'll find junk tucked proudly under your arm.

There are some locations we have to frequent less or avoid altogether if we intend ever to be cured of junkitis.

Frequenting shopping malls (plazas, squares, centers, complexes, or any of their other aliases) is location-lurking suicide: even an innocent amble through will insinuate some junk into your shopping bag. Never go to or hang out in such places if you don't need anything.

Next time you go to a shopping mall, before you buy or look, sit down on a bench and watch the customers. You'll notice the majority of them shuffling along purposelessly, often not after anything in particular, just looking for what they *might* need. The displays, decor, and smell of a mall seem to have a hypnotic hold, especially when people, like overpowered hot rods on a Saturday night, travel up and down the aisles looking for action.

The media—and perhaps our parents, teachers, and friends—have inadvertently taught us that happiness comes from things: that's why when we get "down" or depressed and want a lift we often seek to buy something. That's why people wander aimlessly through malls and curio shops—they don't even know *what* they want. They just crave the experience of buying a new thing every so often. The minute they buy it, the time starts ticking down till the next time they have to do that. And when they do get something, it just triggers the urge for the next and next—all of which compounds accumulation. Just picking up "one little thing" here and "one little thing" there is where the pile of clutter came from.

"Recreational" shopping is a mistake. If you need, want, or have to have a specific something, go for it, but just poking around in shopping malls (or anywhere there is a glamorous array of goods, food, or whatever) is a temptation you don't need. It will seduce you into acquiring things that will needlessly clutter your life.

The Languid Locations

Some locations are particularly perilous because they have a very high clutter quotient or actually *specialize* in things that are junk to most of us (scarcely or non-functional, largely decorative, often expensive "stuff"). Fortunately, we have a clue to this before we ever enter by the very name of the place.

Any place with the word "gift" in its name.

Ye Olde, etc.: when Old is spelled Olde . . . watch out! (Anything with an extra "e" on the end is probably a junk dive.)

Anything with an animal in the name: The Busy Bee, The Bashful

165

Bunny, The Fragrant Frog, The Rumpled Unicorn . . .

Anything that sports an ampersand, or has an "N": (N'Stuff, N'Such) is a dead giveaway.

Anything that substitutes Ks for Cs: The Kozy Korner, The Kountry Kobbler, etc.

For that matter, anything with "Country" or "Corner" in the name.

Trees or plants in names are also suspect: The Tulip Tree, The Boysenberry Bush, The Sassafras Shrub.

Have you ever gone back to an old junk-purchase stomping ground, shuddered, and asked yourself, "How could I ever in my right mind have bought that?" It seems we have to buy a certain number of trinkets a certain number of times before becoming immune. If you haven't reached your junk saturation level yet, don't wait for it! It might be years of unhappiness away.

Garage Sale Sickness

Garage sales have increased about 800 percent in the last decade—the ultimate public confession that the house runneth over, a family fight is inevitable if the junk stays, or they need cash to buy different junk.

The display of all of your junk right in front of your house takes real guts. I couldn't do it if they paid me double the price. A quiet classified ad at least has a little dignity (only people might match your phone number with the worn mattress, the highchair without a tray, or the "like new" exercise bike). The allure of a garage sale is unreal: I've seen people become totally distraught when they hear another garage sale is going on while theirs is in progress. It's not the competition that causes the concern—it's the fact that they can't leave and get in on the goodies at the other sale! Garage sales are *the* place to give you a double-whammy dose of junkitis virus. There seems to be something inflammatory about the sight of someone else's junk all spread out on open display (and for such cheap prices, too!).

It's truly the Great American Junk phenomenon—how ordinarily intelligent, discriminating consumers will suddenly abandon all reason and begin to scoop up armloads of the most absurd stuff imaginable:

- Old half-used bottles of aftershave
- Dilapidated parlor games
- Burned-out appliances
- Tent dresses and double-breasted suits
- Half-dead houseplants
- Moth-eaten uniforms
- Mismatched dishes
- Parts to extinct autos
- Leaky hip boots
- Abused toys
- Obsolete textbooks
- Run-over shoes
- Holey Levis
- Shorted-out electric blankets
- Bald tires
- High-water pants

You name it—and it's selling like hotcakes at your nearest garage sale. It's not amazing enough that the junkee shells out perfectly good money for this trash—

he or she actually experiences euphoric feelings of cleverness and joy at having scored such a hit. These feelings usually dissipate by the time the victim reaches home, however. Having by now returned to full consciousness and taken a second look at the plunder, the hapless junkee goes into a fit of depression.

If you're serious about saving yourself from junkicide, garage sales may well be a pleasure you might wish to forgo.

The garage sale has a few relatives also worth sidestepping. The *rummage sale*, for example, is an increasingly rare species that still lingers on in church halls and school basements, often heavily inhabited by charming chirping ladies. The rummage sale abounds in shabby but genteel junk—worn books, limp afghans, faded plastic flower arrangements, and frumpy 1950s clothing. The *flea market*, on the other hand, is a vigorous and fast-growing hybrid that springs up in shopping malls, parking lots, vacant lots, fairgrounds—anywhere there is abundant open space for display and parking. Here the innocent is adrift in a sea of separate booths featuring a breathtaking variety of junk—old, middle-aged, and even brand spanking new. Velvet paintings, Last Supper rugs, log-slice clocks, hubcaps, novelty booze bottles, comic books, used paperbacks, tattered girlie magazines, and printed T-shirts of every description are standard flea market fare. You even stand a good chance of being able to lay your hands on a genuine ($5) Sears wrench for only $6.50.

Some junk danger zones are less widespread than others—not everyone passes through them—but they're no less deadly for being less trafficked. If you're due to travel these zones soon, begin preventative therapy *now*.

Convention Clutter

Have you ever watched crowds at a convention as they scoop up all those buttons, brochures, booklets, pens, posters, stickers, swatches, samples, and special-release records—and cart them home? We even save the plastic bags they gave us to carry the clutter in, and our plastic badge holders to remember the glory of our name in lights (or at least felt-tip marker). Maybe someday we'll have enough to slip in new cards and reuse them to run our *own* convention (the annual Junkman's Convention?). . . .

Convention "fall-out," by and large, just litters drawers and punctures fingers—how much of this stuff do you have squirreled away? I'll bet my whole stack of play money any of you who've been to a convention or trade show within the past year *still* haven't gotten around to using (or even sorting) the junk you hauled home. Embarrassing, huh?

Sick Junk

Even sick, we aren't safe from the junk virus. Isn't it odd that people keep their hospital junk? As we check out, we clutch our flattened bed fleece and all those little pitchers, pans, and cups, plastic straws, and wristbands—after all, we paid for them—so we load them up and take them home, and never, never use them. They're the sickest green you ever laid eyes on, and every time we see them they remind us of the hospital—the shots and the nausea and that miserable operation. (And how many homes need more than three pairs of crutches?) Why do we keep them? Trying to get our money's worth out of that $2,600 hospital bill? Forget it. If you're saving the stuff for the next time, forget that, too—they'll charge you for it again, even if you bring your own!

Passing Fancy Junk

In the moments when clutter begins to overwhelm us, we never ask, "How did I get all this?" We know exactly how! We instead ask ourselves, "*Why* did I get all this junk?" The answer is often—we fell for the old "fad" or "get in the swim" trick.

When any type of craze sweeps the nation, committed as a lynching mob, a big percentage of us join in. We buy fast,

pay more, and then fizzle out. Homes and cars are stuffed to the gills with seldom-used "good as new":

aquariums	gerbil cages
jogging accessories	hula hoops
video games	food processors
fondue pots	fad style clothes
ceiling fans	movie cameras
string art kits	weaving looms
massaging foot-baths	yogurt makers
wood-burning kits	hot tubs
pet rocks	macrame makings
diet books and plans	hurricane lamps
weights and exercise machines	guitars
metal detectors	trampolines
ceramic molds and kilns	CB radios
pasta machines	walkie-talkies
organs and pianos	slow cookers
stereo headphones	popcorn machines
rock tumblers	wood-burning stoves
adult bicycles	ice cream makers

Most of this is bought on the spur of the moment and before the new smell has vanished, so has our interest. As costly as it may have been, it's now a burden to us. How can we poke fun at the snake oil salesmen and claim-salting victims of the Old West when we're suckered out of millions of dollars daily on things we don't need, or that we use for an hour and keep for a decade?

Beware the "Danger Days" that accelerate the accumulation of clutter

If you think avoiding gift shops, shopping malls, and even garage sales alone is enough to keep you safe from junk, you're riding for a fall.

Custer came to an untimely end because he unwarily rode into an area where the opposition outnumbered him; our clutter defeats are caused by a similar unawareness. When you stop and think about it, we're surrounded by specially scheduled days that circle and bombard us. Study your calendar the way Custer should have studied his war map.

JANUARY

NEW YEAR'S EVE

We insist on starting our year off miserably with too much liquor, rich food, tootie horns, stupid hats, streamers, pages of unresolved resolutions and twenty-seven more calendars than we'll ever use.

FEBRUARY

VALENTINE'S DAY

This high holy day of accumulation rolls around just about the day the last piece of Christmas clutter finally disappears. We only prepare for it a week or so in advance, but manage to swiftly replace the missing Christmas junk with frilly paper doilies, cheap candies stuck together in a gaudy dish bought for the occasion, over-frosted cookies that hang around for weeks in drawers and on shelves, shiny cupid-shaped cake pans to be tucked (or crammed) into storage for next year . . . and who with a grain of romance in their soul could throw away empty embossed candy boxes with lace and ribbons?

APRIL

EASTER

Think of all the awful Easter bonnets and broken Easter baskets, battered chicks and bunnies, baggies of plastic grass, and picked-over jelly beans stashed somewhere; along with the leftover egg coloring kits and peekaboo candy eggs that we'll never eat and never throw away.

MAY

OPENING DAY: FISHING

Full-grown adults (especially the males) become insane weaklings on this day, so hide the checkbook. They buy assorted rods, reels, creels, lures, and hooks, fish-fooling and -finding gadgets, books and bait incubators, tons of real and artificial foodstuffs, attractants, repellents, and special fishing togs, 80 percent of which are expensive (and ultimately destined to dry-rot in the storage room).

JULY

FOURTH OF JULY

We always get twice as many sparklers, wienie buns, coolers, and charcoal briquettes as we need, and more suntan lotion than we could use in three summers—and then spend the rest of the year trying to keep it all out of sight.

OCTOBER

HALLOWEEN

We buy racks of creepy costumes, a bale of orange-and-black napkins, a six-foot paper skeleton and witches for the walls, keep a 50¢ mask with our kid's first trick-or-treat candy crushed on it—and then at the after-Halloween sale buy four more plastic lanterns to store till next year.

NOVEMBER

THANKSGIVING

Got to have ugly miniature turkeys, six extra giant platters, assorted relishes in assorted little awkward display dishes, shedding centerpieces and door ornaments, and an extra meat thermometer in case the other three extras don't work. (And we'll keep those gap-toothed Indian corn ears and dried-up gourds into infinity.)

DECEMBER 25

CHRISTMAS

Keep the wrinkled wrappings, crushed bows, and snarled ribbons, sagging Santa candles, frayed pine cones, faded wreaths, broken bulbs and tree ornaments, every tree stand we ever bought, and the last two surviving pieces of the Nativity set (even if Joseph's head is missing).

SOME OTHERS TO BEWARE OF:

Mother's Day—Father's Day—Memorial Day—birthdays—weddings—anniversaries—any opening day—reunions—graduations—Election Day—St. Patrick's Day—Washington's and Lincoln's birthdays

For some reason we can't just enjoy the spirit of the day—we have to "thing" it to death. It's as if we have to *prove* we're loving or patriotic or happy or thankful. But the proof is in the feeling, not in the accessories.

Celebrity Clutter

Billie Bicep eats Soggie Doggie Flakes, so millions eat Soggie Doggie Flakes. Many don't even know Billie Bicep, or if the flakes killed him, or what—but they'll buy and eat. Miss Doris Dottungorto wears purple pump shoes exclusively—so millions of teens buy (but seldom wear) purple pump shoes. Endorsements and testimonials from the most famous "personality" can't convert junk to jewels: because a guy hit fifty-eight home runs doesn't make him an authority on what to drink or eat; because a woman has traveled to the moon doesn't mean she knows anything about luggage. We are as much authorities as anyone on ourselves and our world.

We seldom see ourselves as celebrities, but we are, all of us—only our degree of exposure varies. You are admired and looked up to by someone—probably scores of someones. When you begin to realize this, you won't be such a victim of celebrity clutter. Don't let yourself revere any mere human to the point he or she can dump junk into your life.

I love heroes—they have been and still are some of the greatest inspirations in my life. When John Wayne died I felt like lying down in front of a truck; when Sophia Loren appears on the screen, my nostrils flare. I think Walt Disney was one of the greatest geniuses who have lived on this earth—but they are just people like you and me, and your friends, relatives, and family. I don't need John Wayne saucers hanging on every wall, or a Sophia Loren T-shirt (it wouldn't fit anyway), or a pair of mouse ears in my closet. My Roy Rogers capgun was my pride and joy, as was my Captain Marvel code ring, when I was a kid, but we all grow up (we hope) and take a saner view of celebrities.

Let your heroes and heroines fill you with feeling, not load you down with junk. Anyway, think how disrespectful it is to blow your nose right in the faces of your Beatle hanky, chew on the eraser of your president pencil, or sit on your Elvis Presley pillow. (And an autograph on something only *guarantees* you'll never use it.)

Endanger Junk? . . . Never!

If you're a tender-hearted junkee you may worry about becoming so junk-free that junk will become extinct. It won't happen. As hard as you may be working to pitch it out of your life, 40,000 companies are actively working to lay more on you. Have you ever noticed when anything reaches the "endangered species" state how it suddenly multiplies? Newspaper headlines now read:

SNAIL DARTER
ENDANGERED SPECIES!

Overnight, snail darter plates and coins and memorial mugs and spoons appear in gift shops and in mailings. People stampede to buy them so they'll always keep in touch with the snail darter (whatever a snail darter might be). Soon there are tons of snail darter junk; though no one remembers or cares about the real, live, almost extinct little darter. Other creatures, famous/infamous people, places, etc., are handled just the same. As soon as something is winding down, the media and manufacturers pump it right back up. Don't have junk paranoia—there'll always be plenty if you get lonely!

Media Mania

Every time new heroes come on the tube or screen we fall in love with them, but the experience is so passive that to keep our love alive we have to shower ourselves and our shelves with the flood of trinketry that follows. The whole environment is remade in the image of some fictitious creature: rings, T-shirts, notebooks, pencils, ponchos, perfume, candy, sleeping bags and sheets and pajamas, watches, shoes, decals, games, books are everywhere. Can you believe it? We pay for it! $10.95 for a $1.99 T-shirt with some nonexistent primordial amphibian silkscreened on the front. It all ends up junk as soon as the theater changes the marquee.

Imagination junk We snicker and chuckle at the kids being suckered in on movie and TV junk (toys and souvenirs), but they can't really hold a clutter candle to our acquisition of imagination junk, whereby we buy miniature replicas and play models of the things we want but can't afford. Thus we have Mercedes and Porsche keychains, Ferrari eyeglasses; if we can't have a boat in the bay, we have one in a bottle; if we can't be a real cowboy, we get the buckle, boots, spurs, hat, and often a bronze stallion for the shelf.

The really gross junk in the line of things we want but don't always get is *women's figure junk.* Anything made to resemble a woman's body, some men will buy. Thus we have female torso drinking glasses, bottle openers, ice cubes, swizzle sticks, toothbrushes, chess sets, ashtrays, and even tire irons. Talk about imagination junk! Can you imagine being eager to use Marilyn Monroe boat bumpers or a Dolly Parton parcheesi set. . . . Gadfrey, I can't "bare" to go on!

Beware of These Junk Seduction Words . . .

All of us are lambs when it comes to the seductive words and phrases that convince us we can't live through the day without knowing what _____ feels or tastes like, if we can't own a _____ of our own. Before soft messages and signs croon you into the arms of Old Mother Junk, make sure you translate them.

The One-Word Wonders

Selected: *Everything* is selected—it could be selected out of the reject pile, the failure file, or the trash barrel.

Imported: Just about everything is "imported" from somewhere—how far away doesn't matter much any more.

Premium: Could be a way of marketing something, not an indication of worth or quality.

Limited: They don't say limited to what or where, or how many.

Model: A small imitation of the real thing.

Special: A term of timing—not value! In the right time or circumstances *anything* can be special.

Exclusive: They haven't dared try it anywhere else.

Handmade: A hand touches the tool or mold that makes everything.

Homegrown: Everything is homegrown (even if it's been shipped in from 4,000 miles away).

Free: Law of the Universe: There is nothing without a price.

Revised: It didn't work (or sell) the first time.

Quality: Quality is just a state (it could be good or bad).

Priceless: Smiles are priceless. People are priceless. I've never seen a *thing* that is.

Distinctive: Distinguishable from other things—isn't everything?

Authentic: Genuine junk!

Reduced: Same junk with a different price.

Layaway: Get it now and let it grow on you before you have to pay for it.

Clutter by Any Other Name Is. . . .

We've evolved gentler, more indirect, euphemistic approaches to most of the unpleasant things in our lives: we can say "portly" instead of "overweight," "sexually active" instead of "immoral," "legally detained" for "in jail." Thus of course we've found some soothing clever names for clutter, too—so we don't have to come out and call it "junk" or "trash" or "clutter" or "worthless objects."

You can do a fairly good job of identifying junk by its nicknames—and they are legion. Cast a harsh eye on anything that you find yourself (or others) calling:

doodads	trifles
odds and ends	trinkets
curios	baubles
knickknacks	gimcracks
gewgaws	folderol
paraphernalia	doohickeys
collectibles	thingamajigs
bric-a-brac	watchamacallits
whatnots	

The Phrase Fresheners

Sometimes, no matter how seductively junk is marketed in the first place, it just doesn't sell. So the advertising people are called in to revamp the campaign and they come up with ploys like these.

On Sale: The most desirable things and places don't have to go on sale.

New, Improved: It failed, and we want *you* to guinea-pig the second round.

Once-in-a-Lifetime: You can be sure that after getting stung this time you'll never do it again.

In Style: It's time again to tell people what they like.

For a Limited Time Only: They've only got a few more left to dump.

May Never Be Offered Again: There are two lawsuits pending.

Backed by _____ Years of Integrity: "The more he talked of his honor, the faster I counted my spoons."

Top-Rated: Only means that it's popular—doesn't say why: it could be the only one in town.

Double Your Money Back: If you can find them.

Only One per Customer: Offer to buy a hundred, they'll love you!

Our Only Concern Is Your Satisfaction: Your money will satisfy that concern.

Ten-Day Trial Offer: They can depend on your procrastination.

Not Sold in Stores: We decided to hit you suckers direct.

First Edition: Is always the worst—mechanically and structurally. All first editions are prototypes, experiments—which means they don't have the bugs worked out yet.

Space-Age Material:	Most likely plastic, sometimes stated as "Space-Age Technology."
Years Ahead of Its Time:	Just hope it doesn't need a part not invented yet.
World's Thinnest, Lightest, etc.:	They made it as cheap as they could.
Doctors Use:	Doctors make mistakes and have bad habits, too.
The Next Best Thing to _____:	Please buy this second-best.
No Artificial Preservatives:	But surely lots of natural ones.
Factory Outlet:	No retailer wants it.
First Class:	Should be the standard, not a degree of excellence.
Grand 2 for 1 Sale:	Easiest way to get rid of two pieces of junk simultaneously.
Custom-Made:	The factory made an error.
Order Toll-Free:	Junk is only a phone call away (we'll include the toll in the purchase price).
Special Edition:	Every edition is special in some way.
For Adults Only:	If you're a twelve-year-old with fuzz on your lip—you're in!
Train or Truckload Sale:	Just about everything travels one way or the other these days.
Laboratory-Tested:	It could have *failed* the test.
Made from Selected Raw Materials:	Probably a tuna can you threw away a month ago.
Largest Selection Available:	Nobody else in the area carries any.
New Fall Colors:	The same old colors with new names.
Almost Too Good to Believe:	It almost fools you every time.
At Last, a _____:	It never was really needed.
Order Before Midnight and We'll Include. . .:	Will you accept a bribe for junking?

Everything tagged with these teasers isn't necessarily junk, but how often do we let phrases like these inflate an object's value—and how often do we end up with clutter because of them? You hear people (who have no idea what that might entail) say, "But it's Swiss-made!" So what? Do the Swiss (or the Japanese or the Swedes or Guatamalan Indians) have a corner on quality? The fact is, well-crafted items can come from anywhere—and so can sloppily built things.

You *Can* Take It With You (Clutter!)

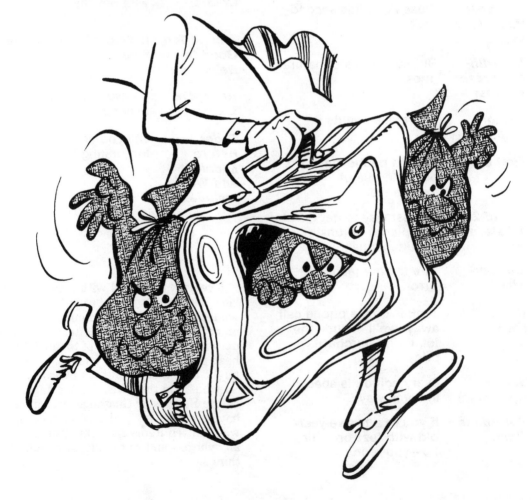

At age fifty-seven, my wife's parents, Vera and Jerry, were comfortable, their family was raised, their health good, they had plenty of friends, and Jerry had a good job. They had just built a little house and I guess you might say they had it made—they could live out their lives in a secure and honorable fashion. But to them, as to most of us, there's more to living than room, board, and a job. Although their situation was pleasant enough, they got to thinking of the routine they'd established in the past twenty years—it just wasn't going to be as exciting for the next twenty very important ones. They'd watch the same trees turn, the same people cruise the neighborhood, go to the same bowling alley (and get the same score), have the same hamburger every Tuesday, the same chicken every Thursday, go on the same vacation every year, suffer through the same weather, and so on. Secure—but dull, unchallenging. Routine, too, can become junk.

Of course, we know we don't have to change geography to change routine, and that problems can travel with us to the farthest mountain cabin or desert isle, but sometimes a change in location, leaving the junk of routine and place behind, can force a freshness into your

life that will make your heart beat with joy again and arouse new feelings (and revive some old ones).

One evening, during the same conversation during the same visit to the same house at the same hour with the same people, Jerry's drooping ears heard someone mention a possible mechanic's job in the wilds of Fairbanks, Alaska. The job wasn't for sure, but for a qualified mechanic chances were good—and Jerry was the *best* mechanic. Three weeks later, eyes blazing, possessions loaded in a new Ford pickup with a camper shell, Vera and Jerry, at an age most people would hole up in fear, left their home of forty years and went to Alaska.

When my wife and I visited them three years later, we discovered a miracle had occurred in their lives. Both looked forty, both bubbled with enthusiasm. We stayed with them two weeks, and every place and person they introduced us to was stimulating and life-brightening. They had experienced floods, dog races, record cold, wild animals, glaciers, and the most majestic mountains in the world. They were irresistibly alive—it was almost impossible to leave them when our departure time arrived.

After ten years Vera and Jerry retired, and still with only a pickup full of possessions, came home (grandkids are hard to resist). Their lives today still have a zing from those ten years of new experience and challenge. They still have the love and associations of their home and friends of forty years, and now hundreds of new friends and memories from Alaska.

When our realm of experience is too confined, we lose confidence—get cluttered. (Isn't just about every unconfident person you know intensely territorial?) We don't give new people or places a chance to touch our heart.

We can have the same experience twenty times—or twenty different experiences. I'm not saying old friends or good old places are junk—just that we need to always be progressing and expanding. We can't stand still and savor a situation too long or it loses its savor. We have to go forward; we'll get junked standing still.

Reflect on this some evening after you arrive home from a twenty-same-experience activity. Maybe a trip to Africa or Australia or South America is out of the question, but if you curl up in your den of routine and security too long, your mate, family, peers, employers will see the junk of routine making you into a dud.

The same goes for the clutter of constantly returning to old stomping grounds and scenes of former glory. Junk locks us into the old; it gives us false security.

It's like that spark of hope we carry around of revisiting and reliving the past. Life doesn't have any reruns: all those people and places didn't go into cold storage the day we left; like us, they grew and changed. And when we go back, the miles are shorter, the hills smaller, the old buildings replaced by new, and no one is in near the awe of us that we expected. We had the chance to wave our banners once; the second time around will bring us little or no applause.

A return to jog memories or show the kids or friends is sometimes beneficial, but make it quick and move on. I used to long at least once daily to return to the ballfield where I once had the ability to bring the crowd cheering to their feet. Thirty years later I did return for a big ballgame—and they could have put a tent over me and sold my performance as an act. I was ill-timed and awkward—when I left in glory I should have left it alone.

Things evolve, turn over—the new comes and the old dies or is left behind. Growth is all! Junk prevents growth, change, moving on ahead to better—in love, jobs, friendships.

There is always more ahead than behind; the past can become clutter to us if we don't learn to live it and leave it graciously behind.

You Can Take It With You . . . But Please Don't

We Americans are a mobile society; if we want to, we can move around pretty easily and change our life experience. We can travel anywhere, any way, any day. We travel to and from work, to and from college, to and from relatives, to and from the places we go just for the fun of it— "vacations." We ride thirty different modes of transportation—even go as far as the moon. We spend more time on the move than in our permanent living quarters, called home. The average one of us moves from one home to another about fourteen times during a lifetime.

Most of this mobility is for a few basic reasons:

1. To have new experiences.

2. To meet new people.

3. To expand ourselves.

Much of our mobility is a quest for self-discovery and self-expression, but most of us don't really gain the advantage of our movement, or reach our real destination, because we're too weighed down by the clutter we carry along.

Most of us who want to get away from it all end up taking it all with us. The very things, the very people, the very thoughts that have ruined our nerves are packed (as much as possible) in the car or suitcase and taken along. And then it has to be tended, sorted, and worried about as much in Mexico as back on the farm in Iowa or the house in Baltimore.

We can't change, expand, meet new people, see new places, or have new experiences when the old junk that inspired us to get away is traveling along with us. Consider a simple trip into the country: we prepare for a three-day trip for five days—not what to do when we get there, but organizing to get there and back in comfort. We end up packing so much there's no place to sleep or ride. Excess baggage always dampens travel; much of it is clutter and ends up detracting from the destination. Truthfully now—when you see someone staggering along with piles and piles of baggage, what do you think? You don't like them, do you?

Where you're going usually has a kitchen sink of some sort, so don't take yours along. The more junk you carry on your journey, the less vacation you'll have from junk.

JUNKEES ARE ALWAYS PREPARED—ESPECIALLY ON VACATION. THEY CARRY WITH THEM:

- **four outfits** for each projected day of vacation—clothes for all different temperatures, weather, and moods
- the **dashing outfits** they never have the courage to wear at home (and won't have the courage to wear there)
- more **perfume** and **jewelry** than they ever wear at home
- **clothes** that are too tight for them at home (and will be even more impossible to wear after several days of vacation feasting)
- at least two **fancy formals** "in case they decide to go to a nightclub"—

but they'll never get off the beach, as usual
- **ten pairs of pantyhose** (after the first sunburn, they won't be wearing any—though they *could* use them to hang themselves)
- **wide-brimmed hats** (hard to carry or pack without smashing, hard to keep on, will block everyone's view if they do wear them and the car's rear window if they don't)
- **food** (in case they get stranded)
- a **can opener** (and an extra can opener)

- a **bathrobe and slippers,** plus
- a **dressing gown** (and high-heeled mules)
- an **extra purse**
- extra **heavy coat** and an extra raincoat
- all the **shoes** they never wear at home
- three **swimsuits** (different styles)
- **umbrella** and backup umbrella
- four boxes of **Kleenex**
- the **multi-vitamins** they never take at home
- six pairs of **sunglasses**
- a **sun lamp**
- a **heating pad**
- **towels** they won't need
- a fold-up **exercise bench**
- **curling iron** or electric curlers (they'll be too busy or too lazy to use either)
- a **flashlight**
- **pruning shears**
- a **croquet set**
- the **craft project** they never get to at home (that somehow they're going to get to amidst the exotic sights and sounds and happenings of wherever they're going)
- the last six months' **newspaper puzzles**
- the copy of *War and Peace* they promised their teacher they'd read back in high school
- their **butterfly/stamp/coin collection**
- **unanswered letters** and undone personal accounting
- three **legal pads** for the short story they're finally going to write
- a **diary** with only three pages filled out (that will return with only three pages filled out)
- an **extra suitcase** (to lug home all those souvenirs)

And we wonder why we come home tired.

If you take it all with you, you might just as well as not go. In fact, a better idea: once you have it all packed, just send all your junk on vacation—you'll both be better off.

If you de-junk your travels, you won't need to bring along medicine for:

- Backache (you'll be carrying a light load)
- Headache (you won't be thinking of junk)
- Indigestion (you won't be eating junk)
- Sore feet (you won't be searching for all that junk)
- Nerves or sleeping (you won't be worrying about junk)
- Waking (you'll be eager to get up)

When you're planning your next trip, take a hard look at what you take and what you bring back: remember, the reason we move or go places is often to get away from the things that make our life cluttered and uncomfortable. Our urge to take our clutter with us destroys the very reason for the change. That's why so many people who run away from troubles at work or home or school don't find any peace or easing of pressure. The very things that caused the problem are still tagging along. We aren't talking here only about the tangible things that fit in a suitcase, car, or moving van, but also junk of mind and heart and habit. Before you begin a project, a relationship, a journey, first get rid of the stuff you don't need to take into the experience with you—it's just excess baggage. It's a lot easier to enjoy life without it.

A few tips for de-junking a suitcase:

1. Remember that just about anything can be replaced easily en route— except maybe eyeglasses and medication.

2. The dry cleaner (or laundromat) where you're going can lighten your load on an extended stay. If you try to bring enough for the whole trip, it'll just crush and wrinkle, anyway.

3. Don't bother to pack *food*—there's just about nowhere in the world you can go and run out of food. The golden arches are everywhere your fallen arches can walk.

4. Don't load up on film—you can buy film even at the edge of the Grand

Canyon, the entrance to Nairobi Park—*every* junk stand has it. And are you sure you shouldn't just buy postcards? (Let *them* take the pictures.)

5. Pack it all up and try to carry it for two blocks—then start eliminating.

Don't Forget the Bags You Carry Every Day

Make it a tradition, before you leave on any trip, to clean out your pockets, pocketbook, and/or wallet. This will work wonders: (1) you'll leave clean and organized; (2) you'll be reminded of how much junk you already have, and how much money you have to spend, just before you head off toward all those souvenir stands—it's a great junk inhibitor.

Souvenirs

In 1976 I took thirty-eight Boy Scouts to the National Scout Jamboree in Moraine Park, Pennsylvania. En route to the camp we toured some famous, picturesque, and historically interesting places like Niagara Falls, New York City, Philadelphia, and Washington, D.C. The boys had paid about $1,000 each for the trip, which included everything—food, admission fees, transportation, etc.—and all had, as recommended, brought $100 spending money. You could more accurately have called the $100 their "junk money," and indeed, it ended up almost dominating the whole trip.

At the spectacular Niagara Falls I observed only one boy once looking over into the awesome roaring tumble of water, absorbing the grandeur and the mist; the others—you guessed it—were lodged in a souvenir store line, shoving to latch on to gaudy mementos of the Falls. When the bus pulled out, hardly anyone had spent any time at the Falls or noticed the breathtaking flowers, trees, and buildings of the park grounds. They were all sorting through the flags, pennants, pens, pencils, mugs, beanies, whistles, and other cellophane-wrapped trinkets stamped out in the Orient. Fifty percent of it broke before they got home, and 95 percent of it was entirely worthless a month later. One boy had bought a two-pound brick of chocolate that demobilized him at future stops; he was so sugar-junked he couldn't walk far enough to watch a 300-foot ship be spectacularly raised to the Lake Erie channel. In New York, few boys had time to look up at the Statue of Liberty, they were so busy buying little metal models of it. In Philadelphia, Liberty Bell frisbees eclipsed the Bell itself. In Washington, some boys, bedazzled by the souvenir shops, sidestepped the Smithsonian. They were so busy collecting junk they missed the collection really worth seeing.

But my Scouts were only small-time clutter collectors compared to us adults. During a trip to an historic Alaska town I noted that the majority of the people who had spent thousands of dollars to get there spent most of their free time wandering the shops, buying expensive souvenirs. An elderly couple from Colorado bought a rare Inuit seal-skinning knife—absolutely no place for anybody else in the world to legally use it—while their companions invested in some intricately carved caribou-antler buttons. ("Hey Betty, can you and Jim come over tonight and see our authentic caribou buttons?") Gilded gold pans and little plastic bags ($1) of Mt. St. Helens dust were also selling briskly—and we wonder why our lives erupt with junk! But the epitome of valueless souvenir collecting was well represented by a couple of prime little items people flocked to buy—actually paid good money for, and carried home to show friends or set on the shelf. One was a lump of horse manure, sprayed with varnish—with a few wires for legs, wings, and a beak, it was selling for $5.99, a genuine "Turd Bird." In the next town the gift shop stocked a genuine varnished moose dropping, likewise wired for antennae, wings, legs, etc. It was a "Moosequito," a better bargain at $3.99.

Many of the souvenirs we buy and lug home are of about equal value.

We are souvenir-aholics; we feel we must buy. But almost everything we buy on vacation is junk—or ends up that way. We go to travel, to see new and different cultures, people, lands, places, scents, sounds, and to store the experience in our being—to replenish our souls, not our shelves.

We often are so obsessed with mummifying memory with a souvenir that we're oblivious to the actual event or place we want to remember.

Often I've seen the spectators at big-league games so buried in buying (beer, popcorn, programs, hats, bats, helmets, badges, pins, keychains) that they never see the game.

Disneyland is one of the most fascinating places I've been; yet I watched three-fourths of the visitors there spend the majority of their time and money in the junk shops buying food and trinkets, letting the genius of the operation go unsavored.

Once I was with a couple of other cars full of tourists at Needle Rock on the island of Maui. The air was clean, the mountain and jungle enthralling. Three large tour buses drove up—and right behind the three buses came four van-type pickups. They shot in like race cars, the drivers jumped out of their vehicles,

folded down the sides, and opened up built-in cabinets and display cases. Zap—four instant souvenir shops. All eyes left the natural beauty of the land and like possessed spirits, the visitors stampeded, shoved, and pushed to get at the counters of the very same things they had in their hotels and on every street corner at home in San Francisco. They loaded up on cheap jewelry, enameled rocks, smiling sea shells, plastic leis, and shark combs, and wrestled their treasures to the buses, forgetting the reason they came to that spot in the first place.

Souvenirs not only dilute the rapture of the moment, they cast their shadow over the entire trip. What is it, as you are flying or cruising, you suddenly worry about in one of your twelve suitcases? A $75 shoe getting crushed, a $350 suit getting damp or wrinkled? *No*—it's the $2.25 glass souvenir or the swan-shaped bottle of perfume that keeps you awake in the stateroom at night.

Commemoratory Evidence

Perhaps we think people won't really believe we were there, at Famous Fountain, so we feel we must return with evidence. We think about taking a picture or making a sketch—but that doesn't seem to have the whammy of a genuine commercial item, so we buy and return with some ridiculous commemoratory samples:

- a **lava cinder** from Craters of the Moon Park
- a genuine **Japanese fan:** You can buy it cheaper almost anywhere (including Sioux Falls, South Dakota).
- **sand** from Death Valley: Could you or your friends tell it from sand from the Indiana dunes or South Carolina?
- a **piece of bark** from an Australian Eucalyptus: Long Beach Park has 500 matching trees—with bark.
- Dodge City **Saloon mug:** A perfect replica of the one Whiskey Pete spat in just before he shot Mole Morgan. One Wheaties box top and 50¢ will get you a matching set!
- a varnished **redwood plaque** with a maudlin Moon-and-June message: "God bless this little house of mine, that tolerates this tacky sign"—bought at Whitewater Falls, West Virginia.

- a **can opener** proudly imprinted "Carlsbad Caverns": Is this something you'll want to look at every time you reach in the drawer?

- a genuine carved gritstone **chess set:** Those knights and kings are really demonic-looking, but no one else has one even close to this baby.
- a complete annotated **tour guide** to the Old Trojan Mine: A little gem to show your friends who can't understand a bit of it without seeing the mine. And of course *you'll* never read it again, but it can go on the shelf.
- one adolescent **orange tree** or sawed-off saguaro: It wasn't easy to get home to Wisconsin through quarantine and customs, and should last at least three days before the north wind nips the life out of it.

We buy all manner of often expensive souvenirs to prove to friends we were there. It would be cheaper and more legally convincing to carry a pocketful of 25¢ affidavits and get them signed by the locals.

Show-and-tell is great—for third graders. What do you end up doing with all this?

Not All Silly Souvenirs Come Off the Shelves

A sharp English editor friend of mine pointed to a grotesque piece of driftwood decaying away at the back of his house. "We got that on the north shore of Ireland, carried it on the car, when we ferried, and onto the train. Riding I had to carry it under my arm to avoid poking someone's eye out. It sat too tall on the luggage rack for parking garages, it shed all over us; what a tussle it was getting the bloody thing here, but finally we did. It's a prize piece of grotesque driftwood, but what to do with it, I don't know." (He seemed to have just shifted its rotting spot.)

When we seek to crystallize an experience in things, it's always disappointing. That hunk of rock from the ridge has no grandeur on an end table; those multicolored pebbles leave their magic in the stream bed we plucked them from. That beautiful little bird's nest just sags and gets wispy on the shelf.

And sometimes the "free" souvenirs we labor to acquire (that cactus by the roadside, at the risk of a fat fine and gravel scrapes on our new pumps, not to mention the chance of being flattened by a passing semi) are as costly as the boughten extravanganzas.

Some friends of mine have a summer cottage on a river that feeds into Lake Michigan. They also have a beautiful old wooden powerboat—a classic. One day they were toodling along the shore of a cove far upriver, spotted a large and very nifty-looking log—and decided it would look great in front of their rustic cottage. After securing a line to it they revved up the boat (powerful enough to pull three skiers) to yank the log off the beach. They did manage to get it off the beach—but in the course of pulling it home they pulled the transom off the boat, to the tune of several thousand dollars' custom boat repair work. The log looks real nice in front of the cottage.

Souvenirs Cost

The big cost over the course of time is the amount of our life's energy spent caring for them—but oddly enough, when it comes to "souvenirs," we lose all price perspective, even at the point of sale. We'll pay $5 for something worth 5¢; I've watched people pay $28 for a cross-eyed bear that cost $1.50 to produce.

Even the best-controlled junker weakens when in another country—we'll travel a thousand miles to buy something that generally was available in our hometown, pay twice as much for it, and protect it on the trip better than our own health.

A 98¢ shirt will go for $10 with 3¢ worth of ink and a message on it. Cheap travel bags worth $2.49 at the five-and-dime store at home will cost us $9.95 away, and we pay it gladly, because it has a garish silkscreen of El Capitan on it.

Would you go to a tourist trap in your own town and drop four bucks on a raccoon tail or a varnished beach rock? Would you spend $10 on a plastic model of your city hall, or the big cloverleaf and overpass outside town? Of course not.

Don't buy junk under the guise of souvenirs! On your next trip try to bring home more memories and less memorabilia.

Bursting the Rubble Bubble

Remember when you finish a vacation and come home and sort through all the things stuffed in your bags and suitcases and one by one retrieve all the souvenirs you so carefully selected? As you take each out of its now-ripped and wrinkled paper bag, your heart sinks lower and lower with every one you lay out on the bed. The glue on some has already crumbled. The eyes have already fallen off the rubber snake, the water is leaking out of your little snow scene, the musical pencil sharpener is already out of tune. As you appraise the lot of them, you see a collection of 100 percent clutter—how could you have been so stupid! Now you have to tend these things, clean them, store them, make excuses for them, and try to figure out what to do with them.

Clutter Bugs

We can clutter ourselves and take our own luster away or throw it in the environment and do the same. I walked the shore of a lake in the Northwestern Rockies and the sights and sensations of this beautiful spot were despoiled with (I took out my pad and scribbled a list on the back):

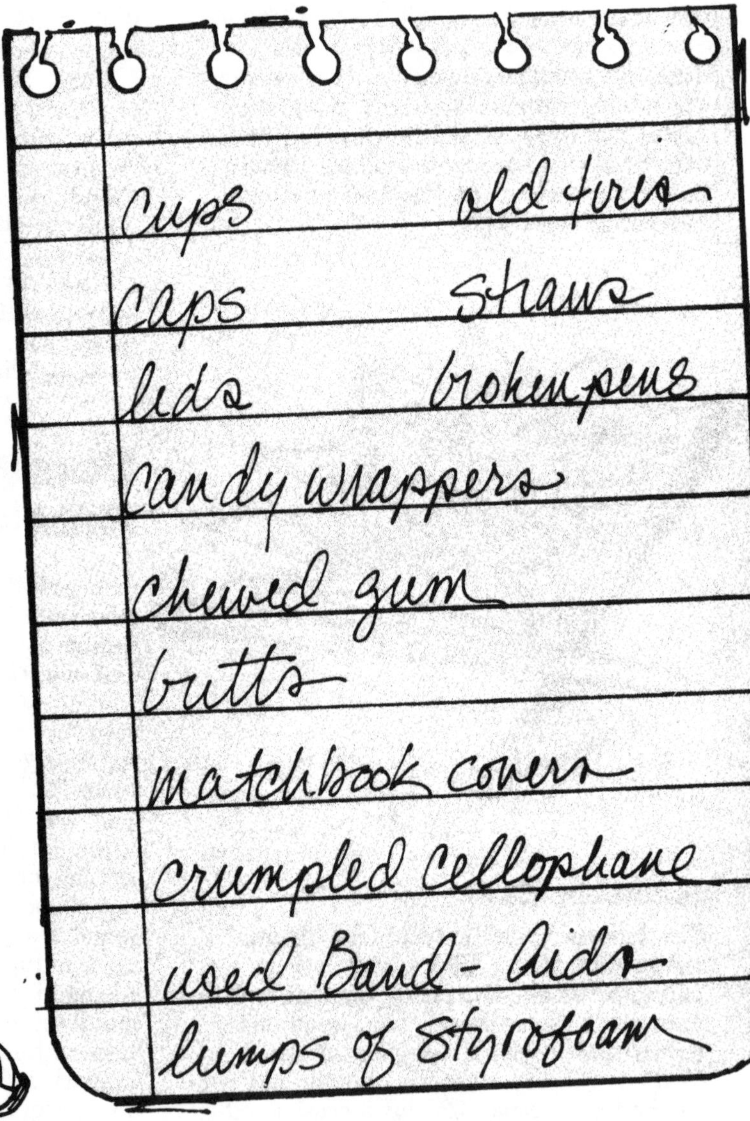

cups   old tires

caps   straws

lids   broken pens

candy wrappers

chewed gum

butts

matchbook covers

crumpled cellophane

used Band-Aids

lumps of styrofoam

Ran out of room on my pad. . . .
How do you feel about these additions to the landscape? A walk down the beach, street, or through the neighborhood will be a great incentive to de-junk.

Animal Litterers

Before all you animal lovers see what's coming and refuse to read on, let me bare my soul about animals. I've raised, fed, cared for, and been around more animals, birds, and fish than most people see in a lifetime and I love them. I think children need a pet as much as they need a good breakfast. I've fed rows of pretty kittens in the barn with warm squirts of milk from the cows; I have huge trout in the pond out back that I like too much to catch and eat. I don't even kill bugs—I capture them and turn them loose outside. The friendship of animals does a better job of restoring us to our senses than most things, but in some environments and situations, pets get cluttered and cheated and the junk that results outweighs even the love we get from them.

Recently we drove through the Canadian Rockies, and more awe-striking, sweet-smelling country I have never set eyes and lungs on. While everyone stretched when we stopped at a rest area, I did some people-watching. Sixty percent of the cars or motor homes that stopped would let out a poor cooped-up dog or cat. Then their owners walked them over to the nice lawn and shrubby rest area to do their little job of pooping or piddling all over the place ("Not on *my* tires—over there so other people can step in it"). In one area, nine vehicles with animals stopped and everything from Great Danes to pet panda bears pottied on and over everything. Remember, this goes on all day, every day. It's likely that more than 200 sweet little pets did unsweet things to that area in one day, and the next and the next. Have you smelled a rest area, park, or pet-walking street lately, or tried to get through one? It's like an obstacle course. I'll admit that inside the restrooms where the humans do their thing isn't much better, but at least it's *contained*. The sanitation and health requirements for a house with two people living in it are an engineering nightmare of a septic tank or sewer systems. Yet in many places animals can clutter and litter and junk up yards and parks at will.

Carefree strolls through the park, lolling on the grass, playful tussling with your toddler are just a few of the joyous activities greatly inhibited by the junk left by dogs. No wonder some states require owners to recover their animals' nuisances.

There Is a Solution to Clutter

In Fact, There Are Many Solutions. . . .

ONE

You could *have your clutter cremated* and have a daily or weekly viewing of the vase containing the remains, if deep feelings are still there for your junk. It can remain with you, in spirit and condensed form.

TWO

You could *microfilm it* and carry every bit of your junk everywhere you go.

THREE

You can *seal it up in the cornerstone* of your new house, and it will finally have value when it's dug out centuries later—as an *artifact*.

BROKEN CLOTHESPIN:
Under stairs, in cigar box,
between gerbil cage and
croquet mallet, left of coffee
can of sink stoppers. Cross
check chafing dish, on top
of plastic bucket behind
garage door, and shed.

FOUR

You can *move a lot*—into places that are too small!

FIVE

Our modern computers might be the ultimate solution to the modern-day problem of junk. With a computer you have two choices for keeping track of your junk.

a. You can simply *program all your junk onto a disk*—what, where, when you last saw it, etc.—and when you get to longing for it you can call up that file so you'll know exactly where it is.

b. Or even more useful (because we seldom actually use junk), you can *program all your junk into a visual format*. Then when you get lonesome for it, or want to check on it, you can punch computer recall—and there it is to radiate security and be enjoyed, while taking up no appreciable room.

SIX

You can do nothing. Actually, doing absolutely nothing about the junk that has overcome you is the most common approach. This is also called retreat. It is totally chicken-hearted; you will retreat again and again, and junk will multiply.

SEVEN

Retrench. When any of your junk—things or personal habits—threatens you and your comfort zone, you hide it in a better place, pack it in tighter, contain it like nuclear waste so it won't contaminate its surroundings—thus we become slaves, servants, flunkies to junk.

EIGHT

Planned riddance. Might facing up to junk be the best solution? Face up to it—it won't fade out!

Turn the page and let's get started.

What is junk?

If we could all throw out each others' clutter, we'd have no trouble deciding, but our own—well, that's a different story.

Knee-deep in our own junk, we are a one-person hung jury. Everything we possess has its attachments—seemingly into the very nerve center of our bodies and sometimes to the rational core of our brains. But we have to judge and sentence our own junk—no one can (or should have to) do it for us.

My opinion of hats, for example, might differ from yours.

Hats

Hats, I feel, exist for three purposes: Practicality, decoration, and to look stupid.

The practical hat is useful, even necessary. These are hats used for building and doing, like hard hats to keep rocks off your head, sombreros to keep the sun out, helmets to keep bullets out, miner's hats to see where you're going and so on. Such hats aren't anywhere near being junk, if they're used for their intended purpose.

The decorative hat (or vanity hat) includes the big parade jobs with "fruit salad" stacked on the head for style, plumed hats that make people in church sneeze, safari helmets or Australian bush hats, coonskin caps, Yukon derbies, captain hats, Sherlock Holmes hats—all of which I feel are a waste of money, effort, and raw material out of their proper context. Unworn decorative hats clog a lot of shelves and closets, but you might like them and use them and they do your psyche a lot of good, so it's hard to make a universal judgment on these.

The "to look stupid" hat I won't even apologize for calling junk. These are wolf faces, pig ears, stuffed fish, bawdy

beercan, or the wing and antler types. Who in their right mind would skull around in one of these? A derby with flipping propellers or deeleybobbers or a baseball cap with curling antennas can only top a total moron, in my opinion.

Pretty harsh on your junk, aren't I? (Thank goodness we can't really judge each other's junk!) If you happen to be a model, an entertainer, or an actor, have grandchildren or like to play cowboys and Indians—or if nothing lifts your heart more than the hat that tops your outfit— many hats in these last two groups wouldn't be junk at all. Only *you* know the immediate and long-term value of your hatrobe and if some are junk you can throw them in the ring to start off your de-junking pilgrimage.

For another example, almost every military person I know has a hand-carved wooden water buffalo on his desk. They're ugly and always dusty and chipped, they always get knocked over and shown off to uninterested guests— but for some reason they're tolerated. If I were to judge your junk and you pastured one of these hideous things, there would be one last moo. But for all I know it may be a sacred reminder to you of the person who saved your life in the rice paddy under machine-gun fire and you'd never part with it.

I also think gum chewing is clutter, that no one with any class would be caught chewing in public. *You* may find it a harmless habit that relaxes you. Fortunately, we don't run others' lives, and must analyze our own selves and possessions to determine what's junk. Some things that keep *your* life fresh might be smothering mine; some things that help keep me well might make you sick. There's no way I or anyone else can assume your junk-judging duties.

Empty tin cans are clutter to 99 percent of us, but not to the person who uses them for constructive projects, or earns money by recycling them. Parties can be total junk, ruin your life—or they can add a sparkle to it. It depends, of course, on the party and its effect on you. *You* have to judge that.

Anything that crowds the life out of you is junk. Anything that builds, edifies, enriches our spirit—that makes us truly happy, regardless of how worthless it may be in cash terms—isn't junk. Something worth $100,000 can be pure clutter to you if it causes discomfort and anxiety or insulates you from love or a relationship.

Most active things are not junk, most inactive things are. But you have to determine the degree of activity that makes something meaningful to you. Whatever contributes to a happy, free, resourceful, sharing life isn't junk to you—but it might be someday. Our needs and values change—with our age, location, mates, and degree of self-development. We should keep our eyes on the new horizon of life coming and that means that some of the tools, places, and things we used to operate in the old horizon, although once good and valuable, might now be junk. As we reach out and grow up, we have to learn to throw out.

The pioneers provide us with an excellent example of this. Heading west, they loaded up all their possessions and precious treasures—including heavy hand-carved furniture, elaborate table settings, trunks of clothes, decorative gates and headboards, and oversized clocks.

When they reached the rough-hewn trails and steep terrain of the hills they were forced, if they were to survive, to lighten their loads, to discard some of their good stuff; it was, although costly, clutter to them at that moment. Others coming along the trail found the valuables free for the taking, but they too had to judge it as junk (and leave it behind) because it stood in the way of their greatest goal—their destiny. So it is with junk: that which restricts our living, loving, thinking, and feeling is junk, be it a thing, habit, person, place, or position. You alone have to make this judgment, because only you fully understand your position in life, your goals, your emotional ties, the time you have available, and the limitations of your physical self and space.

The silliest little trinkets or souvenirs of people or places aren't junk if they give you enjoyable participation. If, on the other hand, you just possess them, they just sit on the shelf and you never even look at them, they probably are junk and should be thrown out of your life.

Consider the story of a family traveling by car on a long vacation to Alaska. At one of the first gift shops, the father shook a wise bony finger at the three travel-weary grade-schoolers and said, "Now don't you kids buy any junk with your hard-earned money, you hear?" The kids bought some beef jerky, a 98¢ travel riddle book, an animals-of-Alaska game, a cheap turquoise ring, and one of those

$3.98 automatic paper birds that fly. While the parents lingered in the gift shop, the kids went out on the freshly mowed park lawn, wound the bird up, and threw it back and forth, screaming with delight, running, jumping, laughing, and breathing the fresh Canadian air. At every stop they did it. The paper bird was the finest thing going. As they rode along, they played with the game and told riddles—thought about and questioned them—and everyone felt and examined the "real" turquoise ring. In four days that bird provided those kids with more exposure to nature and good feelings than they'd had for a long time. On the fifth day, the bird, beat to a frazzle, gave up the ghost.

When they got back in the car, the parents unloaded: "You stupid kids, that's what you get for buying junk, what do you have now for your money, the riddle book is worn out, the bird is broken, and that ring, if you keep passing it around, will soon be gone. Spend your money on something nice like we did. You'll have something to show for your vacation." (The parents at the same stop had bought four cups of coffee, a varnished wall plaque that contained the words "ass," "hell," and "damn," a $2.75 women's glamor magazine, and an ugly $43 etched ivory figurine.) The kids, with downcast eyes, felt guilty and learned there and then that one of the main purposes of a vacation is to bring back stuff (junk). The kids' stuff wasn't junk—it enhanced, stimulated, and accelerated their feelings for each other and the beautiful country they were traveling through. The parents' figurine was packed away and hidden—it had no value; the paper bird beat it a hundred times over. *Junk depends on your use of something, and what it does to your life.*

Don't Let Hard-Earned Cash Buy You a Hard Head!

I wanted a top-of-the-line slide projector. My expert camera man sold me a handsome model and twenty trays to go with it. The unit, impressive as the name engraved on it might be in other circumstances, was a dog—a failure of design. I got annoyed and then angry with it and badgered the company to make it work. *They* were so discouraged with that model, they'd quit making it— or parts for it. But do you think I could dump that bright mechanical dinosaur and all its accessories? No, and twelve years later I gave it to my son-in-law, who now in Skagway, Alaska is beating and kicking and cursing it and trying to decide what to do with twenty expensive-looking slide trays.

One of the biggest reasons we keep junk is that we hate to admit mistakes. Often we acquire a thing, a job, a habit that we absolutely hate the minute after we get it. But we don't get around to taking it back (or quitting, or stopping), though it's a constant pain to maintain, to own, to be around. In general it makes life miserable but we keep it—why? Because we don't want to admit we were wrong or greedy for a moment or made a bad judgment.

Once I bought a pair of "El-Crako" ski bindings and had them mounted. The bindings cost $56.50 and I thought they were great—until statistics and experience showed that they led the leagues in leg-breaking, premature ski releases, and every other binding failing possible, so I took those new expensive bindings off and put on some good Nevadas. But the ones I had removed were so shiny and I'd paid so much for them and after all, they were hardly used. . . . I put them in a gallon can and kept them.

Over time I moved, sorted, and shuffled them from place to place because they cost so much, were nearly new, and I would be admitting I made an error. But I would never use them and it would be immoral to give them to a friend— what good were they except to clutter my mind and shelf? (I finally dumped them while working on this book.)

I've done the same with notebooks. I bought some expensive jobs that looked handy and revolutionary, but the stupid things wouldn't hold standard-size paper and wouldn't open right, so I went back to using a $1.69 one and left the nice leather ones on the shelf. They didn't suit me any better when I tried them again five years later, so I pitched them, wondering why I ever kept them in the first place.

There's nothing wrong with making mistakes—cautious living and five accomplishments only get five things experienced a week. Only those who belt in and do fifty things a week and make twenty mistakes get thirty experiences to the good and gain confidence; they generally end up years ahead in living and enjoying life. Mistakes can be tolerated as building experiences, but don't hold fast to your mistakes—pitch the evidence!

Don't Be Prejudiced by Pride

It was a cool morning and I was dressed for the hike into the hills, when a wiser and older man I barely knew stepped up and said, "You ought to take that last heavy coat off, you aren't going to need it, and you'll get hot later." Like any other twenty-five-year-old I knew how to dress, and what business was it of his? I kind of resented him questioning my decision—so I wore it. Half a mile up the hill, I knew I'd made a mistake, but decided to pretend I was enjoying being overwarm. One hour later the sun was beating down and I was heating up like a pressure cooker. I still hated to admit that his suggestion to shed the coat back at the car was right, so I suffered with it for another hour. I was so dehydrated I felt like a shriveled hide, when about three that afternoon some people came by headed back to camp and asked if they could take the coat back to lighten my load. Humbler than I was in the morning, I gave them the coat and began immediately to enjoy a bright, beautiful, carefree afternoon in the mountains.

When you find yourself resenting having to, or being told to throw something away or give something up, consider first and foremost the reward, the end result—how you and your life will be without it. Nothing is more stimulating than being rid of some thing or habit (or even person) that has held you down. When you pause with the decision in mind or hand—shall it go or shall it stay with me—when logic and even emotion can't manage to help you reach a decision, ask yourself, "What will my life be like without this?" Don't think about *it* (the thing)—think about *you*, your life, your freedom.

Some Junk-Sorting Guidelines

Is it clutter or is it not? Is your de-junking fever being cooled down by cold feet? Are emotional ties and guilt diluting your ability to be ruthless and strong? If indecisiveness sets in, here are some guidelines that may help.

IT IS JUNK IF:

☐ it's broken or obsolete (and fixing it is unrealistic)

☐ you've outgrown it, physically or emotionally

☐ you've always hated it

☐ it's the wrong size, wrong color, or wrong style

☐ using it is more bother than it's worth

☐ it wouldn't really affect you if you never saw it again

☐ it generates bad feelings

☐ you have to clean it, store it, and insure it (but you don't get much use or enjoyment out of it)

☐ it will shock, bore, or burden the coming generation

If you can check one or more of the above truthfully, then it's probably junk. Do yourself, your house, and posterity a favor—pitch it! It's robbing you of peace of mind and space.

IT'S NOT JUNK IF IT:

☐ generates love and good feelings

☐ helps you make a living

☐ will do something you need done

☐ has significant cash value

☐ gives you more than it takes

☐ will enrich or delight the coming generation

If you can check a few of the above comfortably, then it's probably *not* junk—enjoy it and feel good about its place in your life.

The Final Judgment

Let me repeat: I'm not claiming the position of the Great Wahoo of Junk-Judging. I'm presenting some views (perhaps tinged with a little personal opinion) to help stimulate new thoughts in your hoarding soul—but the decision of what to keep and what to dump out of your life is all yours. Age, sentiment, and "I may need it someday" all have their legitimacy. Think about a fire extinguisher—it fits many of the criteria of clutter as it hangs there for twenty years. It's not the latest style, it's ugly, it never moves, it's never used, it costs money to have checked and re-checked—but it's certainly worth having when it's needed *once* in that twenty years!

The ultimate evaluation is up to you. I'll share my observations and others' contributions in this volume, but what is and is not clutter is for you to determine—by the use and benefit an item is to you, the actions it encourages you to take, and the effect it has through you on others. A piece of garbage isn't junk if it enriches the quality of life. And a beautiful, valuable, and expensive thing can be total junk if it detracts from your joy of living and loving.

How to Leave It and Love It (Clutter!)

We wake up one morning and suddenly realize that we're buried in problems— almost insurmountable ones. The more we think about them, the more they seem to multiply. We drag ourselves out into the day, through our home full of things we're struggling to pay for, things we seldom use. Listening to news about everyone else's struggles, we glance in the mirror and see how everything we've eaten over the years has stacked up on us, how everything we hate about ourselves seems to show in our eyes. We get to work, and see the IN basket triumphing unmercifully over the OUT basket. We light a cigarette or go for coffee and a Danish to help us face the work, and we *still* can't face it. When we finally do find our desk top, we find a disconnect notice for a bill we misplaced. At these discouraging times—any discouraging and depressed time, before you reach for more aspirin, a ticket to run away for good, or a shoulder to cry on—reverse it all. Decide to finally get rid of the clutter that's causing your bad day, plaguing your life and mind—all those things you don't need. Throw out your junk first—

before you swing into that miracle plan to rearrange your life for maximum efficiency, or set in motion that complicated strategy of self-improvement. It's as simple and logical as throwing away the shoes that are blistering and cramping your feet, or dumping out the rotten apples at the bottom of the barrel before you try to wash it out. The time you invest in de-junking will pay you back several-fold—you'll save all those *future* hours detouring around, moving about, cleaning up, and agonizing over junk.

It's amazing how many problems go away when junk does. Once something is eliminated, its capacity to clutter and foul up your life is gone. Your life is simplified—and you're free to operate on the important things, not thrash in the piles. Get rid of the clutter that makes you spin your wheels, that causes you the stress, and there'll be no stress left to get rid of. You'll break out laughing when you realize how little effort will be needed to reorganize, restore, regain control of things. De-junking is a true miracle that will happen to you; and I guarantee it's the best antidepressant going.

There's a lot to be said for simplicity—how it feels, and how much we need it. De-junking is the most direct path to simplicity there is. You'll have a wonderful feeling of completion and accomplishment and self-mastery when you hold to an anti-clutter campaign in

your life. Enjoy the most refreshing experience in the world—that great sigh of relief when you're totally (well, 95 percent) free of junk!

Besides, while you're de-junking you'll probably find some things you've been looking for for years—such as the flash unit for the camera, your lower dentures, the hardware for the electric garage door opener, etc. . . .

When Is the Best Time to De-Junk?

When is the best time to rip in and start casting out? Immediately after you've determined that the junk is junk. If you wait for further confirmation, you'll fall back in love with the clutter in your life and keep it. To be more specific, here are some guidelines reported by successful de-junkers:

MORNING:

Light beats darkness for evaluating things. You're more objective in the morning, have more energy to dig and throw. The earlier the better—5:00 a.m. tossing is exhilarating—plus the garbage truck hauls it away at 7:30 and then when you crack in the afternoon and run to retrieve it—it's gone!

SUNDAYS, VACATIONS, and LONG WEEKENDS:

Are probably the best times to reflect, analyze, and file, to review your values and strip yourself of burden (90 percent of your burdens are junk-related). Sunday usually follows a trying recreational Saturday; maybe what caused you to be "overdone" (too much food, too much sun, too much shopping) should go out of your life.

FALL:

As the trees shed at the end of the season, so should you shed some of your worn and tired treasures. It's time to store some, sell some, and dump the rest so they won't press and depress you all winter. Besides, you're going to collect more over the holidays and need some room for it.

On a few of those brisk autumn days or evenings, instead of going "out" and adding clutter to your life, stay home and get rid of some of what you've got. You'll find it entertaining and exhilarating, without any hangover.

De-junking when angry is pretty effective—we need to take aggression out on something. We clean house fast and effectively when we're burnt up over something, and it's when we're angry that we're the least sentimental. However, if you're so mad you're full of disdain for someone (or something) you'll often not make good decisions and will be sorry later (maybe at the dump trying to dig something out). If you're experiencing a peak of energy and motivation (you just got a promotion or lost ten pounds), run with it. And de-junking is the perfect pastime for those moments when you're trying desperately to put off something else.

Eight years old is probably the time to start individual accountability for de-junking—and the older you are, the more you have to de-junk!

Is probably the best time to start. Don't wait until your storage runs over or someone is threatening to leave you before remorsefully de-junking, or until you are forced to by some circumstance that won't allow you the time to do it right.

What to Wear:

When de-junking, never wear clothes with big pockets or room to stash. Wear pocketless apparel—like a suit of armor, a bathing suit, a straitjacket, or a hospital gown, and you won't be tempted. And if it's the second time around, wear dark glasses—very dark. In any case, loose-fitting (but not baggy) comfortable clothes and sturdy low-heeled shoes are a good idea, and be sure to wear something you won't be afraid to get messy in the throes of de-junking.

Tune In to a De-Junking Channel

Mood makes a great difference when de-junking. Remember, you aren't just throwing out things, but habits, experiences, places, even people that have been a part of you for years, perhaps decades. Moody, clinging, sentimental music ("Auld Lang Syne," "Memories Are Made of This," "Bringing in the Sheaves," "Send Me the Pillow You Dream On," "They Can't Take That Away From Me," "Carry Me Back to Old

Virginny," sad country western songs or hymns, golden oldy ballads won't do it—put on some rousing music that will make you want to charge, change, chuck, and cheer.

Good music to de-junk by: John Philip Sousa marches, marches from Verdi operas, polkas, "The Good, the Bad, and the Ugly," "Sixteen Tons," "So Long, It's Been Good to Know Ya," the 1812 Overture, "I've Got You Out of My Bin," "Climb Every Mountain," football fight songs, the Anvil Chorus from *Il Trovatore*, the William Tell Overture (the "Lone Ranger" theme), "Fifty Ways to Leave Your Lover," "Burning Memories," "There'll Be Some Changes Made," "Nothing Can Stop Me Now," etc.

Should You Go It Alone?

Most of us don't like friends or companions to meddle in our beloved clutter, but when we're overcome and reach the depths of junk depression, we will perhaps find it advantageous to do a little companionship junking. It really does help to have someone standing by when you seize something and hold it up and weigh its worth. They'll probably say one of two things:

"Gads . . . you'd keep *that* thing . . .?"
And it's final, out it goes.
Or as their greedy eyes light up:
"Ooohhh, gimme that . . . can I really have it?" And again, it's gone for good!

If de-junking yourself and your premises gets to be too emotional an undertaking, reformed junkees also testify that it's helpful to find another struggling junkee and trade. Let them have at yours and you have at theirs. It's easy to de-clutter someone else's house; you can be as objective as a ranger roaming a forest marking trees to be felled. You—the ranger—are only using your expertise to identify; you don't have

to actually throw anyone else's junk out (besides, you're probably too young to die). Just tag or mark it—and the decisions are made! And you'll probably have to agree with some of the tags on *your* treasures. . . .

One of the biggest disadvantages of being a junkee is that your pack-rat reputation will inspire friends to bring their junk to you, thinking they're doing you a favor. You can become the ammo dump for an entire battalion of clutter collectors. One on one is okay, but I don't recommend a neighborhood de-junking party—with that many people around, it's too easy to get distracted from the objective at hand. You probably also don't want anyone but close friends to see your most embarassing junk. For the same reason, if you hire help, go out of town for the people.

The De-Junking Drill and Warmup

Every great event deserves an appetizer:

Exercise 1. Stand in front of a mirror to give yourself a vivid perspective of how your body junk (and the junk behind you) looks to an outsider.

Exercise 2. Thumb your overstuffed library, or some of those newspapers and magazines you've been saving. This will loosen hand and finger joints and your all-important pitching shoulder.

Exercise 3. Visit one of your storage areas blindfolded. The bumps on your shins, elbows, and head will make you "junk smart" and anxious to get revenge!

Exercise 4. Take off the blindfold. Think of three things in your junk you'd like to find just for fun (or to see if they're still there). Whether you find them or not, you'll be ready to attack and destroy.

Exercise 5. De-junking dry run. If you aren't sure yet that you can depart on a disposing journey through your life and place, try a dry run like the Army does when it trains soldiers: attack some real clutter and place it in an imitation waste container. Practice regularly until your anxiety ceases, then use a *real* trash can.

You are now psyched for the final exercise. I guarantee it will move you to jubilant junk-tossing.

Exercise 6. Pretend the carpet cleaners or the movers are coming in one hour and *everything* in every room has to be up and out. This will force into brilliant focus all those layers of junk that've been there so long they've become invisible to you!

Dis-Count What You Can't Count

One division of my cleaning contracting business handles restoration jobs. In each case the victim of the fire or other disaster is asked to make a list of the items in the attic, basement, or other room that was destroyed. To most that's like asking them if they've memorized the Bible. They know the closets, trunks, and drawers were full, but of what? There follows a week of sheer brain-wrenching, trying to account for what, where, how much, etc., for the proof of loss. It proves that (1) a lot of it must have been junk if they can't remember it, and (2) *after* is not the time to account for your possessions.

Making a list of all you own and where and what is a smart thing to do—start in one room and go through everything. Soon you'll find things not worth the ink or the effort to write down and pitch them away.

Another worthwhile adventure is to rent a home video camera and film all your stuff, simultaneously describing what it is and what it's worth into a tape recorder. This is fun, fast, and effective,

and then you can put the video in a safe deposit box. A two-hour tape should do it, and if you find yourself running into two six-hour tapes and beyond, it'll be good food for de-junking thought. I guarantee that either the list or the video will force a de-junking insight into your life! And you never know, you might get an Oscar or Emmy (or maybe a Cranny) for Junker of the Year.

Pace Yourself

Rome wasn't de-junked in a day. You'll get the bends and terrible withdrawal tremors if you come up through your clutter too fast. A two-drawer day is an honorable accomplishment; a two-drawer-and-closet-and-no-cigarette-or-chocolate-bar day is pushing the limit; a six-drawer-and-workshop/attic/garage day could be suicidal. If you try to do too much at once you'll lose your edge and not be nearly fierce enough to get the job done right.

Pace yourself; don't fall for the old "decoy" trap. When you start to de-junk an area (or habit), get the job *done:* otherwise when you go to throw out that old pan you'll notice on the way to the garbage that the yard needs de-junking. So you stop to do the yard, but notice those faded bumper stickers on the car. You start to scrape the bumper and see the toolshed is a mess, stop to rearrange that and find the plants on the porch have to be repotted, so you figure the pan you were taking to the dump is just the thing to put under the plants . . . and as it turns out, nothing was de-junked.

Vary your attack to maintain momentum. Switch back and forth between outside and inside junk. Every time you have a session of ridding yourself of worn-out tires and shabby coats, turn to your inner junk and get rid of an old unpleasant unkind feeling or a shabby habit. It works! You can lose hundreds of pounds of physical and emotional junk in one day!

How to Get Rid of It

Simply dumping it is harsh and not always the only way or wise—so says Gladys Allen, a well-known de-junking engineer (believe it or not, there are professional de-junkers afoot in this country). I like her approach, which is as follows:

Start with three large heavy-duty garbage bags and one box. Label them:

1. **JUNK**
2. **CHARITY**
3. **SORT**
4. **EMOTIONAL WITHDRAWAL (the box)**

Dragging your bags and box behind you, systematically attack *every* room in the house. Assign every junk suspect—every piece of loose clutter, clothing, magazine, toy, shoe, stray animal, unidentified child, etc.—to one of the bags or the box.

1. JUNK

If it's broken, outdated, lost its mate, out of style, ugly, useless, dead or moldy, then it's junk.

1. JUNK (no good)

DUMP IT

2. CHARITY

If it's still repairable or useful (to someone else), if it's the wrong color, wrong style, too little, too big for you, bores you, or is simply an excess, chuck it in the Charity bag. Let someone else worry about it for a change.

2. GOOD (but you don't want or need it)
   It *can* be used . . . by someone
   It *could* be used . . for something
   It *might* be used . . . sometime
(means it won't be used—by *you*)

GIVE IT AWAY!

3. SORT

All your loose, misplaced and homeless stuff that is still useful and needed, but that you haven't figured out where to park, put in the Sort bag. Much of this is probably not located in convenient place to use.

3. SORT (want it, but have no place to keep it)

**KEEP—AND
SORT AGAIN
IN A MONTH**

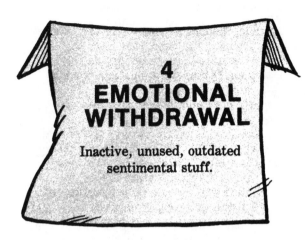

4
EMOTIONAL WITHDRAWAL

Inactive, unused, outdated
sentimental stuff.

KEEP! (in junk limbo for six months)

and then **THROW IT AWAY**

At the end of the junk raid day (or the
end of your de-junking drive) take the
Junk bag to the nearest garbage dump.
Deliver the Charity bag to the nearest
thrift store or pickup point.

As for bag number 3, Sort—it will have
an interesting fate: once it's filled, you'll
let it sit for awhile, as you dread the time
you have to burrow in and assign each
wayward item. The longer it sits, the less
you miss whatever was in there. You're
getting along fine without that whole
giant bag of "good stuff" the longer it
sits, and the less you miss it. Finally, the
prospect of pitching most of it outweighs
the dread of sorting it—and after pulling
out and intelligently placing the things
you do need, it's three bags down and one
to go!

Number 4: The Emotional Withdrawal Box

Have you ever had the experience of
reluctantly trying to let go of the little
hand of your baby so he can climb on the
bus for his first day of school? Or did you
ever try to drop the keys of a faithful old
truck that's been your dependable
companion over many colorful miles into
the waiting hand of the guy you just sold
it to?

These are things you know you have to do, and yet, when the moment to do them arrives, suddenly you're gripped with an ache that almost does you in. Some clutter is like that.

No matter how great our zeal to de-junk our lives, and no matter how firm our resolve to be ruthless and cold as we maraud our cupboards and denude our drawers, still, every now and then we uncover something we just can't bring ourselves to toss into the Charity box.

It's those "emotional involvement" ties again. The funny thing about it is, the object is usually something that would be of absolutely no use to anyone else (and certainly is of none to you), and yet. . . .

Like the day you're attacking your clothes closet and stoically making castoffs out of everything in there except the really current wardrobe. If the hem is too short, out it goes! If the waist is too tight or the lapels too wide or too narrow, out it goes! If it hasn't been worn in the last two years (or the last fifteen), out it goes. If the toes are too pointed or the heels too flat, out they go.

Then, at the back of the closet, you pull out that shortie nightie set left over from newlywed days—a lacy little cellophane number with a matching bikini. "How tacky," you say with a blush (hoping your fifteen-year-old won't walk in just then), and yet—that little reminder from the past will *not* fall out of your hand into the Charity box! You have no intention of ever scampering around in that getup again, yet somehow it seems a sacrilege to discard it.

Do you know the feeling? So what we need to do is get a box and label it "Emotional Withdrawal." Then, when we're mercilessly de-junking with that predatory glint in our eye, and suddenly come upon one of those gripping things that it seems a sin to knowingly discard, then DON'T! Don't upset yourself and lose momentum by trying to argue with your emotions. Just pat it affectionately

and lay it gently into your Emotional Withdrawal box. At the end of your crusade, dispose of your Junk bag, and your Charity bag, and your Sort bag. But write the date in huge letters on the Emotional Withdrawal box and store it away somewhere safe.

Then, six months from the date on the box (or a year if you're really a sentimental slob), go retrieve the box. DO NOT OPEN IT OR PEEK INTO IT. (This is a must!) Because by now, you see, you've forgotten what it was you stuck in there. Or you *do* remember but at least that gripping moment of emotional attachment has passed and you can dispassionately deliver the box to the nearest charity pickup point, or slide it out to the curb on garbage day and never feel a thing but victory—and pleasure over your uncluttered closets and your spacious storage areas.

If you still can't have the Emotional Withdrawal box ripped out of your hands and heart, if sentimental ties clearly demand a retrial, if an appeal to the Supreme Clutter Court is imminent, remark that box "trial pending" and let it sit another six months.

*B*UY—USE—OUTGROW—THROW
Release it so it will release you!

Throw It *All the Way* Away

When I was growing up, we had terrible weeds in our yard, which basically are junk to a nice garden or landscaping. My dad would send us kids to de-junk the pesky plants and soon the spot would be cleaned and looking great. But a few weeks later the weeds would reappear, bigger and stronger than before—because we never did really get rid of them. We didn't pull them up and cast them away as Dad told us to do; we cut them down with a hoe, leaving the roots there to carry on a regrowth. When you throw junk out of your life, don't just wound it like we did the plants—go all the way, pull it out, dump it, give it, sell it, but get rid of it. It's like jumping in icy water or pulling the tape off a bandage—a quick "yank" and it hurts less.

If you don't, the most deadly stage of the junk disease will come the fatal day you creep up on an overstuffed Salvation Army bin. As you step forward to throw your two things in, you'll see something in there you really could use—an old sweatshirt, just right for a car rag, so in go two and out comes one. How much credit will you get for two in and one out? Well, not much, because next time you'll be looking and two will go in and three will come out. That's how junkitis progresses.

The only way to arrest this junker's tendency is, when you decide to do away with something, keep telling yourself how loathsome it is—and tell yourself that all the way to the trash/giveaway bin. If you know you'll weaken, or fish somebody else's junk out, ask a family member (like a long-suffering spouse, no-nonsense teenager, or tough sister) to dispose of the stuff as a favor to you. Or pay a neighbor kid to do it. Be creative—but be ruthless: however you do it, make sure you actually *do* get rid of the stuff.

Here's a scenario of what will happen if you don't.

At long last, that old carpet in the bedroom or living room has to go—it's damaged, stained, and odorful, and you're sick of the color. You select a lush new loom at the carpet store to replace that miserable floorpiece, but whether you or the carpet layers take the old one up, the pangs of pity begin to flow through you. You're suffering, but willing to see it go—until the carpet layer says, "What would you like us to do with this old carpet, haul it away?" Your throat tightens as you look at that neat roll; all rolled up it has assumed the embryonic form in which it was delivered to you ten years ago—a clean edge conceals the threadbare, urine-stained, disintegrating innards. You stammer and then have them drag the moldy heap into the garage or basement. Maybe, just maybe, you can cut out an unworn section or two for the doghouse, the bathroom, the porch, the car trunk. You're so caught up in the concept of using that old worthless veteran, you don't even appreciate your new carpet.

Do you know how many people ruin walls and doors, hurt themselves stumbling over, and get hernias heaving worthless salvaged, worn carpet? If you've fallen for this in the past, don't in the future, or you'll end up with wall-to-wall clutter. Hold your chin high and say, "Haul 'er off, boys," and use your energy rolling on the new carpet.

De-Junk, Don't "Neatspree"

It's possible to be a de-junk hypocrite or fanatic. Remember, the adage "One man's junk is another man's treasure" does have some truth to it. As our lives, age, size, location, and environment change, it all affects what and how much we need. Some real hardhearts say, "If I don't use it for six months, out it goes"; a junkee will bellow in pain at that statement. Somewhere in between you should find the criteria for giving, trading, chucking—or keeping.

One repentant junkee I know got an oversized grill for a wedding present; she threw it in the garbage, right in the

unopened box. In a few years grills were twice the price and there were five in her family instead of two. Think! Just because you don't need it now or have grown tired of it doesn't mean it's junk. Anticipate—don't decapitate. There's always room to store genuinely useful things.

Going on a "neat spree" and throwing out tons of stuff (including valuable items) is thoughtless and stupid. Again, let me caution you not to go on an unmitigated throwout seige just for the sake of taking revenge on a worthless spouse or to work out some aggravation or problem. Some people go on a casting caper and punish themselves by ridding all their (or someone else's) favorite things. Don't do it—think! There's an old proverb about not tearing down a wall until you know why it was built, and that's a saying of great de-junking wisdom. Throwing out the overshoes and umbrella when the sun comes out isn't smart (unless they leak or you've moved to the Mojave).

Recycling—The Great Equalizer

Is ruthless de-junking wasteful? Will you go straight to hell or be pronounced un-American if you trash something worth cash? Nope! A soothing word called "recycling" comes to our rescue here: recycling is the great equalizer, the great escape from bad judgment.

At the age of thirteen I had a serious cash-flow problem and our remote rural location eliminated the prospect of resolving it by getting a job. One morning I heard on a radio show that dried prairie bones (the skeletons of cattle and horses that died on the range) were worth $30 a ton to be ground up and made into fertilizer. Convinced I'd soon be a bone business executive, I threw a couple of burlap bags over my back and began to walk the desert. How many light prairie bones it takes to make a ton (unless you run into a *Tyrannosaurus rex*) is beyond most people's comprehension—I never did get rich, but I felt good because I was not only making a little money, but cleaning up the countryside, and contributing to a product that people benefited from.

Like old bones, much of our clutter can be recycled, and even if we get little or no cash for it, we can help upgrade the environment, contribute to the economy, and have a personal building experience. Just think—those old clothes, papers, cans, and tires you've been stumbling over for years can be reincarnated into a warm quilt, shiny sheet metal, elegant greeting cards, or an NCAA basketball. Glass, paper, cardboard, old cars, lumber, dirty motor oil, blacktop, and numerous other objects can be used again! Think recycle—but be reasonable—don't get carried away into saving credit card carbons and pen cartridges and the little boxes your eyedrops came in. Check with your local recycling center to see exactly what they handle.

Sometimes the Kids Grow Up Before the Skates Grow Old

I saw that title on an ad in the classifieds, and it made the case for de-junking so eloquently that I clipped it and hung it on my bulletin board. So often tools, equipment, work or play things are still in good useful condition when we outgrow them. But then, forgetting that their only value was in actual use, we feel an obligation to preserve them, as if we were trying to preserve the part of our life that they touched. The longer we cling to them after their usefulness is past, the greater the chance that they'll begin to blot out the good memories they once gave us, the reason for our keeping them. Don't turn them from a positive into a negative. They weren't junk, but

we can make them junk—what a disrespectful end for those beautiful skates or that wonderful bike, to be preserved into eternal inactivity. Use those classified ads and share what thrilled and blessed you once. This way it will live to bless you again and again through others.

Or you can do yourself and someone else a favor—and feel good at the same time—if you box and/or bag up all the things that are of dubious value to you and donate them to a worthy cause—Salvation Army, Goodwill, etc.

I feel particularly good about a certain association for handicapped people I regularly de-junk to: they use the junk as therapy—their people sort, price, tag, and sell it in their own thrift store. It's wonderful to know your old stuff is helping rehabilitate someone (and even more wonderful to know someone else is shuffling it around for a change).

A Solution to Lackluster (or Lost Luster) Items:

One of the toughest de-junking problems we face is stuff that's still perfectly good, but that we just don't need or want any more. In such cases junk transfusion is an effective way to keep those good nonused gifts or other useful items from becoming junk. You simply transfer them to someone else who *can* use and delight in them. If you recycle things this way, at least you'll be helping to prevent the generation of new junk. For instance, I gave my old, too-small, still-snappable portfolio to an outstanding twelve-year-old artist; made my trophies and plaques into awards for little Scouts; and we have a genuine samurai helmet in my family that's in its fourth-generation shuffle.

Old how-to or instruction books can be a difficult cast-away. It seems that we all,

for example, sometime in our lives want to be artistic and end up with a few beginner's how-to-draw or -paint books. We do 99 percent of our drawing or painting the first couple of weeks we have them—but we keep them around for years and years. After finally realizing that mine did no instructing sitting on the shelf, I gave them to an up-and-coming young kid and he shed tears of joy to get those encrusted volumes. This works equally well for those how-to-carve-wood books, those very basic cookbooks you don't need any more, and the foreign language course/tape set we all have stashed somewhere.

A good technique for encouraging such transfers is a "giveaway box." This isn't strictly moral, but it works and keeps clutter circulating. My mother came up with this idea. When over fifty, she realized she had an advanced case of junkitis, but being Danish, she couldn't bear to simply throw out all her useless sentimental holdings. She got them out of her hair—and kept most of them in the family—by creating a special giveaway box (junk box) in which these things would wait for a visit from innocent unwary grandkids or neighbor kids. Like all kids, they loved surprises, and quivered with anticipation on the way to Grandma's—eager to make a selection. (And they try to convince us that our mothers love us.)

If You Can't Can It, Convert Your Clutter

Or if you can't give it away, dump it, or burn it, use a piece of junk to make something useful. Look at it for a few minutes and think: What could I make this into that wouldn't be junk, that wouldn't just clutter my life, but actually serve a purpose?

I made a Mickey Mouse backscratcher into a paint-stirring stick—it then got more comments and generated more affection and honor than its giver ever intended.

I made my old floor polisher into a mailbox.

When something is too dear, too big, or too challenging to cast away, try to figure a way to make it useful that will benefit you and others while it preserves the item.

My wife and I bought our "dream" ranch right after we graduated from Idaho State University. Its only structures were a tiny wellhouse and an 1880s log cabin, said to have been built by outlaws in frontier days. The cabin roof leaked and the windows were gone, so it was valueless as a house, barn, or chicken coop, but we love old cabins—so we kept it and built new fences and barns around it. It became more of an eyesore every year but I couldn't bring myself to burn or bulldoze it down; it even sat right where I wanted to build a machinery

shop—but I could never feel good about leveling it.

So, as a family project, we restored the entire inside and replaced the roof, leaving the outside looking exactly as it did originally. It cost us over $8,500 way back then (not counting labor) to convert that piece of junk—but we now had a delightful guest house (which you'll get to stay in if you visit us). It's now a landmark in the community and in our lives, and not junk any more.

Don't go to the extent of using an old hula hoop for a picture frame, but do be alert to possibilities to convert your clutter.

Miniaturize It

On pages 88-111 I explained the concept of miniaturizing: the simple act of taking something and reducing its bulk but keeping its spirit or effectiveness. I've found that even for things I need, full scale isn't always necessary. I make good use, when I travel, of miniature binoculars, cameras, Scriptures, etc. Even maybe-useful-someday information or oversized worthwhile printed material can be converted, via microfilm, from a clumsy file or ledger to a tiny disk or filmstrip.

I have constant need of names, phone numbers, and addresses as I travel. It was suggested by efficiency experts that I take along a prompter (to whisper dignitaries' names as they approach), a computer, or a preprogrammed personal phone system—all of which threatened to double my mobile junk. Instead, I miniaturized: I typed all my active names and addresses on a few sheets, took them to an instant print shop, had them reduced, and bound them in my calendar. Now I have everything at my fingertips in a few neat tiny pages, easy to use and carry. Names and addresses I need just for a particular trip, I prepare the same way.

The Old Soiled and Spoiled Trick

This is a good technique when you have something that is unquestionably pure clutter, but somehow you just can't get rid of it. It will just lie there in sparkling uselessness and taunt you, because anything physically perfect seems to have an immunity to disposal. Have you noticed how passionately relieved you feel when one day such an object gets defaced—a drop of water blotches it, or it gets stained or wrinkled or stepped on? You suddenly have guillotine gumption and can fling it away with no qualms. Its value didn't change, neither did your attitude—you simply found an excuse, a reason to dump it. The junk is gone with no guilt, because "it isn't nice any more." Even induced defacement is moral if that's what it takes to de-junk a hunk of junk—leave it in the rain or on the counter when you deep-fry, haul it around in your car or with you to the beach, turn your kids loose on it. It's sure to get soiled or spoiled, then it can be easily de-junked.

Apply the One-In, One-Out Rule:

If you can't wade into de-junking wholeheartedly, if you can't completely suppress that itchy urge to collect, an effective compromise or cease-fire is possible that will at least halt the buildup. Apply the "One-In, One-Out Rule," meaning if you bring anything new into your collection, something old has to be removed at the same time. This is a great way to warm up for a full-scale clutter cleanout—and learn basic control.

The Tax Write-Off—Another Great Reason to De-Junk

Some of your heaps and piles of things may possibly have cash value—so get the cash, because if the stuff isn't enhancing your life right now, it's doing you no good. Cash it in, give it to someone who can benefit from it, and if it ends up tax deductible, you'll get a double reward.

A friend of mine had an old classic car he was going to restore and sell—someday! It chugged and snorted but never ran too well so it got little use. He puttered around with it and enjoyed it for a few years, then lost interest—but it occupied a spot in his yard for the next ten years. Finally it had to go. Not wanting to sell a used car to a friend, he donated it to the local Scouts. They raffled it off at a fund-raiser for an amazing $10,000. The Scouts loved him, the town loved him, his wife loved him—and his accountant informed him that under the Internal Revenue Code, he could claim the $10,000 as a tax deduction. He was elated, richer, freer—and best of all—de-junked. Something that had been parked in his mind was gone, and really fulfilling things could move in. Your accountant might be a great help in de-junking: call him or her to see what clutter might qualify.

Overcoming "The Great Junk Standoff"

"I won't budge on my junk until my husband budges on his. . . ." The woman who told me this also admitted being on the brink of separation. They didn't mean it to come down to divorce, but each's

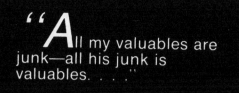

"All my valuables are junk—all his junk is valuables. . . ."

accumulation began to irritate the other—and the kids aggravated matters further by collecting and keeping an equal amount of junk. Patience and tolerance disappeared with the room to keep everything—so they blamed each other. Each sincerely believed his or her stuff was more valuable, and snide cracks and judgmental opinions of each other's junk soon grew to open animosity: "I won't give up my smoking, every-other-night football, or my cow skull collection until you give up those stupid soap operas and that stinking spaniel." And so goes the

Great Junk Standoff. In a standoff, both sides lose, junk wins, and no one lives happily ever after. Don't force a standoff with anyone in your home, office, school, or organization. Trying to use junk as a weapon on someone else is like shooting a pistol backward—it gets *you*, not them. It's like a kid threatening his parents, "I'll go cut my arm off and then you'll have a one-armed kid and be embarrassed."

If you really want to see results (and get the best kind of revenge on your antagonizer), with great ceremony and enthusiasm, nobly and unflinchingly cast off some of your clutter. You'll disarm your opponent, bring instant peace to you and the situation—and give him or her the guilties. Be the initiator—don't expect anyone else to do what you aren't willing to. Go ahead—start right now with a couple of small things. Make sure everyone sees the junk (thing, habit) go—and then watch—your opponent will

immediately be intimidated and miserable until he or she rids himself or herself of something equal to your sacrifice. This works at home, school, work, social clubs. Try it—quit the threats, cutting remarks, bribes, or any such tactics you are using now to get that certain person to cast off his or her junk. Simply lead the way (and don't overdo reminding the other junker what you got rid of). It's the best way to spread the de-junking gospel.

> "All of humankind is divided into two basic groups, the keepers and the throwers-away. The only thing worse than a keeper and a caster slugging it out is two keepers getting together."

De-Junking Is Not Forever

De-junking is a journey, not a destination; a process, not an end product. You don't de-junk and remain de-junked forever, because new junk will keep filtering in to fill the vacancies. It's like fitness or cleanliness—it doesn't last; de-junking from time to time must become a reflex.

So many of us have suffered from a junk habit or junk object, got sick of it, got rid of it, and felt so good to be free we soon forgot how bad being laden was. So gradually, we reacquire the same problem. Slowly and silently we gain the weight back, start dropping our clothes instead of hanging them. Once we get our noses out of problems, we somehow want to stick them back in.

It reminds me of the time my neighbor's Labrador retriever tangled with a porcupine and came whimpering home with a snout full of quills. I held the dog while my neighbor, using a heavy

pair of pliers, pulled two dozen wicked quills, the dog yelping generously with every yank. Painfully de-junked of the quills, you'd think the dog would avoid a repeat of the adventure. Not so—the next evening a whining and pawing at the door evidenced another losing bout with the porcupine. This time quills were in the mouth and tongue. Sad to say, that dog never learned the value of staying de-junked, and after yet more repeat performances, the canine cashed in.

You're smarter than a black Lab—I know you won't get a new snout full of junk if you do a good initial job of de-junking. Especially if you keep in mind the big secrets of staying de-junked:

1. Avoid junk danger zones (see pages 162-177).

2. Don't move into a bigger house.
3. Don't read junk pornography ("things and stuff" catalogs; see pages 112-137).
4. Or read a "trash to treasure"

book. This little X-rated volume tells you how to take the most worthless clutter and give it a whole new visual identity (transform it into something else you'll have to start all over again to justify the discard of). Worthless egg cartons can be made into a stunning snake—it's clever, it's cute, and it's the same empty carton you were hauling to the trash. Now it might manage to fake out common sense. The sole purpose of most of these books is to provide an elaborate, time-consuming, sometimes expensive way to disguise junk!

"What's Bothering You?"

There's no visible clutter left but you still feel junked in? To find what's been called "inner peace," you have to de-junk yourself of the piles of clutter you carry in your mind, or as some call it, your heart.

This junk got there when you, sometime in the past, did something you now regret. You wish you hadn't. It could be a crime, a putdown, a cruelty, a prejudice, a lie, you swiped something—anything you did or said that now haunts you and you find uncomfortable to live with. We all have this emotional clutter. Like our tangible junk, some of us keep it and tolerate its misery and memory forever, but this kind of junk is embedded in our being and can't be de-junked as easily. Often these are little things—their injury and cost are long gone—but we continue to harbor them, so our guilt and unhappiness about it can pop up again, and again, and again.

An employee of mine, while a young serviceman, like his buddies enjoyed leave—but a shortage of cash often held down the high jinks. As mechanics, they occasionally had extra parts after a job and smuggled them off the base and sold them, using the money for leave. They were never caught, but years later, whenever any law or military service agent would call on my office for routine employee security checks, this employee would dart out the back door and hide out in terror. I've known hundreds of people who go through the very same thing—avoid people, situations, and places because of a little problem they had years ago. I've watched petty family or job resentments or jealousies totally alienate and choke off people's enjoyment of life. Holding a grudge is no different from holding a bag of junk; one is visible and the other isn't, but both weigh. Both cheat you. Both restrict life. The reason you haven't been able to de-junk it (forget it) is because this piece of junk isn't just yours—it involves others. (If it is just yours, de-junk it today.)

Emotional de-junking is generally free, but if it involves someone else, pay the simple price of making it right—if you have to come up with a confession, a concession, some cash, a repair, do it. If you can't find a place to start, talk to your religious leader or a friend, but get it out! Go find out the damages, write or call. It will take some nerve initially, but in most cases it's not a tenth as bad as anticipated. In fact, it's often enjoyable—a lifting of burdens, a renewing you never forget. You're free!

The rewards of shedding and leaving behind past grudges, disappointments, and angers are wonderful. Millions of us have stored up and carried such things forever, and because we carry them we nurture them, and like any load it gets heavy after awhile.

Emotional de-junking generally follows a 4-R course:

1. *Remorse*—you're sorry, it was wrong.
2. *Resolve*—you'll correct it.
3. *Restore*—contact the injured party and repair/return/restore it.
4. *Refrain*—from doing it again!

Clutter's Last Stand

The *real* fate worse than death is the probability that **what we are now, we'll remain the rest of our lives.**

We can change our looks, location, age, job, and economic position, but what we are as people, we'll remain if the things, places, people that made us that way stay with us. The anxieties, unhappiness, discomfort, and disgust we're struggling with now might shift position but will remain with us, keeping us the same.

It's discouraging to think that a bunch of clutter could cheat us out of our future—a vibrant, zestful, rapture-filled life. It can! It *is!*

But we can have it all back, revive, restore, re-experience those fine fun feelings and love if we allow some room for them. Right now that room in our homes and hearts is piled with clutter—some we loaded in, some we absorbed, some that was dumped on or given to us. But how it got there doesn't matter nearly as much as now, the time to get it out.

Life doesn't begin at forty, sixty-five, twenty, thirty, when you get married, when you get promoted, or when you have grandkids—life truly begins when you discover how flexible and free you are without clutter.

Remember, any junk or clutter (house clutter, car clutter, mind clutter) can and will sprout into more of the same. We humans wrinkle and wither fast, mentally and physically, from the burden of worthless cargo.

Determining what is clutter may be our own opinion, but whether or not we keep it in our lives may not be strictly our own business. Because we can be sure that some way, someday, somehow, even right now, our clutter will not only hurt us, but drastically affect the lives of others.

Clutter is simply undealt-with junk. Usable things are used, valuable things contribute value, you'll seldom find good things cluttering life—it's the junk, the non- or little-needed that is hung onto for the sheer sake of owning and having. How long it stands and mows you down is only up to you. Clutter's last stand will free the years, the months, the weeks, the days and the hours you've spent hauling, digging, thrashing, sorting, hunting, protecting in the past. With the clutter will go the messes you've battled all your life—and defeating clutter will cost you nothing but a decision.

Remember, everything has a cost to acquire and to maintain. The majority of this cost you pay with your time and energy. To lead the life you really want to lead, you must eliminate the clutter and excess from your mind, home, and habits. It's simple, and one of the easiest ways to be "born again."

De-junking is the cheapest, fastest, and most effective way to become physically and financially sound, emotionally and intellectually happy.

Oh yes—before we close this book and let you get on with it (de-junking), let's clear up this business about our "high standard of living." Our American standard of living isn't so high—it's our degree of luxury and convenience that's high.

Take a hard look today at those you know who "have everything"—automatic back scratchers, rotating tie racks, computerized cars, instant food, world tours, better girdles, fancier foods, unlimited money, lofty positions. Honestly, in the things by which we should measure a life, how do they rate? The chance of unlimited comfort and luxury making you an unhappy, dissatisfied, restless human being would seem to be great.

A true *standard* of living is physical and emotional health, harmony, loving and being loved, sharing, serving, being satisfied, motivated, inspired, joyful, and in control. Our standards for these things can never be too high.

De-junking will truly raise your standard of living, give life back to you from the clutter that stole it from you.

I've tried to give you physical, financial, emotional, and aesthetic reasons to de-junk your life.

If I haven't convinced you yet, I'll back my message with the greatest book of all:

the Good Book (the Bible)

What is the complete, condensed message of the Scriptures? Isn't it totally

De-Junk Thy Life

of greed, envy, covetousness, lust, bad language, pride, cowardice, wasteful living, overdressing, underloving? Because these things crowd out joy, love, fulfillment. It was eloquently said:

"Therefore I say unto you, take no thought for your life, what ye shall eat, or what ye shall drink; nor yet for your body, what ye shall put on. Is not the life more than meat, and the body than raiment?"

"And why take ye thought for raiment? Consider the lilies of the field, how they grow; they toil not, neither do they spin:

"And yet I say unto you, That even Solomon in all his glory was not arrayed like one of these."
(Matthew 6:25, 28-29)

"He that loveth silver shall not be satisfied with silver; nor he that loveth abundance with increase: this is also vanity." (Ecclesiastes 5:9)

There is a time on earth for everything, so says Ecclesiastes (3:1-6)

1: To every thing there is a season, and a time to every purpose under the heaven: 2: A time to be born, and a time to die; a time to plant, and a time to pluck up that which is planted: 3: A time to kill, and a time to heal; a time to break down, and a time to build up; . . . 6: A time to get, and a time to lose; a time to keep, and a time to cast away. . . .

When the Lord commands it, how can we resist?

Like Moses, start kicking junk out of your life.

It will be a resurrection for you, your loved ones, and associates. I think we all agree now that de-junking is absolutely necessary for a high-quality life, so no matter how it hurts—become dedicated and aggressive, decide to cut your way out of the bag of junk and get out.

I'm hoping I've managed to give you a few strong hints of how, where, and when to begin de-junking. There is a time to stop war-dancing and circling around our junk and charge! A time to make our junk tremble in the trenches instead of our cowering from its clutter. Losing a few old habits and heirlooms might leave a tiny wound or two, but *you'll win! You'll conquer! You'll be free!* No blood will spill from your defeated junk—but blood will again begin to flow for life instead of for objects.

Attack with the strength of a lion: start grabbing those junk items that have been smothering you, competing for your time and affection, costing you money and concern, and throw them out, give them away, donate them, sell them, burn them—anything—but get them out of your sight and mind. Ignore the outcries of onlookers who have to crawl out from under their own junk to give you reasons to cling on forever.

As the clutter goes, light will penetrate to you and then you can de-junk in a big way—ten times faster than you accumulated it. The fresh air of relief, of living will begin to envelop you, the exhilaration of true power and control will permeate your being.

Once you've de-junked you won't accumulate again as fast; you'll automatically have a built-in new sense of value that will inspire you to spot clutter and avoid it. The junk will seem to disintegrate by itself—people will give you less (if any), you won't buy any—you won't believe how naturally it works!

Start now—the older you are, the more you have to de-junk. And the longer you've been junked, the happier you'll be de-junked!

You are entitled to a life of love, fulfillment and accomplishment, but these rewards are almost impossible to obtain when you spend your life thrashing and wallowing in a muddle of housework. Time—the time to love, to be, to grow—is the most precious commodity on earth. No one's time should be wasted cleaning needlessly or inefficiently.

A Clean House
How Does Everyone Else Do It?

- Some lie. . . .
- Some have mighty lumpy rugs. . . .
- Some have no children. . . .
- Some have a maid. . . .
- Some convince their husbands to do a little of it. . . .
- Some use only one room in the house. . . .
- Some never let anyone in. . . .

Most of us don't use any of these methods to clean our houses. We represent the 95 percent of homemakers who, often in a state of cobweb confusion at the end of the day, wonder, "Just how does everyone else do it?"

Every time we see another clean-and-organized success story, we end up depressed and frustrated. We try the miracle formulas, quick tips and super systems, but when we find ourselves still not progressing in the war against grime, grit and grubbies, we again wonder why it works so well for others. "Something is surely wrong with me!" we conclude.

Newspaper columns, slick magazines and bestselling authors have tried to provide all the answers for a "perfect home"—and have convinced too many homemakers they don't have a chance. This constant bombardment of get-clean-and-organized propaganda leaves millions of women wondering, "What's wrong with my system? Why am I the only one failing?"

Well, I don't think there's anything wrong with you or with any other woman struggling to run a home (and/or raise kids, hold down a job, go back to school, do volunteer work). Housework is, for a fact, never ending and little appreciated. There are no superwoman homemakers. Most women are barely managing, meeting daily crises and demands, just like you are, wondering too what's wrong with them. It's amazing that no real training is provided for the most complicated, life-affecting job on earth: homemaking.

The superwoman articles, books and commercials are a failure if their intent is to inspire the homemaker to rise to maximum efficiency. Gimmicks, hints, formulas, and magic schedules for living happily ever after aren't the answer. Overestimating or underestimating your abilities in any situation feeds the monster of discouragement. When you're doing your best but see yourself falling short of your goals, it's hard to have a bright outlook or a sense of accomplishment.

Yet I assure you there are proven ways to have a clean house, and they don't hinge on magic, good luck, or genies in a cleaner jug. By learning how to *prevent* housework, and by using *professional* cleaning methods, you can reduce your household chore time by as much as 75 percent. You'll simply learn to clean more efficiently and effectively. My confidence in you and in this statement is anchored in more than thirty-five years as a professional housecleaner—and teaching and listening to thousands of women around the world talk about cleaning.

A housecleaner is born

Fresh off the farm and unappreciative of my mother's labors to provide me with hearty meals, ironed shirts and a clean bed, I found college life a far cry from a comfortable home. My appreciation for that home and mother became keener when I discovered how much of my time and money it took to support myself. For survival, I landed a job bottling pop for seventy-five cents an hour, my first nonfarm job. The funds left after deductions were definitely not enough to get me through college. So I looked for a better paying part-time pastime.

Cleaning yards and houses seemed to be a likely prospect, and so my

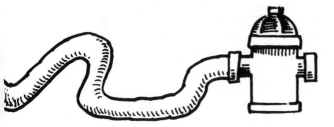

career as a world-renowned house-cleaner was launched. Following afternoon classes, I'd suit up in a white uniform and knock on doors, asking if I could assume some of the household drudgery. I received only a few sneers before I was snatched from the street and given a furnace-cleaning job, followed later by some floors, then some windows. On every job, the homemaker would watch and direct as I'd scrub, shovel and polish. Next came wallpaper-cleaning, wall-washing and cupboard-cleaning. Word got out that an eager housecleaner was loose in the neighborhood, and soon I had more work than I needed. I hired help, taught them what the homemakers had taught me—and the business grew. Carpet- and upholstery-cleaning were added to my list of skills. Soon my business was a large one, in demand in towns outside the college city of Pocatello, Idaho.

Over the next ten years my unique housecleaning business received much public recognition— "College Boy Makes Good." Between newspaper headlines I acquired a vast amount of experience in housecleaning. I ruined grand piano tops, toppled china cabinets, broke windows, streaked walls, suffocated pet birds with ammonia, ruined murals, shrank wall-to-wall carpets into throw rugs, and pulled hundreds of other goofs. But with each job I got better, faster

and more efficient (at cleaning, not breaking). I cleaned log cabins with dirt floors and the plushest mansions in the country. Some days, with five housecleaning crews in operation, I'd clean several three-story homes from top to bottom.

But cleaning skill wasn't the only talent needed to run the company; organization was important. All of us working in the business were full-time students, active in church and civic affairs, and the heads of large families.

My wife Barbara and I had six children in seven years. While operating the business, going to school, and getting a degree, I lettered three years in college athletics and was on the debating team. Because my co-workers and I had no alternative, we *had* to develop efficient methods to clean houses. Fortunately we also received much opinionated coaching and direction from every homemaker we worked for.

In these years of "field experience" is based my confidence that I can show you how to attain greater housecleaning efficiency. Although I now serve as a consultant on building efficiency and maintenance for some of the world's largest companies, I know that the homemaker faces some of the most difficult cleaning problems of all. And to make the matter tougher, housework is something women are expected to do in addition to *homemaking*.

This is why I prefer to use the word "homemaker" rather than "housewife." "Housewife," like "janitor," has come to mean someone who slaves away at menial, boring work. The "home" in "homemaker" is important because home is the most personal, important place for us all. "Making" is a hint that the job can be creative and fun. Making a home a happy, welcoming place means more to life than any high-powered industrial or office job.

The root of housework evil

Do you want to know what the biggest, ugliest housework problem is? It's that 90 percent of all housework is caused by men and children—and 90 percent of all housework is done by women. Like most men, I once viewed, with a certain critical eye, my wife and other women struggling feverishly to get the housework finished. I ached to jump in and show those "disorganized gals" how an expert could square things away.

Soon the opportunity, along with a great lesson, came to me. Fresh out of college, I worked hard washing walls late at night to buy my wife a surprise plane ticket to Alaska. She was delighted to have her first flight ever and a chance to see her mother again. I bade her goodbye and told her to stay as many weeks as she wished, that I would care well for our six small children. (She wasted no time leaving, I assure you.) But my true thoughts were, "Now that I have her out of town, I'm going to shape up this disorganized house and make it as efficient as my business!"

I woke up at 4:00 the first morning and confidently mapped out the campaign of great household efficiency about to be enacted in our home. By 6:30 the kids were up, and they saluted before they went to the bathroom! By 7:30, the beds were made, the dishes were done, and I was rolling to victory. We were putting the finishing touches on a new home, and my project for the day was constructing a vanity cabinet in the master bathroom—an easy half-day's work. I had just started to glue the first board when "Waaa!" One of the kids had biffed another. I ran out and made peace, passed out the storybooks, and again picked up the hammer and board. "Waaa!"—someone cut a finger.

Three bandages and ten minutes of comforting and mercurochrome-dabbing later, I again picked up the hammer (after scraping off the now-dry glue) and had one nail started when "Waaa!"—a diaper to change (a cry that was repeated all day; I'd have sworn we had four in diapers at the same time).

Again I returned to work, and had started the second nail, when *ding-dong* (the milkman; I slammed the cottage cheese into the fridge), then *ding-dong* (the mailman; I ran down and signed for the package), then *ring-a-ling* (the school telephoning—Laura forgot her lunch money). Then *knock-knock*—"Can I borrow. . . ." Then *buzz*—time for lunch . . . *ding-dong* . . . time for bottles. "Waaa!"—diapers again, etc., etc., etc. You would not believe how my morning went. (Or *would* you?) My building project looked like a chimpanzee special—dried glue and badly cut boards all over, and no real work accomplished. I discovered that dressing a kid once is just a warm-up—one of those kids went through four outfits by 11:15. Noon came and another surprise—those little dudes don't appreciate what you do for them, all that work cooking and they threw food, slobbered, and not one of them thanked me. . . .

Nap time came, and would you believe little kids don't all go to sleep at the same time? I've bedded down 600 head of cattle easier and faster than those six kids. When I finally got them all down, no way was I going to hammer, play the stereo, or even turn a page loudly and risk waking one of them! Fortunately, the day ended just before I did. I had two boards up on the cabinet by the time the last baby was read to sleep at midnight. The most famous housecleaner and best organizer in the West . . . had accomplished nothing! I was *so* tired and discouraged. The day before I'd bought five trucks, four people had asked me to lunch—I'd expanded my company into a new area—but that day, nothing!

The next morning, I again woke at 4:00 and again decided I was going to run things like my business. I'd change all the diapers ahead for the whole day! But it didn't work. Leaving out all the gory details of the next few days, my half-day cabinet job, only half-complete, bit the dust.

A week later my wife called to check on things. I pinched all the kids to get them howling in the background so I wouldn't have to beg her to come and save me. She did return at once, and I suddenly got efficient again.

Since this experience, my compassion, respect and appreciation for the homemaker have grown considerably. I realized then for the first time how frustrating, time-consuming, and just plain hard the job of making a home is, and how much patience and ingenuity it takes.

In preparing this book I've tried to keep in mind the hundreds of other jobs the homemaker must perform simultaneously with housecleaning. Laundry, shopping, cooking, mending and errands *ad infinitum* will always be required. Though housework can be shortened, and there *is* life after housework, life *during* housework must also go on.

This is why rigid cleaning methods and plans seldom work. Schedules and demands are different in every household, big houses are proportionately easier to clean than small ones, new houses are easier than old; so homemakers trying to pattern their lives after others are eventually disillusioned—like the determined woman who tried a simple "foolproof" formula for keeping children from getting their dirty fingerprints all over the walls. She had read a "how to run a perfect home" article that advised, "Take Junior, sit him down and say, 'Junior, if you wash your hands three times a day, Mommy will give you a twenty-five-cent raise in your allowance.'" Immediately the woman called her dirty-fingered son in and presented the proposal to him. "I promise," said the son. But the spots were still on the wall. The mother observed her son one morning, and indeed, he was keeping the bargain. He went to the sink, washed his hands and dried them, and repeated the procedure twice more. Then he left to play in the dirt.

It's frustrating to see commercial exaggerations of how well cleaning methods and materials work, especially when they're applied to a house in which everything is already perfect. You're not alone in being offended by the gorgeous TV homemaker in expensive evening clothes who flips her pearls out of the way to mop the floor with Magic Glow. Occasionally an immaculate kid or two tiptoes past or a well-groomed dog ambles through the place, after which the "super-smelling clean-all," applied effortlessly, takes over. But don't be discouraged—there's something wrong with them, not you!

Miracle formulas, tricks, gimmicks and solutions aren't the answer; and if they haven't worked for you, don't let it get you down, because they aren't the key to freedom from housework. The first principle of effective housework is not to have to do it! Being able to do it well is great, but it's greater not to have to do it at all. Your real goal is to *eliminate* all of it you can. In this book you'll learn how to get rid of a lot of it, and the rest I'll show you how to take care of quickly and efficiently.

Just remember that, while getting finished with any housework chore is a worthwhile goal, doing it in teeth-gritting agony is self-defeating. There are "have-to" jobs, no matter how good we are (like bathtub rings, fingerprints, etc.). You'll never escape them. But when you learn to minimize the time you spend on the have-to jobs, you'll finally be able to get to the "get-to" jobs, and they'll both become more pleasant, I promise! There *is* life after housework—and if you do it right,

there can even be life *during* housework.

Once you start finding the extra time that once was all spent on housework, nothing in your home will be mediocre or dull. You'll rip down anything that's faded or ugly and replace it with the prettiest, most colorful, most refreshing things you can find or make. You'll throw out or trade things that don't fit in. If something is torn or worn or forlorn, you'll look forward to taking care of it, not as a chore, but as a chance to better yourself and your home. You'll want to mend it, because it will be mending *you*. Once you have time, you'll be inspired to repair and refinish. The real struggle before wasn't the chore or item you had to service—it was the hopeless feeling that there was never any time for it. A lot of little things that need to be done really aren't work once you can get to them—and once you really believe that you can, you'll start looking forward to them! That's life *during* housework!

At the housecleaning seminars I've taught across the country, I've passed out thousands and thousands of registration cards with a space left for comments, special requests or housecleaning wisdom. This was written on one: "I must tell you, I love to clean. I have a clean house and I've been using the same techniques you use for years now. Everything in my house looks good, but my husband accuses me of being lazy because I don't exhaust myself every day like his mother did. I make lots of handicrafts and things, and he can't get over the fact that everything is clean and yet I still have time to goof off. He is honestly upset. He thinks I have too much fun and don't work enough."

You can't win 'em all. You'll discover in your worrying about how other people do it that 90 percent of the time you're overestimating their results. Even in the cartoon world, Wonder Woman in all her glory never raised children, stabilized a husband, or cleaned and managed a house. Wonder Woman faced only criminals, not housework horrors.

You can be as much a Wonder Woman as anyone you'll meet or read about, if you'll only learn to harness your own resources. Not many others are more efficient or have a neater house than you.

By following the simple secrets in this book, you'll become even more efficient, and will have more time to enjoy life after housework.

WILMA SEEMS TO BE HAVING A LOT MORE FUN EVER SINCE SHE GOT THAT YELLOW BOOK.

The professional cleaning approach won't take cleaning away entirely, but it will give you a lot of extra hours. The time rewards of efficient cleaning are real, and the busier you are, the more you'll appreciate them.

Is It Organization... or Your Energy Level?

"I get the feeling at the end of every day that I haven't gotten anywhere and I'm never going to get anywhere. . . ." This is how a lovely young mother with a brand-new house and four small children rather concisely summed up a basic problem of homemaking: understanding what needs to be done but feeling that you lack the skill or direction to accomplish it. Even if you know what the rewards will be, constantly thinking you aren't getting there will discourage you and begin to prevent you from *wanting* to get there.

The big magic word

The big magic word to homemakers, business managers—in fact, all of us—is "organization." If we could just get ourselves properly organized, we could do anything (so we think). We spend a great deal of time trying to organize ourselves like the superwoman and superman formulas say we should, but still we seem to get little accomplished. We subconsciously figure the "organizing" is going to do it for us.

This is wrong. No organization plan can supply the whole answer or do the work. Is there hope? Yes, and this bit of good news will start this chapter off right: Women are much better organizers than men. I say so, and if you ask any boss, school principal or minister who organizes best, they'll agree with me: Women do! (If you want to prove it, send a man and woman to town, each with a list of things to do and get. The woman will be home in two hours with everything. Six hours later, the man will lumber in, only partly successful and mean as a bear.)

There is no one best way to organize

Organization is an ever-changing process; it's a journey, not a destination. Every minute of every day a new approach is being thought up. Everyone is different in temperament, attitude, build, energy and ambition; every situation requires a different style of organization to get the job done. The secret isn't in how you get organized—it's in *wanting* to be organized and committing yourself to it. Once that's achieved, everything will fall into place. You can organize as well as anyone if you want to or have to. There isn't any "set" way to do anything. You don't have to eat the soup first or second in a meal—you can eat it last!

Your system of organization should fit you personally. It should be tailored to your style, your schedule and your motivation. Some of us are day people; some, night. You run your own life—the clock doesn't run it.

Some organizational myths

I'm convinced that everyone can be organized if they have to be and if they quit trying to follow "know-it-all" methods and formulas. For example, some efficiency experts give this "foolproof" method of accomplishment: They say, in essence, "Sit yourself down and make a list of the things you want to get done. Put the most important ones first. When you get up in the morning, start on the first one and don't leave it or go to the next one until the first is finished. Then go on to the second one and so on until you've finished with the list."

I can't imagine anyone being able to exist (let alone succeed) following that kind of organizational concept. It's grossly inefficient, noncreative, inflexible—not to mention no fun. For years I've worked closely with top executives from some of the world's largest corporations, and I've never met one who worked this way. Yet I know many homemakers who've been trying desperately to organize their lives to fit this ridiculous concept, and they are paying dearly for it, suffering endless frustration because they can't make it work. If I followed that style of organization in my business or personal activities, I'd be twenty years behind!

Look where trying to follow the one-two-three style of getting things done can lead you. Let's say you make a list of the following things to do this week (in addition to your regular chores):

1. Make the kids a birdhouse.
2. Water the garden.
3. Memorize my part of the poem for PTA play.
4. Send Grandmother a birthday card.
5. Get the new lawn in.

Enthusiastically, you tackle the five projects in the down-the-list style outlined by the efficiency experts. While in town, you pick up the birdhouse materials, and soon you get started on the house with full gusto; however, you forgot to get an adjustable bit to make the hole in the front of the birdhouse. So, at a critical point, you're stopped. The one-two-three track compels you to leave the task and take time out to secure the needed tool, which you do at a cost of twenty-three miles of driving and two hours of searching. You then paint an undercoat on the birdhouse, wait a day for it to dry, and then put on the second coat. After two days, task number one is at last finished, so out to the garden next. You turn on the water. Four hours later the water is finally down the rows and task number two is finished. Next you go into the house for a few hours to memorize the PTA poem, number three on the list. Grandmother's card, item number four, you then pick up at the store, bring home, sign and address, and take to the post office. To put a hero's touch on number five, you pick up a book on lawns, work on the lawn for the last three days, and are finished with all your projects in one week!

Efficiency experts might have a week to spend to do all this, but you don't, and neither do I. The tasks could easily be done in a day or more, of course, with a little margin for daydreaming on the side. How? By relying on your creativity and a more flexible system. While in town, before anything is started, pick up the card for Grandmother. While driving on to get the birdhouse materials, mentally build the house so you'll be aware of each thing that has to be picked up. While waiting for the lumberyard clerk to round up the materials, chat with one of the staff about lawn season and grass and at this time get the fertilizer, mulch and seed for the anticipated lawn.

On the way home, turn off the car radio and start to memorize the PTA poem. Once you get home, lay out the materials for the birdhouse and build it. (Oops, we forgot the adjustable bit, too.) Let's stop the birdhouse immediately and go turn on the water for the garden, taking the poem with us to memorize while waiting for the water to get down the rows. Once the water is going, planting the lawn gets attention. Next, phone your brother-in-law, asking him to send his adjustable bit for the birdhouse home with your child who'll be coming by in a while from school. Continue to work on the lawn until you're too tired to hustle. After washing for supper, write out Grandmother's card so the children can take it to the mailbox on their way to school next morning. When your child arrives with the adjustable bit, drill the hole and paint the birdhouse. By this time, you're rested, so you tackle the lawn again. When tired—but finished with the lawn—you come in and give the birdhouse a second coat (you were smart enough to buy a fast-drying primer). By then it's late, but just time for another shot at the poem, and you've memorized it. Now all five things are completed in *one day* instead of a week, and look at the time you have left for yourself.

Impossible to do all that in one day? No. And you can apply this same principle to housework if you rely on your own skills and really want to get it done. Your freedom and ingenuity will produce creative energy. It's simply a matter of "multiple-track" organization. In housework, if you wait until one thing is completed before you start another—the single-track system—you'll take forever to finish and never get around to any freedom to enjoy life. Once you train yourself to the multiple-track method, thinking will be effortless. You'll just roll along, accomplishing things. You won't have to drain your think tank or worry or sweat to organize. It will come naturally.

Here's the secret: The start and finish of a job are the difficult parts. So start the first project at once! As it gets rolling, begin the second. As the second gets in gear, attack the third.

By then the second one is done, so pounce on the fourth, fifth and sixth; and if the third isn't done, start on the seventh. Don't start and finish any two tasks at the same time. Don't start one thing when you're finishing another. Start another project while you're in the middle of three or four, but don't start one at the end of another project. The multiple-track system is the right way to run many projects at the same time—and it's easy if you alternate starting and finishing times.

The way some people cook is a prime example of doing things the most efficient way. I've watched my grandmother, who had fifteen children, prepare eight different dishes for twelve people in just minutes—a miracle. But it wasn't a miracle—just good organization and the multiple-track system. She simply got eight things going at alternate times, nothing starting or ending at once. You've done that, haven't you, when you had to? No sense waiting for water to boil, biscuits to rise, salads to cool, butter to melt. She simply used the waiting time productively.

I've watched a one-track-system mother with one small child crumple in total frustration trying to manage her baby. Five years, a couple of sets of twins and two singles later, she's doing a marvelous job. How? She learned the four- or five-track organization system and applied it! Your mind is capable of it and your body is, too. The success of this system is amazing, and once you get it down, you'll benefit from it in every area of your life.

A large percentage of our housecleaning time is spent "putting out brush fires," as it's called in business— such as spending three days hunting for your dog, because you didn't take three seconds to close the gate behind you. Many a homemaker fails because all her efforts are spent taking care of problems that a little timely action would have prevented. They spend twenty hours a year (and a lot of mental anguish) trying to remove felt-tip marker writing from walls, instead of a minute putting the pens out of reach of the kids; ten hours a year cleaning ovens or stovetops instead of fifteen minutes choosing a pot or pan that won't boil or slop over!

Simplicity vs. procrastination

A great deal of effort is expended as a result of failure to put out a simple timely effort. Here's a common every-day example: doing the dishes later instead of right after the meal. Notice how a simple chore multiplies itself into an insurmountable obstacle of negative feeling and freedom-robbing discouragement. Do you take the time, over and over, to cope with an unsatis-factory situation instead of correcting the underlying problem? For example, do you have to adjust the faucet handle just right when you turn it off so the drip is minimized? Or angle and massage that sticky drawer for thirty seconds every time you use it to get it to slide back in? Or wonder and experiment every time a fuse blows—which breaker switch is the lights, which is the heater, which is the outlet, which is the. . . . I think you know what I mean. (See the checklist on page 304.)

The best "organization" is simply deciding to do things before they get out of hand and dictate to *you* how and when they'll be done. Are you the slave or the master? Simplicity seldom goes hand in hand with procrastina-tion. Do you clean up and put away things as soon as you're through (sim-plicity), or do you throw them in a pile to be rummaged through as they're needed (procrastination)? It only takes a few minutes to iron a blouse. Do you do it well ahead of the appointment, or five tense minutes be-fore you have to dash out the door? (And of course then you have to take out and set up the ironing board for just one piece of clothing—and you risk scorching the blouse in your haste and having to find and iron another.) Do you make your bed when you jump out (simplicity) or just before you go to bed again at night (procras-tination)?

Do you fill out that committee re-port when it's still fresh in your mind and will take only a few minutes, or do it when it's overdue? You've been strongly reminded to get it in, and now you'll spend hours doing so, be-

Clean in the daytime whenever you can. Cleaning at night shortchanges you on helpers, energy, light and safety.

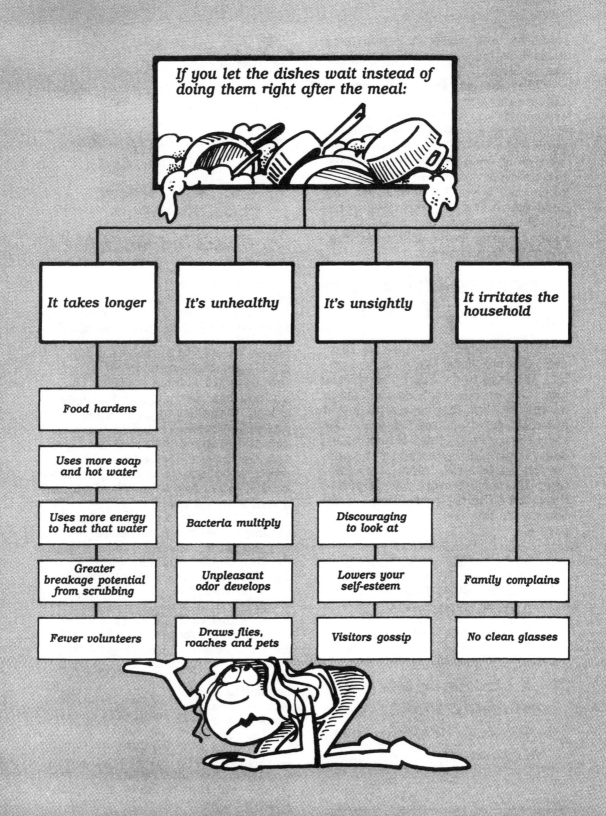

If you let the dishes wait instead of doing them right after the meal:

It takes longer
- Food hardens
- Uses more soap and hot water
- Uses more energy to heat that water
- Greater breakage potential from scrubbing
- Fewer volunteers

It's unhealthy
- Bacteria multiply
- Unpleasant odor develops
- Draws flies, roaches and pets

It's unsightly
- Discouraging to look at
- Lowers your self-esteem
- Visitors gossip

It irritates the household
- Family complains
- No clean glasses

cause by now you've forgotten facts, mislaid evidence, and had to write an excuse letter.

The time gap between doing most things promptly and doing them late compounds and multiplies problems. You end up spending time not simply getting the job done, but fighting and recovering from the problems created because you waited. Doing things when they take less time is not only good scheduling, it makes good sense: It will save energy and motivation to apply to more personally satisfying efforts than housework.

Back to the ever-growing list

Lists are great—as long as they don't run our lives. We all have our lists of things to do. I'd be lost without mine! We don't always *do* the things on the list, but they're always jotted down. At one time, my list grew to seventy-six "immediate" things to be done. It took all my time just to transfer the list to a new piece of paper when the old one wore out. If your list follows the typical pattern, at the bottom are the hard, unpleasant tasks, such as:

19. Clean the oven
20. Clean the 3-section storm windows
21. Volunteer to tend Dennis the Menace
22. Kick cousin Jack out of the front room
23. Go thru 700 old issues of Good Housekeeping

or

38. Tell Jack he's to be terminated.
39. Pour concrete for the back step.
40. Go face the banker and get the loan.
41. Get my wisdom teeth pulled
42. Speak to George about taking a few more baths

We have to be careful with that villain list. We're often so proud of ourselves for even writing something down on our list that we immediately relax. We say to ourselves, "Boy, I'm glad I got that one started." After a few days we suddenly realize that nothing has been done, and we sneak a look at the list to see if that item has disappeared. It hasn't. We're so relieved to know that it wasn't forgotten, we leave it for a few more days. The day before the deadline, we've no choice but to face it, and we generally get the item done in half the time we feared it would take!

A list has one big value, and that's getting things recorded before you forget them. That's all! As for using a list to discipline yourself, forget it. *You* have to do the things—the list won't do them for you.

A schedule won't do them for you either. I dislike the regimentation of set schedules; they're only for inefficient people afraid they're going to run out of things to do. Some scheduling and budgeting of time is needed, but not to the extent that it dictates your every move and mood. You should run a schedule for your benefit, not the reverse.

It can't be illustrated better than by this skit sent to me by homemaker Gladys Allen:

[Aslett arrives at the highly polished door of Ms. Polly Programmed.]

Polly: *[Wearing a huge watch on her arm, feather duster in hand. She's immaculately groomed and dressed.]* Hi, Mr. Aslett, won't you please take off your shoes and come in? *[Dusts him off lightly as he removes his shoes.]* How nice to have a visitor drop by. I have *[checking her watch]* 6¼ minutes' relaxation time before I have to knead the bread and water the alfalfa sprouts.

Aslett: Ms. Programmed, I see that you're busy. . . . I just stopped by to invite you to a little efficiency seminar.

Polly: Nonsense! Now you come right here and sit down. I still have five minutes and thirty-three seconds of leisure time.

Aslett: *[Sits down.]* As you know, Ms. P. . . .

Polly: *[Interrupting.]* Oh, Mr. Aslett, would you mind sitting on this cushion? That one has already been sat on this morning. I like to alternate. The fabric wears much longer that way.

Aslett: *[Moving to another cushion.]* Really? Now, I never would have thought of that.

Polly: My, yes! My last divan lasted seventy-eight days longer just by using that one little trick.

Aslett: What I've come to tell you, Ms. Programmed, is that I've come up with a great new idea for a seminar, and I'd like to invite you to come preview it tomorrow morning at 10:00.

Polly: Ten o'clock Thursday? *[Rushes to a big box labeled "Daily Schedules."]* I've just typed up my schedules for the month. I'll have to check. *[Pulls out a long folded sheet.]*

Aslett: Is that your schedule for just one month?

Polly: One month? Oh, my no! This is my schedule for Thursday. *[Studies it carefully, consults watch, makes a few changes with a pencil.]* Now, what time did you say that would start tomorrow?

Aslett: Ten a.m.

Polly: *[Making a few more changes.]* Yes, yes, I think I'll be able to work it in after all. If I get up at 5:00 a.m. instead of 6:00, I can have my laundry sorted and my Scripture studies done by 7:00. I can get my drapes vacuumed and my children fed by 7:47. While they practice their violins, I can shine the furniture and wash the dishes. They leave for school at 8:19, which gives me just enough time to stir up a casserole for supper and get myself ready. Umm, yes. I should be able to leave here by 9:37 at the latest. By the way, Mr. Aslett, what did you say your seminar will be about?

Aslett: *[Stands up with a sigh, shrugs weakly, unable to speak.]*

Highs and lows

The old up-and-down pattern is entrenched in our style of living—but how devastating it is to human feelings and efficient housekeeping! Most housecleaners unthinkingly roll along in this style. Once a week (or once a month) we clean the house, water the plants, and do everything just so, then we're "up." But immediately the spotlessness and satisfaction attained begin to erode as dust, spiders, children, animals, spouse and guests mount their attack. It's frustrating because we've expended so much dedication and energy getting the house to its peak.

247

One elderly gentleman, recalling his mother's approach to housework, said, "She organized herself and the family so that all the housework (washing, ironing, baking, sewing, etc.) was done on Monday (one day, mind you). What an accomplishment! But she spent the other six days recovering to prepare for the big Monday cleanup again."

This kind of housecleaning approach gets old fast, and it gets you nowhere except an early grave. Even if your house is clean as often as it's dirty, 50 percent of the time, or 50-50, you'll not be rewarded 50-50, because it's human nature to notice and respond to the negative, not the positive. Little is heard about the house if it's clean—but if it's dirty, everybody squawks, gossips and complains. It's demoralizing, but you can't give up the battle. So you buckle down and restore your domain to order and cleanliness.

Hold it. Now that you've got your house in top shape again, try something different.

A little consistency saves a lot of time, energy and discouragement. Avoid the "up-and-down" style of housekeeping. Establish an *acceptable* cleanliness level and maintain it daily. If you really want to be freed from housework drudgery, this one change in style will work wonders for you. When you learn to keep house on a straight line, you'll not only find extra hours appearing, but some of the other up-and-down styles you've been struggling with for years (exercising, cooking, letter writing, reading, gardening, etc.) will follow your housecleaning system and suddenly begin to be manageable. Your home will never stay static. It will be in a constant state of flux, if it's used as all homes should be. Avoid extremes both ways—too much polish is just as disconcerting as too little. Gold-plating a house won't bring you anything but discouragement and worry.

To keep your home in a steady state of cleanliness and livability, you'll learn to wipe down shower walls and plumbing fixtures daily to avoid having to acid-bath hard water deposits monthly. You'll carry in a manageable armload of firewood whenever you enter the house, instead of spending a back-breaking hour lugging a week's worth in on Saturday. You'll wipe up spills immediately, when it's five times easier, faster, and much less damaging than putting it off.

You'll also discover that *eliminating* work does wonders for your efficiency. (See page 288.) And try delegating, say, 60 percent of the daily chores to your family—you'll be amazed how much the need for picking up the house will decrease.

Do your big yearly cleaning each fall instead of spring; you'll marvel at how much longer the house looks nice.

248

By cleaning *after* the open-window, kids-in-and-out-all-day season, you keep all that dust and pollen and dirt from deteriorating your house all winter—with the bonus that the house is cleaner for the winter holidays.

Make yourself a simple cleaning checklist

You may not be able to keep things as antiseptic as Grandma did—you may not even want to. And with everything else you have going, you may rarely be able to get the cleaning done *when* you intended.

But here, as in everything, it helps to have a map or plan of where you're headed (even if you have to take detours, alternate routes, or shortcuts to get there). An outline of the goal helps you feel calm and in control even when the waves of other agendas and responsibilities are breaking all around you. You don't really want a schedule for cleaning, something that prescribes a precise day and time to do each chore; you want a list or reminder of what needs to be done at approximately what intervals.

Here is a sample of the type of outline we pro cleaners use. You may wish to modify or photocopy it and use it for yourself. Just remember that this is only a very general guide—the number (and age) of the people in your household, your climate, and the type of furnishings you have will all have a bearing on how often things need to be done.

Daily

- ☐ Straighten up the whole place
- ☐ Do all dishes
- ☐ Wipe counters and range top
- ☐ Make beds
- ☐ Dump kitchen garbage
- ☐ Clean up any spots and spills
- ☐ Hang up all clothes
- ☐ Read and dispose of mail and magazines
- ☐ Praise any cleaning effort

Exterior
- ☐ Police any litter or left-behind tools/toys

Semiweekly

- ☐ Vacuum most-used areas
- ☐ Do laundry

Weekly

- ☐ Vacuum carpets
- ☐ Sweep or dustmop hard floors
- ☐ Damp-mop floors
- ☐ Dust furniture
- ☐ Change beds
- ☐ Spot clean handprints, etc.
- ☐ Wash door glass
- ☐ Clean mirrors
- ☐ Clean sinks
- ☐ Clean showers and tubs
- ☐ Clean the outside and clean and delime the inside of the toilet bowl
- ☐ Dump all trashcans

Exterior
- ☐ Vacuum door mats
- ☐ Sweep porches
- ☐ Sweep patios
- ☐ Haul off any accumulated junk/trash

Monthly

- ☐ Dust woodwork and high and low areas
- ☐ Catch all cobwebs
- ☐ Vacuum upholstery
- ☐ Vacuum drapes
- ☐ Vacuum blinds
- ☐ Sweep or vacuum carpet edges
- ☐ Surface clean carpeting

- ☐ Rewax heavy traffic areas on waxed floors
- ☐ Damp-wipe seats of chairs
- ☐ Clean out refrigerator
- ☐ Clean kitchen cabinet fronts
- ☐ Clean appliance fronts and tops
- ☐ Dissolve any hard-water buildup
- ☐ Wash/disinfect trash containers

Exterior
- ☐ Wash doormats
- ☐ Sweep or hose walks/driveway
- ☐ Wash easy-to-reach windows
- ☐ Spot clean doors
- ☐ Sweep garage

Quarterly

- ☐ Polish furniture
- ☐ Check and clean or change furnace/ central air conditioning filters

Twice a Year

- ☐ Clean oven
- ☐ Defrost freezer
- ☐ Degrease stove hood/exhaust fan
- ☐ Wash vinyl furniture
- ☐ Turn mattresses
- ☐ Vacuum air and heat vents

- ☐ Dust tops of tall furniture, rafters, etc.

Annually

- ☐ Strip and rewax waxed floors
- ☐ Wash or dry-sponge walls
- ☐ Touch up nicks in wall paint
- ☐ Clean under and behind things
- ☐ Wash hard-to-reach windows
- ☐ Wash or dry-clean drapes or curtains
- ☐ Wash window screens
- ☐ Clean light fixtures
- ☐ Wash blinds
- ☐ Wash/clean blankets
- ☐ Shampoo carpet/upholstery if needed

Exterior
- ☐ Clean drain gutters
- ☐ Wash exterior of all windows
- ☐ Clean screens/storm doors
- ☐ Clean/sweep chimney

Every Several Years or So

- ☐ Wash or otherwise clean ceilings

But remember: Clean it when it's soiled, not when it's scheduled.

How Much Time Does Housework Actually Take?

We exaggerate three things around the house: "I told you kids a million times," "I haven't slept for two weeks" and "All I do is clean, clean, clean."

The last one I know is an overdone appraisal. We only vacuum seven minutes at a time on the average, spend ten minutes once every ten days cleaning the toilets, wash the walls about once every four years. Many of us dread and dread a task that, if you actually clocked it, takes maybe sixteen minutes. Some of the most procrastinated things (however psychologically formidable) are among the shortest. You can de-cobweb a whole house in less than fifteen minutes. No matter how it seems, few of us clean "forever." We probably average ten hours a week actually housecleaning. The bad aura comes not from cleaning but procrustination (yes, it's spelled right—leaving things until they're crusty).

So see how long it takes you to do a chore—and see if you can shave a few minutes off each time you do it. This won't just gradually reduce the time you have to spend on housework—it'll help you plan better (because you'll know how long various operations actually take). And you'll dread a lot of things less, after you realize they're a matter of minutes, not hours.

Remember to tie scheduling and organization to your own personal motivation or energy level. Add to that the conviction that what you have to do or want to do is really worth it, and organization will fall into place. You're a human being, not a machine. You don't start running at full efficiency the minute you're cranked up. If you try that, you're going to end up mighty discouraged. By tying my energy level to production, I can knock out three magazine articles in an hour; but I can't finish one in eight hours when I have the drags. When I'm rolling, I tackle my most active and demanding work. When the drags invade, I file, sort, or do something that requires no creativity or mental energy. In both situations, I'm accomplishing a lot by fitting the task to my mood and personality.

Be yourself and decide what's most important to you. Wade into it during your best hours for that particular chore, and a miracle will happen. (You might end up writing a book on organization and selling it back to the supermen and -women of the world.)

What to Expect From Your Husband and Children

On this subject I'll gladly assume the role of the learner. When you find something that works the miracle of getting husbands and children to take on their rightful share of the housework, let me know so I can tell the thousands of exasperated women I hear from every year.

This lack of cooperation from men and children is a grim reality, all right, but it doesn't have to be. While doing a consulting study for a large Eastern school district, I was introduced to a quiet grade school cafeteria. At the stroke of noon, 420 children converged enthusiastically on the polished lunchroom with trays and brown bags. Forty minutes later the room was quiet again, but not polished. It looked like a tornado had feasted instead of humans. Forks, food and wrappers decorated the floor, the tables, chairs, walls, and even the light fixtures. When we finished the building tour *two hours* later, I noticed the janitor just finishing the cleaning. *Two 30-gallon garbage cans* were required to contain the mess the janitor picked up from that lunchroom.

The next day we were touring a similar school in town: same floor plan, same area, and 412 students. This time we arrived about fifteen minutes after lunch ended—and the place was immaculate! The janitor was scooping up what appeared to be the final dustpan of debris. I was told by the guide that not only was it the last dustpan, it was the *only* dustpan! This janitor had spent fifteen minutes restoring the room and filled only a small pan of dirt, while the janitor at the other school labored two hours in the same area, after the same number of children, and accumulated two garbage cans full. What was the difference? Same number of kids, same community, same size building—but *not the same boss!*

It's not circumstance that causes you to have a messy house and spend two hours cleaning when you could spend fifteen minutes. It's you! The only difference between the schools was the principals. The first principal allowed the students freedom to eat and leave a mess; the other principal allowed the students the freedom of eating and simply added the responsibility of cleaning up their own mess. "Anything you mess up, you clean up" was the fair and simple rule. That meant crumbs, drops and dribbles on tables, chairs and floors. It took each kid seconds to perform the task and unquestionably taught and reinforced the most important ingredient of greatness: responsibility. Any woman who cleans up after a husband or a kid over two years old deserves the garbage cans she has to lug out every day!

I don't ordinarily suggest open rebellion or brute force, but I do offer these suggestions:

1. Refuse to be the janitor for the kids' and husband's messes. Picking up after them is bad for everyone involved. You teach irresponsibility when you assume someone else's responsibility (except those who don't know any better or can't help themselves). Insist that everyone clean up his or her own messes and premises: If they're old enough to mess up, they're old enough to clean up!

2. Write down and post needs. When you ask for (or demand) help, most family members will begin to assist you. Written messages eliminate short memories and the innocent phrase, "I didn't know you needed anything done."

3. Make it easy for them to help. To encourage bed-making, for instance, use one heavy blanket instead of several thinner ones (better yet, invest in European-style comforters that serve

254

as blanket and bedspread). Teach the kids to spread the sheet and blanket and then circle the bed once, tucking as they go. Make sure everyone has plenty of bins and hangers for personal belongings, and the house will be tidier.

4. Be patient. Be persistent. Things don't change just because you say they will. You have to stick with it. The biggest threat to success here is the "If you can't beat 'em, join 'em" syndrome. Hang in there. Refuse to pick up the slack for nonperformers. Don't fall back on "It's easier to do it myself than to get them to do it." The reason is this: If you work to make others clean up after themselves, you'll eventually get them trained and you won't have to worry about it. But if you break down and do it yourself, you'll be doing it for the rest of your life.

5. Use praise lavishly when it's deserved. Appeal to their vanity (this may work especially well on a husband). Remember, you can catch more flies with honey than with vinegar.

6. Leave home or play sick, if necessary.

Sorry I can't help you more on this one! Just remember—it's as much for your husband's and kids' good as it is for yours. So stand your ground!

P.S. My apologies to the 5 percent of husbands and children who already do their share around the house.

The Old Wives' Tales
Ever Hear These?

"Never shampoo carpets when they're new; they get dirty faster."

"Toothpaste and peanut butter remove black marks."

"Start washing from the bottom of the wall and work up."

"Use newspaper to polish your windows."

"Dried bread crumbs clean wallpaper."

Some of these might possibly work, but why go the long way around to get the job done? Spring isn't the best time to clean indoors—late fall is. Who wants to be cooped up with paint and ammonia fumes when springtime blossoms are fragrant? Painting isn't cheaper than cleaning; cleaning averages 60 to 70 percent less. Carpets don't get dirty faster after the first shampooing, if you do it right. Newspapers aren't good for polishing (only for training puppies and peeks at the funnies). Toothpaste and peanut butter do remove marks because they're abrasive—but they also cut the gloss of good enamel paint, and the resulting dull patch looks worse than the original mark.

For centuries, "secrets" of sure-cleaning brews have been passed on to young housekeepers. These formulas are applied unsuccessfully, yet on deathbeds are whispered to the next generation. Hence, even in this day of modern science, well-educated homemakers living in up-to-the-minute homes are still using powdered frogs' legs to remove ink stains from their carpets and crumbled cottage cheese to polish brass doorknobs.

I have yet to find a magic cleaner or solution that will take all the work out of cleaning a house. Less than 5 percent of the hundreds of old wives' tales sent or repeated to me even *worked*. And there's no magic in the bottle, either. The "cleaning cyclone" that whips out of the container isn't interested in cleaning for you when it's getting $150,000 for a minute on TV. Even if that solution—or any solution—is as good as advertisers say it is, it will have little effect on your cleaning time.

It's not what you clean with so much as how you go about it that really matters. So forget most of the old wives' tales you've heard and commercials you've seen and follow some simple professional methods that have been used efficiently and safely for decades.

Whatever you do, don't feel it's your patriotic or economic duty to mix up your own money-saving brew. Some of the results are ridiculous. For example, it's easy to make your own glue, isn't it? Just find an old cow, kill it, and cut off as many hooves as you need for as much glue as you want. Grind them up in your trusty blender, then add. . . .

It's not worth it when you can spend $1.59 and get something better. Besides, it's cheaper than finding a cow and not nearly as messy as killing one.

Homemakers trying to make their own home brew furniture polish can spend three hours rounding up the ma-

terials and mixing up a solution that costs $5.45 for ingredients alone—instead of buying a commercial polish for $2.49 that's tested, safe, and guaranteed not to rot, explode or poison. Remember, *it's your time that's valuable*. A half-century of professional cleaners' records show that out of every dollar spent for cleaning, only 5½¢ is for supplies and equipment; almost the same ratio holds true in the home. Your time and safety are the valuable commodities, not the supplies.

Most home brews are misguided formulations. For instance, most homemade furniture polishes call for linseed oil—a penetrant that conditions raw wood but that, when smeared on *finished* wood (which most furniture is), acts as a sticky magnet to every passing speck of dust. Many homemakers pour chlorine bleach into everything from mop water to toilet bowls, to no avail—bleach is an oxidizing agent that doesn't clean a thing. And don't spend your precious hours grinding and rubbing trying to get vinegar to perform like soap. Vinegar isn't a cleaner, it's a rinsing agent. The "squeak" is what turns you on!

Figuring this from a "free me from housework" angle, using good, efficient—even expensive—supplies and equipment is a cheap way to go if it cuts your time down. For example, if you pay $15 for a gallon of wax, it's a wise buy if it means that whatever you apply it to will only need annual or biennial cleaning and waxing.

Your household tools are your power tools

A gross injustice is usually inflicted on women in this area. Over and over, I see homemakers using an old rattletrap vacuum hardly capable of running, let alone sucking up any dirt. The hose is full of holes, the cord is worn and offers instant electrocution if touched in the wrong place. Every day women wrestle with these machines to do the housework, while in basements and garages sit $400 radial-arm saws and other power tools their husbands haven't used in six months! Men need these macho tools to give their masculinity an occasional boost—while women fight unsafe, ineffective vacuums for hours, every day! Husbands' closets are full of expensive toys that they use one or two days a year, while their wives are cooking three square meals on an electric stove with worn-out switches, or bunching tricot on a twenty-year-old single-stitch sewing machine—daily! The kitchen junk drawer (you know, that drawer with all the parts, spare tools, lids, screws, handles, matches, nails, etc.) is used more by the average man than his $800 solid oak workbench.

In most cases, after an industrious project or two, men seldom use their expensive tools; as investments go, such tools are poor ones. Time is our most valuable commodity, and good housecleaning tools and equipment can save hundreds of hours a year.

My wife, the bread-mixer

A confident husband pulled up in front of a specialty shop, carefully parked his $43,000 Mercedes, and strolled into the store. He paused to examine a new bread-mixer, advertised to cut breadmaking time dramatically. The clerk eased up to him and politely suggested, "Why don't you buy a bread-mixer for your wife?" "Ha!" said the man triumphantly, "Why should I buy one? I *married* a bread-mixer."

This kind of attitude is an unimaginable infringement of one individual upon another. Men are the greatest offenders because traditionally a

and those capable of saving the most time are the ones to purchase. Anything that can be purchased to save time in housework is just as important as a new computer for the business! Buy up! (And don't spend all the money on little-used and often useless "trinket" attachments to cleaning machines or appliances; concentrate on solid, basic tools and supplies.)

What's a homemaker to do?

If you can read, you can forget the witch potions and the glamorously packaged, overpriced household cleaners you've been using. The Yellow Pages in almost every phone directory in the world list janitorial-supply stores. These are (generally) wholesale outlets where commercial cleaning companies buy many of their supplies. It's here you'll find the items I refer to in this book that can't be bought at the supermarket or hardware store. Professionals buy the rest at a local supermarket, same as you do. The prices at janitorial-supply stores vary, but I've never run into one in the multistate area where I've cleaned that wouldn't sell to a homemaker.

Wholesale or retail? Well, you can get either price. And either is better than the price of comparable supplies at the supermarket. The best way to try for a wholesale price is to walk in with dignity and authority, squinting confidently at the shelves of cleaning material and equipment (few of which you'll recognize the first time), and say, "I'm Mrs. Van Snoot of Snoot, Snoot, Frisky and Melvin (you, your husband, cat and dog; the more you sound like a law firm, the better). I need one gallon of metal interlock self-

man's time has been considered to be of greater value. Tradition has validity, but not here. No one's time is worth more or less than another's: for every one of us, time is to love, to feel, to be, to experience, to serve, to relax, or to edify self. Position, sex, status, age, etc., have no bearing on the matter. Too many men think that they married a bread-mixer, maid, taxi driver, gardener, nurse, laundress— forgetting that their mate is entitled to the same share of "time" that they are. The average man reacts almost violently when his wife quietly asks for a $75 pressure cooker to make meal preparation more efficient and provide better nutrition for the family. The same man will slap a $149 telescopic sight on his rifle (used once a year at hunting time) and never even bother to mention it to his wife.

On this earth, no one's time is worth any more than anyone else's. I used to send my wife to town or on errands to do "the piddly things" because my time was worth "so much"— after all, I could get $50 to $100 an hour for consulting jobs. I was way off base. Any woman's time is worth what any man's is.

Take a hard look around your home. The tools likely to be used most polishing floor finish." This usually convinces the seller that you're official, and he or she will generally offer you the contractor's price, since most suppliers are great people and run "hungry" establishments. If the supplier asks you a question like, "Do you want polymer or carnauba base?" don't lose your nerve. Just say,

Give me the house's best-selling brand.

(Forty janitorial companies can't be wrong!) I'm sure if you don't get the contractor's price, you'll at least get a discount.

Which supplies to use: where and when?

I'll discuss these as we cover each area of cleaning. Just remember this: There's no magic in the bottle or machine. The basics of effective cleaning are extremely simple, and you need just a few professional supplies. A chart at the end of this chapter lists the basic tools you'll find useful. A home will be well prepared for efficient cleaning and maintenance if it's equipped with the items listed. (If you can't find them, write me at the address on page 264 and I'll send you a mail-order catalog.)

Proper supplies— big returns

There are more benefits from using the right equipment and supplies than merely doing a (1) faster and (2) better job. There are: (3) safety— you'll be using fewer, simpler items that will be safer to use and easier to store out of children's reach; (4) cost— in the long run you'll spend a lot less on cleaning supplies if you select and use them properly; (5) depreciation— using proper cleaning supplies and tools reduces damage to and deterioration of the surfaces and structures you're cleaning; (6) storage—fewer and more efficient concentrated supplies take up less of the storage space you probably don't have enough of anyway.

If your cleaning closet is full of fancy cans and bottles—Zippo, Rippo, Snort, Rubb Off, Scale Off, Goof Off— I promise a roomier closet when you learn the secrets of proper cleaning. Many of those chemicals and cleaners crammed into every cupboard and under every sink aren't all that effective. They use up valuable room, they're safety hazards for children, and many of them actually damage household surfaces.

Most homemakers' cleaning supply storage areas (under the sink, the pantry, the closet) look like Tom Edison's chemical cache just seconds before the explosion. Many of these things simply get wasted: We have so many, we forget to use them.

Canned expense

The aerosol can has pressured itself into the lives of all. Cosmetics, hair spray, deodorizers, medicines, lubricants, paints, even food—just about everything comes in aerosol because we've been convinced it takes too much effort to do any more than push a button. We've carried this principle

Limit your use of aerosols—they're expensive and bulky. Buy concentrates whenever possible.

supply store and buy four or five reusable commercial plastic spray bottles. Buy your chemicals, cleaners and disinfectants concentrated, in gallons. Mix them with water at the suggested dilution ratios and put the solutions in the spray bottles. Label the bottles with a waterproof marker or make sure each chemical is a different color, lest you end up cleaning windows with upholstery shampoo. These plastic spray bottles are unbreakable, durable, won't nick cupboards, and are extremely efficient and economical to use, whether for heavy-duty cleaning or smaller "keep-up" jobs.

Cleaning concentrates are also now available in little plastic packets (like those little single servings of catsup or mustard), preventing waste and wrong dilution, and making storage and handling a cinch. They're premeasured for use in a bucket or spray bottle—just snip them open and mix

over into our housecleaning systems, paying dollars for pennies' worth of cleaners and compressed gas. Yes, they are convenient, and they may use a propellant that doesn't harm the environment. But considering the small amount of cleaner you get this way, how easily the nozzle clogs, and the dangerous can you have to dispose of afterward, it's cheaper and more environmentally sound to dilute your own concentrated cleaner into good plastic spray bottles.

They last and last, you can see what's in them at any time, and you can control the spray (mist or stream). Some bug killer, paint and grooming products are hard to beat in aerosol, but when it comes to cleaning, I'd go with the spray bottles for speed, economy and safety.

To replace most of the aerosols you now use, go to the janitorial-

Cleaning concentrates are now available in "single-serving" plastic packets. Since they're premeasured for use (either in a bucket or a spray bottle), mixing is easy—and storage is even easier.

Concentrates are 80 percent cheaper than ordinary "household cleaning" products. They take a lot less room to store, and, because they're professional products, they do a better job.

with water as directed on the label. Being able to bring a year's worth of cleaning supplies home in a small sack and store them safely in a little lockable drawer instead of under the sink is the thing of the future. And using concentrates reduces the number of aerosols we use, and the number of empty containers to be disposed of.

When mixing up cleaners from concentrate, fill the bottle with water before you add the concentrate. You won't have four inches of foam in the bottle this way, and it prevents chemical splashes, too.

Neutral cleaner

Neutral cleaner is a cleaner that's mild and safe enough for most any surface because it's neither acid nor alkaline. A detergent doesn't have to

be strictly neutral (have a pH of 7.0) to qualify—it just has to be somewhere close. Most neutral cleaners have a pH in the range of 7 to 9. Professionals use these cleaners for many light-duty cleaning jobs such as floor-mopping and wall-washing, which call for streak-free results with no detergent residue. Give yourself a big supply of neutral cleaner to handle the majority of the cleaning chores around the house safely and inexpensively by going to a janitorial-supply store and getting a jug of "neutral all-purpose cleaner concentrate." (It's even available with a pump-dispenser top.) Then just dilute with water as needed and use.

When using any kind of cleaner, commercial or household, *read the label.* Don't sniff (and for heaven's sake,

262

You need only four basic cleaners

1. NEUTRAL ALL-PURPOSE CLEANER: Neither alkaline nor acidic, so it can be used for almost any type of cleaning. Safe for most surfaces.

2. DISINFECTANT CLEANER: For bathrooms and other areas needing germicidal action. Buy only a quaternary type—it's relatively nontoxic and won't damage most surfaces.

3. HEAVY-DUTY CLEANER/ DEGREASER: A high-pH cleaner with good emulsifying action for tough cleaning jobs where grease is a problem.

4. GLASS CLEANER: Usually alcohol or ammonia based, so it evaporates quickly without leaving streaks or residue. For cleaning small windows, polishing mirrors, appliances, tiles, etc.

For most general cleaning purposes and "keep-up" cleaning, use a 1-quart spray bottle. Just add concentrate to water according to directions.

don't taste) to see what's in the jug; a rose will never smell the same if you get a strong whiff from a commercial ammonia bottle. And be sure to properly dilute cleaners. Our tendency is to say, "If a little does a good job, a lot will do better." This is as silly as saying, "If a teaspoon of baking powder will make the biscuits rise, then a cup should do wonders." We often gluggy-glug-glug too much soap into the water and actually destroy the chemical's dirt-suspending and grease-cutting action. Read the directions! Remember, you don't clean alone. You have two helpers, water and chemicals; they'll do most of the work.

"Miracle" solutions and "magic" tools aren't the only carry-over from old wives' tales. Newspaper and magazine household advice columns are everywhere. "Helpful hints" often only add frustration. In a recent "Forty Ways to Save Time in the Home" article, I found only one tip that was unquestionably beneficial. Be discerning, and check sources when you choose housecleaning advice.

You can do without advice like "Drop a couple of rose petals in your vacuum bag so you can deodorize as you clean," or "Color-coordinate all your bathrooms so the towels will match and you'll always be ready for unexpected company." What you need to learn most of all is how to choose and use supplies and materials so as to use fewer hours of your time to have a cleaner home than you've ever had before. Life after housework is life left over for happiness—for family, for friends, for self—and you're entitled to that. In the following chapters, I'll explain how to do this as we cover each major cleaning area in detail.

By the way—did you know that a paste of strawberries, wheat germ, ground glass and baking soda will polish the bottom of a Boy Scout's cooking kit? (But so will a 6¢ scouring pad!)

Professional Equipment & Supplies

ITEM	SIZE/TYPE	USE	SOURCE
CLEANING CLOTH *	Made from 18"x18" piece of cotton terrycloth	Replaces the "rag." Can be used for most cleaning jobs; especially effective in wall- and ceiling-cleaning. Folding and turning inside out provides 16 cleaning surfaces. (See pages 372-377 for details on how to make and use a cleaning cloth.)	Homemade; also available from the Cleaning Center
MASSLINN CLOTH *	11"x17", disposable	For dusting. The specially treated paper "cloth" collects dust instead of scattering it. Leaves soft sheen on furniture, doesn't create buildup.	Janitorial-supply store
LAMBSWOOL DUSTER *	Lambswool or synthetic puff on 24" or 30" handle	Picks up dust by static attraction. Extremely useful for high dusting, picture frames, moldings, blinds, books, cobwebs, houseplants, etc.	Janitorial-supply or housewares store
CELLULOSE SPONGE	Various sizes; 4"x6"x1½" is a handy size.	For any washing or absorbing job. You can cut a sponge to fit your hand. Always squeeze, never wring.	Discount or paint store
SCRUB SPONGE *	Two-layer nylon and cellulose	Use where gentle abrasion is needed; always wet before using. Use the type with a white nylon side on fixtures, sinks, showers, etc. Good in the bathroom and kitchen. The slightly larger scrub sponges with a harsher green nylon side should only be used on nondamageable surfaces—not on enamel, plastic, fiberglass or porcelain.	Discount store or supermarket
SPRAY BOTTLE *	22 oz. or 1 qt. plastic with professional-quality trigger sprayer	To fill with diluted concentrated cleaners for spot cleaning, bathrooms, small windows, or other general cleaning duties. Keep several around the house in convenient locations.	Janitorial-supply or discount store

The cleaning compounds described in this chart and elsewhere in this book are no more dangerous than many preparations found on supermarket shelves. But since most janitorial supplies do not come with child-proof lids, be sure to keep them out of the reach of children.

For your convenience, those items marked * are available by mail. For more information and a free catalog write to: The Cleaning Center, P.O. Box 39-H, Pocatello, ID 83204.

ITEM	SIZE/TYPE	USE	SOURCE
DRY SPONGE*	5"x7"x½" natural open-cell rubber	(My favorite cleaning tool.) Use on flat-painted walls and ceilings, wallpaper, lampshades, oil paintings. Cleans many surfaces better, faster, and less messily than liquid cleaners. Discard when dirt-saturated.	Paint store or janitorial-supply store
WINDOW SQUEEGEE*	Brass frame, rubber blade. Ettore is a good brand. For the average home window a 10" or 12" blade is best; for very large panes, use a 16" or 18" blade.	Strictly for window cleaning. Avoid contact with rough surfaces so rubber blade will stay perfectly sharp. For high windows can be used with extension handle (see Optional Professional Equipment Chart).	Janitorial-supply store
DUSTMOP	14" or 18" cotton head, rotating handle	For use on all hard floors. Fast and efficient; lasts for years. Use dust treatment (see page 318) for best results. Shake out and vacuum head regularly; launder when dirt-saturated, then re-treat.	Janitorial-supply store
SPONGE MOP*	10" or 12", professional-quality sponge mop with no-stoop, easy-pull wringer and changeable head	For damp-mopping in homes with a small amount of hard flooring.	Janitorial-supply store
LONG-HANDLED FLOOR SCRUBBER*	Long-handled tool with 5"x10" nylon scrub pad	Also called a Scrubbee Doo or Doodlebug. For effortless scrubbing of hard floors, showers, baseboards, glass, concrete—almost anything. I wouldn't trade mine for a gold-plated floor machine. The holder comes prepacked with pads of three different strengths for light, medium and heavy-duty scrubbing. Dustmop and wax applicator heads also available.	Janitorial-supply store
FLOOR SQUEEGEE*	18" push-pull. Ettore is a good brand	For floor-cleaning, picking up water, and drying sidewalks and garage floors. Use instead of a slop mop when stripping or refinishing a hard floor. See pages 316-330 for detailed instructions on using a floor squeegee when stripping a floor.	Janitorial-supply store

ITEM	SIZE/TYPE	USE	SOURCE
BOWL SWAB *	Cotton or rayon head on plastic handle	Enables you to use bowl cleaner neatly and safely. Swab is used to force water out of toilet bowl (see p. 370), soaked with bowl cleaner, then swabbed around interior of bowl.	Janitorial-supply store
MATS (indoor and outdoor) *	3' × 4', 3' × 5', or 3' × 6' — nylon or olefin fiber on vinyl or rubber backing for inside or covered exteriors. Use a synthetic grass-type or rough-textured nonperforated mat for outside.	Help keep dust, grit and other debris from being tracked in. Absorb mud and water from foot traffic.	Janitorial-supply store
UPRIGHT VACUUM *	12" 6 amp commercial beater-brush model with 12" head. Don't buy half a dozen attachments; get a long cord.	For carpet and rug vacuuming.	Janitorial-supply or vacuum store
WET/DRY VACUUM	10-gallon metal or plastic tank. Be sure you get one with a rust-resistant tank. And get squeegee, upholstery and edge tool attachments with it.	Can be used like a canister vacuum for all household vacuuming, as well as to pick up water when scrubbing floor, to pick up spills and overflows.	Discount, hardware or janitorial-supply store
NEUTRAL ALL-PURPOSE CLEANER *	Concentrate — gallon or packet size	Dilute as directed for mopping, spray-cleaning, cleaning painted surfaces, and all general cleaning where a disinfectant isn't needed. Won't damage household surfaces.	Janitorial-supply store
DISINFECTANT CLEANER *	Quaternary type, concentrate — gallon or packet size	Dilute as directed for use in bathroom-cleaning and wherever else sanitation is essential.	Janitorial-supply store

ITEM	SIZE/TYPE	USE	SOURCE
*FAST-EVAPORATING GLASS CLEANER**	Concentrate—gallon or packet size	Dilute as directed to clean mirrors, small windows, appliances, chrome, etc.	Janitorial-supply store
*HEAVY-DUTY CLEANER/ DEGREASER**	Concentrate—gallon or packet size	For tough cleaning jobs where grease is a problem (vent fans, top of refrigerator, etc.).	Janitorial-supply store
COMMERCIAL WAX REMOVER	Nonammoniated, 1-gallon size	For removing wax from hard floors.	Janitorial-supply store
*FLOOR FINISH ("WAX")**	1-gallon size, metal interlock self-polishing	To protect all hard floor surfaces— wood, tile, linoleum, sealed concrete and no-wax floors.	Janitorial-supply store
*OIL SOAP**	A mild soap often made of vegetable oil	Safely cleans and leaves a soft sheen on wood furniture, paneling, etc.	Discount store or supermarket

Optional Professional Equipment

ITEM	SIZE/TYPE	USE	SOURCE
EXTENSION HANDLE*	4' to 8' aluminum or fiberglass, rubber handle	Lightweight, easy to use. Extends from 4' to 8' to safely reach high places. Fits squeegees, window washing wands, paint rollers, etc.	Janitorial-supply store
WINDOW WASHING WAND*	10" or 12" aluminum holder with fabric head	Use to apply cleaning solution to windows prior to squeegeeing. Great for high windows and high dusting. Fits extension handle.	Janitorial-supply store
WET MOP*	16 oz. rayon/cotton; Layflat is a good brand. Screw-type handle enables heads to be replaced easily.	For damp-mopping if you have a great deal of hard flooring.	Janitorial-supply store
MOP BUCKET*	18-quart metal or plastic with self-contained roller wringer.	If you wet-mop, the self-contained wringer saves injuries from hand-wringing. Use for mopping or as a punchbowl at a janitor's wedding.	Janitorial-supply store
PUMICE STONE*	Small bar or block of pumice	To remove accumulated hard-water ring in toilet. (Not for use on tubs, bold-colored fixtures or tile.) Always wet before using.	Janitorial-supply store
PHOSPHORIC ACID CLEANER*	Professional-strength (8% or 9%), 1 quart	To remove mineral deposits from tile and fixtures.	Janitorial-supply store

ITEM	SIZE/TYPE	USE	SOURCE
PROFESSIONAL ALL-PURPOSE SCRUB BRUSH	Nylon bristles and handle; also called utility brush	For cleaning textured or indented surfaces without getting your hand wet or scraped.	Janitorial-supply store
CLEANING CADDY	Plastic (pick a bright color so it's easy to keep track of)	The easy way to carry all your supplies with you as you clean from room to room. Use a caddy, too, to keep all you need to clean a particular area (such as the bathroom) right there in the room.	Discount store or janitorial-supply store
ANGLE BROOM *	Professional-quality plastic broom such as the Rubbermaid 2021, with split-tip nylon bristles.	For quick cleanups, sweeping small areas, and doing edges and corners before vacuuming or dust-mopping.	Janitorial-supply store
PUSH BROOM *	Professional-quality with 18″ or 24″ head, nylon bristles, handle brace	For sweeping sidewalks, driveways and unsealed concrete.	Janitorial-supply store
PET RAKE *	12″, crimped nylon bristles	For removing pet hair from furniture, bedding, carpets and clothing.	The Cleaning Center

Green clean

In the old days, "white" and "shiny" was what we were all after. Now, with ozone depletion, pollution, litter, algae overgrowth, toxic waste, and too much solid waste of any kind to worry about, keeping things "green" is the battle cry of concerned cleaners. None of us wants to ruin our home planet while cleaning, so strong solvents, acids, and other dangerous chemicals and abrasive cleaning materials are getting pretty unpopular in the social circle of the clean. I agree, the real clean is green, and here are some simple, practical things you can do to help out:

1. Buy good, solid cleaning gear and take care of it
Brooms, squeegees, vacuums, etc., can last twenty-plus years. That means less energy and fewer raw materials used manufacturing, and less worn-out tools being disposed of.

OK ...THIS IS DEFINITELY 20TH CENTURY STUFF... SEE THAT BOTTLE OF CLEANER? THAT EXPLAINS THE ABSENCE OF VEGETATION WITHIN FIVE MILES...

2. Simplify
You don't need fifty different cleaning preparations, scores of cleaning machines and attachments. Reread page 233.

3. Use concentrates
If you get premeasured cleaner concentrates (see page 261), you can bring a year's worth of supplies home in a small sack. Fewer bottles and containers will be left to litter and to bury. Not transporting all that water also saves on shipping and energy costs.

4. Do it right
Skillful cleaning cuts 75 percent or more of the time you spend cleaning, and that means three-quarters, too, of all the lights, heat, water, gas, and other energy consumed cleaning. And it prevents premature wear and destruction of paint, carpet, hard flooring and other household furnishings and surfaces.

5. Use no more than you need
And use the gentlest cleaner that will do the job (see page 275).

6. Take advantage of preventive measures
Use mats, maintenance-free design, sealing, etc. This will cut down the need to redo or to clean at all, saving energy, supplies, packaging, etc.

If we all took just these six steps tomorrow, it would help a lot every day. Remember, you don't have to wait until everyone else does it. Be a leader: think green, and white will take care of itself.

Relax, & Work Less

A big event was coming to a small town and in preparation, the townspeople resolved to clean the hardwood floor in the village recreation center. They decided to scrub all the dirt and old wax buildup from the floor and apply a new coat of varnish. The committee in charge chose four of the best housecleaners and the building janitor to do the job. It took the group of seven most of a Saturday to finish it. Six hours they labored, spending a total of forty-two hours to get the floor ready for the finish application.

Four years later, after much hard use, the floor again needed attention. I had a free day, and since I enjoy cleaning floors, I volunteered to do the job at no charge. I refused the help of other volunteers and the janitor and instead used my sons, who were twelve and eight years old. We showed up at 10:30 and went home early for lunch at 11:45. The job was completed perfectly in 1¼ hours, or for the three of us 3¾ total hours, much less than the 42 hours used by the group. We used three fewer mops, half the cleaners and strippers, and one-tenth the hot water—and did a much better job.

I'm not any faster a worker than most of you, nor did I have any secret tools. Any of you could have done the same thing, using a valuable principle of cleaning: Relax, and work less. To relate this principle more directly to the domestic front, let's take a glimpse of Betty Betterhouse in action.

It's been an unbelievable morning. In addition to her own seven children, fourteen friends and relatives, caught in a snowstorm, were overnight guests in her home. They consumed dozens of whole-wheat pancakes, eggs, and other breakfast goodies. Two hours later, Betty finally saw her unexpected guests depart and the children off to school. She then turned to restoring her kitchen to livable condition. Drops of batter, jam and grease covering her stove and countertop were now hard and dry. Betty began scrubbing one end of the counter furiously. Finally loosening (or wearing away) the spattered batter in one spot, she'd move on another few inches to grind some more of the droplets away. Fifteen minutes of exhausting effort later, the counter was presentable.

Eliminate— Saturate— Dissolve— Remove

Betty could have saved more than ten minutes and been easier on the countertop surface if she had used the cleaning principle my sons and I used on the floor. You could call it the universal law of cleaning: Eliminate—saturate—dissolve—remove. You can do 75 percent of your cleaning with your head, not your hands—because 75 percent of soil removal is done chemically, not by elbow grease. Scrubbing to clean something went out with beating your clothes on a rock by the riverside.

Betty needs only to sweep all the loose food particles from the countertop (*eliminate*: 15 seconds). She should then soak her dishcloth in soapy water and generously wet the entire area (*saturate*: 15 seconds), giving the liquid a few minutes to soak and loosen the spatters (*dissolve*). Then she merely has to wipe the mushy residue off (*remove*). Just a few minutes for the entire job.

Of course, many of us have been doing this for years, not only on our countertops, but on appliances, floors, walls, sinks, tubs, shower stalls, automobiles, and four hundred other places that might have used Betty's old time-consuming system. Hard soap crust on the bathroom sink where the hand soap sits can take several minutes of scrubbing, but if it were sprayed or dampened first, it could be wiped off in seconds. Almost everything will clean *itself* with water and the right chemical. Water is practically free and with a few cents' worth of chemicals it can replace hours of your time if used according to the principle outlined above. It's incredibly easy to apply the right solution and wait.

Leave. Read. Rest!

Apply more solution in another area, or do anything you want while the solution's chemical action loosens and suspends the dirt. Unless you get your kicks out of scrubbing, there's not much reason to scrape and grind soil off.

The basic principles of cleaning

Cleaning should be done with your head, not your hands ... in *four basic steps*:

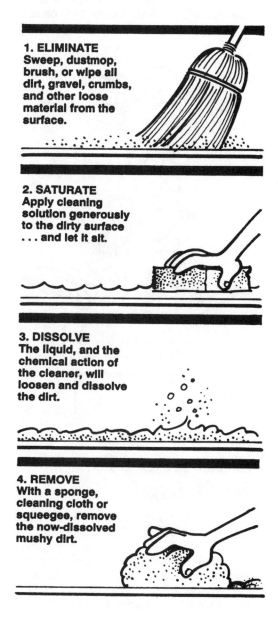

1. ELIMINATE
Sweep, dustmop, brush, or wipe all dirt, gravel, crumbs, and other loose material from the surface.

2. SATURATE
Apply cleaning solution generously to the dirty surface ... and let it sit.

3. DISSOLVE
The liquid, and the chemical action of the cleaner, will loosen and dissolve the dirt.

4. REMOVE
With a sponge, cleaning cloth or squeegee, remove the now-dissolved mushy dirt.

I've watched people try to clean the grease and dust settled on top of their fridge. They wipe the cleaning solution on—and before it has time to break the gunk down and release it from the surface, they start scrubbing furiously. Let the solution do the work! By using the simple principle of eliminate—saturate—dissolve—remove in all cleaning, you can cut time and energy expenditure as much as we cut the floor job for the town recreation center.

On your house floors, for example, remove the large, obvious objects (forks, overshoes, yoyos, dog bones), then spread the solution on as large an area as you can handle before it dries out. As you're finishing at one end of the room, the solution you first laid down is working actively on the dirt, old wax, spots, stains, and marks. When you return to the first area and begin to mop, wipe, or lightly rub it clean, the area you just left is now under heavy attack by the liquid, and most of the cleaning will have been accomplished by the time you get there with the mop.

When we cleaned the big floor in 1¼ hours we spent almost no time scrubbing. We spread the cleaning solution and I ran over the surface with a floor machine (I could also have used a hand floor scrubber—see the Equipment Chart, page 264). I didn't try to grind or scrub the floor clean—I covered it quickly to loosen the surface dirt so the chemical solution could do the work. By the time I reached the far end of the room, the solution spread on the first part had dissolved and suspended the dirty old wax. The next pass over the same area caused every drop of dirt and wax to come off. We immediately squeegeed the floor and picked up the gunk with a plain old dustpan and put it in a bucket. (This eliminated the need for a "slop mop.") The floor squeegeed

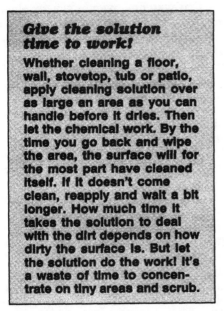
(see Equipment Chart, page 264) clean, then only needed to be mopped with clear water. One mop bucket did the whole floor!

Abrasion evasion

Using powdered cleansers and steel wool to grind dirt off surfaces has become a ritual with too many homemakers. With the same generosity they use to apply powder to the baby's rump, they coat their sinks with cleansing powder and attack them with brisk rubbing. You can actually hear the results as the grinding abrasion quickly removes stains and spots—along with the chrome or porcelain on the unit. The cleanser then has to be flushed off. Some of it will set like concrete in the gooseneck of the sink drain, on the floor, and on the fixtures. The light scum that remains on the sink or tub has to be rubbed and polished off, again wearing away the surface. The damage is gradual but inevitable. On fiberglass or plastic sinks, tubs and other fixtures, the damage isn't even that gradual. Fiberglass isn't as tough as the old porcelain and

enameled iron. It damages easily and, once damaged, is a pain to clean.

Even more important, you lose time cleaning by the abrasion method. You should be relaxing to the cleaning principle *eliminate—saturate—dissolve—remove*. It really works. Discipline yourself to use it, and you'll reward yourself with two hours of free time out of the four hours you once wasted grinding and scrubbing away!

Beware of buildup!

In cases where all the dirt and wax won't quite come off and scrubbing seems called for, it's generally your own fault—by failing to perform good, regular cleaning, you've allowed a thick layer of wax and dirt to build up. Buildups of various kinds are the greatest obstacle to simple cleaning; they're best exemplified by the old villain hard water. Look at the brand-new sparkling tile in your shower, or your exterior windows. They're going to get hard water on them from use, accident or irrigation. Residue starts with an innocent thing called a drop. A drop doesn't seem much of a bother, because if unmolested, it will evaporate away.

At least it will *appear* to leave. A closer examination reveals that each drop has something called mineral salts, which slide to the bottom of the drop as it evaporates. Though the drop appears to have vanished, a slight deposit of mineral salts remains. Beginning so insignificantly and unseen, it's ignored. Again water is splashed on the surface, new drops form in the place occupied by previous drops, and leave their mineral marks to unite with the existing residue. Six months, sixty showers, or twenty sprinklings later, that innocent first drop has become hard-water buildup. If kept clean daily, or in many cases even weekly, it's a two-minute instead of a twenty-minute job. If done annually or "when I get around to it," it's a surface-dam-

aging, chemical-squandering experience that greatly embitters one's attitude toward sanitation.

Less is best

When faced with a cleaning problem, always try to solve it with the gentlest cleaning solution or approach first. Don't call in a backhoe when a shovel will do. Aggressive cleaning methods may be necessary for very difficult situations, but they can also injure or destroy household furnishings and surfaces. As a cleaning product salesperson once put it, "Only get as tough on a stain as the stain demands." If rinsing with water will remove a stain, why start bleaching it? Don't reach for the heavy-duty cleaner till you've tried the all-purpose cleaner first. Don't scrub when you could soak. Don't scrape with a knife or razor till you've tried your fingernail first. Don't resort to a metal pot scrubber till first a white, then green nylon pad proves powerless. Less is best!

Grease removal

Removing grease is something we're especially interested in after our hands start sticking to the stovetop or the cupboard doors. Grease buildup occurs inside and out, as dirt is trapped and glued to things by airborne oils from cooking, heating, smoking, candles, auto emissions, etc. You'll have a real struggle cleaning greasy things if you don't use the right solution. Grease is acid, so a cleaner from the opposite end of the pH scale—alkaline—is what's needed to dissolve it.

This is why ammonia—which has a high pH—works. The more alkaline a cleaner, the more grease-cutting power it has. A lot of heavy-duty cleaners on the market are designed to dissolve grease, and janitorial-supply stores sell "degreasers."

I attack grease in two ways:

1. *For light degreasing*—Fill a spray bottle with a solution of heavy-duty cleaner. Spray it on and let it sit longer than usual. Give the surfactants in there time to loosen, dissolve and suspend the grease film. Then wipe dry with a cleaning cloth (see page 381).

2. *For heavy degreasing*—Fill a bucket half full of degreaser solution. Use a white-backed scrub sponge to apply a generous coat of the solution (not so much that it drips and runs) to the surface and let it sit on there as long as you can. Then scrub, rinse and wipe dry to a luster with a cleaning cloth. If necessary, repeat the process.

When you do have to scrub

The right scrubbing tool is the key. If you're cleaning something with deep crevices and textures, then a stiff nylon brush will reach in and dig out the dirt. The kind you want will have a handle to keep your knuckles unscraped and your hands out of the dirt and chemicals. See the Equipment Chart, page 264, for the type pro cleaners use. For most other surfaces nothing beats nylon scrub pads. They have just the right degree of rub to remove rebellious residue, and they have more total contact with the surface than a brush does. The white nylon type can be used safely on most household surfaces—just don't scrub too hard or too long on soft finishes such as plastic or latex paint. Use the more aggressive green nylon pads to

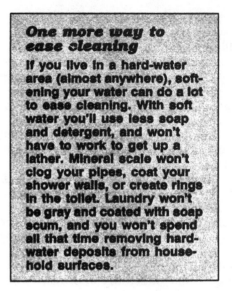

One more way to ease cleaning

If you live in a hard-water area (almost anywhere), softening your water can do a lot to ease cleaning. With soft water you'll use less soap and detergent, and won't have to work to get up a lather. Mineral scale won't clog your pipes, coat your shower walls, or create rings in the toilet. Laundry won't be gray and coated with soap scum, and you won't spend all that time removing hard-water deposits from household surfaces.

remove more stubborn spots and deposits on nondelicate surfaces. The brown or black pads are too harsh for anything but wax-stripping, concrete-cleaning, etc.

Always keep any surface you scrub wet. This aids the action and reduces the chance of damage and scratching. Add more solution when you need to so the surface doesn't dry while you work. If you use a brush, remember that brushes don't hold cleaning solution—you have to pour or spray the solution on first. Rinse the surface occasionally while you work, especially if it's textured or indented, to check on your progress and remove loosened soil. (See page 285 for the right direction in which to scrub.)

Don't bear down on a brush when you use it—that actually lessens the cleaning action. You don't believe me? Go get a brush out of the cabinet, any brush, and scrub lightly, daintily, with just a wee bit of pressure. Notice the points of the bristles are really massaging the heck out of things, loosening the soil and working the soap and solution in, around and under it. Now press "eight axe handles hard" and notice how the brush flattens. Now when you go back and forth, the cleaning ends of the brush aren't doing a thing—the only part of the brush hitting the surface is the sides of the bristles, which are smooth as a bundle of eels. When you add in the slipperiness of soap, that "cleaning action" isn't even tickling the surface!

I had a bristle brush under a 150-pound floor machine once, and my cleaning instructor told me to stick my hand under the edge of the brush. I thought it would rip my finger off, but the sides of the bristles gliding over my fingers were so smooth and slippery they didn't even clean my fingernails. Likewise, notice the next time you sweep a floor how a light stroke allows the bottoms of the bristles (where all the work is done) to contact the floor so they don't miss a sesame seed. Just as light taps of a hammer are usually more effective than a full hard swing, so it is with cleaning.

Keep your working stuff near you!

I've heard claims that a homemaker walks eight to fifteen miles a day doing housework. I wouldn't doubt it. I used to walk one mile per room until I learned to keep my cleaning tools within reach. Too many peo-

ple place their tools and buckets in a central "cleaning station" in the room and constantly walk three, four, even five or six steps back and forth during a project. They spend half of their time and energy traveling.

If you need the exercise, continue to use a central cleaning station. If you want to get the job done and have energy left for a tennis game or bowling or other personal sporting around, figure out how to keep your tools (sponges, buckets, cloths, screwdriver, etc.) within your reach. (For example, if you wash cupboards, set your tools on the counter instead of on the floor. Same with painting.) If you hang the bucket on the ladder or hold it in your hand, it will save the bend and dip all the way to the floor and back up. Try it—you'll be amazed at the time and effort you save!

To keep your tools rounded up and ready at all times, to pick up and use and then put back away, a little plastic cleaning caddy or "maid basket" (kind of like a miniature janitor's cart) is hard to beat. Cleaning aprons sound good on paper but they don't make much sense unless you clean steadily for several hours or so. They also make it hard to bend over, and you bump the walls as you work. I keep a caddy in every area that needs frequent cleaning, filled with whatever is needed to clean that area. Buy a bright color so you can see it easily and don't stumble over it or have to search for it.

More Professional Secrets (For You... at Home)

Since I wrote the first edition of this book in 1981, I've constantly been asked—on radio and TV and at my seminars and in letters—for more "secrets of the pros"; more things we professionals do that make a big difference in the time cleaning takes and in the quality of the results. So here are some more ways to make your cleaning life easier.

Outsmarting interruptions

It's the same old frustrating story: you get right in the middle of something (and have a good head of steam) and someone knocks on the door, the phone rings, the kids start to shriek, you run out of supplies, something breaks, you run across something that you have to stop and deal with or handle. You might call them *interruptions*; I call them housework's number one enemy. Interruptions occur in every activity, but housework has such a humble status, people will deem you not really occupied and think nothing of asking you to stop at their convenience. Life just won't go on hold while we clean. I, too, have literally hundreds of interruptions and demands for immediate attention every day—nearly as many as the average mom—during my work time. If I yield to them all, just like you I'll suffer a mortal efficiency loss, besides being discouraged—if not driven to the rubber room. Here are three things you can do to control interruptions:

1. Wield your mop at unpopular times!

Early, late, on holidays, during lunch—the times when everyone else is sleeping, playing or eating. It's exactly like traffic time. You can go during the most popular to and from times (rush hours)

and count on losing an hour to interruptions (stops and slowdowns)—or go a bit earlier or later or by a little different route and cover the same miles in fifteen minutes. I can write or clean more from 5:00 to 8:00 a.m. than all the rest of the day put together, because there are no interruptions. Society, business, friends, relatives and even kids close down at times. Find those times, grab the bucket and run with it.

2. Clean in short bursts

Cleaning doesn't have to be one long session or giant project. Some of the most efficient cleaning is done in short bursts, which add up to a lot of things done. Fifteen-minute time fragments are much harder to interrupt than a four-hour block of time that you've set aside. Even the busiest of us have small pieces of time available every day, and what are you doing with them now? If you just take advantage of the five-, ten-, and fifteen-minute time fragments that fall your way every day, you may never have to spend all Saturday cleaning again. Take advantage of those TV

commercials, phone calls that leave your hands free, waiting time, etc.

3. Don't yield!

Simply say no. Most interruptions aren't mandatory, like so many of us think. The phone, for example: When it rings, most people run to get it as if they were possessed. Yet most of us haven't had more than one or two true emergency calls in our whole lives. One of my college professors used to say, "My life and home isn't open to any fool with a dime." (Make that a quarter now.) When I'm right in the middle of pouring cement, or up on a ladder painting, and someone comes by or calls, stopping would be a real problem, so I don't. Or if I'm on a job where stopping and then reassembling everything would double the work, I just keep on going. "But Don, it's Ms. Eclair from *Toothpaste Today*" (like God calling). Well, if she were in the middle of writing an editorial, I wouldn't expect her to break her concentration and drop everything to talk to me. So I'll call her back.

Let me share a little secret about interruptions with you: Once you refuse to lay your life and time out at will to family, friends and passing salespeople, they'll begin to adjust their timetables and curb their impositions on you. *You* are the one who sets the mood for the amount of meddling in your schedule. *You* can control it. I'm not saying to force them to make an appointment with you for everything, I'm saying demand appreciation of the value of your time—it works.

When is the best time to clean?

As we all grow more and more aware of time (and ever more short of it, it seems), this is a query I often hear.

Finding the time to clean in a world busy with "better" things to do *is* a big question, especially since cleaning doesn't usually top our morning list of "exciting things to do today." When I started looking at when I clean and at others who seemed to have the cleaning problem licked, I noticed that none of us clean in prime time. A lot of us can't, because we work outside the home during what we think of as "prime time"—but *not* cleaning during prime time is my philosophy anyway.

When we feel good and are really rolling on some other project, stopping to clean means stopping to do something someone else is just going to mess up again, anyway. It produces a certain resentment in us all. When you have momentum elsewhere, that's just not the time to stop and spit-polish a house, even if things are dirty and you've scheduled it, because you'll hate every minute of it.

I don't and won't clean during my prime time. Cleaning isn't hard, nor does it require maximum physical or mental powers—so when body and spirit are in a lull or at loose ends, when I'm not doing much anyway, that's when I jump in and clean.

It's stimulating, exercising, and best of all, I know I'm not squandering my most precious time to do it. So it's almost like getting free time.

If you clean when you're running out of energy you'll find that cleaning gives you a mental second wind and even a physical boost; it can actually be a way of recharging yourself.

And since cleaning doesn't take your full attention, you can do other things while you clean that refresh your mind and spirit, so you almost get "double duty" out of the time. For instance:

1. Note and create

I carry a pad and pencil in my pocket and jot down ideas, impressions, things I suddenly see or understand while shoveling away at clutter and dirt. Some of our best thoughts and inspirations come during half-attention times, and cleaning is certainly one of those. I've often written more creative things in half an hour of cleaning than in half a day at the typewriter with a 200,000 word thesaurus by my side.

2. Rhapsodize

You can listen to music, and then you can *listen* to music—truly hear and savor it. When most of us listen to music our minds are too occupied to pay much attention. When you clean, music can really raise the goosebumps, because cleaning doesn't take concentration and it really benefits from a rhythm backup. I wouldn't be surprised if the Lord ordained cleaning just for the purpose of allowing us a way of appreciating music to the max.

3. Teach the family

How many honest opportunities are left in the world to teach children the basic principles of cooperation and responsibility? Fifty years ago most of the world was agricultural, and parents were with their children all day, week after week, sharing chores. Today about 5 percent of us are down on the farm, and the rest of us hunt and strain to find experiences and challenges to share with our family. Cleaning is one of the few things left. You can formally sit down a fourteen-year-old and lecture about the value of self-esteem and discipline . . . or visit and converse while you clean together. You tell me which will have more impact. Busy hands always beat a moving mouth in getting a message across.

4. Daydream

I have to credit daydreaming with many of my greatest accomplishments. It's not just soothing, it's a source of endless ideas. When you're operating a machine at the construction site, typing ninety words a minute, or doing anything that takes your full attention—including driving—daydreaming is an inefficient if not dangerous thing to do. But with cleaning, you've done it all before—you know how to handle the vacuum, the squeegee, the sponge—so you can click into your "wouldn't this be a great world if" mode as you sail through the soap scum.

5. Focus on the rewards

Whenever I'm assigned to something, before I launch into it, I think first and only of the end result, the rewards after the project is finished. When I start on a room, deciding how and with what to clean it is just reflex; how neat and inviting it'll look when I'm through is what I really focus on. All during the cleaning process I concentrate on the end result. Even those stove rings that are so slow to surrender the burned-on crud, I imagine them as the shining halos they'll be when I'm done, and it makes the work something I actually *want* to do. Weird, maybe, but it works! Remember, all the rewards don't come from life's fun and play activities; most of them in fact come from the tough and responsible ones.

A few more rewards for us cleaners: *Satisfaction*—that you used your skill and the result was good. *Pride*—it sits there looking great and you know *you* did it. *Relief*—it's finally done and you won't have to do it again for a while!

What can I do with the kids when I clean?

Living out West where the average family size seems to be sixteen, this is a question I hear constantly. There had to be a few cleaning problems I haven't solved, and this is one. You can't put off cleaning until the kids are in college. You learn to clean around their schedule—as long as you have to. The baby will boggle you, the teens try you, the grandkids grind down all thought of ever conquering cleaning with kids. But kids actually mold some of the world's best cleaners, giving them eternal surprises and only fragments of time to handle them in. Here are a few ways to lengthen your leash:

- Most of the principles of interruption prevention (see pages 278-280) will work with kids, especially the off-hours approach. When they're down or on nap idle, watch how quickly and cheerfully (and quietly) we clean!

- Shift the overseeing of the younger set to your mate for the occasion:

"One of us does the floors and one of us does the kids ... Which will it be, Wilbur?"

- Send the kids to the neighbors to play. (You can return the favor later in the week when they're trying to clean.)

- Hire a babysitter for a few hours a couple of days a week, or make arrangements with a nearby preschool. Or you might just decide to spend the money on a housekeeper (see page 292). Grandparents are great at watching kids while you clean (and they don't mind feeling genuinely needed either).

- When you *don't* have the kids, do as much "cleaning as you go" as you can. Clean the shower while you shower, the tub as the water goes down the drain, etc.

- A very young child, as long as he's not wet or hungry, should be happy to watch you sweep or fold laundry for a while from a portable baby seat, cradle, playpen or baby "corral" set on the floor nearby—especially if you keep up a lively dialogue or have on some peppy music. There are also nice portable battery-powered baby swings.

- Set up a play area in a basement or other room. Promise a special reward if the kids remain in the area until you're done. (Use a kitchen timer to let them see how much time remains.)

- Certain carefully chosen light chores (such as dusting with a lambswool duster or spot-cleaning) can be done with baby nestled in a carrier across your chest. Baby backpacks leave your hands freer, but they're less safe since you can't see what's going on back there.

- There's always TV, that awful time-eater that converts intelligent offspring to bug-eyed brats. To gain a little time for cleaning, it is slightly better than tranquilizing them. Go for a good, long video.

- Let them help! Even after raising six of our own and leading Scout troops and church youth groups numbering into the hundreds, I continue to be amazed at how much work a kid can do. By the age of eight—the official age of accountability—they can do almost anything as well as adults. And you tell me something better to do with kids while cleaning . . . than having them help clean!

When they're really little, you can buy them their own toy cleaning supplies: vacuum, broom, dustpan, etc., and let them pretend while you do the real thing. During the toddler years, take some of the cleaning activities and make a game of them. Low dusting, as we call it in my business, is ideal for toddlers. Give them a dustcloth or lambswool duster and have them compete with you to reach a finish point. Three- and four-year-olds delight in vacuuming with small hand-held vacuums, and are especially handy for going after those crumbs under the kitchen table. Toddlers also like to shop. Let them use a wagon or a toy shopping cart to "police"—what we pros call picking up the clutter in the area before you vacuum.

Try to stick with sessions of no more than ten minutes so you hold their interest, and keep the games fresh so they don't get bored. Give a prize or a treat when the game is finished. Just bear in mind that cleaning with the kids is a healthy activity for them, but it can be a little aggravating for the "supervisor." When you work with kids, be sure to allow extra time for "training," and reconcile yourself to the fact that they're not going to do things the same way you would.

Yes, you could probably do a better job in half the time, but what you teach them outweighs the little extra effort you have to put into it.

As kids get older, they can help a lot more and even do major jobs themselves.

No sweat . . . and little strain

The wonderful thing about watching professionals perform is that they always make what they do seem effortless. Just remember, when you see pro window cleaners squeegeeing an acre of glass at a stretch, they do that every day and you don't. Try to imitate it, and you can quickly get sore and even injured. How can you keep cleaning casualties at a minimum?

1. Get help

Few of us get hurt doing regular housework. It's that "spring" cleaning campaign, the once-a-year effort and strain, that has the greatest possibility of leaving you with an ache or pain. It's always that giant reach or heavy lift that we justify by saying to ourselves, "It's only this once." That's all it takes. When is anything large or cumbersome moved upstairs or down, for example, without smashed fingers, chipped finishes or grazed walls? An object doesn't have to be super-heavy—"awkward" is enough to put undue strain on the spine, and back injuries are the number one cause of claims in the cleaning industry. After years of seeing even professional cleaners get hurt in such situations I have one directive that I know and live by: Get help. Even the macho man or aerobically fit woman needs help sometimes. Two people reduce the weight and risk by half, and three is even better. Help speeds things up, too.

OK, BOY, C'MON NOW, BEHIND THE TOILET. C'MON.

2. Reduce bending and reaching

"Never trust a maid with clean knees," they used to say. That was probably true in Great-grandma's day, but today if you get your knees dirty cleaning, you aren't doing it right. Bending is tiring and gets old faster than we do. Minimizing bending and reaching is the secret of fast, tireless cleaning. So ask, "How can I put a handle on this?" of every cleaning operation you come across.

Use a long-handled floor scrubber (see Equipment Chart, page 264) for all those chores you used to do on hands and knees. You can also use a long-handled floor scrubber to scrub things like shower walls, grimy outside windows and house siding.

Extension poles (see page 312) make high reaches a cinch and keep your feet on the ground. Extension poles can be used on lambswool dusters and paint rollers as well as squeegees. And they can be used to extend your reach down as well as up.

Another way to reduce reaching is to get a taller ladder or have someone hold the ladder and hand things to you.

3. Lift the right way

When lifting (light things, too) up from the floor, lift with your legs. Let yourself down to the level of the object with your leg muscles, rather than bending over it with your back. After you have a good grip, use your leg muscles to lift you and it back up.

4. Use the right-sized tools

Forget about oversized buckets, for example. You won't be able to lift them when they're full, and you'll slop, spill and strain yourself trying. If you clean with my two-bucket system (see page 385) you won't need more than two

quarts of cleaning solution, anyway.

In all your cleaning tools, get the right size. Ever try hiking in a shoe that doesn't fit? That's about where you are with a tool that's too big or too little for the job at hand. Buy not only buckets but sponges, handles, vacuums, etc., to fit you and your cleaning chores. Or adjust or whittle them to fit if you have to.

What's the best direction to clean?

- Top to bottom. When you dust, start at the top and work down, and the same when you wash walls.

- North and south, east and west. When you scrub anything, you want to go in four directions—first north and south, then east and west. That's because almost everything, even seemingly flat surfaces such as concrete or vinyl, has a grain or texture, even if you might need a magnifying glass to see it. When you scrub in circles, you really only clean and massage one side. When you scrub back and forth, you only get two sides. When you go in all four directions you agitate all the sides of the area and loosen the dirt more quickly and effectively. And you're far less likely to miss places. The carpet-cleaning people taught me this, and once I put it into practice, boy, did it make a difference in all kinds of cleaning.

- Back to front. If you clean a room from back to front (toward the door), you save steps because you walk through the room just once and then work your way back out. If you clean in the other direction, you walk through the room at least twice and probably more.

- Clockwise. Clockwise is another efficient approach, but some people may work better moving around a room toward their left, so for them counterclockwise may be best. This is a matter of taste, but the important thing is to start in one direction and keep going that way.

Switch-hitting

You probably know what this means. Most people are either right- or left-handed and do most or all of their work from that side, but some "switch-hitting" batters can swing from either side (so they can instantly adjust to either a right- or left-handed pitcher). Switch-hitting gives you an edge in cleaning, too. Once you're

really rolling on something, the longer you can keep it up, the better off you are. Once you pick up the duster, dust it all. Once the broom is in your hand, sweep it all. You get in a kind of rhythm this way, and it's a lot faster than stopping and restarting forty times in one afternoon. So when one arm gets tired, switch to the other and don't stop. It'll be awkward at first, but if you can learn to do it you can pick up hours in a day of work.

"Holidays" or misses

In six years as a high school and college athlete, there's one move I never mastered: the "squint stretch" over a newly waxed floor to see if I missed a place. After the applicator is rinsed and hung to dry, the wax bottle put away, and all the furniture back in place, finding a flat or dull spot on the floor can ruin the whole job, as well as your ego. These misses with mops, paint rollers, brushes or wax applicators are what the professionals call "holidays." How do we avoid them? Simply by crossing the area twice for total coverage and then once more for security. Whether cleaning, painting or waxing, pass over every surface a minimum of three times. Do this and your work will never go on holiday. The extra passes take half the time it takes to crane your neck enough to spot all the misses you'll make in a fast single pass.

Give yourself a janitor closet

Even the best cleaning supplies won't do much good if you can't find them when you need them. Since most homes don't have a janitor closet or any respectable space for cleaning materials, you need to engineer your own storage space. First, about 70 percent of the cleaning stuff under your sink is only used once a year, if then. De-junk this antique collection down to the things you really use. Then get a plastic cleaning caddy. Put what you need for the sink area in it, and if you don't have small children you can even leave it under the sink. When it's time to clean you can just snatch the caddy out, set it on the counter and clean from it. That way you won't set acid or corrosive cleaners on household surfaces and leave rings and burns. Keep a similar caddy of supplies anywhere else you clean frequently.

For the big stuff—brooms, mops, buckets, squeegees, the vacuum and its attachments—pre-empt a closet, perhaps near the kitchen, and even if you have to remove shelves to do it, make yourself a cleaning center. Suspend all you can off the floor; hang brooms, mops and brushes by their handles on nice, sturdy hooks (so they get enough air circulation to dry fast and won't warp out of shape). Be sure you hang a treated dustmop, too. If you lean it against the wall or leave it flat on the floor the oil will wick out and may leave a stain. Keep cleaning chemicals on an eye-level shelf (safely out of youngsters' reach) with the labels turned toward you. Keep dangerous cleaning chemicals, insect spray and even plastic bags on one or two high shelves. Use wire racks or bins if you have room to mount anything; they allow air circulation so stored cloths and sponges can dry. I generally clean my scrub pads and squeegee and drop them into the bucket I'll use them with, so they're easy to find and all ready to carry off to the cleaning site.

Don't allow any squatters here. Is your rug shampooer seldom used? Then store it neatly in the garage.

Dress for success

● Shoes

You don't want any high heels or sandals when cleaning, and *never* go barefoot. You're on your feet a lot when you clean, so wear shoes or boots with good support and traction tread. (And to live to clean another day, go for rubber soles when working on wet floors.) Athletic shoes are excellent because they're light, yet sure-footed. Trying to clean in those old, tired slippers will fatigue you fast and greatly increase your chance of tripping and slipping. Besides, you'll feel lean and mean moving around the house in your Reeboks.

● Clothes

I've heard of people cleaning in the altogether, but it only gives new meaning to the term "buffing." Besides, it gets drafty when you take out the trash. You don't have to clean in your aerobics outfit, but I do recommend that you wear loose, comfortable clothing such as a sweatsuit. It's tough to stretch and bend in tight jeans or a miniskirt. I always like to wear a long-sleeved shirt and leave the shirt tails out when I clean. This saves your arms from scratches and burns, and any dead spiders that fall will end up on the floor, not in your pants. (P.S. If you look neat and attractive while you clean, you'll feel better about it.)

● Rubber gloves

Are a cleaner's best friend—use them when you need to. They protect your skin from harsh chemicals, protect your nails, and keep your hands out of yucky, germy messes. Long contact with even mild chemicals can dry out your hands, and some of the more toxic ones will not merely irritate or burn your skin but be absorbed right through it. (Get the good latex gloves with a comfortable flocked lining. I use one size bigger than my hand size for easy on and off.)

● Safety glasses

Were invented to protect you from splashes of acids or strong alkaline chemicals, especially if you're working above your head. If in doubt, don't go without—it's not worth the chance of losing your eyesight. (And no, regular glasses aren't just as good.)

Cleaning you can ignore

Remember, as a kid, when someone did you "dirt," you snubbed them, made believe you didn't know they were there? We all did it, and it was a bad thing to do to people. But it's not at all a bad approach to some of our cleaning chores. Lots of us clean innocent things that don't really need it. Many times I've been led through a home to look at a tub, floor or fixture that won't come clean, and I've been amazed. The thing would have lasted thirty years, but it was on the way out after only ten, because...

"Ma'm, you've cleaned it to death, actually worn it out cleaning it up!" We all know an Annie Septic or Sam Overshine who does this. You could call it overkill, and plenty of us do it because we feel guilty if we don't clean things regularly.

Yet our outdoors is largely paved today, so we don't track in half the mud, gravel, dirt and straw they did in Grandpa's day. Modern homes with better weather stripping, carpeted floors and entryways, and fewer cracks and holes around windows and doors let in less dirt and dust. Soot and smoke from heating was a big problem thirty years ago, too, and it's almost eliminated today.

When I was in college, my cleaning crew and I often had five homes a day to clean. We had faithful clients who always called us for their annual big cleaning—washing down every wall and ceiling, shampooing all the carpet, cleaning all the windows, even painting. As their children grew up and left home, the housekeeping load was lighter, but out of habit they'd still call us to do "spring cleaning" that could have gone undone. Sometimes my cleaning water would be clear as a glass of 7-Up after cleaning three rooms! "We can't find any dirt," I'd tell the owners. And they'd say, "But Don, it's been a year..."

The following are a few tasks you could trim back on, and relieve yourself both of cleaning effort and a guilty conscience:

1. Windows

Glass is a nondepreciable material. No matter how dirty it gets, it doesn't rot or get ruined. If you have to let it go a little while, it won't hurt a thing—just give you a little visual pain (no pun intended). Besides, as long as you're not confronted with it close-up (it's not the top of the coffee table), even dirty glass gives the illusion of clean.

2. Vacuuming

An important procedure, to be sure, but only regularly necessary in the traffic patterns. Lint under furniture and on the edges of the carpet doesn't hurt a thing, so the rest of the carpet can be done semimonthly or even less. Meanwhile, a hand vac can catch those few dustballs or cookie crumbs.

3. Closets

Need to be *de-junked* a lot, but when it comes to actual *cleaning* (walls, floors, ceilings)—closets just don't get dirty. You might want to clean the closets once when you're moving into an older home, but then forget them for at least the next decade.

4. Ceilings

People seem to clean the ceiling every time they do the walls, which is really overkill. Ceilings just don't get the same fingerprints and bumps that walls do, so leave them till about every third or fourth time. If a heat register mars a section of a ceiling just clean the buildup around the vent—don't feel like you have to do the whole thing.

5. Pits

We all own something with a pitted or indented surface (generally a floor), and it drives us crazy trying to get it really clean. This is a flaw in the design, not in your cleaning prowess, so don't let it get you down. If the dirt doesn't lift out or dissolve away with one or two passes of a scrub brush, then leave it and call it shading. No one will know. When the dirt fills in to the top of the pits, just call it a "design correction." (You can also alleviate the problem by filling the pits with clean wax.)

6. Silverware

I've never understood this one. People polish silverware and put it up, just so they can take it out and polish it again. When they're busy feeding their faces, most people won't notice whether it's stainless steel or sterling, anyway.

7. Carpet shampooing

My wife and I went ten years in our new house without shampooing the carpet, and I own hundreds of commercial carpet shampooers, some right on the premises. The carpet continued to look good though we had seventy and eighty kids over for church socials, two hundred employees for picnics, and fifteen grandkids dragging pet goats, muddy boots and old deer hides. Commercial matting inside and out at every entrance and regular vacuuming of traffic areas will do a lot to delay the need for shampooing. You have to judge when to do it, but don't shampoo every year just because that's the schedule. Your home may only need it every two or three years.

8. Cobwebs

These aren't the ultimate index of housework neglect—they can appear overnight. You could argue that they actually aid cleaning by trapping dust and airborne grease along with the bugs. A daily cobweb safari isn't necessary, and if guests are freaked out by a fresh one, be sure to thank them for spotting it for you.

9. Absentee maid service

(For when you're gone.) Yes, there are those so clean-conscious they have a maid service come in once a week, all four weeks they're away on vacation! Why bother? A waste of money, cleaning supplies, electricity and gas.

10. Inside the cupboards

Most of us could get by honorably for ten or twenty years just wiping out the bottom of the shelves. But I see lots of people empty the entire cupboard every year to wash or paint ... it's nonsense.

11. Towel washing

You can use a towel for a week before it's actually dirty (remember, you only *dry* yourself with towels, after you're already clean). Who needs four towels per person per week, including one so big you drag it on the floor trying to dry yourself? Why not save lots of water and washing time?

12. Bathrooms

Okay, we may go potty in there, but bathrooms are actually one of the most sanitary places in a home. Ninety percent of a bathroom is hard surfaces such as tile, porcelain and metal, which don't absorb dirt. And when we're in there, we're usually washing ourselves. If you don't clean the bathroom daily you won't disgrace yourself or endanger your family.

13. Interior chrome and stainless steel

These are usually water spotted, not dirty. It's nice to have gleaming chrome, but your guests would probably rather focus on you than the coffee table frame. As for trying to keep chrome faucets unspotted—why try to create the impression they're never used?

14. Brass and copper

Can either be left to develop a handsome natural patina, or laboriously detarnished every couple of months so that they can develop a new coat of tarnish that will have to be removed again. Which makes more sense?

15. Furniture polishing

No, you don't have to pour or blast on a puddle of polish every week—or even every month. Applying too much oil or wax to furniture may look good briefly, but it creates a sticky, gummy mess in the end.

16. Drying dishes

Guess what—letting them drip-dry in the drainer isn't just easier, it's more hygienic.

If it hasn't been used and it isn't dirty, don't clean it just because it's there. I'm not asking you to relax your cleaning standards, just to examine them. What, in the name of life and love, is of more value—germ-fighting or heart-lighting? Cleaning for the sake of cleaning is silly and unnecessary; cleaning to make things sparkle instead of just have a healthy glow is generally a waste of time and effort.

Gang-cleaning

Sounds like a street rumble, but it's the term we pro cleaners use to describe cleaning as a team instead of by one oppressed cleaner alone. For example, we had an eight-story building to clean once, and each floor took one person eight hours. So we had eight cleaners every night for eight hours, one on each floor, which also

meant the lights on each floor were on for eight hours as everyone worked alone, solely responsible for "his" or "her" area. Then we tried putting all eight people on one floor: one getting rid of the trash, one dusting, one doing desks, one doing bathrooms, two vacuuming, one straightening up, etc. Suddenly we did the whole building in six hours, and the lights were only on one floor at a time, which won us an official award of recognition for the phenomenal savings in energy this meant throughout the whole company. Plus, in the "gang" there was less piddling around and no foot-dragging—the team members motivated and disciplined each other. We humans are social animals, so naturally we enjoy performing in groups more than (pardon the pun) alone in a vacuum.

When more than one person cleans at once, it has the spirit of a team effort. It's easier to take because the total time that each person needs to spend on chores is a lot shorter. Team-cleaning is faster, more fun, less boring, and it even makes de-dirting a social experience. Like many of you, I like to work alone, but you can't really ignore the old adage that many hands make light work. They do, espe-

cially in cleaning. Once everyone knows you're all in this together, some bright spirit will set the pace and watch everyone try to match it!

If you have a gang around, you probably have a megamess. So see if you can organize them for even one hour of group-cleaning. You'll see results, not just arguments about whose turn it is to clean and whose it isn't. And best of all, the work gets done *quickly*.

To clean well as a team, you need a good coach or manager to set things up, just as in any other team sport. In your home *you* get to be the coach (even if it is a working coach). Everyone doesn't just grab a cloth or sponge and start cleaning. Assign specific duties to each person on the team. Each of you takes a different job in the same location: One does windows while another dusts and spot cleans, or one is inside the window and the other is out (you know *that* already, but I bring it up to tell you not to argue over whose side that last little spot or streak is on—it isn't worth a lost workmate ... or a marriage).

When it's time to do a really thorough vacuuming, one person can move the furniture out and back. Or when you do high cleaning, have someone at the foot of the ladder hand things up, saving the cleaner many trips up and down. When you wash walls or paint, it really speeds things up to have an extra pair of hands to help move heavy furniture, remove and replace decorations, go get the tool you forgot, and change water and towels when your hands are in the grime or paint.

After all the tasks are divvied up, the gang starts in on the target area and everyone completes assignments as swiftly as possible. Then the coach makes a quick inspection to ensure quality before everyone moves on.

The secret of successful gang-cleaning is a little bit of planning before you begin. Just as in a football play, everyone has a job to do, a time to do it, and a way to move to get it done. Here's the plan for the living room: Huddle with your two preteen kids. "Okay guys, here's the play. We're going to hit the living room. We'll start at the right of the door as we go in. Hank, you take this sack and pick up all the trash. Work to your left around the room till you get back to the door. Then place the trash bag outside the door. I'll move in after Hank and do the high dusting with this lambswool duster and work my way around the room hitting cobwebs, the top of the bookshelves, lamps, high corners, the top of the valances, and anything else above six feet. Lisa, you follow me, doing the flat surfaces with this treated dust cloth, hitting everything below six feet, including around the legs of furniture and chairs. Hank, as soon as you're done trashing, go back in and help Lisa dust, but you start on the left side of the door and work your way back until you and Lisa meet. I'll follow you guys with a vacuum and by the time you're finished, I should be close behind. I'll make sure we didn't miss anything while you go on and start the dining room. Any questions? Remember, we want to move fast but get the job done well. We've got the #1 team in town, so let's get going."

Gang-cleaning makes people feel as if they're accomplishing something. If you make it a game and even a little bit of a competition, they'll hardly notice they're cleaning. This isn't magic, of course. You still may meet resistance. But when you work right along with the team, it helps a lot to motivate them.

Remember, this doesn't have to be done on a nice, fat, valuable Saturday morning. Forty-five minutes with a gang some evening can clean any house so it'll never need to be touched on a weekend.

Call in a pro

When things get out of hand, when you're in over your head, when there's just too much on the agenda—get help. That's what the professionals do, and they're never ashamed to do it. There are more than one hundred thousand cleaning companies and maid services in the United States. Even where there isn't an official licensed cleaning firm, there are dependable individuals who clean house on a regular basis (which many people in fact prefer over "big company" service).

What kind of professional help?

Just as housework is often more than whisking up a bit of dust and adjusting an off-center lamp, so is there a difference in the types of professional people you can hire. Many maid services are essentially a sort of skim service. They often won't do any of the real housework, like cleaning outside windows, ovens or carpets, washing walls, or stripping and waxing floors. They may do these "big jobs" for a special hourly rate, but usually they just scoot in and dust, vacuum, make beds, straighten, touch up— and go.

Maid services charge by the house or by the visit. Should you use a franchised service or an independent? Independents have both more to gain and more to lose by pleasing or not pleasing you. Think about what the services offered will be worth to you, not only in terms of cost but in terms of time freed for other things. How many hours of help, how many times a week or a month, does your household need to prevent minor chores from backing up?

Hire a maid service on a trial basis to begin with. You might have to go through a few to get the maid you like and trust, but give it a while and you'll find someone reliable who works at a reasonable rate. When you find somebody good, talk to him or her about returning weekly, monthly or whatever. You need service you can count on, and if those you hire know they'll be getting regular work, they can give you a better price.

A professional cleaner (as opposed to a maid service) is the heavy-duty dude. These are the people equipped to do the big jobs calling for big, heavy equipment. Call pro cleaners when you have a big, one-time or seasonal job.

Picking a real pro

You're the only one who can decide when and if you need or want a professional to do your cleaning. But the cleaning business has a high turnover and failure rate. When you decide to go outside, how do you make sure you pick the right professional? Here are some guidelines from someone who knows the business inside out:

● *Don't just believe all the claims on the brochure*

Get and check references. Sure, they'll always give their best, but some are better than none. Remember that you'll probably use this person or outfit for years. They'll be in your house and around your children and valuables often when you're gone, so taking the time to check them out with a few phone calls or letters is well worth it—just as if you were picking a doctor for surgery. Finding out who your well-satisfied friends or neighbors use to do their cleaning can save you some detective work.

● *Ask how long they've been in business*

Anyone who's been around less than a couple of years would make me nervous. If someone lasts in this business over three years, they're generally worth a try.

● *Get a bid*

Anyone who knows the business knows what a given job involves and can give you a bid—not merely an estimate, but an actual price. Have them spell out what they will do, when, and how much it will cost. If someone says they won't, can't, or don't know, they won't get a foot in my house to experiment. Most real professionals have a form that fits all of this and a place for them, you or both to sign. Get it in writing, and hold them to it.

● *Never,* never *pay in advance*

Only 6 percent of a cleaning job is material, so paying in advance is neither necessary nor wise.

● *Get proof of insurance*

We never feel we should have to worry about such things, but an accident that happens on your premises to someone without professional insurance can easily end up your problem. This is one reason you contract work, so the pro will furnish the skill, the muscles and the tools, and assume the liabilities. The cleaners you want will not only be insured but bonded. Remember, however, that even if they do have insurance it doesn't protect the contents of your home. If they ruin a couch cleaning it, they're not insured for workmanship, generally just liability—another reason to choose wisely the people who will be within your walls.

● *Find out who will come on the job*

It's seldom the sharp, clean-cut person who gives the bid. Too often the ones who show up are surly, fresh recruits who can barely read house numbers, and you have to train them. Once a contractor knows you expect and demand the best, that's generally what you'll get.

Prevention: Keeping the Enemy Out

*What do we do with
the dirt on the farm?*

*It flies from the road
and comes straight
from the barn.*

*It pours through the
windows and tracks on
the floors.*

*We give up and just
plant our garden
indoors.*

—Marilyn May

Mats: a must

A new hospital, nestled in a valley with one of the world's most famous ski resorts, had been in operation for two years when its housekeeping personnel retired. Replacements were needed and a professional cleaning service was contracted. Following careful measurement of the space, occupancy and conditions, and after interviews with the retiring staff members, it was concluded that twelve hours of work was required each night to clean the offices, public area, entrances and medical administrative wing. When signing the contract, the owner of the janitorial company made one explicit request: both entrances to the hospital were to be covered with vinyl-backed nylon mats running at least fifteen feet inside both entrances. There had been no mats before, because it was thought they might detract from the hospital's alpine beauty. The hospital's administrator agreed to order the doormats that day.

The cleaning company began its service and was spending twelve hours plus a few extra daily to keep the place up to standard. They wet-mopped nightly, used six treated dust-control cloths on the floor, and had to scrub some areas every week with their floor machines. Anticipating the difference the new mats would make, the cleaning company owner had the sweeping and vacuuming crew keep track of residue collected from the floors throughout the building. Each night a gallon can was half-filled with gravel, sand, thread, pine needles, and every other thing common to a resort area. Three weeks later, the mats arrived and were installed at both entrances.

The first night the mats were in place, the hours of work dropped to ten, and the sweeping residue was reduced to half a quart of gum wrappers, toothpicks, etc. After one week, the new mats reduced the cleaning to nine hours per night. The dust cloths were reduced from six to two, wet-mopping was reduced to twice a week, and dusting to every other night. Cleaning supplies were cut more than 50 percent. The mats cost $240 and were paid for in less than one week in labor and cleaning supplies saved. The hospital noted that fewer people slipped and fell at the entrances, and the mats lasted for four years!

Proper matting alone can save the average household approximately 200 hours of work a year, slow down structural depreciation, and save more than $100 in cleaning supplies. The cost of matting for the average home is about $120. But the 200 hours is big savings for you. That's thirty minutes a day cut from your chore time.

The reasons for such savings are easy to understand if you simply ask yourself, "What is it that I clean out of my house, off my rugs and hard floors, off the walls, off the furniture, etc.?" Dust and dirt are the obvious answers. Where does it come from? Almost 100 percent of it comes from the outside. How does it get inside? Eighty percent of it is *transported* in (the rest leaks through cracks, is airborne or originates inside). The average five-person home accumulates forty pounds of dust a year—dust

Mats protect your house.

295

composed of everything from air pollution particles and topsoil to dead insects and pet dander. Most dirt or residue is carried into the home via clothes and feet.

Professionals estimate that it costs $600 a pound to remove dirt once it's inside. It costs *you* even more in time:

1. You shampoo carpets because of that dirt embedded in them.

2. You strip and wax the floor because of that dirt embedded in it.

3. You change furnace and air conditioner filters more often and dust, dust, dust because of that dirt circulating in the air.

4. You wash clothes more often because of that dirt.

5. Your cleaning equipment and supplies are used up and wear out faster because of that dirt.

Proper matting will:

1. Keep your house cleaner.

2. Reduce the need for shampooing, waxing and washing.

3. Absorb sound.

4. Enhance safety.

5. Improve appearance.

All this saves you both time and money. It takes one piece of equipment and a few minutes to get dirt out of a mat. It takes ten pieces of equipment and hours to get it out of your home!

Where is your carpet the dirtiest? At the entrance, on about a three-by-four-foot square where the matting should be. It's only logical—if dirt doesn't get in, you won't have to round it up. As a person criticizing mats once

said, "Bah! I hate doormats—all they are is dirt catchers!" I rest my case.

Taking advantage of good matting is the smartest, easiest and least expensive thing you can do to cut your housecleaning time. It's easier to vacuum or shake out a mat daily than it is to chase dirt all over the house. Look at the hospital. The distributed dirt and debris were reduced from one-half gallon to one pint. Mats will perform a great service in your home. Don't take my word for it—try it! You'll cry over the lost years of labor

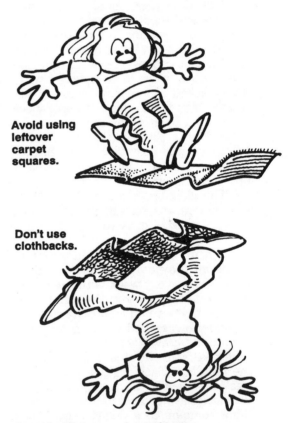

Avoid using leftover carpet squares.

Don't use clothbacks.

Get rid of link or perforated mats.

296

How to mat an entrance

EXTERIOR   **DOOR**   **INTERIOR**

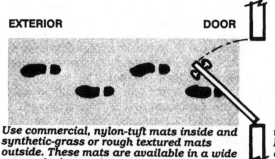

Use commercial, nylon-tuft mats inside and synthetic-grass or rough textured mats outside. These mats are available in a wide range of colors and can be obtained in rolls or in pre-cut sizes at a janitorial-supply house. For best results, the mats should be long enough to allow four steps on each.

and money you've wasted by not getting adequate mats sooner. Instead of scrubbing your floor weekly, you could end up doing it annually. (I've even had one commercial building go *five years*, and the floor finish still looked good.)

If you have good matting, all the fine gravel, grit and dirt that hangs on the bottoms of shoes and scratches and soils things will be out of action. Waxed floors last a long time when they aren't abused by grit. Next time you go into an office building, notice the difference in the floor on the lower level as compared to the upper-level floors. Even if the traffic is the same, the upper ones will last twice as long and look twice as good because the grit doesn't get to them. Traffic doesn't hurt a floor much—it's the abrasiveness of dirt that creates havoc. Keep it out of your home, and you'll keep yourself out of the crouching, scrubbing position. Now, that's the sensible way to clean house—not to have to do it in the first place!

Here are some matting pointers that will advance your goal of gaining thirty "free" minutes a day.

Some mats to sidestep

Avoid decorative mats. We all love to see our name in print—even on a worthless rubber doormat. Get rid of it! It isn't doing much good, and the time it takes to clean around it is probably greater than the cleaning time it saves. Link mats (the kind made from little slices of old car tires wired together) are ineffective for most homes and extremely dangerous for wearers of high heels. Coco mats are more trouble than they're worth because they don't absorb well and they shed. Have you ever tried to clean a coco mat? That alone should convince you not to buy one!

For outside the house, the synthetic-grass-type mats or any rough-textured nonperforated mat with a rubber back is good. These won't rot, they're easy to clean, and they'll knock the big stuff off the shoes or boots of the person coming into your home. Try to get one at least five feet long to cover three or four steps. The exact type of exterior mat to buy depends on the space available, overhead cover (awning or porch), your home and landscaping style, and how bad thievery is in the neighborhood.

On the Inside

The first thing to do is get rid of any carpet samples or scraps you're using for "throw rugs." These items are, indeed, appropriately named. The jute backing and curling edges throw their users into the hospital. They're unsafe, unattractive and, more to the point, inefficient. Get rid of them!

To maintain mats:

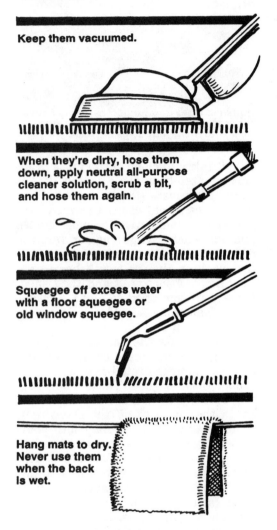

Keep them vacuumed.

When they're dirty, hose them down, apply neutral all-purpose cleaner solution, scrub a bit, and hose them again.

Squeegee off excess water with a floor squeegee or old window squeegee.

Hang mats to dry. Never use them when the back is wet.

At any janitorial-supply store, you can buy commercial grade, vinyl- or rubber-backed nylon mats. This type of mat for inside areas helps to reduce falls and trap loose dirt—the same dirt you'd be cleaning from everything in the house. They are efficient, will last up to fifteen years, and are available in a wide variety of colors. They come in widths of three, four

or six feet, and in any length. The nylon creates a static charge that actually helps pull particles from your shoes and clothes. The mats will absorb mud and water from foot traffic and hold it in their roots. They won't show dirt easily and can be vacuumed like any other carpet.

Some mats will creep a little on some surfaces, and a "rug hugger" type with a textured back can be purchased if you get tired of retrieving the carpet. Or you can get polyester "sticky pads" from a hardware or janitorial-supply store to keep your present mats from creeping or bunching.

An often-forgotten area in our homes that should also be well matted is the garage entrance. Plenty of sawdust, oil stains and project residue get tracked into the house from the garage. Fine silt, sand and gravel often get caught up in the snow that lodges under a car and falls loose on the garage floor. When it melts, the sand and grit are carried into the house by foot. Concrete dust and garage-type soils and dirt are abrasive to carpet and waxed floors.

Apartments, condominiums and motor homes need to be matted, too. The slightly smaller amount of dirt and debris that might get to the eighth floor of a modern apartment building is multiplied by the fact that it's gritty city dirt that has a smaller area over which to distribute itself—hence the soiling and damage to the dwelling can be as acute as in a large, dust-surrounded farmhouse.

A three-by-five-foot mat is an excellent all-purpose size. It's wide

---

It takes one piece of equipment and a few minutes to get dirt out of a mat. It takes ten pieces of equipment and hours to get it out of your home.

enough to cover an average doorway, long enough to cover four entrance steps, and light enough to handle and to clean. An extra three-by-twelve-foot runner can be rolled up and kept for remodeling, parties or wet weather. This extra mat will be a good investment if your traffic, lifestyle and location merit it. It would be an especially good idea for a newly built home, since it's common for a family to move in before the landscaping is completed. The several months of working on the yard generates a lot of mud, and the resulting damage is often unnoticed because the house is new.

Not only will you save thirty minutes a day when you install adequate matting, but your doorways and entrances will be better looking, quieter and safer. Get mats before you start to clean, and you won't have to start as soon or work as long.

Other preventive measures

Now that you have your mats lying in wait for all that creeping dirt, you ought to set up a few more culprit catchers for the things that cause housework. Remember again, the idea isn't to get faster, bigger or better tools to beat the dirtiers. The first principle of cleaning is not to have to do it in the first place. . . .

Cure litter

Make it a hard-and-fast rule in your home that everyone picks up his or her own litter and is responsible for personal belongings. And make it relatively simple for everyone to abide by the rule. Provide waste containers for *every* room in the

The trouble with cleaning up litter is that when you're finished you're right where you should have been before you started!

299

house, and outside where the kids play. Empty the containers frequently, before the contents become attractive to germs, insects and larger animals.

Make sure there are shelves, drawers, racks, hooks and toy boxes enough for everyone to put away belongings quickly and easily. If there's a place to put it, chances are 60 percent better that it'll end up where it ought to (rather than on the couch, the bed, the floor, the stairs).

Prepare

Putting a cover over or under anything that needs protection when you clean, paint, etc., will save all kinds of unnecessary cleaning. We're always tempted to skip this little step and we always pay for it later—with a lot of extra work, if not with ruined objects. So get out those tarps, dropcloths or old newspapers and use them.

Get it out of the dirt zone

What's up and out of the way won't have to be cleaned, and that's the name of the prevention game. So make sure all your unused but needed stuff is hung or cupboarded out of the way of daily traffic that will soil and abuse it.

> **Wrinkles: a condition of creased, crinkled and crumpled that we get with age, and our possessions get when not folded or hung carefully. A little prevention can save a lot of ironing.**

Animals

There's no getting around the fact that house animals create housework and cause damage, but you can mini-mize it. My choice, depending on the animal and where you live, is to keep it outside, but that's not always possible. If you do have an indoor/outdoor pet, consider installing a pet door so it can come in and go out at will. This saves wear and tear on the people door if your pet's a scratch-at-the-door type (and it saves you from being the animal's door person).

Both cats and dogs should be brushed regularly and their claws trimmed. Your vet can show you how to do this. Dogs should be bathed as soon as they start smelling "doggy." An inexpensive pet rake will be a big help in coping with shedding hair (see Equipment Chart, page 264).

Vacuum pet hair off upholstered furniture. Better yet, keep animals off furniture, or designate one chair that's theirs, and keep a throw cover over it that you can wash easily.

Build your cat a good scratching post. Make sure it's tall enough for the cat to stretch full length, and weight the base so the cat can't tip it over. If you cover it with carpeting, use the loopy kind that will engage the cat's claws. But a harsh, scratchy surface like woven sisal, or even highly textured fabric like burlap, is better than carpeting of any kind.

Use a disinfectant cleaner when you clean up after animals.

Pet problems can often be traced to problems with the training process. It's important to spend as much time training your pets as you do loving them. This will reduce pet accidents to a minimum. After you train your pets, make sure that you're trained, too. If you're too tired to change that litter box or take your dogs out to relieve themselves, then you have to take the credit for the puddle on your carpet. Pets try to please you. But when they can't wait any longer, it happens. Pets demand responsibility. Don't allow your pets (and your household furnishings) to suffer for lack of it.

Mildew

Mildew looks bad and can be damaging, but it isn't really a cleaning problem. Mildew is a fungus that thrives on moisture and temperatures between 75° and 85° F. There are five ways to prevent or retard mildew growth:

1. Never put anything away wet (laundry, camping gear, etc.).

2. Well-lighted areas don't agree with mildew. Light prevents its growth and can even kill it.

3. Proper ventilation helps prevent mildew spore growth.

4. Cleaning all mildew-prone areas with a disinfectant solution will slow down or stop growth.

5. Put packets of silica gel in small, enclosed, chronically mildewed places (drawers, shoes). The gel can absorb moisture and minimize mildew growth. Reusable bags of calcium chloride (such as De-Moist) are available for larger areas such as damp rooms or basements.

Cigarette mess

One of the most effective preventive measures you can take is to eliminate smoking from your home. In commercial buildings almost 30 percent of cleaning costs stem from smoking residue, waste and damage.

All of us pay a small fortune for the smoking habit—it costs taxpayers millions of dollars daily. Smoking also causes a high percentage of fatal and damaging fires, and can make many jobs unsafe.

Smoke dirties the windows, yellows the light fixtures (so you don't get all the light you pay for), soils and ruins the acoustical tile of the ceiling, smells up the upholstery, and burns and damages the carpet and floor. Eyes water, lungs fill with smoke, clothes and hair are saturated offensively. Who would consider taking out a miniature incinerator and burning paper, leaves, and trash whenever they got the urge? But that's what a smoker does.

In trying to correct the problem, we designate special smoking areas, make better filters, bigger ashtrays, better vents and room deodorizers, better gargles and tooth polishes, develop lung transplants, etc. But this is like building a bigger drawer, closet, or garage when the others get full: The problem is still there, doing damage, it's just contained.

The simplest, cheapest, most effective approach is to de-junk the habit; then the problem will be cut off at the source.

Keep up

Finally, remember: Dirt by the inch is a cinch; by the yard, it's hard.

Don't get buried alive—clean as you go. Who wants to finish an overhaul, a paint job, or any project and have to clean the entire mess at the end? Clean and put everything back as soon as you finish using it. If you let it all pile up for a big cleaning spree, it's emotional and physical suicide.

And *don't clean things that aren't dirty*. (See "Cleaning You Can Ignore" on pages 288-289.) You can go months without doing windows and vacuuming in certain places. Too many people think they have a moral obligation to do it "every day" or "once a week" or "once a month."

You clean to prevent unhealthiness, ugliness, and depreciation. If a little dirt or dust causes none of these, darned if I'm going to flounder around with a broom and a bucket.

Design away cleaning

Cleaning faster and better isn't the only way to reduce the time and expense of cleaning and maintaining a home. How about designing it away?

You've said it, you've thought it, you've seen it. When you were working on or with something and stopped to say: "Who designed this? It's twice as hard to clean or fix this way. If it had been better/simpler I could have serviced it in minutes instead of the hours it's taking now." The women who have done most of the cleaning for so long have thought of many design ideas that would eliminate or ease some hard cleaning chores. However, men, who do little cleaning, have done most of the building, and so for centuries the same hard-to-clean, -reach, -lift and -move things are built into our homes. Maintenance-freeing design has long been needed, but is only now coming into its own. We'd all like to make things easier to care for, and the logical place to start is the place we spend so much time: our home.

"But my house is already built, so I can't have a maintenance-free home!" *Wrong!* About three-quarters of the possible time-saving changes you can make are in what we professionals call rollover items, like paint, carpeting, furniture, drapes, fixtures, appliances and decorations. In five to ten years these often need replacing anyway, so why not do it with something much easier to clean? It's a sneaky, brilliant, fun way to solve cleaning problems and get rid of the time (and agony) they take.

The more I heard women say "Why do they build things like _____?" the more intrigued I was by the subject of designing to reduce cleaning. So I asked my audiences to share their thoughts on this, and all kinds of bright ideas came rolling in on the best way of all to save cleaning time: Design It Away!

When my collection of material on this subject grew to three-box size and my daughter was working her way through school designing kitchens, we realized there was enough there for a book. After several more years of research and investigation, we assembled

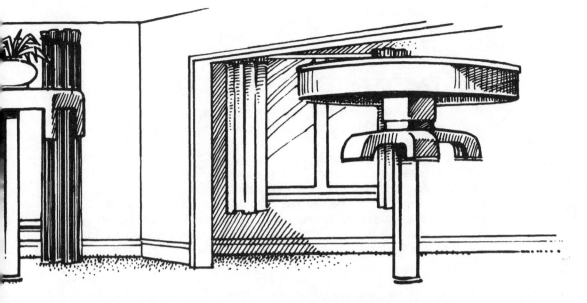

all of this material into a nice volume called *Make Your House Do the Housework*, which Book-of-the-Month Club members and tens of thousands of other people have been using to inspire them in their remodeling, redecorating and new home building. In *Make Your House Do the Housework* (check at your local bookstore), there are hundreds of good ideas for cutting cleaning through low-maintenance design. You'll learn about the wisdom of approaches like camouflage, built-in, wall-hung, better arrangement, artful elimination, and choosing the smart surface, material and color. The thrill and beauty of it all is that when you change even one single thing to reduce its maintenance requirements, those savings in time and effort are repeated day after day, multiplying even one little improvement into thousands of hours (and a lot of cleaning supplies) saved, and a lot of safety risks avoided, too.

Start thinking about it seriously and your blood will boil with anticipation. Design is one sure way to cut cleaning out of your life!

FLOOR CLEANING   PLAN I

HYDRAULIC LIFT FURNITURE

COMPRESSOR AND TANK

Check ✓ *before you clean it*

Fix those items that always slow you up and cause you to do everything more than once (or actually *add* to your cleaning chores).

Some things aren't worth doing. Some *can't* be cleaned. Others will look tacky even when they're clean and orderly. Taking care of these items first will not only make cleaning and maintenance easier, but will make you feel better (which makes everything easier).

Eliminate or remove anything that bugs you—that's inconvenient, no longer functional, or that you just don't like. *Remember*: The first principle of efficient cleaning is not to have to do it in the first place. Check these things before you start:

☐ **Be sure you have plenty of convenient, roomy litter receptacles. You'll do less cleaning and picking up.**

☐ **Be sure you have enough towel racks.**

☐ **Be sure all closets have an adequate supply of hangers.**

☐ **Eliminate furniture you don't use or need. It has no value and magnifies your cleaning chores.**

☐ **Eliminate excess playthings (child or adult). Unused tennis racquets, snowmobiles, motorbikes, TV games that have fallen from favor, old hobby supplies, puzzles with "only one piece missing."**

☐ **Get anything that can be wall-mounted off the floor. It'll make cleaning a lot easier and will curb accumulation. (And eye-level things are easier to see and safer to use.)**

☐ **See that your cooking exhaust is vented.**

- [ ] Stop all dirt and air leakage into the house around windows and doors, etc. Cracks in the foundation, too, let dust and moisture into the house, causing damage and additional cleaning time.

- [ ] Make sure your vacuum works perfectly.

- [ ] Seal all concrete floors for easy maintenance.

- [ ] Paint or seal (varnish) all surfaces that can't be easily dusted, washed or cleaned.

- [ ] Repair/replace all damaged surfaces. Paint, patch or panel so they can be easily maintained.

- [ ] Alter any physical surface or appearance you don't like. Paint it, sand it, cover it or give it away.

- [ ] See that drawer hardware is tight and that drawers slide easily.

- [ ] Make sure that all doors close tightly and easily. A light sanding and two coats of polyurethane or varnish will make wooden doors bright and easily cleanable, and doortops smooth and easily dusted.

- [ ] Be sure that all windows slide and lock easily—and seal any cracks.

- [ ] Repair every leaky or dripping fixture.

- [ ] Fix or tighten all clotheslines, stair railings, etc. Check all the hardware around the house. Remember, a 50¢ screw or bolt can save a $5 hinge . . . a $50 door . . . a $500 robbery . . . a $5,000 fire!

- [ ] Replace burnt-out light bulbs and tighten any parts of light fixtures that need tightening.

- [ ] Get rid of shin and head bumpers (such as sharp edges or protruding legs) on woodwork, furniture, or anything that bashes you every time you pass by or straighten up.

- [ ] Adjust every shelf to the height you really want and need.

Don't Be Caught Streaking Windows

The dreaded task: At my house-cleaning seminars I always spring the question, "How many of you like to clean windows?" This is always good for a chorus of groans from everyone present. Occasionally, about two out of every thousand will raise an eager hand indicating that they, indeed, do enjoy cleaning windows. (Further investigation reveals why: Both have maids to do the job!) That leaves almost 100 percent of homemakers who hate window cleaning.

The reason is simple. After hours of laboriously polishing windows, you think, "At last. I'm finished!" But hope is dashed when the sun comes up or changes angle. Streaks and smears suddenly appear out of nowhere, magnified for all to see. You again give the window the old college try—and the smears and streaks only change places. Re-arming yourself with more window cleaner, rags and gritty determination, you work even harder and faster to get the windows clean, but they seem only to get worse.

Night falls, and so does the curtain, on a crestfallen and discouraged worker. The next morning you go downtown and eye the fifty-story solid glass buildings, the huge store-front display windows, and mumble, "That glass is beautiful . . . but I never see anyone cleaning it. How do they keep it so clean?"

The reason we seldom see window cleaners isn't because those windows don't need to be done—most commercial windows have to be cleaned more often than house windows. But professional window cleaners only take minutes, not hours, to do their job. Homemakers can be just as effective on their own windows if they learn the basic techniques used by professionals.

The first move toward successful window cleaning is to rid your storage cabinet of all the "glass gleam" garbage you've been trying to make work for years. The main reason your windows streak and seem to get worse is the oily, soapy gunk (including homemade concoctions) you smear on them. Pounds of it have been put on, and only part of it wipes off. Gradually you've built up a layer of transparent waxy material that you spread around

every time you try to clean the window. It not only creates an impossible cleaning situation, it also primes the glass surface to hold dust, bug spots and airborne particles. The result is windows that have to be cleaned more often.

Take heart. It hasn't been your fault all these years. Even the chief window washers for New York City's tallest all-glass buildings couldn't get windows clean without streaks if all they used was the stuff sold to most of the public.

The right way

To recover all those lost polishing hours, let's learn to do windows professionally. Go down to the janitorial-supply store and buy a professional-quality brass or stainless steel squeegee (see Equipment Chart, page 264).

Spraying and rubbing are self-defeating — as you can see as soon as the sun comes up or changes direction.

Ettore brand is the best! Don't go to the local supermarket or discount house and buy those recycled-truck-tire war clubs they call squeegees. These won't work well even in a professional's hands.

There are even tilt squeegees available now that are only slightly more expensive than a standard squeegee. They have a handle that enables you to tilt the blade so you can clean several windows from a single spot (you don't have to stand directly in front of each window to clean it). I saw a man stand on his front porch with one and clean all of the upper and lower story windows without changing location!

Go to a janitorial-supply store and buy a professional-quality squeegee. Make sure the rubber blade extends ¼" beyond the frame at both ends, and keep the blade undamaged — don't do anything but clean windows with it.

Pick up some window-cleaning solution, which can be either ammonia, or ordinary liquid dish detergent. Both will work well if you use them sparingly; resist the tendency to add too

Six steps to sparkling windows

1. Put a capful of ammonia or a few drops of dish detergent in a bucket of warm water. There is always a tendency to add too much soap or detergent — this is what causes streaks and leaves residue.

2. Wet the window lightly with the solution, using a clean sponge, soft-bristle brush or window washing wand. You don't need to flood it. You're cleaning it, not baptizing it! If the window is really dirty or has years of "miracle" gunk buildup, go over the moistened area again.

much chemical or detergent to the solution—this causes streaks and leaves residue. One capful of ammonia or four or five drops of dish detergent is plenty for each bucket of warm water.

Before starting to squeegee, I always take a damp cloth and run it around the entire outside edge of the window. This removes the cobwebs and debris that collect around windows, so

3. Wipe the dry rubber blade of your squeegee with a damp cloth or chamois. A dry blade on any dry glass surface will "peep-a-peep" along and skip places.

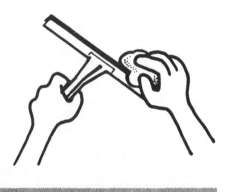

4. Next, tilt the squeegee at an angle to the glass so that only about an inch of the rubber blade presses lightly against the top of the window glass (not the window frame or the house shingles). Then pull the squeegee across the window horizontally. This will leave about a one-inch dry strip across the top of the window.

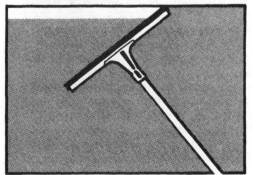

5. Remember all those drips that came running down from the top of your clean window when you tried squeegeeing once before? Well, by squeegeeing across the top first, you've removed that potential stream. Place the squeegee horizontally in the dry area . . .

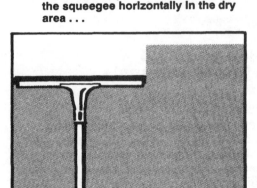

6. . . . and pull down, lapping over into the dry, clean area each time to prevent any water from running into it. Wipe the blade with a damp cloth or chamois after each stroke. Finish with a horizontal stroke across the bottom to remove the water puddled there.

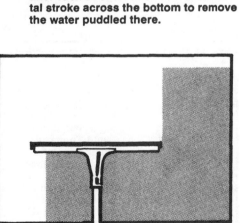

they won't end up on the window itself during cleaning.

A window can be cleaned from either side or from the top using this technique. Always be sure first to squeegee off that top inch of the glass to eliminate potential dripping. Wipe off the bottom of the window sill with your damp cloth when you're finished.

Never wash windows in direct sunlight if you can possibly avoid it. The solution will dry too fast and streak the glass. If you have to clean in bright sunlight, be extra sure not to put too much cleaner in the water, and squeegee *fast!*

How to get rid of those last spots

After completing a window, you undoubtedly will detect a tiny drop or squeegee mark or two and a little moisture on the edges of the glass near the frame. Your old tendency was to snatch a dry cloth and with a fingertip under it wipe off the edge. I can assure you this will leave a finger-wide mark right down that edge. Once you notice that, the temptation will be to wipe it again, this time with a bundled cloth. Then you'll have a four-inch mark and will have to reclean the whole window.

After squeegeeing the window, just

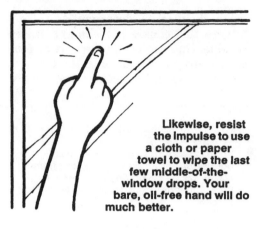

Likewise, resist the impulse to use a cloth or paper towel to wipe the last few middle-of-the-window drops. Your bare, oil-free hand will do much better.

leave those little beads of side moisture. They'll disappear and you'll never see them. Your friends won't, either, unless they bring their opera glasses with them.

As for middle-of-the-window drops or tiny squeegee lines, do not use a cloth. (*Law:* There is no such thing as a lint-free or mark-free cloth in window cleaning.) Because you've been working in the solution, your bare hand will be oil-free, and you can use a dry finger to wipe marks away without leaving a blemish.

The squeegee method really is as easy as it sounds. It's three to five times faster than the old way. It will use only a penny or two worth of cleaner and leave your windows pure and clean to repel particles and dirt.

It's worth the effort to work on your squeegee technique for a while, since it will be awkward at first. And all of that accumulated gunk might take a little extra effort to remove. Once you catch on, you'll love it and wish you had more windows to do.

Learning to clean windows quickly and effectively will change your outlook on life. You'll cherish the cute little handprints, enjoy watching frustrated insects slip off the glass, and even tolerate the sweet birdies who occasionally befoul your windows.

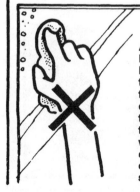

As for the tiny beads of water left at the edge of the frame, leave them! They will evaporate unnoticed. Avoid the temptation to wipe with a finger or cloth or you'll end up with a ½" streak.

Problem areas

Squeegees will work on any normal household window (but not on textured or stained glass, for instance), and they come in sizes to fit the task at hand. Squeegees can also be cut with a hacksaw to custom-fit small panes if you so desire. Pull the rubber blade out of the channel before cutting, and then cut the rubber about one-quarter inch longer than the remodeled blade (so it will extend one-eighth inch at each end).

Close quarters cleaning

There are times and places in small, confined areas where a spray bottle of fast-evaporating glass cleaner is more efficient to use (small panes, handprints on glass entrance doors, decorative doors and windows, etc.). You can obtain an inexpensive solution of this type in concentrated form from a janitorial-supply store, dilute it with water, spray it lightly on soiled glass, then buff it dry with a cotton cloth or a "hard" (read "cheap") paper towel (the soft, expensive ones leave lint like crazy). *Don't* use newspaper. Only slight sheens and streaks are left when you clean this way, and they're seldom noticeable in such small areas.

My advice regarding tiny little windows is to let them go as long as possible, because the optical illusion created by the small surfaces hides marks, specks and smudges. When they do need cleaning, depending on their size, use either a squeegee or a spray bottle filled with glass cleaner.

If you're not too particular, I'd just brush off the outside, hose them down to rinse them, and call it good. I don't think any window in a home is worth hours of work. Big windows show dirt and streaks more readily than small panes, which look more "romantic" when they're a bit hazy.

Mirrors

Once people get enthused about a squeegee, they want to use it on everything, even mirrors. *Don't!* Notice some mirrors have black circles under their eyes (black edges)? This means too much moisture was used cleaning it and the moisture dripped, leached, or otherwise worked its way to the edge of the mirror. When the cleaning solution hit the silver on the back, the chemicals oxidized it. In fact, you shouldn't even spray a mirror (or TV or computer face) with a spray bottle because of possible renegade moisture. Instead, spray into a soft cloth and then wipe. For mirrors, too, a glass cleaner is best. It's fast, inexpensive and safe (as long as you keep it off the edges!).

For no-smudge mirrors, use full-length downstrokes when you wipe. Then with a final swipe across the bottom, eliminate that start-and-stop line.

Plexiglas windows

Plexiglas should have been called plexiplastic because it doesn't clean like glass at all. Solvents can eat right through it, and anything slightly abrasive (including ordinary dust) will scratch, cloud and mar it. So "soft" is the word—soft cleaner, soft cloth, soft touch. There are special Plexiglas cleaning solutions that help clean and clear it—don't use anything else!

Don't attempt to wipe—or squeegee—Plexiglas before you rinse it well with water to remove any particles; otherwise, they will catch underneath your cleaning cloth or squeegee blade and scratch the surface. And if you squeegee, keep your blade extra clean and make sure the window *stays* wet the whole time you work on it.

Thermal windows

Many of the thermal or double-pane windows will fog up when cold, so if the streaks don't come out, check: They're probably on the inside. You can't clean them; 95 percent of the time if you want this kind of streak gone it means a new window!

Cleaning outside windows

As a precleaning precaution, look at the window carefully before whipping out your fine cleaning tools. Often the window, frame and sill are plastered with bird droppings, mud, hornet nests, and spider webs complete with dried flies. If so, give it a quick hose-down first to flush it off. It only takes a minute and makes the final cleaning neater and safer for your squeegee blade.

If you have to clean glass outside on a below-freezing day, mix your cleaning solution 50-50 with some "antifreeze"—isopropyl or denatured alcohol.

For dead bugs and other debris lying in the bottom of a sliding window channel, spray generously with neutral all-purpose cleaner and let it sit for five minutes, till it all turns soft. Then wrap a cleaning cloth around a screwdriver blade, insert it in the track, and run it up and down to dislodge and absorb the dirt. Repeat until the channel is polished clean. It sounds primitive, but it's the fastest and best method I've found.

High windows

When windows are out of reach for easy hand or ladder squeegee work, a pole or extension handle of any length you can maneuver will work on the same principle surprisingly well. Clean glass always looks good. A few tiny smudges or drips won't hurt anything, so don't try to be a perfectionist. It isn't worth the stress or time. I use an Ettore extension handle that extends from four to eight feet. Even second-story windows are quick to do, and your feet never leave the ground. You don't need a ladder and there's no safety risk.

When you use an extension pole, instead of wiping the squeegee after each stroke, just hit the pole with the palm of your hand to release excess water from the blade.

Washing high windows

When windows are out of reach for easy hand or ladder work, a squeegee handle of any length you can maneuver will work with surprising accuracy. I use a handle that extends from four to eight feet. A few tiny smudges or drips won't hurt anything, so don't try to be a perfectionist.

EXTENSION HANDLES

Second-story windows can be done easily and your feet never leave the ground. No ladder is needed and there's no safety risk.

Hard water deposits

If you have hard-water buildup from sprinkling your lawn or irrigation, don't use abrasive cleanser or the glass will cloud and scratch. If it isn't too thick and hasn't been on there too long, phosphoric acid cleaner will remove the deposit. Spray the solution on, let it work a minute, then scrub it with a white nylon scrub sponge until it dissolves. Rinse and repeat if needed. If you have a real accumulation welded on, it'll take several applications, with the phosphoric acid left on for a longer time. Don't lose patience if it doesn't wipe right off. If after all this it's still white and opaque, your window may be etched and damaged. No cleaner I know of can repair this. Replace the glass or draw the drapes. Keep hard water off your windows with regular maintenance or an adjustment in your sprinkling system.

Keep your eye on the blade

If your squeegee blade gets damaged and starts leaving a line of solution on your windows, pull it out of the channel, turn it over, and snap it back in. When the blade finally wears out, just buy a new blade and snap it into the squeegee channel. (Be sure ⅛ inch of the blade extends beyond each end of the channel.)

When window casings and trim get older, paint and putty chips catch under the squeegee blade and make cleaning miserable. New aluminum or well-maintained wood won't give you any grief. Taking the time to sand and repaint or reglaze will save you many cleaning hours.

Window scraping woes

A lot of window damage is done when paint, labels or mortar are being removed from windows. Here's the right way to go about cleanup operations on glass:

1. Before you start scraping a window with anything, try to soak the foreign material off with plain water. Then try a solvent such as De-Solv-it.

2. Always keep the glass surface wet when scraping.

3. Use only razor-sharp blades or flat razor-type tools in a one-way forward motion, then lift the tool off the glass and make another forward stroke. Never go back and forth. Pulling the tool back and forth will eventually trap a piece of grit or sand behind and under the blade, which will scratch even a wet window. (You'll never rub *that* one off with a de-oiled bare hand, either.)

Dragging a scraper backward or back and forth can trap sand or dirt under the blade, causing it to scratch the glass.

4. Don't use abrasive scrub pads or compounds on window glass.

5. Be *careful*. Too much pressure, or an abrupt or careless motion, could get you a nasty cut as well as a broken pane.

In general, windows are high-maintenance areas, and there's a lot more than glass to keep clean and dust-free. Fortunately, just as professional window-washing methods can have glass looking its best with minimum effort on your part, a little attention to technique can keep your screens, blinds and curtains looking sharp.

How to clean . . .

Drapes

Buy good-quality drapes, and check regularly to make sure they stay hung properly. Vacuum drape tops and sides occasionally. When you clean the floor near full-length drapes, protect them by slipping the bottom of the panel through an ordinary clothes hanger and hooking the top over the rod.

You can refurbish drapes not dirty enough to be cleaned by running them through the clothes dryer on a cool setting. (*Don't* do this with fiberglass drapes; they'll leave an irritating residue in the dryer that will transfer itself to clothing.) Be sure to remove the drapery hooks first.

Since drapes are relatively inexpensive to dry clean, get estimates from different shops. It's often less of a hassle than doing them yourself.

Check your drapes by slapping them in the sunshine. If they've been collecting dirt, you'll see it. If they're faded and threadbare and the dirt is all that's holding them together, it's time to go shopping.

Shades

If window shades are going to come clean, a dry sponge (see page 379) will do it. The sturdier plastic or plastic-coated shades can be damp-wiped with a neutral all-purpose cleaner. Remember that shades get sun-rotted and discolored over time, so don't be disappointed if they don't look resurrected when you're finished.

Screens

When your screens become embedded with dead bugs, tree sap, dirt, bird droppings, and other unsightly debris, take them down. Carry them outside, spread out a big cloth, old rug, or piece of canvas, and *lay them flat* (this is important to avoid damage) on it. Mix up a light neutral cleaner solution and scrub them with a soft-bristled brush. Rinse the screens with a hose, give them a sharp rap with your hand to jar most of the water loose, and let them finish drying in the sun.

Blinds

Whether the old venetian type or the newer minis, blinds are such a pain to clean that some homemakers have cheerfully given up the privacy and easy light adjustment that blinds undeniably provide. If you haven't yet reached that point, you might never have to if you clean blinds this way.

The big secret of blind maintenance isn't any "magic fingers" you send away for. It's simply dusting of-

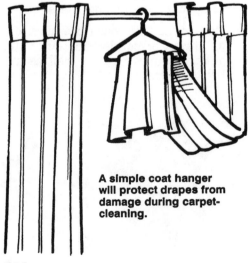

A simple coat hanger will protect drapes from damage during carpet-cleaning.

ten enough that the dust doesn't have a chance to blend with airborne oils into that stubborn, grimy coating we all know and hate. This means at least a monthly run over the blinds with a lambswool duster (see Equipment Chart, page 264), making firm contact with the surface. Close the blinds before you start, and when you've done one side, close them in the other direction and do the other side.

Vertical blinds don't collect dust and airborne soil as swiftly as the horizontals. But they should be dusted frequently too (quarterly might be enough here), for the same reason. Cloth-covered verticals should be done more often because their soft surface will absorb dirt, which if left on will soon be baked in by the sun. Don't use a lambswool duster or treated dust cloth of any kind on cloth-covered blinds—again because of their absorbency. Vacuum them with a dust brush attachment instead.

Sooner or later blinds will need to be washed. Don't try to do this without taking them down; washing blinds in place is slow and messy, and you'll curse yourself for attempting it. Don't wash them in the sink or bathtub, either. Take them outside. Find a slanting surface, such as a driveway, if you can; if not, flat will do. But you *must* lay down an old quilt, blanket or piece of canvas first, and then lay the blinds on it to prevent them from being damaged.

Let each blind out to full length and close it, making sure the louvers are flat. Lay the blind down on the cushioning cloth and scrub in the direction of the slats, using a soft-bristled brush and neutral all-purpose cleaner. Then reverse the blind and wash the other side. The cloth will get soapy and help clean the blind.

Hang or hold the blind up and rinse it with a hose (a helper is very useful at this point). Shake the excess

water off and let the blind dry thoroughly before rehanging it.

There is a nice little tonglike tool called a "Tricket" we professionals use on jalousie windows that makes quick work of washing vertical blinds, since you can do both sides at once. You wash them with the sponge inserts, then squeegee them with the miniature squeegee blades.

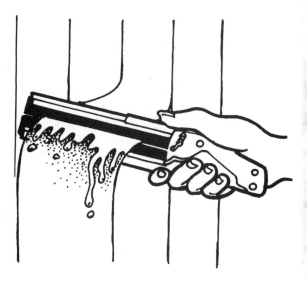

A tricket makes quick work of washing vertical blinds, since both sides of each blind are cleaned with a single stroke.

Clean cloth-covered verticals a couple of times a year by taking a cloth dampened with carpet shampoo solution and lightly wiping the surface.

The most painless way to clean blinds is to send them out to a professional for ultrasonic cleaning. (Just look in the Yellow Pages under Blinds—Cleaning.) This gets the slats, ladders, cords—*everything*—sparkling clean.

315

Floors Under Your Foot & Rule

The floor, more than any other part of the house, projects the overall image of your home. The chances of anyone's noticing that all-day sucker stuck to the patio door, the half-eaten wiener on the bookcase, or the cobweb across Grandpa's picture are lessened if the floors are clean and brilliant. Fortunately, maintaining beautiful floors is one of the simplest jobs in the house. (Trust me.)

The term "hard floors" didn't originate as a description of the effort needed to clean them; it's simply used to distinguish them from soft floors (carpets). Hard floors include vinyl, linoleum, wood, ceramic and other tiles, terrazzo, cork, dirt (nothing under it) and good old concrete. All hard floors have their purpose, and they all have to be cleaned and maintained.

Proper floor care can be a lifesaver for you physically and emotionally. There are four reasons for you to learn and apply good floor care:

1. Appearance

A beautiful floor is an exhilarating experience for the beholder and a reward for the homemaker.

2. Protection

Even the hardest surfaces will scuff, wear and dull with grinding foot traffic, spills and chemical cleaners. A wax or other protective finish covering the surface lessens abrasion and other damage and lengthens the life of the floor. Even "no-wax" floors need a dressing or finish to prevent an eventually dull and damaged surface.

3. Cleanability

Soil, dirt, spills, marks of all kinds and abrasive residues are much simpler to clean from a smooth, well-waxed or finished surface. Sweeping a well-used unwaxed or unfinished tile floor will take you 25 percent longer than sweeping a highly polished one. A coat of wax or other finish on the floor is like a coat of varnish on a bare wood picnic table: It keeps soils and oils from penetrating the surface. Wiping something from the top of a protective nonpenetrable finish takes only seconds. It sure beats spending hours trying to scrub it out once it has soaked in and stained.

4. Safety

Contrary to what most people think, shiny, well-waxed and properly maintained floors are generally much less slippery than bare floors. Bare, porous, worn floors have a slick, flint-hard surface whether wet or dry. A coat or two of wax or acrylic finish actually cushions the floor. This could be compared to laying a thin cloth or cover over a bare plastic tabletop: it creates a surface that won't let things slide around. Thus a coat or "cover" of wax makes most floors less slippery.

A waxed floor is safer

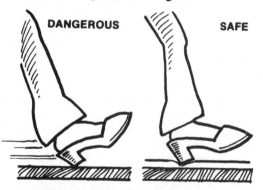

DANGEROUS   SAFE

Clean, waxed floors are safer than bare, untreated floors. Wax "cushions" the surface and actually helps prevent slipping.

Another reminder: Floors require less cleaning if you provide adequate entrance matting (see pages 294-305). Hundreds of hours of floor problems and worries will disappear if you install adequate matting at entrances to stop dirt and abrasives from getting into your house. Some discoloration and wear of waxes comes with time and exposure to sunlight. But most discoloration of wax or finish and deterioration of flooring material comes from dirt penetrating into the wax and eventually to the floor surface. Keeping the surface clean will greatly prolong the life of the finish.

I'm often asked whether hard or soft floors are easier to keep clean. The answer is, it depends. In high-traffic or high-abuse areas, hard flooring is better. In low-traffic, low-abuse areas, carpeting is easier and faster to care for.

How to clean hard floors

Again, the most important factor in saving time and keeping maintenance of your floor to a minimum is simple: Keep it clean! That doesn't just mean removing roller skates, cat toys, coins, combs and clothes, either. It's the dust, grit, gravel, sand, food crumbs and other such substances that remain on floors, abrade them, and eventually get ground into powder and embed themselves in the surface that cause your cleaning woes. Once all this "dirt power" is on the loose, it will destroy a floor rapidly. Keep hard floors well swept (even when you can't see dirt and dust).

You can, of course, vacuum a hard-surface floor, and it does get all the dust and crumbs from corners and hard-to-reach crevices, but on a large hard floor (wood, tile or vinyl) vacuuming is slow, noisy and inefficient. However, on small areas of hard-surface floor right next to other vacuum jobs, it's smart maneuvering to just hit it with the vacuum while you're at it (and it saves stooping with a dustpan). Don't use a vacuum with a beater bar

on a hard floor, especially wood—even if the beater doesn't dent the floor it can, at its rapid rotation rate, fling grit or gravel into the floor and chip the surface. The wide brush head on a canister is designed for hard floors.

Where possible, use a commercial twelve- or eighteen-inch treated dustmop. It's faster, more effective, and will last much longer than anything you can pick up at the supermarket. Brooms stir up dust all over the place and leave fine unseen particles that will be ground into your wax and eventually destroy the finish. A good dustmop is much faster and does a much better job than a broom. There's no comparison, especially if you have a good-quality commercial dustmop with a full-circle swivel head. It will cover a lot of ground quickly and is flat enough to get under furniture. It will gather gravel, paper clips, gum wrappers, safety pins, and the hundred other items that find their way to the floor. It will also pick up and hold the dust. A dustmop is unbelievably effective on sealed concrete basement and garage floors, especially if it's treated to pick up dust.

The care and feeding of dustmops

Treat your dustmop by spraying the head with a little Endust, furniture polish or commercial dustmop treatment, or by taking the head off the frame and pouring a few tablespoonfuls of furniture polish into the pocket. Let it sit overnight (at least twelve hours) before mopping.

Before you start, use a counter brush or angle broom to detail the edges so you don't leave a lingering buildup in the corners. If you use a broom to do this, run it along the tops of the baseboards too and use the angled point to clean out corners.

When you mop, use "s" strokes and keep the mop in contact with the

Dustmop

Get dust and dirt off the floor regularly—preferably with a dustmop.

A 14–18" commercial-quality dustmop will pay you dividends. It cleans hard-surfaced floors better and faster than any broom.

floor, but don't bear down on it; pressure isn't necessary. The mop will turn and swivel under furniture (one of the advantages of the professional-quality mop). Always lead with the same edge and don't lift the head from the floor until you're finished or you'll lose your dust load. Mop next to the baseboard last.

If you have only a small amount of hard flooring, do it by hand with a cleaning cloth (see pages 378-389) or dust cloth. You won't need a commercial dustmop.

When you need to sweep

The corn broom has been around a long time, and can serve well if you remember it's only for dry work. If you do sweep anything wet, don't set the broom on the straw end to dry or it'll develop a permanent curl.

I've switched to the nylon angle head type. The bristles have fine split tips, to get up even the most minute stuff, and lots of springy strength to pull the rocks and toys along, should you need to sweep that hard. The angled head reaches into corners better, and it suits our natural sweeping stroke better. And these plastic brooms shed less and last and last (which is easier on the pocketbook and

our dumpsites)—water, snow, chemicals, or chasing the chickens won't hurt them. I wouldn't be surprised to see the witches switch to them soon!

For outdoor or rough-surfaced expanses of hard flooring, a push broom is what you want—with an eighteen- or twenty-four-inch nylon bristle head and good, sturdy handle braces.

To pick up the final whisk of dirt that the dustpan and broom won't get, I grab a piece of paper out of the garbage, or from an old newspaper or magazine, and wet it (if no one's looking, I just lick it). Then I wipe the area with it, and those tiny particles all stick to the wet paper. Not a speck will be left on the floor.

An angle broom suits our natural sweeping stroke better.

Damp-mopping

The most important operation (after sweeping) is damp-mopping, which is done to remove the light layer of dirt, settled airborne grease and sticky spills that accumulate from daily use.

The equipment needed to wet-clean your floors depends on the amount and type of hard-surfaced floors you have. During the last twenty years, wall-to-wall carpet has found its way into more and more of the new homes built, often leaving only kitchen and bathroom with hard floors.

If a hard floor is in the center of the house where considerable travel over carpeted areas is required to reach it, that hard-floor finish will last for months, if it's kept clean. You could do it by hand in about fifteen minutes a year. A sponge mop (see Equipment Chart, page 264, for the superior professional model of these) is adequate damp-mopping equipment in 80 percent of modern homes.

If you have several rooms of vinyl, linoleum, quarry tile or wood floors, as well as a big game room, garage, converted patio or storage area, some basic labor-saving floor tools would be a good investment. The Equipment Chart on page 264 outlines what I'd suggest. Get a good twelve- or sixteen-ounce string mop, preferably a rayon/cotton Layflat, and a good mop bucket (the built-in roller wringer types are good, and so are the small versions of the commercial handle squeezer type). Wheels on a household mop bucket aren't necessarily what you want, since we rarely move the bucket when we just mop the kitchen floor; besides, wheels make a bucket heavier and more awkward. But you do want *something* to squeeze the moisture out of your mops so you don't have to tromp on them with your foot or do it with your bare hands. Wringing mops by hand is finger suicide: The things your mop picks up—pins, glass, etc.—will lacerate your hands. The price of a small commercial mop bucket might shock you, but gasp once or twice and buy it anyway. It will be a time-saver and greatly contribute to the quality of work you can do.

How to damp-mop

Dipping a mop in a bucket of plain or soapy water and swabbing the place down is not mopping. It gives the floor a temporary wet look, but when it dries it won't look much better than it did to begin with. Magnificent moppers remember these basics:

1. Use the right solution.
Mopping with plain or vinegar water is an exercise in futility, wasted wear and tear on a good mop. Without a surfactant (chemical that helps the solution to penetrate) and emulsifier (to help break up and dissolve the dirt), moisture alone does little to a floor or to the soil on it. On the other hand, too strong a solution will degloss the floor and cause filming or streaks. So use just a bit of neutral all-purpose cleaner (one ounce per gallon of warm water). You want to cut the dirt but not the wax or the finish.

2. Sweep or dustmop the floor thoroughly before you start.
Even better, vacuum it. (By failing to do this, more people soil their floors mopping than by any other method.)

3. "Frame" the floor first.
Run the mop around the edges of the floor, to a point ten to twelve inches from the baseboard. Then when you mop the middle (see number four following), stay ten to twelve inches away from the wall. This eliminates the buildup that mopping can deposit along the baseboard. Slapping the mop on the baseboard is a bad idea that will result in a filthy edge.

4. Mop all the rest in a "figure 8" from side to side out in front of you.
Mopping like this is less fatiguing because you use the big muscles of your

Figure 8 pattern for damp-mopping

midbody and hips, rather than your wrists and arms; it also covers more ground in less time. You also overlap more, so there are fewer missed spots.

5. *Keep your mop clean.*
Always wring the dirty water into a slop bucket before you dip the mop back into the cleaning solution.

6. *Flop your mop!*
Or turn the mop head over, often. Water is heavy, so when you pick up water with a mop it will always accumulate at the bottom of the mop as you work with it. This is why you need to flip the mop over every two or three strokes, to get a drier side. When you use a mop to apply solution or "scrub," you flop it to get to a cleaner side. When you've flopped the mop several times and it won't pick up any more water or it's completely dirty, then wring it out.

7. *Go over the floor twice.*
Make *two* passes over the same surface:

the first to wet and dissolve, the second to remove. So first spread the solution out over the floor (but don't flood it), and let it sit on there a minute (or a little longer if the floor is extra dirty) so the cleaner can attack and emulsify the dirt. Then wring the mop dry and go over the whole area again, removing all the moisture and dirt possible. If you've mixed up the solution right—not too much cleaner—and mopped the floor good and dry on the second pass, you'll be done. If you put on too much solution and leave it on too long, it'll cut the wax. And if you don't make a second pass to remove your cleaning solution, there'll be lots of detergent residue when the water evaporates, leaving the floor sticky and cloudy.

Mop miscellaneous

- The telltale four: If you find more than four mop strings in the bottom of the bucket after cleaning the

floor, it's time to get a new mop head. With all the time they spend wet, they do disintegrate after a while.

- Why do you want a rayon/cotton rather than all-cotton mop? Because the strands will be stronger, so there will be fewer of them left behind on the chair legs and in corners.

- "Damp-mopping" means what it says. Wring all the possible moisture out before putting mop to floor. Excess water runs into cracks and corners and down to the subfloor, and it won't do any good for anything in any of these places.

- Keep a green nylon scrub pad handy when you mop so you can make quick work of stubborn "glued-on" spots and spills.

- Watch the handle when you raise a mop to put it in the wringer. Pro cleaners know only too well that you can wreck ceiling tile, break light fixtures, and be injured by falling glass.

Wax it!

As I said earlier, most hard floors need a protective coating. Floors will wear out much faster if they're not protected. Floors claiming to be "no-wax" will also dull in traffic areas if not protected by a finish of some kind. The "never need to wax" claim just doesn't hold up. If you expect such a floor to stay shiny in heavy traffic areas, it needs a dressing.

First, take the old wax off

Once the hard floor is prepared by sweeping and you know the old wax or finish is due to come off, it's time to make that hard job an easy one. Arrive at the scene with two buckets: an ordinary bucket and a mop bucket.

Fill the mop bucket three-quarters full of clean water; don't put cleaner in it. Mix some warm water and wax stripper in the ordinary bucket. A detergent cleaner will do fine for a light scrub, but if you want all the wax off, use a commercial wax remover. Ammonia cuts wax, but it can also cut the plasticizers in the floor if you leave it on too long! A nonammoniated commercial wax remover will do the best and safest job.

Dip your fresh mop into the solution and apply to the floor generously so that the solution can attack the old wax or dirt. Cover as large an area as you feel you can clean and take up before it dries. (About ten by ten feet—you'll learn how much to do if it dries on you once.) Remember, use the basic principle of cleaning explained in chapter six. As soon as the solution is on the floor, old wax and dirt begin to be dissolved and suspended and can soon be wiped off easily.

This may be a bit optimistic, because chances are you have some spots where wax is built up thick as cardboard and hard as a bullet. It will need scrubbing or scraping, and possibly another application or two of solution. If so, scrub (and not on your hands and knees, either). Get a hand floor scrubber (see Equipment Chart, page 264). It has a long handle with a plastic "gripper" on its end that holds a five-by-ten-inch nylon pad. Edges, especially, are easy with one of these little gems. I think one hand floor

> **Do all your hard floors at once if you can. Whether you mop, wax or vacuum, it's a lot more efficient to get out, clean up and put away all your equipment just once. (Cleaning up the wax applicator, for example, can take as long as waxing one whole floor.)**

The right way to remove old wax

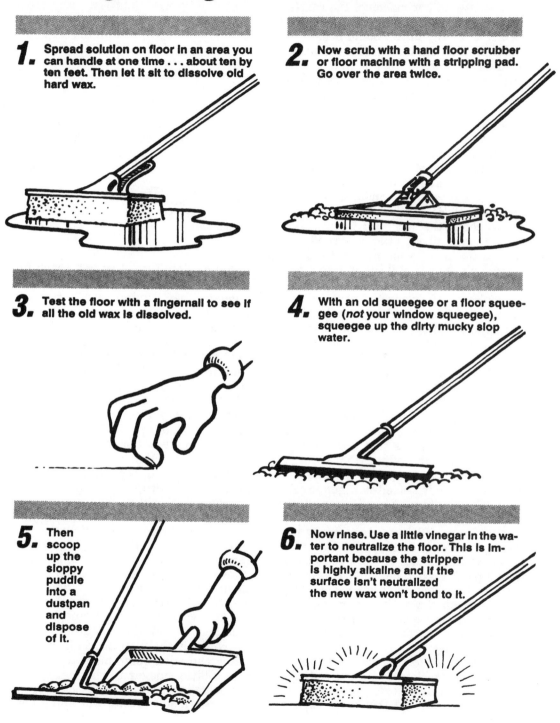

1. Spread solution on floor in an area you can handle at one time . . . about ten by ten feet. Then let it sit to dissolve old hard wax.

2. Now scrub with a hand floor scrubber or floor machine with a stripping pad. Go over the area twice.

3. Test the floor with a fingernail to see if all the old wax is dissolved.

4. With an old squeegee or a floor squeegee (*not* your window squeegee), squeegee up the dirty mucky slop water.

5. Then scoop up the sloppy puddle into a dustpan and dispose of it.

6. Now rinse. Use a little vinegar in the water to neutralize the floor. This is important because the stripper is highly alkaline and if the surface isn't neutralized the new wax won't bond to it.

323

scrubber could outdo five of those small electric twin-brush scrubbers. If you do use a floor machine, the single-disc models are at least twenty times better than the little double-brush units. Watch the classified section of your paper and you might find a $350 twelve- or thirteen-inch commercial unit for $40 or $50. Use nylon scrubbing and polishing pads under a floor machine for best results. Brushes are almost worthless. For wax removal, the brown or black pads are the best.

When the solution on the floor looks gunky and creamy, it means the dirt and old wax are coming loose. Before you clean off the stripper and gunk, check the scrubbed floor with your fingernail. If, after a scrape across the floor, your nail looks like your son's, wax is still there. Use more solution and if necessary scrub a little. If you're on the verge of passing out from exhaustion, you're in an ideal frame of mind to resolve not to let your floor ever get in this condition again.

Most floor-cleaning time is spent trying to get wax off unused areas, such as under the lamp table and TV, and off the edges of the floors. Previously, when you rewaxed the traffic paths or worn areas that needed it, you also gave the edges, the areas beneath furniture, and all the other places that didn't need it a generous coat. This system of application was repeated year after year. A traffic pattern area will come clean easily because there's no buildup, but the thick areas will need lots of work to get the buildup off. Next time, don't rewax the floors where you don't use them. Once you've given the entire floor one coat of wax and more coats are to be applied, put the additional coats *on traffic areas only.*

Now, back to cleaning the floor. The floor is soaked and scrubbed, the wax and dirt are loosened, and it's a mess. Don't pull out that mop and try

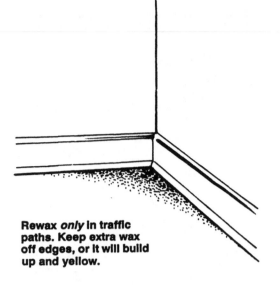

Rewax *only* in traffic paths. Keep extra wax off edges, or it will build up and yellow.

to sop or slop it up. Instead, reach for a simple, inexpensive tool called a floor squeegee (see Equipment Chart, page 264). Or you can use an old window squeegee you have lying around (not your nice new one, which should be used only for windows). Squeegee the gunk into a puddle on the uncleaned area (mind you don't squeegee it down a heating vent), and use an ordinary dustpan and empty bucket to quickly scoop the gunk up. (I once met a woman who uses her turkey baster to suck it up, but I'm sticking with the dustpan.) The squeegeed area (except for a possible drop or two from the squeegee lap) will be almost perfectly clean. A squeegee will do a great job on all hard floors—even fairly rough concrete, or vinyl floors with relief designs (the little crud-catching indentations or pits that really are the pits to clean). If the floor has some deep bad cracks between tiles you can use a wet/dry vacuum with a squeegee attachment to pull the liquid out.

Now for the mop. Rinse it in clear water and then damp-mop the area. Add a little vinegar to the mop water to neutralize any alkaline residue from the cleaner so the wax will apply better. If the floor was really gunky, rinse again with clean water. Let the floor dry, and that area is ready to wax. Repeat this process until the whole floor is finished. All the gunk will end up in one bucket to be dumped in the toilet (*not* the sink). The mop water will remain fresh and work for the entire floor because it only rinses the squeegeed floor. (And just think: You never had your hands in filthy water.)

When the floor is dry, apply a first light coat of wax to the entire floor. Put two more thin coats on your traffic paths; don't rewax areas that don't get heavy wear. I'd use a good commercial metal interlock or polymer finish, obtainable at any janitorial-supply store.

Wax wisdom

- Just because it shines doesn't mean it's clean. Those mop-and-shine products lay a gloss on top of your floor that reflects light. When you're finished, where's the dirt? Under the wax. Likewise, be sure to remove the grimy scrub water before applying any finishing product, or you may just have shiny dirt.

- Pros wax floors with a clean string mop, but a full-sized (thirty-six-ounce) mop is huge. The next time one of your small mops gets older or hardened at the ends, trim it to six- or eight-ounce size and wax with it, just as if you were damp-mopping. It's faster than an applicator and it applies wax perfectly. Rinse well with hot water afterward or you'll have a plaster-hard wax mop!

- Most floor finishes and waxes are delicately balanced chemically. Mixing them with water or other

wax—or even waxing over an unrinsed floor—will cause them to yellow, powder, streak and perform poorly. Use them pure.

- Three's Better than One: When applying floor finish or wax, remember that several (two or three) thin coats beat one big heavy coat. It's better for looks, durability and even drying!

Tile floors

There must be four hundred brands, five hundred styles, and at least a thousand different colors and patterns of clay and masonry floor tiles to choose from. And it's pretty clear from all the calls, letters and questions I get concerning "their new tile" that everyone thinks they picked the wrong one. Seldom does any tile give you all you expected, but many tile problems can be cured with a little adjustment in approach and cleaning product, especially by simply coming to understand and accept just what you *do* have in the floor tile you have now. Tile in general has a very hard surface made to take abuse and wear and to require a minimum of maintenance. Generally it does just that, but the stickler is that tile comes in everything from a slick, glossy surface to a dull, porous one. Your tile could be one of these or of the many variations in between.

Lots of people who have bought the shiny tile call me and say, "I don't like the shininess. It shows every streak or bit of dirt. What can I do?" Well, that is the tile's nature and personality, the way it was designed—its slick surface reflects light and so the shine. Shiny surfaces also won't hold finish or "wax"; it powders and flakes off because the surface is too slippery to bond to. But that same slick, hard surface won't allow dirt or spills to penetrate and is easy to clean. (As to how to avoid streaks, see point #1 following.)

The next most frequent question I get about tile floors is, "I can't make my 'Mexican tile' floor shine!" That's right. Unglazed clay or quarry tile like this was designed rough and porous to provide traction, and it absorbs rather than reflects light so it won't shine. If you put enough coats of sealer and finish on, some shine will come, but it takes a lot of applications and continual maintenance. Again, you won't change the personality of the tile.

A few more truths about tile

1. Remove the residue

Two of the most common mistakes on shiny tile are mopping in a way that leaves soap residue behind (which kills the luster), or mopping with plain water, vinegar and water, or something that doesn't cut the grease and dirt so the floor stays dull and sticky. You have to mop or scrub a tile floor with a good cleaner (such as neutral all-purpose cleaner), making sure you mix it up exactly as the manufacturer recommends, no stronger—and then make sure you get rid of all the traces of that cleaner when you're done. To accomplish this, rinse-mop with plain water afterward or add a little vinegar to the rinse water (it doesn't clean, but it will neutralize any alkalinity left on the floor). Check this out if your ceramic tile isn't as sparkling as you want it. If I had lots of tile I'd get a little thirteen-inch single-disc floor polisher from a janitorial-supply store and, with a white nylon pad, buff or "burnish" the tile after it's been cleaned to remove hard water and other stubborn stains or deposits and bring up its natural luster. It only takes a minute or two.

2. Coat it

If you have one of the more porous types of tile and insist on some shine, you can put a coating (sealer or finish) on it to fill the pores, prevent dirt penetration, and give it a bit of a glow.

Since I don't know which of the five hundred tiles you may have out there in Stamford, Miami, Albuquerque or Billings, I suggest you go down to the local janitorial-supply store and ask what they would recommend for tile of your type or what the local contractors use to enhance floors like yours. Then you'll know what you can use and where to get it. But be sure the floor is properly prepared first—well cleaned, rinsed and neutralized if necessary, or the finish will quickly flake or powder off. Finish will also fail to adhere over any greasy or oily spots.

3. Grout

On most tile the grout is the biggest problem. The mortar between the tiles gets porous (or was that way to begin with), so dirt and stains get in it and, when you clean, they don't come out. Any untreated masonry like this, just like a plain cement garage floor, will absorb everything and quickly get cruddy. Clean and rinse your tile floor well, especially the grout (you may need a degreaser to get out all that embedded oily dirt). Then get some grout sealer (Color Tile stores have it), take a little brush and seal the grout; it will be well worth it. The sealer, usually a silicone, fills the pores of the grout so that it resists dirt and buildup.

4. The secret of intelligent selection

All of you who *were* going to get a tile floor, don't panic! I was once very gun-shy on tile, but now I'm putting mostly tile floors in the maintenance-free house

I'm building. The secret is that for years my wife and I viewed tile that was already in use. Some tile, especially in shopping malls, always looks beautiful, and with little maintenance. Contact the architect of the place with the tile you admire and find out what it is — "showroom selection" is often maintenance masochism.

> If you have carpet butting up against ceramic tile flooring, be sure to replace any metal bar in your vacuum beater with another brush. The metal bar (great for bouncing the carpet to loosen soil) can chip your tile if you happen to lap over onto it.

Coping with concrete floors

Dust-mopping concrete floors is a trick most of us haven't heard of. Concrete floors, believe it or not, are almost equal in square footage to carpet in many American homes. Unfinished full basements are common. People often intend to finish them, but they wait many years — "until we can afford to finish those two bedrooms and a family room in the basement." Two-car garages are also a mass of concrete flooring. Both of these areas bear a constant flow of traffic back and forth into the "finished" part of the house. Concrete absorbs and holds stains and marks and produces much destructive material (dirt, grit, sand, etc.), so it's responsible for more cleaning time than you might realize. The surface of concrete (which is made of sand, cement, lime and additives) will perpetually "bleed" dust and grit, which if not cleaned up regularly eventually circulates through your house.

Go get your broom right now and sweep your basement or garage. Leave the pile of residue, and go back and sweep again just as carefully. The second pile will amaze you, as will the third if you sweep again. Because concrete is textured and porous and "bleeds," vacuuming it is really the only way to get it dustless, and after use, it will again be dusty. If you want to eliminate hundreds of hours of direct and indirect adverse results from concrete floors in your home, seal the concrete. You've walked on many a sealed floor in supermarkets, malls, stadiums, on ramps, around pools, etc. It looks like it's varnished. Sealed concrete is easy and practical to maintain and will last for years.

You can seal your own concrete floors

Concrete has to cure at least twenty-eight days after pouring before it's ready to seal. It's best to seal it before it's used, because oil stains and other fluids may penetrate and will be difficult or impossible to remove, and the seal will magnify any pre-existing marks.

On either old or new concrete, sweep up all surface dirt and remove everything possible from the floor (furniture, tools, etc.). Mop on a solution of strong alkaline cleaner or, better still, etching acid diluted in water. (Your janitorial-supply store or paint store will have these.) Let it soak in awhile. It will break and release the lime and debris on the surface of the concrete, leaving a good, firm, clean base. If the floor is old and marked, scrub it with a floor machine (or your trusty hand floor scrubber). Even if you don't scrub, apply the solution and let it sit. Then flush the solution off, using your floor squeegee. Rinse with a hose. Allow the floor to dry for five or more hours.

You can get penetrating seal at paint or janitorial-supply stores. The

I JUST CAN'T DO A THING WITH THIS FLOOR!

them have written or called me with fears and worries about wood.

Wood is a warm, handsome surface that will last and look good indefinitely if you treat it right. The old way to maintain wood floors is to apply a penetrating oil and then put a layer of solvent (or "spirit") wax over it. This does protect the floor to a degree, but it doesn't give it a hard, permanent, waterproof coating. It's also a lot of work, and the floor always looks like an Alaskan barroom floor needing only a layer of sawdust and a moth-eaten moosehead to complete the atmosphere.

The better way to go is to apply two or three coats of polyurethane-type finish or varnish to a wood floor. Like a thin sheet of glass, this will seal the wood off from moisture, wear and abuse. Any maintenance you do after that isn't going to touch the wood itself. Water doesn't hurt well-sealed wood if used wisely, which means used sparingly and not left on for long. Be sure the sealer or finish is intact (no cracks or worn spots), because once moisture gets into wood it swells the grain and pops off the finish; it can even discolor and warp the floor.

Once the floor is well sealed, pick any spills up quickly, dustmop or sweep it frequently to keep it free of dust and grit, and damp-mop it occasionally with a light neutral all-purpose cleaner, getting that water on and

latest generation of water-based concrete seals are wonderful! Apply the seal, according to directions, with any applicator that will distribute it in a nice, thin, even coat; let it dry. Most concrete seals are self-leveling so it should turn out okay, but I'd advise a second coat to make sure all the "etched," rough surfaces are filled. (Don't try to save the used applicator. It isn't worth cleaning out.)

Once the seal is dry, you have a shiny, glossy, smooth (not slick) surface that can be waxed and maintained just like any hard floor. Stains, oil spills, etc., can be wiped off without leaving the usual ugly penetrating mark. Sealed concrete finish wears well. Chips and scrapes can be touched up with a small paintbrush or cloth.

Wood floors

Homeowners are in awe of their wood floors; literally thousands of

Keep wooden floors covered with a protective polyurethane or resinous floor finish. If moisture penetrates wood it will swell and pop off the finish; then the wood deteriorates rapidly.

off quickly.

Even a well-varnished floor will look dull when it's worn and scratched, so that's why I personally like to wax them. You can use paste wax, but it's slow hands-and-knees stuff—a nice liquid acrylic with 23 percent solids (such as Top Gloss) will work as well with much less effort. The wax keeps the polyurethane (which is protecting the wood) from getting scratched. But don't try to wax freshly sealed wood, or the finish won't stick. Use the floor for a month or two to reduce the gloss, and the wax will adhere.

Refinishing wood floors

Shy away from sanding wood floors except as a last resort. An eighth of an inch of wood taken off a three-quarter-inch floor really affects its performance. Cracks, crowns and cupping will appear and squeaks will develop.

Sometimes, especially if you're rehabbing a much-abused old house, you'll have no choice but to sand down the floors. But chances are, if your wood floors are old and ugly-looking, the problem's not the wood, but the layers of yellowed, cracked finish. If you sand it down, the old finish will

gum up the belts of the sander, and it will be a mess. Plus, you lose part of your floor. Instead, try this: Buy a gallon or two of varnish or paint remover and apply it generously to the floor. The old varnish will instantly crumble and release its hold on the wood. Scrape it well, then use your trusty floor squeegee and dustpan to pick up the mess. This should leave the floor bare. If some old varnish does remain, use a little more remover and scrape some more; it will come off.

Then go over the entire floor lightly with a screen-back sanding disc. Apply one coat of polyurethane or varnish—thin it down so it will soak into the wood—and then one or two coats more, the number of coats depending on the condition of the floor. Soft or cracked wood generally needs two coats to achieve a good gloss.

You won't believe how good your floor will look or how easy the job will be. Just be sure to read all the directions that come with floor care products, and don't be afraid to ask the dealer questions.

P.S. It's clear to me that a small book on the subject of caring for wood in a home—especially floors—is really needed. I'm working on it, so be sure to send *me* your questions and concerns about wood so I can include them.

To move heavy furniture and appliances easily without scratching the floor—

A thick towel slipped under each leg will help the unit slide for easy cleaning access.

Remember daily maintenance for protection

After you've expended all the time and effort to get your floors clean and shiny, keep them clean daily and they'll last for years. Remember, it's the spills, crumbs, sand, dust, etc., that create the conditions that make you work. If a few black marks get on the floor, they'll be on top of the wax, and easily removed with the moist nylon cleaning pad on the end of your hand floor scrubber. The most efficient way to keep hard floors clean is to dust-mop them daily.

A few final words about floors

Remember, good matting at exterior and interior entrances will save you more floor work than all the gimmicks, tips and miracle floor formulas combined. Avoid "one-stroke" miracle combinations that clean and wax your floor at the same time. And if anyone in the family has shoes or other footwear that leave black marks, I'd make a quick Salvation Army donation of them (the shoes, not the person!).

Some floors are much easier to maintain than others, so don't break your neck trying to match your neighbor's shine. Some floor material, because it's cheap, damaged, porous, discolored or just plain ugly, is almost impossible to make look good. When you put in new flooring, stick to

A quick review of floor care

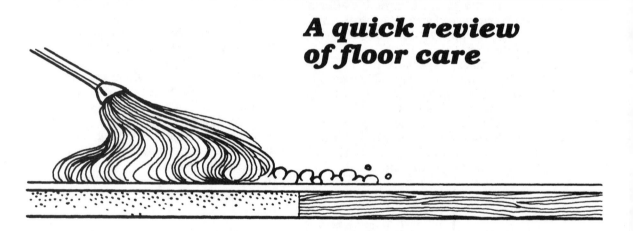

VINYL OR LINOLEUM

All vinyl, asphalt and even "no-wax" floors must have a coat of wax or polish applied so that dirt and debris from foot traffic won't damage them. Keep such floors dustmopped and damp-mopped regularly, even if "they don't look dirty." Damp-mop with a light neutral all-purpose cleaner when soiled; rewax regularly in the traffic patterns.

WOOD

Make sure wood floors are sealed with a good resinous or polyurethane "membrane" finish so moisture and stains won't penetrate the wood. Then treat wood floors like any hard flooring. Sweep, dustmop and damp-mop to maintain, but go light on the water, and don't let it puddle on the surface.

tested, reliable surfaces.

Some floors need three or four coats of wax to build them up to a gloss. A good shine will hide a multitude of sins. If a floor won't shine, or is difficult to maintain, consider replacing it or carpeting it.

Pick a good-quality flooring. Remember that solid colors are tougher to maintain and keep looking good. Try to avoid flooring with grooves and indentations—it's literally the "pits." Smooth-surfaced floors are nicer—and much easier to keep clean.

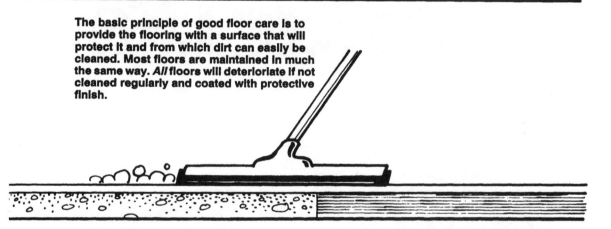

The basic principle of good floor care is to provide the flooring with a surface that will protect it and from which dirt can easily be cleaned. Most floors are maintained in much the same way. *All* floors will deteriorate if not cleaned regularly and coated with protective finish.

CONCRETE

Raw concrete will "bleed" dust and sand. Once interior concrete has cured, it should be cleaned thoroughly, let dry, and then sealed with a concrete seal. The resulting protective finish lets it be maintained like other floors. Never paint concrete floors, because most paints will peel and chip off concrete.

STONE, BRICK, CERAMIC OR QUARRY TILE

The dozens of types of tiles available make it difficult to recommend a single method. If you have one of the more porous kinds of tile and are unhappy with it, ask the dealer (or your local janitorial-supply store) for a sealer or finish appropriate for your kind of tile. Remember that tiles intended to have a highly textured or "rustic" look will never shine no matter what—so don't waste your time and energy.

How to Clean Carpets for a Softer Life

"Never shampoo a carpet before you have to, because once you do, it will get dirty faster." (Old Wives' Tales, continued). That's like saying, "Never wash your socks after the first wearing, because they'll get dirty faster." There are plenty of soothsayers around quoting great carpet wisdom to the homemaker, most of which costs you time and money. With some simple professional techniques, you can get the job done, keep your carpets looking sharp, and minimize your maintenance time. My company cleans and maintains several million square feet of carpet every night. What I've learned in the process applies to household as well as commercial carpet.

Buy quality carpet

"Which carpet is best?" If I had a dollar for every time I've been asked that, I could carpet the parking lot at your favorite mall! Carpet is so much better today than it was twenty or thirty years ago that if you stick to a good, reputable dealer and a Stain-Master, Stainblocker or other soil-resistant type, it'll be hard to go wrong. The fierce competition in the carpet industry has forced the quality up; almost all of it is nylon now and stain-resistant, and it's good! Don't bargain for the basement cost—better carpet is better, period! Pay the few extra dollars per yard to get the better grade, and have it installed professionally. You'll get thousands of dollars of benefit in comfort, durability, enjoyment and ease of maintenance. Choose what you like, but make sure you get good stuff.

Selecting carpet color, style and material is generally a personal privilege, but living with it (especially maintaining it) may not be a "privi-lege" if you don't choose wisely. For example, commercial carpets are so tightly woven and low-pile they're now referred to as "soft floors," not carpeted floors. Don't get too commercial-minded and buy the "wear like iron" style. Believe me, it *feels* like iron when you roll around on it with the kids or tackle a "living room floor" project. Go for the highest-quality domestic instead, and you'll be better off all around. The feel and the looks are a large part of the value of home carpeting. Much low-pile or indoor-outdoor carpet is difficult to maintain, not because it gets any dirtier than a thicker, plusher carpet, but because of its short pile and the solid colors it usually comes in. Every tiny piece of litter or trash is highly visible on it, and little bits of thread and similar material resist being vacuumed off; a good, deep pile can tolerate, undetected, just about anything from crumbs to catcher's mitts. There's nothing wrong with letting your rug help you out a little—as long as it isn't physically destructive to the carpet.

A homemaker will often spend hours selecting an exact shade, not realizing that once it's in place and in use—under different light conditions, and underfoot being soiled—the color won't be the same as the color you chose for even a tenth of the time the carpet is in service. Color is one area where you should be cautious.

There's no way you can keep airborne soilants from industrial burning, home heating gases, family cooking or foot-borne street oils from any carpet. All carpets will get soiled with time. Light golds, yellows, whites, pastels or flecks will serve you well if you live "el plusho" and your house is only a showplace. However, if you have children, grandchildren, animals or home-study groups, those elegant light carpets will be a disaster. Light solid colors show soil and are difficult to shampoo, and often show "cow trails."

Patterns and textures tend to hide soiling and wear.

Use common sense when you choose carpeting. Think of the maintenance. Deep pile is harder to vacuum than medium pile. Although the old standby, wool, is lovely, I'd choose nylon, a synthetic, ten times over for stain resistance, wear and cleanability. Oriental, Indian and woven rugs must *always* be cleaned professionally. These and other area rugs *cause* housework: Area rugs present two surfaces (instead of one) to clean. They're always being kicked and wrinkled, and they're easy to trip over. But they *are* beautiful. If you have to have them, hang them on a wall.

Kitchen and bathroom carpet

I'd *never* have carpet in a bathroom. There is a 100 percent chance that moisture (new and used) will get on the carpet, as will hair spray and other grooming residue. It will stink, harbor germs and look ugly. Bathroom carpeting takes much more time to care for than hard-surfaced flooring, and it deteriorates rapidly. Don't do it!

And in the kitchen? Where bread always falls jelly/mayonnaise/salami side down? Where meat juices run over the edge of the counter and dirty dishwater splashes out of the sink? Where pressure cookers of potato chowder explode and casseroles of baked beans are dropped? Don't you have better things to do than clean carpet?

High-abuse areas such as bathrooms, kitchens, garages, studios and workshops should have the lowest-maintenance, easiest-to-clean flooring possible. It will certainly save you time and grief, and probably money as well.

If you're in doubt anywhere here, my daughter and I did a book called *Make Your House Do the Housework* which covers carpet from every angle for looks, durability and ease of upkeep.

Regular maintenance is important

Carpet in a home or lightly trafficked commercial area is easier to take care of than a hard floor if it's maintained properly. Its biggest problem is neglect. A carpet that looks okay is often used and abused, going unnoticed until it's too late. Then the owner of the neglected carpet says, "Huh, I wonder why the fur is all falling out" or "I can't remember what color it used to be. It must be time to clean it." At this stage most people wake up to the fact that carpets have to be maintained. But by then it's too late. Cleanup attempts are generally futile, and the owner becomes displeased with the carpet, unjustly blaming the problems on the salesperson or manufacturer.

You might think that carpet wear and damage result only from foot traffic. Wrong! Excessive carpet damage or wear results from a combination of foot traffic, furniture pressure, and residues (such as sand and grit) that are allowed to remain in the carpet. Any sharp, abrasive particles or articles on or at the base of the carpet fibers are, as the carpet is walked on, ground against each other. In time, the fibers that aren't cut or damaged are soiled. The carpet wears out and gets soiled from the bottom as well as the top. Thus, to maintain your carpet properly, you've got to keep off or remove surface litter, dust, grit, wet soils and the old airborne soils before they become embedded in your carpet. Another reminder: Good matting will eliminate a big share of this, especially wet soils and grit. Airborne dust you have to live with. Litter you can pick up or vacuum. The real culprit is embedded dirt.

Enter the vacuum . . .

Vacuum cleaners were invented to get surface dust, embedded dirt and litter from carpets efficiently. Few vacuums make as much impression on the carpet as they do on the user, who thinks noise, chrome and suction are the ultimate. For ages, vacuum salespeople (all equal in wind velocity to their products) have unloaded shiny, overpriced machines on customers fascinated by suction and attachments. Neither of these is that important in maintaining your carpet and saving yourself housecleaning hours. After showing you how a vacuum can do everything but brush your teeth, the sales approach is to drop a steel ball on the floor and suck it up into the vacuum. The gullible potential customer thinks, "If that vacuum can get a big steel ball off the carpet, sand and gravel will be a snap!"

Wrong! First, the steel ball trick is a volume maneuver that any vacuum, weak or strong, old or new, can do under the right conditions. Just get a steel ball slightly smaller than the hose and the ball is easily slurped up. Now take a piece of thread and mash it onto the carpet so it has a little static bind. A vacuum cleaner strong enough to pick up a piano bench will

often have trouble picking up the thread because there's no "displacement lift." We've all tried to get up a thread, haven't we? Likewise, suction alone won't remove the embedded particles of dirt, grit and sand. It will remove only the surface soil because, as with the thread, the displacement lift isn't there. The carpet fibers stand in the way to effectively hold the embedded dirt, grit, and all those other villains grinding away at your carpet. A good "beater brush" vacuum is what's needed to pull those babies out of the pile.

Beat it!

Vacuums with a beater brush, or beater bar, are distinguished by a rapidly rotating brush that beats, combs and vibrates the carpet. This loosens and dislodges embedded dirt and soil so the suction can pull it up into the vacuum. Most beater brush heads will adjust to different heights and won't wear out carpet under normal use. On some models of vacuums the beater bar may be called a "brush roll," and on canister vacuums it's usually contained in a "power wand" type of attachment.

Are you the one in seven?

National studies show that one out of every seven homemakers needs a new vacuum cleaner. If you're that one, get it before your spouse spends the money on a new router or a fancy new computer program he'll use just once or twice during the rest of his life.

A vacuum is indeed "the" tool of cleaning. But which one should you own? A good question, since there are hundreds of them, all shapes and sizes — and a lot of them are excellent. A lot of them are also too big, too small or too expensive. Many fill some special need better than another, but for all-around, all-purpose use in a

Rugs and carpets must have good regular care with a beater-brush vacuum to keep dirt out of the roots.

home we want one that's easy to use, maintain and repair. I like uprights the best, and I've used Eurekas at work and at home for more than thirty-five years. The ideal? I would buy two vacuums: first, an upright beater-brush type. (I hate canister-type vacuums that drag behind you like a ball and chain.) Go a step further and get a commercial upright. These are almost like the regular model sold downtown—except they generally have stronger motors, longer cords, a heavy-duty beater bar, a more durable turn-on switch, and a better-quality bag. Just be sure you choose a model you feel comfortable handling. You should be able to buy a first-class commercial upright for $250 to $350.

Resist buying a boxful of extra attachments that do everything from painting to pan-frying. Most of them are trinkets, and gradually the gadget accessories break or get lost, and eventually the machine is only used for what you needed it for in the first place—to vacuum! Ninety-five percent of your vacuuming can be accomplished with just two or three basic tools.

My criticism of attachments is well documented by your own experience. That big display box of nickel-plated gizmos to hook up to your vacuum is a dandy selling point. But it gets shuffled, unused, from closet to closet for years until the box disintegrates. Then the tools themselves are banged around but never used. Finally, after twelve years, you need the goose-necked anteater attachment to vacuum the glove box of the car. Then you can't find it. If you're buying an upright, forget the attachments.

Just get a sturdy, simple upright. Do be sure to get a vacuum with a long cord—who among us has not wished a hundred times that the vacuum cord was "just ten feet longer"? An extension cord is a pain and cuts

your efficiency greatly. Every time you need to use it you have to hunt it down from the family member who borrowed it for some other purpose.

For your second machine, invest in a tank-type wet/dry vacuum. You'll be money and time ahead.

Commercial uprights are available with either cloth or disposable paper bags; some have a second type of cloth bag that zips open so you can replace the paper bag inside. Cloth bags are reuseable, so you aren't always buying disposables and then having to find a place to store them (due to popular demand, some uprights such as the Eurekas now have a bag holder right on them). I like cloth bags best, but it's a matter of taste. Disposables, on the other hand, can be changed more quickly, don't make a mess when you do, and keep you from handling all the germs, pollen and dust that fly around when you empty a regular vacuum bag. Disposables can be popped out and put right into the trash. In seconds, you're back on the road again.

If you use good doormats, you'll cut down vacuuming intake considerably, and a cloth bag will last a long time. Cloth bags need to be emptied *before* they're a third full and shaken well to keep them from becoming impregnated with soil. If you lack a suitable alley, north forty, or yard to do the airing, disposable bags might serve you better. When bags get too clogged, you'll smell dust when you click the vacuum on. If you see dust pouring out when you start the vacuum up, you've waited too long.

There is a trick to easy cloth bag emptying. After you remove the bag, turn it upside down, holding your hand over the opening, and shake the bag vigorously for a minute or so. All of the clinging dirt within will fall to the top of the bag, and then you can just hold the bag over a waste container, slide off the bag clamp, and let the ball of dirt plop into the waste can. This way there'll be minimum spills, and you won't get dust all over.

Watch a cloth bag while the machine is on. If it blows out like a big balloon the pores are beginning to fill up with dust and the air flow is being constricted. This means reduced suction and pickup. It's time to replace the bag. You can vacuum the bag inside and out, but sooner or later, you'll have to replace it. Don't try to wash the bag, either—it'll negatively affect its operation, and the bag will still have to be replaced soon.

The wet/dry vacuum

A wet/dry is a vacuum that can be safely used to pick up both dry material and liquids. Generally this is accomplished by a simple filter adjustment. Wet/drys are great! They are the vacuums to buy a few attachments for, and the first one should be an extra-long hose.

A wet/dry will not only clean up floods and spills and empty the fish tank, it's great for carpet edges, drapes, floors, furniture, rafters (another reason for a long hose), car upholstery, campers, boats ... the list could go on and on.

A small (ten-gallon capacity) wet/dry is the best size for the household. Those twenty-gallon units will tempt you, but stay with the small—remember, you'll be carrying it full of toilet overflow, diluted doo-doo and other unpleasantries better not slopped out of the tank when you go to empty it. And getting out and muscling around a jumbo wet/dry is a job you'll start wanting to dodge. Wet/drys range in price from $49.95 (on sale) at K-Mart to $120, or you can go high society and get a deluxe stainless steel tank

type at a local janitorial-supply store for several hundred dollars. I warn you, when your neighbors and relatives see what a wet/dry can do, you'll have to buy them one for Christmas, so shop accordingly!

The upright and wet/dry vacuums together are approximately a $500 investment and will take care of all your basic vacuum needs.

Special-purpose assistants

The following helpers make special vacuuming jobs a snap:

- Hand vacs, for quick pickup of little messes like a few cracker crumbs on the couch or the litter the kitty kicked out of the box. We're much more likely to clean it up *now* if we don't have to get out a whole big vacuum rig and plug it in. There are even hand-helds (like the Eureka Step Saver) with beater bars that can handle things like embedded stair tread grit.

- Self-propelled vacuums are not just for the weak or lazy. When they first came out, I wouldn't use one. (After all, John Wayne would never use a self-propelled vacuum.) I have two now, and they're nicer than cruise control.

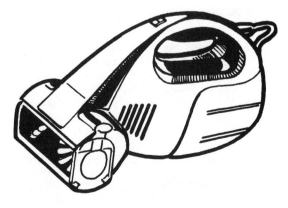

A hand vac with a beater bar, the Eureka Step Saver.

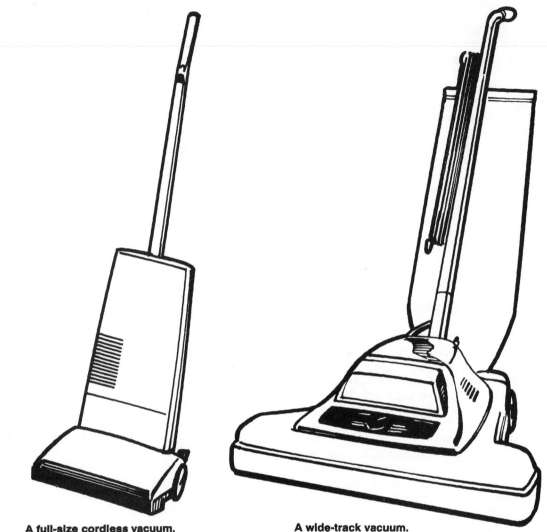

A full-size cordless vacuum.

A wide-track vacuum.

- Full-size cordless vacuums like the Eureka Freedom are battery-powered and can go up to thirty minutes without recharging. Light, quick and easy to use—all the advantages of a cordless vac in a larger size.

- Wide-track vacuums like Eureka's wide-track upright with a sixteen-inch head (instead of the usual eleven or twelve) zooms over the carpet in no time. If you have a big home with lots of carpet, like my wife and I, it'll cut a third off your

vacuuming time. This is one secret that janitors with their acres of carpet have known for years.

Cord control

Two ways we pros keep vacuum cords out of the way: (1) Hold the cord in your free hand, or (2) drape it over your shoulder and vacuum your way into a room or area instead of going all the way in and then vacuuming out (fighting the cord all the way).

Built-in vacuum systems

These beauties—also called "central vacs"—are still one of the best-kept secrets on the market. Watch them take off in the next ten years!

My first experience with a built-in vacuum came when I opened a closet in a house we were cleaning. I winced in startled fright at what I thought was a giant coiled python ready to strike. Its sedate reaction identified it as the longest vacuum hose I'd ever seen. "Wow, there must be some hunk of a vacuum to fit this baby," I thought. The owner later showed me the little wall receptacle where the hose inserted and turned into an instant vacuum. In the next year or so I only encountered or heard of a few more, but the more I saw of them, the more I liked them. And all of their owners seemed to be in love with them.

As I met ever more homemakers across the nation in my seminars and tours, "What about central vacs?" became a question I was asked at every other stop. I began to seek out sources of the central vacuum and had a hard time finding one or two, and my builder and supplier were as uneducated as I. Now in the '90s at least seventeen companies are hard at work selling America central vacs.

Installation is what most of us wonder about, but the vacuums fit easily in new homes and without much difficulty in the already-built ones. Dealers have videotapes to show you how to install them yourself, or they will do it for you. A central vac averages around $1,200 installed, but that's a bargain considering the time and energy it'll save over the years. I'm putting one in the maintenance-free house I'm building in Hawaii and in my twenty-five-year-old masonry home. If you need a source, write to me and I'll send you a list of companies who can direct you to local distributors.

Here are the pluses of the central vac:

1. It saves wear and tear on the house (the vacuum hitting furniture legs and baseboards, etc.).

2. It's the cleanest vacuum going. Residual dust has no home here—it goes out of the room.

3. Since the motor's far away in the basement or garage, it's amazingly quiet.

4. All you handle is a light hose, so it's super easy to use, especially for those once-a-day pickups or once-overs.

5. It's a permanent investment. You can buy one regular vacuum after another and end up with nothing to show for it, but installing a built-in is like putting money in the bank. It's there for good, and it increases the value of the house.

But the nicest thing about central vacs is their simplicity—no vacuum to drag out, no canister to drag around, no cord to keep flipping over furniture (or pulling out of the socket). Central vacs also have *lots* of power, so don't go sticking it on your skin to test the suction.

If you're installing a central vac

The hose of one of these is a little awkward if it's too long; I'd put in a few more receptacles so you can use a short hose.

And here, too, you'll want beater brush action to bounce dirt out, and the manufacturers do make a beater brush head for the hose. If you get the air-driven type of beater head you won't have to worry about needing an electrical outlet at or near each receptacle, to plug the power head into. Be sure to put a couple of outlets in the garage and anyplace you have stairs.

Put the receptacle in the garage near the exterior door, as three-quarters or more of your vehicle vacuuming will be on the driveway, not in the garage.

Mount all the receptacles and switches high—it'll save a lot of bending over.

A vacuuming in time. . .

A good carpet-cleaning program will free you from hours of work and emotional anguish. Clean carpets look and feel better, and they last longer. A regularly maintained carpet means less frequent shampooing, less time expended on carpet care, a longer life for the carpet, and more compliments from your guests!

The ideal carpet care plan is to (1) keep all possible dust, dirt and abrasive material from getting on the carpet—the job of good matting; (2) regularly remove all litter and extract harmful embedded debris from the carpet—the job of a good vacuum; (3) keep grime cleaned off the top of the carpet so that it doesn't have a chance to penetrate—the job of effective surface cleaning.

Install a good set of mats as explained in chapter eight, and vacuum carpets and mats regularly. Don't wait until you can see the dirt. Just because it's possible to camouflage crumbs, dog biscuits, pins, pennies and peelings in deep pile doesn't mean you should overdo it. Keep all materials detrimental to carpeting out of the carpet. I've seen homes go for ten years before the carpets needed shampooing, all due to good matting and regular maintenance. Avoiding unnecessary shampooing is wise because shampooing is expensive, whether you do it yourself or have it done professionally.

Professional secrets of better, faster vacuuming

Always police the area first, to get any large debris off the carpet. A quick bend to pick up an object by hand is a lot faster and smarter than wasting ten minutes—and who knows how much repair shop money—trying to dig it out of your vacuum.

When possible, plug in to a strategic location that will allow you to vacuum the maximum area and avoid backtracking.

You don't have to vacuum every square inch every time. Spend most of your time on the traffic areas—that's where the dirt really is. Under and behind furniture and other out of the way or unused areas can go for two weeks or more without hurting a thing (including your honor). Likewise, don't sweat the edges—where the vacuum won't reach and the foot never treads. Once every two weeks or so before vacuuming, sweep along the baseboards to flick anything there out to where the vacuum can reach it. Occasionally run over the corners and edges with your canister vac and crevice tool or dusting brush. Any dirt (mostly dust) there won't wear out the carpet, since we don't walk along the walls.

Slow, deliberate strokes pick up better and are faster in the end than zipping over one area three or four times. Let the vacuum work for you. It needs time for the beater bar to loosen the dirt and for the air flow to suck it up. If you watch a lot of vacuumers, you'll see that much time is spent in overlap. This is a waste of time if you have a beater brush assembly on your vacuum. Overlap each stroke an inch or so, but avoid running the machine over the same area twice, except as might be needed in badly soiled, high-traffic areas.

If you have a room that's especially dirty, you may have to resort to overlapping, up and back vacuuming strokes. But this takes a lot of time, tires you out, and usually isn't necessary. In rooms or halls that are too small for effective maneuvering, instead push the vacuum to the end of the stroke and then pull it back to cover the next strip of carpet. After you've pulled the vacuum all the way back, push it forward again and repeat the process. This method is quick and will do an effective job 90 percent of the time.

Vacuum carpeted stairways regularly; the corners only need to be wiped with a damp cloth occasionally.

● Stairs

Don't get on your hands and knees— vacuum the center traffic areas of the steps with your beater brush vacuum. This will remove even deeply embedded dirt. As for the edges and corners that rarely are tread upon, just wipe with a damp cloth to pick up the visible surface dust, and occasionally hit 'em with your canister when you do the edges in the rest of the house.

● Area or throw rugs

Take them to a nearby carpeted floor for vacuuming. If you stand on one end of the rug and vacuum away from you, it won't get sucked in.

● Vacuuming carpet fringe

Those fringes on area rugs and carpets are just laying there waiting to be sucked up and jam your beater brush. Outsmart them by quickly sweeping them out of the way (over onto the rug they're attached to); then you can vacuum by and pull up that previously hidden dust and dirt. Or you can bleed off the vacuum suction (that means open the little valve on the hose so the vacuum won't have as much suction).

Edges are only a visual problem because traffic wear is impossible.

Sweep when they're dusty.

It will then pull up the dust bunnies, but not the fringes. You can use the suction adjustment when you vacuum drapes, too.

Always keep your vacuum on carpeted area while it's running. I've ruined a beautiful wood floor by running a low-adjusted beater bar type vacuum over it. The metal part of the bar thumped the floor on every rotation and dented it (at great expense to me, since our insurance covers liability but not stupidity).

Don't abuse your vacuum

Eighty percent of vacuuming problems are caused not by a loose nut on the machine, but by the loose nut running it. The personality and habits of the user can take a great toll on vacuums. For example, I gave two heavy-duty commercial vacuum cleaners for Christmas in 1965, one to my mother-in-law and one to another relative. My mother-in-law's vacuum still looks and works like new (she's had it twenty-six years now). The other one lasted less than thirteen months.

The unintentional (or sometimes intentional) vacuuming of coat hangers, Scout badges, marbles, overshoes

Never feel under a beater vacuum to see if it's working.

Make sure the beater and belt are working properly.

WRONG!
Kicks dirt out and away from vacuum.

RIGHT!
Pulls dirt under vacuum to the intake.

and scissors is what hurts vacuums. Those clicks and clanks you hear when the vacuum picks up one of these or similar articles generally means the (usually plastic) blades of the little gizmo that generates suction, called the impeller or the turbulator fan, are being sheared off. If you're vacuuming more and enjoying it less (getting up less dirt), you had probably better re-

place the fan. It's not uncommon to have a fine-running vacuum without suction, and a beat-up $5 fan is generally the reason. (If it's not the fan, then it's probably the beater brush.)

Note: A strong bar magnet screw-mounted to the front of your upright vacuum will pick up tacks, pins, needles, scissors, can openers, or any other metal object you might miss before vacuuming. It will save injuries to crawling babies, wrestling kids and nice, new vacuum cleaners.

Vacuum health check-up

The biggest secret of efficient vacuuming is *keeping your vacuum well maintained*. Your vac is your second most important set of wheels, so take care of it and check it regularly, just like your car.

● Don't let your bag "overeat." Anything more than 50 percent full will sap your vacuum's cleaning energy and strain the motor. Keep cloth bags emptied and shaken out so the pores in the cloth won't get clogged. To avoid leaks, keep the bag clip tight.

- Never run over the cord or pinch it in doorways. Avoid using extension cords; they lower your vacuum's performance.

- Protect the plug. Remove it from the receptacle with your fingers, not by pulling on the cord.

- Tighten the screws in the handle every so often or they'll work loose and fall off. Keep the handle clean—it's easier to grip, and healthier too.

- Keep the rubber bumper in place to protect your vacuum as well as your furniture and baseboards.

- Make sure the brushes on the beater brush aren't worn to nubs (if they are, you can slip in a new brush insert—it's easy). Check the beater occasionally for cracks or jagged edges that can snag carpet pile.

- The right pile adjustment on your vacuum gives the beater brush room to move to loosen deep dirt. It also ensures that the suction will be able to carry the debris into the bag. Set the brush to its highest setting, completely up off the floor, and turn the vacuum on. Lower the setting gradually until you hear the brush come in light contact with the carpet. If you set it lower than that ("I'm really gonna chomp the carpet"), you cut off the air flow and slow down the beater.

- Make sure the belt is tight and that it's on right. If it's worn, replace it. Don't buy cheap imitation belts, only genuine original manufacturer's parts for your make and model. If the belt runs hot, clean the motor pulley of threads, glaze and accumulated dirt.

- Make sure the beater or roll bar turns easily and is free of thread, string and shoelaces. String wrapped around the bar will pres-

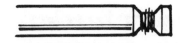

sure the bearings and cause them to turn harder and even heat up. Hooking the point of scissors under them is the best way to remove things like this.

- If you seem to have a lot less suction these days, have a vacuum repair shop check the fan. The fan is what creates the suction, and the blades might be worn down or broken. For a few dollars you'll have your vac like new again.

A new vac fan

A worn vac fan

- Dust the exterior of the machine, and wipe off the power cord occasionally!

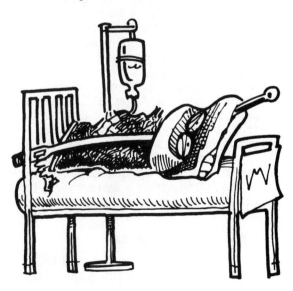

Soil retardant

If your carpeting isn't one of the newer types with soil resistance built right into the fibers, it's generally a good idea to treat with soil retardant.

A soil retardant is a chemical treatment that helps carpet resist soiling and helps prevent water- and soil-based spots and spills from becoming hard-to-remove stains. Water-based soiling agents especially, such as soft drinks, milk, coffee, mud and winter slush, cause big maintenance problems as they soak into carpet fibers and backing, rapidly deteriorating appearance. Soil retardants can be applied to *clean* carpet, old or new. (It's often applied during manufacture, so chances are your new carpet has it. Ask, when you buy a carpet.)

The best-known brand of soil retardant is Scotchgard, made by the 3M Company. If applied correctly, it can be a real boon. After spending time in the 3M testing labs observing control blocks of carpet, treated and untreated, I was impressed. Apply Scotchgard yourself following the directions on the container, or have your dealer do it for you. You can even purchase carpet and upholstery shampoo containing Scotchgard.

But just because carpet is protected by a soil retardant doesn't mean you can relax. You must still keep up your regular schedule of cleaning and maintenance. The chemical types of soil retardant have to be reapplied every time you deep-clean (shampoo) the carpet. Carpets with soil protection locked right into the fibers themselves must be cleaned according to the manufacturer's instructions, or you can undo their stain resistance and void the warranty.

Antistatic agents

Static electricity is the mild shock produced when you touch a metal object after walking across a carpet. It's the result of friction. While not harmful—unless you have a home computer that will go on the blink—it can be irritating. And static electricity can actually pull dust particles from the air. By eliminating static, you keep your carpet cleaner.

Some carpeting contains a small amount of stainless steel fiber to dissipate static electricity. For carpeting that lacks this feature, applying an antistatic agent to the carpet periodically, or simply increasing the humidity in the room, can help the problem.

Shampooing the carpet

There comes a time in the life of all carpet, regardless of how faithfully you have vacuumed, removed spills and spots, and kept mats at the doors, that it will have collected enough dirt and soil deep in the pile that it just has to be washed or "shampooed" out. Some people shampoo the carpet every year (which is probably too often), and some every ten years or when they can see it start to twitch and move by itself. The grime usually sneaks up on us, like weight gain or weeds in the garden—by the time we realize it, it's too far gone. Its location, color, and the amount of traffic it receives will have a lot to do with when a carpet needs to be cleaned, but there are several ways to determine when shampooing is needed:

1. Look for a clean place (under the couch, a saved remnant, etc.) and compare it with the rest of the carpet.

2. Feel it! Yes, dirty carpet feels heavy, matted and sticky.

344

3. Rub it with a white towel dampened with carpet shampoo. The dirt and soil will show up like a red flag.

4. Smell it. Musty, dusty carpet has a smell we all know too well. Get down on your knees and sniff a few times.

5. You can see a three-foot grimy circle around the TV chair or the dust storm that follows you when you walk across the carpet!

Okay, it's ripe. Besides that, company is coming, and you're holding your third daughter's wedding reception at home. You have two basic choices to get the job done: Do it yourself, or call a professional. (And once it's clean, start a regular surface cleaning program—see page 349.)

I'm the first to push independence and "doing your own thing," but I caution you about the pitfalls of shampooing your own carpet. It's not necessarily a complicated job, but don't be deceived by the propaganda of trouble-free, money-saving, automatic, do-it-all machinery. The operator of the machine has to have some knowledge, the ability to adapt to different carpet-cleaning requirements, and understand how much moisture and chemical to use. Otherwise a poor cleaning job, overwetting, or fiber and backing damage will result. It amazes me that people will spend $2,500 for a carpet, then attack it with powerful cleaning gear without any experience whatsoever.

Another pitfall is cost-value miscalculation. Take, for example, a 14×20-foot living room carpet, which a professional might do for $30. A pair of homeowners (one of whom is missing a fishing trip) will drive ten miles across town to rent a big steamer or rug outfit for $15. Then they'll buy $5 worth of chemicals, skin up the family car getting it all in, and drive another ten miles home. They'll unload the

heavy equipment, grunting and groaning. Then they'll move furniture, read directions, spend most of Saturday cleaning carpet, and probably will have to drive back for more shampoo. The results will be questionable.

Once they're finished, it's a repeat performance of loading and driving to return the equipment. At the end of the day, they've spent $35 on gas, rent, shampoo, etc.—not to mention their time. They are dead tired; have

experienced a smashed hand, three arguments, two dogfights—and come Sunday night the carpet still isn't dry in places. I've cleaned carpets for thirty-five years, and always do my own because I know how and have easy access to the equipment. But I would never do my own if I had to round up and rent the mediocre machines available and go through all that. I couldn't afford it and wouldn't enjoy the hassle.

If you insist on doing it yourself, see pages 347-348 for some ways to improve your results.

Professional carpet cleaning

There are also pitfalls to having your carpet done. Not all so-called professionals *are* professionals. Some "carpet cleaners" are opportunists who were franchised or hired for a big kill; their training has been by trial and error. The method used in shampooing carpets is important. That TV before-and-after demonstration of a great contrast once a little foamy carpet shampoo is rubbed on is deceptive. That isn't cleanliness you behold, but the "optical brightening" most carpets exhibit when wetted. After a light foam job, many carpets appear to gleam and sparkle, but they can still be filthy.

This has been the story with most home carpet-cleaning and is in fact the reason you so often hear: "Never shampoo your carpets, for once you do, they will get dirty faster." They *do* get dirty faster, but only because the surface was grazed with a dab of shampoo, and the dirt and soap were carried by the moisture down to the bottom of the fibers, only to emerge quickly when the carpet is in use again. (Remember—ask yourself, when you clean, where the dirt goes.

If you can't figure it out, the dirt probably isn't coming out.) Also, many shampoos leave a soil-attracting residue on the carpet fibers.

Great deals?

You will be approached by mail or by phone with the "mist" method, the "dry-foam" method, the "liquid" method, the "dry-powder" method, and the "steam" or "extraction" method. I would be cautious of any of these on my carpets because they are all in some way obsolete or ineffective. For example, "steam" isn't what it's cracked up to be, but when steam cleaning hit the market, it positively revolutionized carpet-cleaning. It wasn't the steam itself but the extraction process that was so valuable: Hot cleaning solution is pressure-injected into the carpet, and a super-strong wet vacuum is used immediately to pull almost all the moisture back out.

It's my opinion that steam extraction alone generally won't clean an old, dirty carpet. I know the water extracted from the carpet is impressively muddy, but remember that the dwell time between the solution's being injected and removed is so brief that it can't dissolve much of the goop adhering to the fibers. Rotary motion or scrubbing action is needed after the solution is applied to loosen all the dirt and deep-clean the carpet. This should be followed by extracting (rinsing) to remove all dirt, soap, etc.

If you do decide to have your carpets done rather than do them yourself, first make sure there's a good, professional carpet cleaner in your area. (*Always* check references.) They'll do a better job than you can, and probably save you money over doing it yourself.

Be sure to get a firm price quote. And ask which method they use. If they say "steam" or "extraction," request a truck-mounted unit that heats the solution to 150° and has the power to actually steam-clean your carpet. Request that they prespot and prespray any stains.

If they say "rotary," make sure that after they've scrubbed the carpet it is rinsed with hot water by the extraction method. That means, if nine gallons of liquid go into the carpet, they get eight-and-a-half gallons back out. Some professionals call the combination of rotary scrubbing and hot water extraction "showcase" cleaning. It's the most expensive but does the best job.

How to do a better job if you do it yourself

All kinds of places carry rental shampoo equipment, from the simplest to the two-gorilla size guaranteed to beat up your car and give you a hernia loading and unloading. Companies such as Bissell and Sears also sell scaled-down hot-water extraction units.

Equipment like this doesn't have the horsepower to truly deep-clean the carpet all the way down to the roots—suction isn't strong enough and the water doesn't get hot enough. These units are probably better suited for surface cleaning (see page 349). If you follow the manufacturer's directions, the best you can expect is a fair job of shampooing. Let me give you some better directions, whether you use them to surface clean or shampoo. You can do a couple of important things at home with a small extractor that will double your shampooing speed and efficiency.

When you shoot the cleaning solution in, the filthy water you pull right back out gives the illusion that your carpet is really getting cleaned, but that dirty water is just the easy surface dirt that comes off as soon as the carpet is wet. The little sprayers shoot the solution in, but before it can attack

the tough, stuck-on dirt—the aged dog doo, the smashed raisins, the ground-in jellybeans—the vacuum pulls it back out. We pros call this problem not enough "dwell time"; in other words, the solution isn't in the fibers long enough to exert any chemical action, only to dissolve the loose, easy dirt.

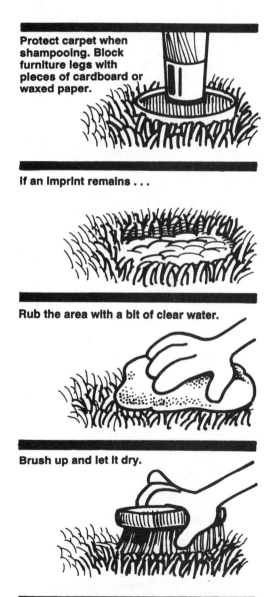

Protect carpet when shampooing. Block furniture legs with pieces of cardboard or waxed paper.

If an imprint remains . . .

Rub the area with a bit of clear water.

Brush up and let it dry.

The good professional carpet cleaner using an extractor system does one of two things, either of which you can do:

1. Scrub the carpet briefly before you start to extract, using a rotary floor scrubber or "buffer," or even just by hand with a cleaning cloth or towel. Just dip up some shampoo foam (not lots of water) and work it into the carpet so it can attack and emulsify the dirt clinging to the carpet yarn. Then when you come behind, with the extractor shooting hot water into the carpet and pulling it out, it's like a flushing rinse; a lot more of the dirt comes out, a lot faster.

2. Use a carpet prespray solution at least five minutes before you start shampooing. *Lightly* spray the carpet, using a hand spray bottle or even a weed sprayer, if the job is a big one. You don't want to soak it, just mist it

to wet the surface, where most of the dirt and airborne oils are. Spray a little heavier in the traffic patterns where the dirt is thicker and worked in. The solution will loosen and release the soil and as your carpet lays there, panting and wounded, you pass over it with your trusty extractor unit—*snort, bobble, squeak*—your water will *really* be dirty now, and you can sigh confidently that you do have most of the dirt.

Rental extractor units such as Rug Doctor have a little scrubber built into the head, which is fine. But even with these it's better to first apply the solution lightly with the scrubbing tool but not the vacuum; then, on the second trip, give it the full business, all controls on. This way you'll have given the shampoo time to "deterg the dirt."

If you do a lot of shampooing, go to a janitorial-supply store (or see page 264 for a mail-order source) and

A home-size hot water extraction machine.

get a gallon of shampoo concentrate. It's much cheaper than the stuff they sell with the machines.

Surface cleaning to delay shampooing

Most homeowners put up with increasingly dirty carpet until they can't stand it anymore, then they spring for an expensive steam-cleaning job. They could learn something from those who maintain carpeting in commercial buildings. These people have learned the value of regular surface cleaning to keep carpets looking good and to stretch out the time between deep cleanings. Surface cleaning is just what it sounds like—a spiffing up of the surface of the carpeting, as opposed to deep cleaning (such as extraction cleaning or shampooing), which takes more time but cleans the carpet clear down to the base of the fibers.

There are various ways to surface clean carpeting, and a home extraction machine, as described earlier, is one. Dry powders (Host, Capture and Amway dry carpet cleaners are some good ones) can be applied by hand or with a machine (purchased or rented) specially designed to scrub them in; with many models you have to use a regular vacuum to remove the powder afterward. There is also the system professionals use called "bonneting." This is a process of taking a yarn bonnet (a yarn pad or disc two inches or so thick) dampened with a special solvent cleaner and simply rubbing it on the carpet. Or if you have a floor machine, you can use it to massage the surface of the carpet with the yarn bonnet. We use it at night on the traffic lanes of commercial buildings, and they're dry in an hour. Bonneting

doesn't deep-clean and it does leave a speck or two of residue, but it's widely used in the professional field and I use it in my own home. I've been in a Bell System office in Pasadena, California, that has used this method for seven years. The carpets, even in the reception area, are clean and new-looking, though they've never been shampooed.

The bonnet treatment is fast, easy and inexpensive. After you moisten the bonnet with carpet-cleaning solution, you wring it out in your roller mop bucket, then mount it under the floor machine and run it over the carpet. The machine moves the pad in a rotating motion on the carpet, and the bonnet picks up and absorbs surface grime and soils. When the pad becomes dirty, turn it over and repeat the process. When both sides are dirty, rinse the bonnet clean in the mop bucket, wring it out and repeat the process.

In a home, a once-a-month bonnet-

A few more do-it-yourself carpet-cleaning cautions

- Vacuum well before you start.
- Don't let the solution sit too long before you extract it.
- Don't overwet! Keep the wand moving and only make one pass to wet the carpet. Overwetting can cause the backing and pad to rot, mildew or even shrink.
- Use a good-quality shampoo in the recommended dilution. Using cheap shampoo or too much shampoo can cause rapid resoiling.
- Ventilate!
- Long-napped carpet may need to be raked or swept to a stand-up position to dry.

ing would be plenty. It does take a certain solution such as Argo Sheen to produce the best results, so check with a professional supplier if you plan to try the bonnet system. A janitorial-supply store can direct you to the right chemical to clean with and a bonnet to fit your floor machine.

You can also use a plain old terry towel or a hand applicator (a dustmop-looking tool), such as that made by Argo Sheen, to bonnet. (The Oreck Company also now produces a little twelve-inch oscillating scrubber perfect for bonneting.)

I like surface cleaning because it holds carpets to a consistent level of cleanliness and replaces the old inefficient up-and-down approach to cleaning. There is something spiritually uplifting about a clean, fresh expanse of carpet.

Spots and stains

Spots, stains and spills on carpet are just as upsetting in the home as they are in the commercial buildings I clean.

There are two basic approaches to take to carpet spots:

One way is to keep just two different spot removers on hand: an all-purpose spotter for water-based substances (food, blood, etc.), and a solvent spotter for tar, grease and oil stains. (If a particular problem keeps recurring in your household, you may want to select in addition to the two spotters and keep on hand—bacteria/enzyme digester, for example, if you have pet "accidents" or children in toilet training.) These spotters are available at janitorial-supply stores, and are very effective. If there's a stain they won't remove, you can call in a professional to get the spot out chemically or to doughnut-cut that piece of carpet and plug in a new piece.

If you're a do-it-yourself type, keep handy a spotting kit (see page 352) and consult the stain chart following. A janitorial-supply store will carry any of the items not available at the supermarket or discount store. Both the kit and chart are useful in the laundry room, too.

Remember, keep cleaning solutions and tools safely out of reach of little children. I would suggest you store your spot removal tools and supplies in a small plastic carrying tray. This will organize your supplies for quick attack on spots.

It's important before you try to deal with it to know what a stain or mark on the carpet *is*. What base is it—water or oil? You must match the base of the stain to the base of the cleaner—for instance, a water-based detergent solution won't make much of an impact on oil, but a petroleum-based solvent spotter will dissolve it immediately.

Smelling and feeling a spot will help you determine what it is. You can also ask other household members (nicely) if they know anything about how the spot got there. If a spot is darker than the carpet, you have a chance of removing it; if it's lighter, that means the substance bleached the fibers and the spot will need to be plugged (unless you can rearrange the furniture).

Bleaching a stain—even with the relatively mild hydrogen peroxide—is a last resort, and I don't generally recommend it, unless you want a little adventure or a new *white* spot as a conversation piece. Before you bleach, *always* test the carpet or fabric in an unobtrusive place.

Red stains—from barbecue sauce to Kool Aid to melted cherry popsicles—have always been among the worst. But now there are special professional products such as Red Out designed just for this purpose, so if you have a stubborn red blotch somewhere,

How to remove carpet stains

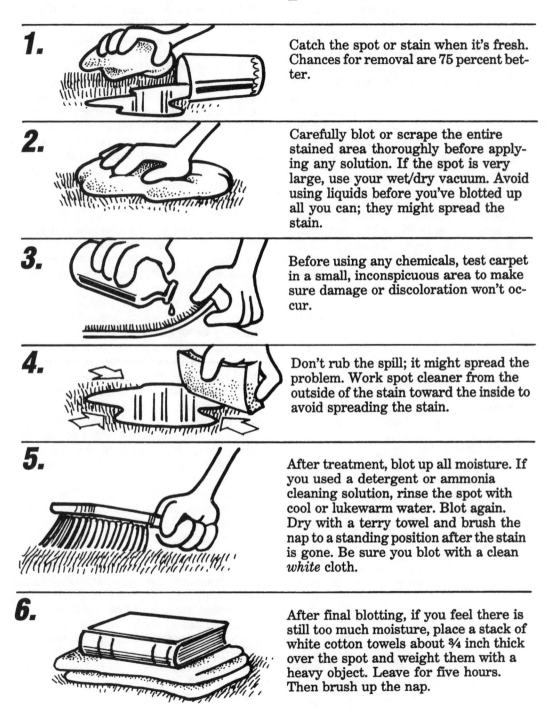

1. Catch the spot or stain when it's fresh. Chances for removal are 75 percent better.

2. Carefully blot or scrape the entire stained area thoroughly before applying any solution. If the spot is very large, use your wet/dry vacuum. Avoid using liquids before you've blotted up all you can; they might spread the stain.

3. Before using any chemicals, test carpet in a small, inconspicuous area to make sure damage or discoloration won't occur.

4. Don't rub the spill; it might spread the problem. Work spot cleaner from the outside of the stain toward the inside to avoid spreading the stain.

5. After treatment, blot up all moisture. If you used a detergent or ammonia cleaning solution, rinse the spot with cool or lukewarm water. Blot again. Dry with a terry towel and brush the nap to a standing position after the stain is gone. Be sure you blot with a clean *white* cloth.

6. After final blotting, if you feel there is still too much moisture, place a stack of white cotton towels about ¾ inch thick over the spot and weight them with a heavy object. Leave for five hours. Then brush up the nap.

351

check with a pro carpet cleaner.

The critical difference in spot removal on carpet as opposed to other fabrics or hard surfaces is drying. Carpets are low and there's no such thing as air circulation under them, so whenever you wet them you better pull that moisture back out with a dry cloth (blot) or even a wet/dry vacuum, if necessary. Get out all the moisture you can, and if it's still wet place a fan near the spot. If carpet stays damp it will rot, mildew, breed bacteria, smell, and the floor underneath can even warp and buckle!

If you have wool carpet or upholstery, try to avoid wet-cleaning it. Use dry-cleaning solvents whenever possible. Call your dealer for advice.

Be patient—give the chemicals time to work. Don't expect all stains to come out immediately—most take some time.

Most old stains and spots can't be removed, and some chemical stains are permanent damage that can't be reversed, so don't get your hopes up too high about that three-year-old acne medicine stain you've had the lamp table over. It might have to remain until you replace the rug!

Spot removal kit

Bear in mind that there is no one miracle stain remover; most stains require a combination of chemicals and a several-stage attack.

Keep the following things on hand to attack fresh spills: (1) a spotting brush (available at janitorial-supply stores) and a scraper (a dull butter knife will serve the purpose); (2) clean white terry cloths (you always want a *white* absorbent cloth when working with stains so you can check for colorfastness and see if the stain is coming out or not); (3) neutral detergent such as liquid dishwashing detergent (dilute 20:1 for spotting); (4) clear household ammonia (don't use on silk or wool); (5) white vinegar (dilute 1:1 with water for cotton, linen and acetate); (6) solvent dry-cleaning fluid such as Energine, Carbona or Afta; (7) hydrogen peroxide (3 percent solution) for bleaching; (8) enzyme digestant such as Biz (soak washables in a solution of digestant for up to an hour; mix into a paste with water and apply for 15 to 30 minutes to dry cleanables); and (9) denatured or isopropyl alcohol. If you have pets, stock a bacteria/enzyme digester also, such as Out! Pet Odor Eliminator.

Pretreat whenever possible. Apply a laundry pretreat or just some liquid laundry detergent, or powdered detergent made into a paste, to the stained area for 15 to 30 minutes prior to washing. This will loosen the stain so the washer can flush it away. You may need some gentle persuasion, too, which means a little physical assistance or "agitation." A stain is generally locked or lodged into the fibers of any fabric; you usually need to gently push or pull it out.

If it's a mystery stain, first try a dry solvent. If it's still there then try a water-based spot remover.

In the following instructions, the terms "sponge" or "feather" are used frequently. Their meanings are as follows: **Sponge**—Lay the stained article face-down on a pad of clean, white, absorbent cloth and use another such pad, dampened with the spotter, to push the spotter through the stained fabric into the pad below. **Feather**—Rinse and dry a spot from the outside in, to blend in the edges and avoid leaving a ring.

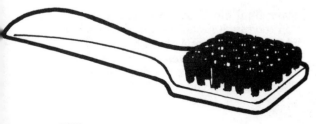

Don Aslett Spot Removal Chart

STAIN/SPOT	METHOD
Alcohol (Liquor, Beer or White Wine)	*Blot up all you can and sponge the spot with water. Sponge with vinegar; blot; rinse. If stain remains, use digestant, and if that doesn't do it, bleach with hydrogen peroxide.*
Blood	*Blot or scrape up all you can; soak old blood stains in salt water or digestant for several hours. Blot with cool water. Blot with ammonia; rinse. Bleach with hydrogen peroxide if necessary. If stain remains, try commercial rust remover from a janitorial-supply store.*
Candle Wax/Crayon	*Scrape off all you can first with a scraper or butter knife. Put a clean, absorbent cloth over the spot and iron with a warm iron to melt and absorb the wax into the blotting cloth. Remove remaining residue with dry-cleaning fluid.*
Chocolate	*Scrape off all you can. Sponge with dry-cleaning fluid. Sponge with detergent solution; blot; rinse. If stain remains, bleach with hydrogen peroxide.*
Cigarette Burns	*For slight discoloration, rub with dry steel wool, vacuum up the debris, then apply detergent solution. Trim off blackened tufts with scissors. For bad burns, have a professional "doughnut cut" the damaged area out and plug in a new piece.*
Coffee	*Blot with detergent solution; rinse. Blot with vinegar; rinse; air-dry. If stain remains, sponge with dry-cleaning fluid. Bleach any remaining stain with hydrogen peroxide.*
Grass	*Sponge with water. Sponge with alcohol (exception: use vinegar if you're working with wool, silk or acetate). If stain remains, use digestant, then sponge with detergent solution; rinse. Bleach with hydrogen peroxide if necessary.*
Greasy Foods	*Gently scrape off all you can. Sponge with dry-cleaning fluid. Sponge with detergent solution. If stain remains, use digestant, then sponge with detergent solution; rinse. Bleach any remaining stain with hydrogen peroxide.*

STAIN/SPOT	METHOD
Gum	*Use aerosol gum freeze from a janitorial-supply or dry ice to harden the gum and make it brittle. Break into pieces by striking and scraping with a dull butter knife, then pick up the pieces. Remove residue with dry-cleaning fluid.*
Ink (Ballpoint)	*Sponge with detergent solution; rinse. If stain remains, saturate with cheap hair spray and blot. If still there, try alcohol, acetone or non-oily nail polish remover and a bleach safe for the fabric, in that order. If yellow stain remains, try commercial rust remover from a janitorial-supply store.*
Lipstick/Shoe Polish	*Gently scrape off all you can, being extra careful not to spread the stain. Blot dry-cleaning fluid through the stain into a clean, absorbent pad. Sponge with detergent solution; blot. Sponge with ammonia; rinse. If stain remains, try alcohol, then hydrogen peroxide.*
Mildew	*Dry-brush to remove as much of the mildew on the surface as possible. Sponge with disinfectant solution; blot. Sponge with ammonia; rinse. Bleach with chlorine bleach if safe for fabric; if not, use hydrogen peroxide.*
Milk/Cream/Ice Cream	*Sponge with detergent solution, then with ammonia; rinse and air-dry. Sponge any remaining stain with dry-cleaning fluid. If stain remains, use digestant, then sponge with detergent solution and rinse.*
Mustard/Catsup	*Scrape and blot to remove all you can. Sponge with detergent solution, then with vinegar; rinse. If stain remains, bleach with hydrogen peroxide.*
Nail Polish	*Blot acetone or non-oily nail polish remover through the stain into a clean, absorbent pad (test first for fabric damage—use no acetone on acetate, modacrylic, silk or wool.) For sensitive fabrics, use amyl acetate (banana oil), available at pharmacies. Flush with dry-cleaning fluid; air-dry. If stain remains, try alcohol, then hydrogen peroxide.*
Oil	*Absorb fresh oil with cornmeal or fuller's earth (available at pharmacies), then sponge with dry-cleaning fluid. Feather edges to avoid leaving a ring. If stain remains, sponge with detergent solution; rinse and feather.*

STAIN/SPOT	METHOD
Paint	*If fresh, flush with either mineral spirits for oil-based paint or detergent solution for latex. If dry, soften with lacquer thinner or paint stripper (test first for fabric damage), then flush with appropriate solvent.*
Rust	*Use commercial rust remover. Home remedies such as salt and lemon juice are slow and not always effective.*
Soft Drinks	*Blot up all you can. Blot with detergent solution; rinse; air-dry. If stain remains, soak with glycerin for thirty minutes and rinse.*
Tar/Grease	*Scrape up all you can, then remove residue by blotting with dry-cleaning fluid. Blot with detergent solution; rinse.*
Urine/Pet Stains	*Scrape up all the solid matter you can and blot out all liquid possible by placing an absorbent towel on the spot and standing on it. Apply a bacteria/enzyme digester according to directions. When dry, remove any remaining stain with detergent solution; rinse.*
Vomit	*Scrape up as much as possible, then rinse the spot with water. Blot with detergent solution. Blot with ammonia; rinse. If stain remains, use digestant, then sponge with detergent solution; rinse.*

Remember, when spills or stains occur, you need to act immediately. Get those spots when they're fresh and manageable, before they can set. For complete stain removal instructions for even the toughest stains, see my book, *Don Aslett's Stainbuster's Bible.*

My free catalog lists a full array of professional supplies and books to help with your every cleaning need. Write to me: Don Aslett, P.O. Box 39-H, Pocatello, ID 83204; or phone (208) 232-6212.

What to Do About Furniture

"What should I do about furniture?" is a question homemakers ask me repeatedly. My own attitude toward furniture is, "I dislike moving it, and I dislike buying it even more." A woman has a finer appreciation for furniture because she's often the one who chooses it, plus much of her time is spent maintaining its appearance.

In an attempt to eliminate both my furniture frustrations, I designed most of the furniture out of a home we built in the resort mountains of Sun Valley, Idaho. Our living room had an octagonal conversation pit padded with vinyl cushions. Twelve or thirteen people could sit and visit comfortably. A plush padded two-stair landing where ten or twelve more visitors could sit faced into the living room. This house didn't have a single piece of furniture except for the beds and the dining room set. I built the stereo and bookcases in, to eliminate cabinets and stands. Pedestal beds were built to the floor and other such adjustments were made to eliminate the clutter and upkeep of furniture. Our home was not only beautiful but usable for family and groups of up to forty, and I didn't have to buy or move furniture!

But for most of you, furniture not only must be bought and moved, it must be cleaned. So the question becomes, "How do I keep my furniture looking nice without a lot of time and effort?"

Attempts to answer this question

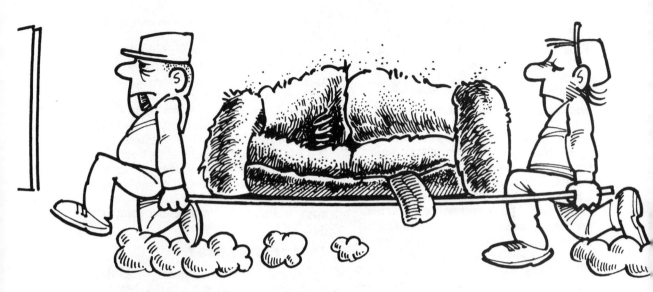

have greatly stimulated the sales of "miracle" furniture polishes. Think about the messages given by thousands of TV furniture polish commercials: "fast and easy"; "polished clean and lint-free"; "see yourself reflected"; "Brand X shines your dingy furniture better than Grandma's beeswax and turpentine and it smells woody, lemony and expensive."

Furniture care isn't that simple. There *are* some ways to cut the time spent caring for furniture and make it last longer. Notice I said "ways," not "way." It isn't done with a squirt of magic aerosol furniture polish as a TV or magazine ad might suggest.

My approach to furniture-cleaning is more preventive than maintenance-oriented. Buy high-quality furniture—well-manufactured furniture, though it may be expensive to buy, costs less in the long run. Cheap furniture loses its crisp, elegant look rapidly and becomes conspicuously dull and shabby-looking. Once in this decrepit condition, it takes a lot of time and supplies to maintain it. And it rarely looks any better cleaned and polished than it did

before you started. Select carefully and get good quality. Paying a little more cash will save a lot of your most precious commodity, personal time.

Choosing furniture with an eye to cleanability

The design and style of furniture you choose will determine how many hours per day, week or year you will have to give to maintaining it. Elaborate grooves, carvings and decorations take more time to keep looking good. And the more kinds of material furniture is made of (or a room is decorated with), the more time and types of equipment and supplies it will take to clean.

You are the sole judge on this one. If the prestige or decor of your home calls for the elaborate unit, you have to decide the long-range value of own-

Which chair leg would you rather clean?

ing it. No matter what you have in mind, check the furniture and make sure all the surfaces *can* be maintained. The wood should have a finish—not just an oiled surface or a colored stain, but a transparent varnish-type coat, called a "membrane finish," to prevent dirt and cleaning materials from penetrating into the wood. Natural or bare wood that needs constant "feeding" or oiling is a pain to maintain and will look dull and discolored before long. Lighter wood furniture shows less dust, is easier to make look good, and remains that way longer than darker furniture.

Metal should have a smooth finish, not be pitted or engraved. It should have a baked enamel or other hard-surfaced coating. Stainless steel and chrome are durable, but require a lot of effort to keep clean and bright.

Glass used as an overlay on a desk or table looks good and doesn't show dust, fingerprints, etc., too badly. But clear glass see-through units—coffee tables, end tables, breakfast tables—act like a magnifying glass. *Everything* shows—a piece of lint will look like a caterpillar carcass.

Is it cleanable?

Fabric will generally be the most used and abused part of furniture. Spillage on furniture is as common as on carpet, believe it or not. Some fabrics look superb, but stains and marks on them may never be removed. Ditto with unfinished cane and wicker furniture. But if you have your heart set

on it, spray-enamel or spray-polyurethane cane and wicker the minute you have it inside the door; this will make it somewhat cleanable (depending on what you spill on it).

Scotchgard, which you can buy at the supermarket or hardware store and apply, is a lifesaver for most upholstery and for you personally. It is an excellent protection for most fabrics, making them more maintainable, because the fibers are protected. But if a big bowl of borscht gets upended and sends a tidal wave of red over the table and onto a Scotchgard seat, you'll probably need to consult the spot and stain removal chart (pages 353-355).

Is it restorable?

Some fabrics look great when new, or newly cleaned, but after a few people sit on them, they become matted or shiny. You've all seen velvet or fur-type material after it has been sat on: a rump print remains, and you have better things to do than go around brushing up cushions to make them look good. Pick a fabric that "restores," or comes back to life, after use (or that doesn't need to "restore"). Select a hard-finish fabric for dining room chairs that are used constantly. White or light-colored fabrics (especially solid colors) show and accent every spot. Fabrics with some color blend or a pattern hide dirt better. Again, this is a matter of taste—but try to make it easy on yourself. Remember, furniture exists for your use and comfort.

Keeping furniture looking nice

Convinced that the secret of furniture maintenance is in the bottle or can of polish, the majority of us use too much of it. We build up layers of gunk, which result in more work and sometimes even surface deterioration. A treated cloth that leaves no oil or residue, yet picks up dust, is the best way to go. Throw away your feather dusters (alias dust spreaders). They are the least effective duster going. You can purchase treated paper dust cloths at your local janitorial-supply store. They're called Masslinn cloths, and they'll last and last; when they're dirt-saturated you can throw them away.

The pro approach might give you new ideas about furniture cleaning. My company cleans thousands of desktops, tabletops, chairs, stands, racks and cabinets every night throughout the United States. In most of our cleaning, we wipe with Masslinn cloths to remove dust. When finger-marks have to be removed, we use a light spray of neutral all-purpose cleaner or a water-damp cloth to wipe, then dry-buff to a natural sheen. We avoid using polish where the finish can maintain its own luster. You could also use a solution of one of the oil soaps made for wood, followed immediately by buffing with a dry cleaning cloth.

If you use an aerosol polish, use

it seldom and lightly. Select one type of polish and use it consistently. The reason for this is simple: Often your furniture surfaces will come out dull and streaked because your new polish isn't compatible with the old polish.

Types of polish

● Clear oil treatment

Usually some kind of oil (mineral or vegetable) and solvent blend, used to "feed" bare wood. Has a wet, glossy look when applied, but a dull sheen after it soaks in. Will become an oily, sticky film if used on varnished or membrane-finished wood.

● Liquid or paste solvent

Hard to apply. Excellent water and abrasion resistance. Low gloss, but durable.

● Oil emulsion polish

Cream type with same drawbacks as clear oil.

● Water or oil wax emulsion (aerosol or spray)

Contain a variety of waxes, silicones and polymers, generally in a water base. They have all the components of a good polish: they protect your furniture, enhance its beauty, and make it easy to dust. Used once a year or so they *are* good, but if you use them every time you clean they'll lay a thick layer of gunk on your pretty wood.

If you have raw or natural wood surfaces in your home, they'll need to be "fed," or treated to keep them from drying out and cracking. Rub on clear oil treatments such as lemon oil. Take your time so the wood can absorb it, then wipe off the excess.

However, I think feeding wood is a ridiculous waste of effort and material. Besides, if grease or ink get on bare wood, it's ruined. Either low-gloss or satin-sheen finishes are available that seal the surface, forming a glasslike membrane through which that beautiful grain will still be bright and clear and fully visible. Marks and stains will end up on the finish instead of on the wood.

If you wish to apply (or reapply) a varnish or polyurethane membrane coat to ailing wood surfaces, it's easy. First, clean the surface with a strong cleaning solution—a strong ammonia solution, wax stripper or degreaser if it's been sealed; solvent if raw—to take off all dirt and oils. Let it dry until any swollen grain goes down. Take care of any nicks or raised spots with a few strokes of superfine sandpaper, then wipe with a tack cloth or a cloth very lightly dampened with paint thinner to pick up any dust or lint on the surface. Finally, apply the varnish or polyurethane, paying attention to the directions on the container. It may take two coats.

Dusting

One of the simplest ways to keep your furniture looking nice is to keep it dusted. The frequency with which you need to dust depends on how dusty or polluted your area is, how readily your furniture shows dust, and how finicky you are.

Dust causes more mental anxiety to you than it does physical damage to your dwelling, so don't get your duster feathers ruffled. Dust is visually offensive and may strain your emotions when visitors drop by, but it does little harm unless someone in the family has an allergy. (Dust on floors, carpets and electronic equipment, however, *does* cause deterioration.) If I had a place I had to dust more than weekly, I'd move!

You can reduce dusting to a minor duty if:

1. You place and maintain proper matting.

2. Your vacuum works well and you use it. Empty your vacuum bag frequently, because if you vacuum when it's full you'll *create* dust.

3. You clean or replace your furnace and/or air conditioner filters regularly.

4. Your home is weatherproofed (door and window seals, caulking, etc.); weatherproofing keeps dust out, too.

When you dust, don't use clouds of aerosol polish or puddles of oily wood treatments, because after a while, you'll create a waxy buildup that will not only look bad and be sticky and more difficult to clean, but actually attract and hold dust. Dust high places first. This gets the dead flies and other crud off the ledges onto the floor, from where it can be vacuumed easily. Always dust *before* you vacuum so that the crumbs and ashes and orange seeds in the corners and crannies of the furniture won't end up on a neatly vacuumed floor.

> **Dusting drill: (1) Dust before you vacuum; (2) work top to bottom; (3) a weekly once-over-lightly is enough for the average house; (4) monthly, hit door frames, window blinds, valances, light fixtures; (5) dust lofts and rafters at least twice a year, using an extension handle.**

Use the right dusting tool. *Don't* use a feather duster. The air movement a feather duster causes will blow particles all over and you'll chase dust for hours. Instead, use one or more of these tools:

1. A Masslinn cloth. This is the disposable chemically treated paper dustcloth I mentioned earlier. It picks up (in fact, attracts!) dust and small particles and is excellent for fine furniture. It will snag on rough surfaces (but any surface that rough should be vacuumed). When a cloth becomes saturated with dust (after about three months of daily use in the average-sized dwelling), simply pitch it and use a new one. These cloths leave a nice nonsticky luster on wood and other finishes and cost only pennies. They're available at janitorial-supply stores.

2. An electrostatic cloth. I'll admit its name — the "New Pig" — is ugly, but the cloth isn't. It's made of a new electrostatic fabric developed by DuPont. Without any oil or treatment of any kind it picks up and holds dust and lint and even gnat eyebrows. When it gets filthy (which it does because everything clings to it), just toss it in the washer. It can be laundered and reused one hundred or more times — now *that's* a dust cloth! I was skeptical at first, but it really works.

3. A water-dampened soft terry cleaning cloth (see Equipment Chart, page 264). Make sure it's thoroughly wrung out so it's only slightly damp. A damp terry duster won't damage surfaces or create extra work; it will hold and remove dust and other residue. Make sure, when you use one, to keep switching to a clean side so it won't become a dust distributor. When it's dust-saturated, use another cloth. On glossy surfaces, buff behind the damp cloth with a dry cloth.

4. A lambswool duster. This is a fluffy ball of (sometimes synthetic) wool on the end of a long handle. It

> **Cobwebs come off easily if you flick them off, rather than rub them in. The lambswool duster is the best tool for the purpose.**

looks like cotton candy on a stick, but almost magically picks up dust and fine particles by static attraction. It's especially good for dusting high and low cobwebs and venetian or mini blinds. Shake it outside after use, and vacuum it when it gets dust-saturated. Lambswool dusters can be bought at a janitorial-supply store or a local housewares store.

Becoming a dust detective

The big trick to dusting is learning where the dust collects: the corners, tops and bottoms of walls and furniture, light fixtures, wall hangings, and any horizontal surface, is the answer. The greatest amount of dust isn't at eye level, as most of us imagine. Natural air currents in the house deposit dust and dirt eighteen to twenty-four inches from the ceiling, and two or three feet up from the floor, and this happens even if no one is in the house! There's plenty of it down low where our feet kick things around, and pets lounge, and the fluff from higher-up settles. The floor (especially a carpeted floor) is full of it, and as we stir it up it lands on the lower rungs and lower half of furniture legs. Take a good look down there and see.

Dust one room at a time with a lambswool duster. Hit the higher areas first, using the side of the duster like a large paint brush, taking care to cover the whole surface and overlap a little. Don't forget those havens for dust known as screens and lattice that may look okay at first glance. Dust and cobwebs really snuggle in here; you have to look close. Even those who dust the top of the door casing trim usually forget the inside of the frame down both sides of the door. Static electricity accumulates here as people, pets and air pass through, so you'll usually see lots of fuzz there. As for that low dusting: with that long

handle on a lambswool duster, you hardly even have to bend at the belt.

Cleaning fabric upholstery

As part of your routine cleaning, keep both vinyl and fabric upholstery vacuumed. Use your upright on the seats of couches and chairs as you vacuum the carpet, or go over the whole piece with the upholstery attachment of a wet/dry or canister vac. Slight surface dirt or hair and skin oils on fabric or vinyl can be removed with a cloth dampened in a carpet shampoo solution. Then wipe with a damp rinse cloth and rub dry with a towel. This kind of surface removal works well if you do it often enough that the headrest, armrests and seat don't have a chance to get too dirty.

When upholstery really gets dirty, you probably ought to call a professional if you want to clean it right. But it *is* possible to do it your-

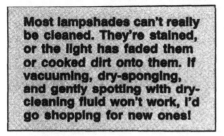

self. If the fabric is thoroughly soiled, it should be washed with an upholstery cleaning solution or shampoo, then rinsed out. This is where problems arise in a do-it-yourself upholstery cleaning job. Cleaning solution is scrubbed on the dirt and the upholstery fabric seems to be cleaner. Actually, the surface dirt has been loosened and has sunk deeper into the fabric along with the cleaning solution. The fabric appears clean, but it isn't. The fabric is soaked with chemical, which leaves it sticky and matted down. The dirt and moisture have to be removed with an upholstery extractor attachment or a good wet/dry vacuum. Soon after the cleaning application, rinse with clear water and use the extractor again. But be sure to use water sparingly—don't get the backing or filling material wet!

Napped fabric should be brushed upright (all in the same direction) before it dries.

To remove stains on upholstery, apply the same principles you do with carpet (see pages 332-355). A surface spot can be wiped or cleaned with an applicator dampened with cleaning solution and dried with a dry, absorbent cloth. Spotting kits with professional instructions are available from most large carpet distributors or a janitorial-supply store.

Always be sure to check manufacturers' cleaning instructions. If your upholstery has been treated with soil retardant, it will usually have to be reapplied after deep-cleaning.

Appliances

One of the most important principles in cleaning appliances, as in any cleaning, is to keep them up. If you let your oven or refrigerator go forever, of course it's going to be a depressing and time-consuming chore.

Frequent, easy, spray-and-wipe cleanups will keep your kitchen appliances looking new indefinitely. Most appliances have an enamel surface: acrylic, porcelain or baked. It's tough and stain-resistant, but not tough enough to resist abrasives. So don't use scouring cleanser, metal scrapers, or steel wool or abrasive (colored) nylon scouring pads on your appliances; these are damaging to enamel, stainless steel and plastic surfaces alike. *Do* use the following: a solution of neutral all-purpose or heavy-duty cleaner (or even plain old hand dishwashing detergent and water) in a spray bottle; a soft white nylon scrub sponge; and a dry cleaning cloth (see page 381) to polish the surface dry right afterward. For those stubborn, dried-on, cooked-on spots, spray and let the solution sit awhile to soften them. Remove and soak the removeables: grills, drawers, drip pans, covers and kickplates. If you want an appliance exterior to really shine, use glass cleaner to polish it. To clean under and behind appliances, just use a radiator brush or vacuum dust brush—but unplug any appliance before you start poking around in back of it (so you'll be sure to live to enjoy how clean it is). Now for the particulars:

Stoves

Spend more time soaking, and you'll spend less time scrubbing. Remove the burner pans and any other parts you can, and dump them in hot, soapy water while you clean the rest of the unit. (If you really need to, you can use a green nylon scrub sponge on the pans to remove the baked-on crud.) Spray and wipe the top, back and sides of the stove. Stop right here if you have the wonderful new solid elements—and consult your owner's manual. Some of them are cast iron, which can tolerate abrasive scouring pads, but others, like some flat-surface ranges, are downright delicate and can even be scratched by a dirty sponge!

If you come across a hardened spot or spill that doesn't come off an ordinary stovetop easily after the

> ### De-slob your knobs!
> Knobs—yes, knobs and dials on stoves—are undoubtedly some of the dirtiest things in the house and are rarely if ever cleaned. They really get bad because they're grooved or serrated for easy grip and often have other little ridges and crevices that catch and hold the crud. *Surprise!*—most knobs and dials slip right off or only need a little simple screw loosened so they can be removed. Toss them into the dishpan (do them right away so you don't forget about them) and give them the "old toothbrush" (scrubbing) treatment if necessary. Then clean that greasy spot *under* the knob or dial before you put it back.

spray-and-sit-for-awhile treatment or even a workover with a white nylon sponge, scrub it gently with a plastic or stainless Chore Boy-type scrubber (keep the surface wet while you scrub). Rinse the pad well in hot water afterward, or grease and grime will harden in it.

Ovens

All of us who still have the old-style ovens clean them the same way, and it's always a tough job. Don't forget to wear rubber gloves, and make sure there's plenty of ventilation—oven cleaner is nasty stuff (for nasty work). I like to put a dropcloth or blanket on the floor in front of the oven when I clean it. Newspaper too often just strains any spills, which end up "eating" your floor. Apply oven cleaner, and wait, and wait some more. (I'm a "wait-over-nighter," myself.) This is the most important step; the chemical needs time to loosen and dissolve all those drips and spatters and stone-hard lumps. When you've tested for the fourth time and the stuff finally seems to be coming off, wipe off the bulk of the now-brown, murky cleaner with paper towels that you can just throw away. By now you should almost be able to see the actual surface of the oven. Reapply cleaner to any black patches that remain, and let it work through them. Don't scrub—just keep applying oven cleaner as long as you need to and let the chemical do the work for you. Simply wipe away the dissolved mess after each application.

When you're done, be sure to remove all traces of oven cleaner with a damp cloth rinse so your next quiche won't reek of chemicals.

Refrigerators and freezers

If you wipe up leaks and spills as soon as they happen and do a quick shelf once-over every week or so with a sponge dipped in clean dishwater, you may be able to avoid the all-out, all-over-the-floor cleaning routine altogether. Regular reconnaissance in there will also keep your hard-earned food dollars and carefully saved leftovers from being wasted. An open box of baking soda in the fridge will help keep odor away, and three tablespoons in a quart of water makes a good deodorizing solution for an overall wipe-down. A neutral all-purpose cleaner is fine, too. Let the solution soften hardened-on food; don't scrub except with a white nylon scrub sponge. Wipe dry with a cleaning cloth. Wash all removable parts in the sink and thoroughly dry them before you put them back.

Stove hoods and exhaust vents

These can cause fires if they get too grease-laden, so don't neglect them. Check the manufacturer's instructions if you can. Generally, you take off the grill, remove the filter, and unplug the unit if you can. Soak the aluminum mesh grease filter in hot dishwashing detergent solution (stubborn deposits might require a strong degreaser solution), or wash it alone in the dishwasher. Rinse in hot water. While the grease filter soaks, use paper towels to wipe off the worst of the sticky, fuzzy grease inside and outside the hood and on the fan blades. Then use a cloth or, if necessary, a white nylon scrub sponge dampened with heavy-duty cleaner or degreaser solution. Deeper cleaning might mean removing the motor and fan assembly; never immerse these parts or spray anything on them or allow water to drip inside. But do wipe off the fan blades and remove the grease and lint from the motor housing. Dry everything, replace the filter and reassemble.

Shorter Visits to the Bathroom

The restroom in the commercial building was a sight to behold. A line of sinks stretched to infinity, and the toilet stalls looked like the starting gate at Santa Anita. This huge restroom was used by 250 people, and it just radiated cleanliness. The chrome glistened, and the porcelain of the sinks and toilets sparkled germ-free—and the matron only spent an hour per day to keep it that way.

Clean your bathroom in 3½ minutes

Considering the average home bathroom's size and use, and that matron's production time, you should be able to keep your bathroom in that same immaculate condition in 3½ minutes a day! Sound impossible? Not if you put some professional techniques to work. The "commercial approach" to cleaning your bathroom is simple and will save you time—the secret, of course, being to spend a few minutes each day keeping it clean rather than indulge in a big once-a-week clean-and-scrub siege. The preventive approach here—maintaining your bathroom regularly and efficiently—is smart.

Again, tools and supplies are important. You'll have to bite your lip and disregard most of the old standbys such as abrasive cleansers, deodorant sprays, magic toilet spices, perfumed blocks, wonder wicks and blue bowl seltzers. The following is a regular cleaning program that eliminates the need for these.

Essential supplies

To avoid wasted time, damage to fixtures and poor results, go to the local janitorial-supply store and purchase scented or unscented disinfectant cleaner concentrate—it's what hospitals use. (Get a *quaternary* cleaner; its active ingredient is ammonium chloride. Avoid the phenol-based cleaners; they're too toxic for home use.) This liquid, if diluted according to the directions on the bottle and used correctly, will clean quickly and efficiently, and eradicate or retard bacterial growth. This will eliminate not only smells but the need for the expensive perfumed preparations you've been using.

I and most other pros use this kind of disinfectant cleaner (nicknamed a "quat"), but if you clean *often* enough, most cleaners sanitize pretty well. So you could use pine cleaner or (if you live in a hard-water area) phosphoric acid cleaner, too. The secret is regularity, not letting soap scum, dirt and mineral deposits build up to stone hardness and thickness.

While at the janitorial-supply store, pick up one plastic spray bottle for each bathroom so the bottle can be left in the room. Once the spray bottle is filled with the water and disinfectant cleaner in the correct proportion, the only other tools you need are a cleaning cloth and a two-sided scrub sponge of cellulose and white nylon mesh (for dislodging any persistent residue).

Your daily bathroom cleaning routine should be something like this: Spray and wipe the mirror if it's spotted. If not, leave it alone. Next, spray the hardware, sink and countertops (spray ahead so the cleaner will soften and break down soil); wipe and buff the surfaces dry. They will sparkle. Do shower stalls and tubs next. Do toilet stool last. (See pages 370-371.)

Once the upper fixtures are clean, fall to your knees (one minute won't hurt you). Spray the floor and, with the already-damp cleaning cloth, wipe it up. This method is a lot faster and better than mixing up mop water and fumbling around with a mop in a fifteen- or twenty-square-foot area.

For daily bathroom maintenance

Use germicidal or disinfectant cleaner diluted from concentrate.

Dilute according to directions into a plastic spray bottle. When spraying disinfectant cleaner in a confined area like the bathroom, adjust the nozzle so the droplets will fall when you spray. If the mist is too fine, you'll inhale particles and irritate your throat.

Spray the mirror, fixtures, sink and countertops. Wipe and buff dry. Next do the shower stall and tub. Then the toilet (base last!) and floor. Remember that odors are caused by bacteria. A clean bathroom won't need deodorant.

The benefits of preventive maintenance

It takes only minutes to clean a bathroom the spray-disinfectant way, and if you leave a spray bottle and cloth in the room, you can get your bathroom spotless while you wait for Junior to go potty or for the sink to fill up. The system works only if you clean the bathroom regularly, however. This keeps hard water deposits, soap scum, toilet bowl lines and other soils from building up and cementing on. The basic reason you needed abrasive cleansers and acids (and dynamite) to clean the bathroom in the past was that buildup accumulated to the point of no return and had to be ground off instead of wiped off.

Don't use powdered cleansers and steel wool to grind dirt off surfaces. In most of the many thousands of houses I've cleaned in my career, the sinks, tubs and shower units—porcelain or plastic—have had damage from improper use of acids, cleansers and abrasive pads. The grinding abrasion that removes spots and stains also re-

moves chrome and porcelain. This is a great reason to use the disinfectant cleaner/spray bottle system from the start. Your chrome, plastic, fiberglass, marble and porcelain will remain bright and sound.

If you have damaged fixtures, you'll have difficulty no matter what you use, because porous surfaces collect gunk quickly and clean up slowly. Many of these surfaces—especially the shower area—will benefit from a coat of paste wax, which helps repel the scum and hard water buildup. (Just don't wax the shower *floor!*)

A squeegee in the shower is worth a truckload of "de-limer"

After attending my seminar, many a housekeeper minimizes the problem of shower buildup by simply hanging a 14-inch squeegee in the shower. It takes only fifteen seconds for the user to leave the wall dry and clean after a shower. (Besides, squeegeeing in the nude is a unique experience!) But if you let hard water dry on your bathroom surfaces over and over again, the built-up minerals practically need to be chiseled off.

It's not a bad idea to wipe the shower chrome (faucets, etc.) too while it's still wet. Use your bath towel to dry it after you dry yourself, and you'll leave it nice and shiny and prevent mineral deposit buildup!

What if you already have hard-water buildup on your walls and fixtures? A professional-strength phosphoric acid "de-scaler" (for home use you don't want anything stronger than 9 percent) will dissolve it faster and better than supermarket de-limers.

For old, stubborn soap scum, try the above first (often the hard-water deposits on a surface create little "shelves" of mineral that hold scum). If that doesn't work, use a degreaser

or soap-scum remover from a janitorial-supply store.

Be careful with those things the hint-and-tip books tell you to soak in tubs and sinks overnight (such as oven grills, blinds, crusted camping gear, tools, etc.). Extended exposure to some

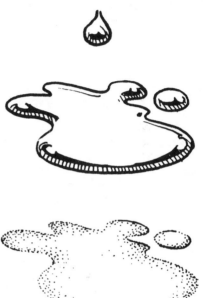

When a drop of hard or soapy water lands on a surface and dries, the minerals and other residue dissolved in it collect at the base of the drop when it evaporates. Every time the surface gets wet, new drops add to the accumulation—and this will keep building up into a hard, solid deposit. That's why it's smart to clean regularly (especially showers and windows) and not give buildup a chance to happen.

Hard water is fast and easy to clean up when fresh, but like cement if you wait!

normally harmless cleaners will often pit the fixtures.

Keep your drains running free by pulling out the stopper every month or so and cleaning the collected hair off it (encouraging hair care to be practiced elsewhere than over the sink can prevent this). Boiling-hot water poured down a drain periodically ought to handle any soap scum buildup that might slow drainage down.

Cleaning toilets

Briskly scrubbing inside a toilet bowl with a bowl brush for a few seconds each day will retard buildup and remove discoloration and lines. When you do your daily spray-cleaning of the bathroom with disinfectant cleaner, spray and wipe the entire outside of the toilet from top to bottom. Contrary to popular belief, it's the outside of the toilet that's most unsanitary. Be sure to do the base of the toilet last. This will prevent you from transporting the worst germ concentration to the faucet handles. Every couple of weeks, pour a little disinfectant into the bowl, swish the water around, and let it sit awhile. Remember, it's the *outside* of the toilet—under the seat and around the rim—that's germiest and will begin to smell if not cleaned frequently. The cold water that enters the bowl with every flush discourages bacterial growth there.

If you need to remove old buildup in the toilet, do it right. Don't pour steaming acid into the water-filled bowl and slosh it around. Dilution with water neutralizes the power of any bowl cleaner. Instead, a couple of times a year, grasp a swab (see Equipment Chart, page 264) and push it quickly up and down in the bowl toward the "throat" of the toilet. All the water will vanish (no free advertising intended). Then give the swab a light

Basic bowl cleaner technique

For daily maintenance, scrub briskly inside the bowl with a bowl brush. You only need to use acid bowl cleaner a couple of times a year. When you do . . .

Don't pour bowl cleaner into the water.

Do force the water out of the bowl with a swab or bowl brush.

Soak the swab with bowl cleaner, lightly coat the bowl—and flush to rinse.

application of bowl cleaner and coat the inside of the toilet bowl. Let the cleaner sit on there a few minutes, then flush to rinse. Reapply, let sit, and rinse again as necessary until all the deposits are gone.

If a ring remains, don't get excited and acid-bath the whole unit. The ring is the result of hard water deposit that's left as water in the toilet evaporates. A pumice stone will remove almost any ring (be sure the surface is wet or it will scratch).

Remember to swab the bowl regularly to prevent buildup. And don't stake your hopes on "miracle" toilet cleaners that promise to make the job fun and easy—there's no such animal out there yet. The "automatic bowl cleaners" that go in the flush tank are a help in keeping things sanitary, but aren't a substitute for periodic deep-cleaning. Even if you can't see the ring, it's still there—you just can't see it because it's bleached white. You still need to get in there with your bowl swab now and then to keep it from building up.

> Still finding hair clinging to the bathroom toilet, sink and walls after cleaning? Before you start, wet a dab of toilet paper and swipe up all the fugitive hair first.

How to get rid of bathroom mildew

When warm, humid weather and spores of mold team up, those little black spots of mildew can grow on everything, including drawers, closets, books and shoes. But aside from the basement, mildew's favorite home is the bathroom.

For the first twenty years of my life, I thought mildew was something that only appeared on roses and al-falfa. Since entering the cleaning business, I've been bombarded with the mildew question: "How do we get rid of it?" The best way to get rid of it is to prevent it. See pages 294-305 for household-wide tips for preventing mildew.

Using disinfectant in the bathroom and shower areas discourages mildew growth there. Chlorine bleach kills mildew, but won't prevent it from returning; you can only do that by altering conditions favorable for its growth. But drying out a bathroom that several people bathe and shower in every day is difficult, so all you can really do is keep cleaning with disinfectant—and hitting mildewed grout with a weak chlorine bleach solution (1 part bleach to 5 parts cool water), as long as the tile isn't made of plastic and you're careful not to get the bleach on anything that is.

Doorknobs, purses and telephones

If people were asked to list the most unsanitary objects in the home, most of them would remember the toilet but forget doorknobs. It wouldn't hurt, while armed with a spray bottle of disinfectant cleaner, to go through the house and spray and wipe all the doorknobs occasionally (and the light switches, chair backs and telephone receivers).

Another unsanitary item that all women should be aware of is the purse. Purses are often placed on dining tables (right next to the salad fork) after having been set on the floor alongside the toilet in a public restroom. Avoid this unappetizing practice! Set your purse by your chair—and use the purse shelves or hooks provided in public restrooms, when available.

Success in High Places

One of my customers had a husband full of ambition and desire to clean, but he was terrified of high places. She would hire me to wash all the high areas, saving the low stuff for him. One year while doing his low section, he was on a plank just a foot off the floor when he was seized by the phobia. He lay down on the plank, dug his whitened fingertips into the wood, and froze. His wife, unable to talk him down from that dizzying height, ended up calling the fire department (siren and all!). They finally dislodged the husband's death grip on the plank and got him onto floor level safely, but he was never sound enough emotionally to assist in cleaning again.

Be sure to adjust or limit the reaching of tall areas to fit your resources, age and nerves (and your helpers' bravery!). But don't be buffaloed by hard-to-reach areas. "Once I got up there, it only took ten minutes" is the wail of many "end-of-the-day" housekeepers. The many hours it takes to get going is the bane of cleaning in high places. Easy access contributes greatly to success in such cleaning, yet the shaky old ladder and unsteady step stool are about the extent of most homes' scaffolding. More energy, time and emotion are used going up and down the ladder or stool than actually doing the job. And all of our effort, worry, tool procurement and arrangement seem to be focused on the few minutes we'll actually perform the job, instead of trying to save the hours getting in position to start it.

As a professional housecleaner, I have to weigh the same factors a homemaker does. The equipment needed to reach the work has to be light enough to be manageable, and small enough to fit in tight areas and keep from scratching walls and woodwork. It must be *sturdy* and *safe* enough to ensure no falls. The following is the basic equipment that more than thirty years of housecleaning have taught me to use.

A good ladder

A plain old common ladder is one of your best all-around tools. It's versatile, manageable and safe . . . if you choose the right model. For household use, the perfect stepladder height is five feet. Four-foot ladders are too short to work on 8-foot ceilings; a 6-foot ladder is too high, and it nicks up the house when you carry it around. A 5-foot ladder is just right for most household cleaning operations. Instead

A five-foot ladder is just right for household cleaning.

4-foot   6-foot   5-foot

373

of buying several creaky wooden ladders for $20 each during your lifetime, buy a 5-foot heavy-duty commercial aluminum ladder for $35 to $50. You'll never regret it. It's strong, safe to use anywhere, and will probably outlast you, even counting the ten years it may add to your life. It can be used outside on rough terrain, and neither bad weather nor dry storage will hurt it.

For higher reaches every household should also have a tall ladder such as the ones firefighters use, and I feel the perfect one for this purpose is an 18-foot, two-piece extension ladder. It will collapse to 10 feet for storage in the laundry room or inside the stairwell and lengthen out safely to 16 feet—enough to get the cat out of the tree, put up the aerial, or paint the trim every five years. Aluminum is lighter, but in an extension ladder for home use, I prefer wood or fiberglass for safety and electrical protection. Don't paint wooden ladders; paint hides breaks, cracks and flaws and is slippery when wet. Instead, use boiled linseed oil to maintain wooden ladders. It penetrates the wood, keeps water out and slivers in. A coat every five years will keep a ladder happy.

Make yourself a box

To reach high cabinets, curtain rods, etc., people usually climb on the harmless-looking kitchen stool or bench. These have a narrow base and a deceptively sturdy top. But they're too unbalanced and risky to use as a standing or cleaning tool. To replace the old bench—and the equally unsafe chair, which has battered many a body—a simply constructed box of three-quarter-inch plywood is inexpensive and far superior. I'd suggest dimensions of 15 × 20 × 28 inches or smaller (see opposite). The telephone companies have a similar unit they've used safely and effectively for years. It's called a "three-position stool." Laid flat on its side or end, it gives you three low heights to work from. Hand holes can be cut in the box's side to move it, and it can serve for storage when it's not in use. It can also serve as a baby crib, an extra chair when company comes, or a place to hide the puppy on Christmas Eve.

Walk the plank for safety

The last and most useful tool to help you conquer the unreachable places is a sturdy, ordinary 2 × 12-inch plank eight to ten feet long. Purchase it at a lumberyard and make sure it has no loose knots, cracks or weak areas. Redwood is good because it's light and rot-resistant. (Pine and hemlock will also work all right, but they're not nearly as light.) Sand off the corners and rough edges for ease of handling, and it's ready to use. Don't paint or varnish it or it will be slippery when wet. You'll use the plank for many things. It is one of the best "under $20" investments you'll ever make. The idea is to combine the stepladder, extension ladder, box and plank in a number of ways to reach your working area easily, safely and without wasted motion. If you need to reach higher areas than can be reached with this combination, rent the necessary equipment, because you'll seldom use it around the house.

A plank, though it may be scary at first, is safe to work on if you're reasonably awake. You'll soon get used to the slight spongy "give" you'll feel. Planks were only fatal to blindfolded pirates when they had to walk

This simply constructed box is inexpensive and a far better way to reach the high places. I'd suggest dimensions of 15" × 20" × 28". You can make it larger or smaller to custom-fit you or your stepladder.

Materials needed:
1 4' × 8' sheet of ¾" exterior plywood
1 pound of No. 8 finish nails
1 bottle of wood glue
sandpaper
1 pint of clear varnish or polyurethane

Just lay out the following plan and assemble per directions. If your husband has traded in his $300 power saw to buy a new vacuum, no sweat—a $39.95 sabre saw will work fine!

Laid flat on its side or end, it gives you three low heights to work from. Hand holes can be cut in the box's side to move it. Use it for storage when it's not in use.

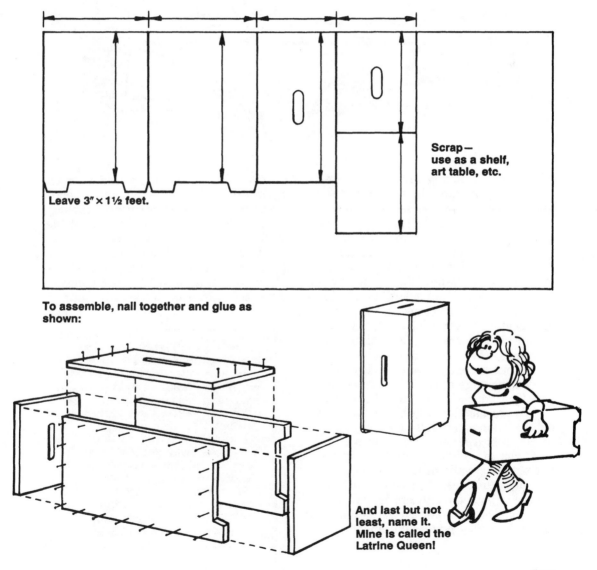

Scrap— use as a shelf, art table, etc.

Leave 3" × 1½ feet.

To assemble, nail together and glue as shown:

And last but not least, name it. Mine is called the Latrine Queen!

375

For maximum stability, be sure your plank extends a few inches beyond the end of the box and beyond the ladder rung it's set on.

off the end. Looking up at the ceiling and moving toward the box end of the plank puts you in the same circumstance as the pirates. That's why you should always keep an extra sponge or empty bucket at the end of the plank so a nudge of the toe reminds you to stop walking. (This is a case where "kicking the bucket" is an aid to longevity.) The plank-and-ladder combination is especially effective to use in high stairwells. On stair landings and other open areas, you can figure out a combination (such as the one on the page opposite). It will make you love yourself for your brilliance.

You're usually only about two feet off the floor when you do ceilings in a house from a ladder. When in a stairwell, you are higher over the stairs, but with the walls of the narrow landing on both sides of you and with a ladder at both ends, there is little risk of falls. I've seen twenty ladder accidents for every plank-and-ladder accident.

Regular or extension ladders must be tilted at the proper angle to keep them from slipping down or tumbling over. One foot out from the base of the wall for every four feet up is just right. Keep your cleaning solution, tools, paint, and other working materials as close to you as possible by wearing a pocketed apron or by setting your

Be sure to adjust or limit the reaching of high areas to fit your age, nerves and bravery. If you have an overwhelming fear of heights, don't do it—you'll get hurt. If you have no fear of heights, get smart—you *can* get hurt. If heights make you shake in your boots, find a couple of daredevils and bake them some cookies. Let *them* climb to clean off that flyspeck, change a light bulb, paint or wash the ceiling.

To clean a stair landing

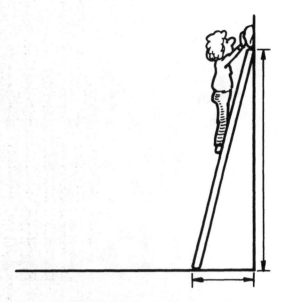

Lean your extension ladder (padded with a towel or dry sponges) against the wall with the base angled into the stairs. Open your stepladder at the top of the stairs. The plank, set across a lower rung of the stepladder and a rung of the extension ladder, puts you in a safe, convenient position to clean or paint the walls. Padding the "wall" end of your plank if it touches the wall will protect the wall.

To use a ladder safely: Angle one foot from the wall for every four feet of height. Never stand on the top rung.

gear on the plank. Ascending or descending a ladder or plank for every dip depletes strength, wastes time, and exposes you more often to mishap.

One "trick" I've tried without much success is moving a stepladder without moving the buckets or tools off it first. I bat about 60 percent. The other 40 percent has cost me wet carpets, skinned shins, painted faces, and trips back to the starting gate. It is also extremely risky to tie or lay a plank on planters, metal railings, fireplace mantels or other trim. Most of these were designed to be looked at, not to support 150 pounds or more of plank, cleaning tools and person. Place ladders and planks on supports where strength is certain.

A cleaning towel (see page 381) slipped over each of the ladder's upper legs will keep it from marking up your walls. A dry sponge (page 379) under each leg will prevent it from slipping if the surface the legs rest on is questionable. Tennis shoes on your feet will prevent *you* from slipping, too.

A final word of advice: put your name on your ladders and planks. When your neighbors spot them, they will be only too happy to try out your new way of reaching high places.

Simplified Wall and Ceiling Cleaning

I once bid to wash walls in six large offices, a long hall, lobby, entrances and storage areas in a Massey-Ferguson tractor dealer's office. Back in the '60s when a dollar was a dollar, I was the low bid at the price of $275. Our new crew was busy on the scheduled day, so I tackled the job alone. Seven hours later, I had it finished and more than a few compliments on the quality of the job. On another occasion, I washed all the walls, ceilings, and woodwork in a modern three-bedroom home in less than one day—alone. Now, I'm no more a "super" wall and ceiling cleaner than you are. In fact, I'm certain that many of you could keep up with or beat me on my best day, if you'd use the same approach I did.

There are two reasons why wall and ceiling cleaning will become one of your favorite housecleaning tasks when you do it my way: (1) It's easy and trouble-free, and (2) the delight of seeing the surface come clean is great! In fact, you'll find washing your walls and ceilings so easy and satisfying, you'll want to wash your friends' walls and ceilings just to show off. Your days of struggling with a bucket of grimy wall-washing solution will end as you finish this chapter, if you follow the simple principles it sets forth.

We outlined the basic principle of cleaning—eliminate, saturate, dissolve, remove—on pages 271-277; here's how that principle applies to the technique and tools of wall-cleaning. Your height, your arm strength, and the degree of dirt accumulated doesn't make much difference in the time and effort it takes to clean walls and ceilings. Using your head and the right tools *will* make a difference.

The versatile dry sponge

One of the first and most important (and least-known) tools of housecleaning is a rubber sponge, called a dry sponge. It works just like a rubber eraser, removing and absorbing dirt. Dry sponges are generally tan or red and come on handles, or as flat 5×7×½-inch pads. The pad is by far the better way to go because it has a larger number of usable surfaces.

Dry sponges come wrapped in cellophane, and when you unwrap them they feel dry and spongy. Never, *never* use water on them or get them wet—not a drop—or they will become useless for cleaning. Most people use dry sponges for cleaning wallpaper. (Now more of you will know what I'm referring to.) They are excellent on wallpaper—much better than "dough" wallpaper cleaners that crumble and stick!

On ceiling acoustical tile and on most flat oil- or latex-painted walls, one swipe of a dry sponge will remove the dirt. It won't remove fingerprints or flyspecks or grease—only the film of dirt. In most homes, dry-sponging the ceiling will leave it perfect. I've washed behind a dry sponge many times, not believing that the sponge could get all the dirt out, but it did—every bit of it! In fact, on many porous walls or painted surfaces, even where the dirt is embedded deeply, a dry sponge is superior to washing. Even on walls that are smoke-damaged, ten minutes of dry-sponging the room prior to washing will reduce washing time and expense by more than 50 percent. When dry-sponging, you don't have to stop to dip or rinse. Just get to the surface and swipe in four-foot lengths (or shorter if your arms are shorter). The sponge will absorb the dirt and begin to get black. It will hold the dirt as you clean along, but as soon as it reaches its saturation

Dry sponges are great for cleaning wallpaper, oil paintings, and smoke or soot damage. Dry sponges also work well on acoustical tile ceilings, masonry surfaces, and most flat-painted walls and ceilings. The proper way to hold a dry sponge (illustrated here) utilizes each pad's eight surfaces.

point, turn and/or refold the sponge and keep going. The residue that falls from the sponge won't stain or stick and is easily vacuumed up after the job is done.

Each pad-type sponge has eight good surfaces, if used correctly. (The handled dry sponges are great, except that once their single cleaning surface is saturated, the sponge is no longer usable.) When a dry sponge is black on both sides, throw it away. Washing it doesn't work. Dry sponges cost less than $2.00 and are worth ten times that for the job they do and the time they save.

A dry sponge won't clean enamel or greasy surfaces, so don't be disappointed when you make a swipe across the kitchen or bathroom wall and nothing dramatic happens.

If you go into the bedroom and make a swipe across the ceiling or outside wall and can't see where you've just been, those surfaces don't need cleaning, and the rest of the walls probably don't either. Just clean the light fixtures and the woodwork and take off the rest of the hour you allowed for bedroom cleaning.

Once the dry-sponging is out of the way, the remaining areas, not cleaned with a dry sponge, will have to be washed. You can accomplish this rather simply if you use the right tools and methods.

Your rag is your worst enemy

There is no question that the most famous household cleaning tool is the simple little item known as a "rag." Your rags have been salvaged from ancient sheets, tattered curtains, worn-out jeans, feed sacks and other fabric scraps. Using a rag to clean with is like using a rake to comb your hair: ineffective. For five hundred years cloth manufacturers have worked to develop fabrics that repel liquids and stains. They've succeeded, and we have scores of fabrics today that resist moisture—which makes them terrible cleaning tools. Yet we can't seem to resist saving trouser legs, old tricot slips, and a thousand other unsuitable fabrics for cleaning rags. Don't do it!

I'm certain that one thing that makes the professional a three times faster—and better—cleaner than the homemaker is the fact that homemakers are hung up on rags. Rags are only good for paint cleanup, stuffing rag dolls, blowing your nose, attracting antelopes in the Wyoming desert, or signaling surrender when the cleaning gets you down. Henceforth, the term "rag" must be banished from your housecleaning vocabulary and from your basket of cleaning tools. The rag in your housecleaning tool bag will be replaced with an item called a "cleaning cloth."

The noble cleaning cloth

A cleaning cloth is made from a new or salvaged heavy Turkish (cotton terry) towel. I've had a lot of questions as to what kind of toweling to use. The big worry is that the poly/cotton blends aren't as absorbent as the old pure cotton towels. Not so! They're an improvement! The polyester is used for the base fabric and the cotton to make the pile (nap). Moisture rarely gets to the base anyway, and the polyester dries faster and resists wrinkles. (A wrinkle-resistant cleaning cloth—now *that's* class!) But do be sure to use toweling with a high cotton content.

First cut an eighteen-by-eighteen-inch piece of toweling. Then fold it over and sew the long side together, leaving it open on both ends like a tube. By

---

How to make a cleaning cloth

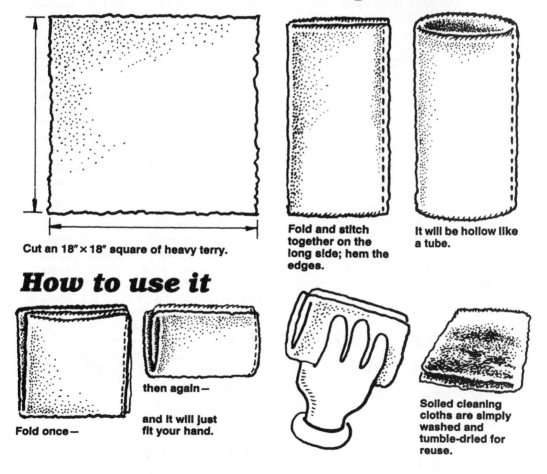

Cut an 18" × 18" square of heavy terry.

Fold and stitch together on the long side; hem the edges.

It will be hollow like a tube.

How to use it

Fold once—

then again—

and it will just fit your hand.

Soiled cleaning cloths are simply washed and tumble-dried for reuse.

By changing sides and turning it inside out, you have sixteen sides to clean with.

folding the tube twice, you have a hand-sized surface of thick, absorbent terry that will efficiently cover every inch of surface it passes over—even get down into bumpy-textured walls and floors. It's not like the old linen bedsheet that just streaks and smears the film around. (We wouldn't think of drying *ourselves* on a piece of sheet after a bath.)

If you refold your cleaning towels correctly and use both sides, you have eight efficient surfaces to use; turn the towel inside out and you have eight more. Sixteen surfaces on one little cleaning cloth! (Terry cleaning cloths are great to protect the hands from scrapes, cuts and ripped fingernails, too.) I often clean all the walls of a large room using only three cleaning cloths. When you finish and the cleaning cloths are damp and dirty, throw them in the washer.

You don't have to use much detergent, because the towels will be full of the cleaner you've been using. If you wash the towels while they're still wet, they'll come out as clean as they were before you used them (although in time they'll get dingy and battle-scarred; they'll still be clean, just stained). Be sure to tumble-dry them! If you hang them on the line they'll be stiff as a board and impossible to use the next time: Twenty cleaning cloths will clean your entire house and, if washed properly, will last for years.

Your basic wall-cleaning tools

The dry sponge and cleaning cloth are the main professional tools you need for your wall-cleaning, so don't prepare a long list of materials and equipment. The rest of the items you probably already have around the house, so round them up: one empty bucket (plastic won't skin up the furni-

ture or sweat like metal does); one bucket half full of warm water; an ordinary cellulose sponge (preferably about 1½ inches thick; make sure the other dimensions fit your hand); and some neutral all-purpose cleaner (I always add a little ammonia to cut grease—besides, I like to see my hands shrivel up!). That's it!

I know what you're thinking now. "Man, wouldn't a two-compartment bucket be great!" No, it wouldn't. They are, without question, one of the most worthless instruments ever palmed off on a housecleaner. Just try to pour dirty water out of one side and keep clean water in the other—or to carry the thing without any intermingling!

Mix your cleaning solution following directions on the container. Make sure your cleaning compound is one capable of cutting the dirt you want to remove. Ammonia or neutral all-purpose cleaner will be fine unless you're dealing with an extremely grease-laden kitchen, where a little degreaser added to the solution will make the job much easier. For bathroom walls, you might want to use a disinfectant cleaner.

Before beginning, reinforce your attitude. I've read books and articles on cleaning house that say, "Allow yourself a day to a week for each room." You're going to clean it, not rebuild it! If you hustle, you should be able to wash a room in thirty minutes, but you'll probably want to allow yourself an hour (maybe more if you anticipate being interrupted). Prolonging a simple job will wear down your initiative and determination.

Cleaning procedure

You have your ladder or scaffolding in position, and now you're ready to begin my method of wall-cleaning. You won't have to cover everything because there will be little or no dripping. (If you have a grand piano that a drop might hurt, don't take the chance—throw a dropcloth or sheet of light plastic over it.) Upholstered furniture can usually be moved out of the way rather than covered. A drop of cleaning solution won't hurt anything if it's removed immediately; if it's not, it may spot or ruin the finish.

Placing your bucket of solution in the right place is extremely important; it should be where you don't have to climb thirty feet to dip your sponge. *Always keep it as close to your working area as possible.* Spilling solution was a major problem in my beginning housecleaning days. I finally learned to set the bucket next to me near the wall—not in back of me, nor on a table, nor in the middle of the floor. Be sure to set it in a visible spot. The most common spillage problems involve tripping over buckets or knocking them over while moving a piece of furniture. If you do spill it on carpet, run for the wet/dry vacuum and get all the moisture out you can. Then rinse with clear water to get the ammonia (or other cleaning agent) out. Again, remember to fill your buckets only half full (if you fill them to the brim they'll be top-heavy and can easily spill), and keep the dirty bucket dumped in the toilet regularly (after each room), for if it spills you'll have a tough cleanup problem.

Take your sponge and dip it into the solution about one-half inch (not all the way in). This will give you plenty of solution to wet the wall or ceiling, yet leave the rest of the sponge dry enough to absorb any water that otherwise would splash into your eyes or run down your arms, down your back and into your shoes.

I know all the books say to start at the bottom of the wall and work up, because if you dribble on the lower unwashed wall from the top, it might stain: an old wives' tale. Anyone who tells you that doesn't know how to wash walls. In extreme cases with, say, fifty-year-old paints or spectacularly dirty walls, it might be wise, but I think it's discouraging to start at the bottom, get it clean, then go on to the top and dribble on the clean wall. I can't stand to back up and redo an area I've already done. So I start at the top and recommend that you do the same.

How large an area you work on at one time depends, of course, on (1) your reach; (2) how soiled the surface is; and (3) how fast the solution will dry on the surface. A three-by-three-foot section is just about right for the average person. Quickly cover the section with the solution on the sponge. Don't press hard or water will spurt out and drip on the carpet and your head. Gently spread the liquid on the surface. By the time you get to the end of the section, the initial application of solution has worked the dirt loose. Now go back to the starting point and again go over the area gently. Don't squeeze the sponge! By now, the dirt should be loosened by the chemicals in your cleaning solution and will come off and soak into the sponge. In the other hand, folded to perfection, is your cleaning cloth, with which you quickly wipe and buff the area before it dries. No rinsing is necessary. The wiping will not only remove the remaining cleaner and dirt, but will polish off the scum that so often streaks washed walls.

Now the critical procedure: Hold the sponge over the empty bucket and *squeeze*, don't wring (you only wring your hands or a chicken neck). When you squeeze the sponge, the dirty solution will go into the empty bucket, leaving the sponge damp and clean. Again dip the sponge one-half inch into the bucket of cleaning solution and repeat the process until the room is

To clean a wall

A bucket half filled with a warm ammonia or neutral cleaner solution . . .

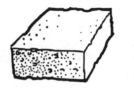

an empty bucket . . .

a sponge . . .

a cleaning cloth.

1.

Dip the sponge about ½ inch into the solution.

2.

Start at the top of the wall and spread the solution to dissolve the soil. Then go back over the wetted-down area with your sponge and wipe to remove the soil.

3.

Wipe the sponged area with a folded cleaning cloth.

4.

Squeeze (don't twist) the dirty sponge into the empty bucket.

Then dip the sponge into the solution again and repeat.

5.

When you finish, the bucket that started out empty will be full of dirty water.

Your cleaning solution will stay crystal clear—the chemical will always be working full strength.

Go easy on the solution. You'll be shocked what too much will do for you!

bright and clean.

You'll notice that the empty bucket is beginning to fill with filthy black gunk, while the cleaning solution is still crystal clear. The sponge you dip into the bucket of solution each time is a squeezed-out hungry sponge (not a sponge full of dirty cleaner), so the dirt never touches your cleaning solution. This means that every drop going on each new section of wall is powerful, unpolluted cleaning solution that will do most of the work. The old method you once used — scrubbing, dipping your sponge in the solution, wringing it, and scrubbing again — always left your cleaning water murky and filthy and thus without full cleaning power. It would streak the walls and have to be changed every fifteen minutes, taking up a lot of time and wasting a lot of cleaning solution. With the two-bucket method you don't spend time scrubbing, just applying and removing. And the towel dries and polishes walls three times as well as the old rags you once used.

"Outside walls" (the inside surfaces of exterior walls) will be dirtier than inside or "partition" walls, so don't be surprised. If you can't see where you're going when you wash, forget it — it doesn't need washing!

Two-bucket benefits

Besides doing a 70 percent faster and better job, the two-bucket wall-cleaning technique has two more great "Life After Housework" savers:

1. You'll never dump and refill another bucket of solution. One bucket of water and fifty cents worth of solution will do all the walls in your house!

2. The dirty water . . . you will love it. In fact you will have a special relationship to it. Before, all your evidence of toil and accomplishment went down the drain; now you have it for show. I've seen people save it for days. (Bottle it and place it on the mantel.) I guarantee it will be the best, most heartwarming exhibit in your housekeeping museum.

Enameled walls

When cleaning enamel-painted halls, kitchens or bathrooms, use the same procedure, with one simple adjustment: Keep the drying towels cleaner and drier, because enamel needs more polishing with a drier buffing cloth than flat paint. Wipe marks won't show on flat paints, but they will show even on perfectly clean enamel. Those circular wipe marks that you can't see when you finish (but can later in certain light) are caused by rags; rags can't/won't buff-dry your walls. I was called back on many jobs during my first year of cleaning to remove streaks that weren't there when I left. Since that day twenty-five years ago when I began to use terry cleaning cloths I haven't been called back for a single case of "enamel streak."

P.S. Plain sheetrock can't be washed. It's just paper over gypsum

How to clean:

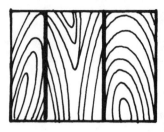

PANELING. Same procedure as for painted walls. Use neutral all-purpose cleaner or oil soap solution, keep the sponge nearly dry, and then, buffing with the grain, dry completely with a cleaning cloth.

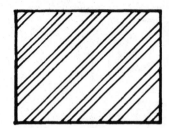

WALLPAPER. Use a dry sponge and clean with the flow of the design.

VINYL WALL COVERING. Use the cleaner recommended by the manufacturer, keeping the sponge nearly dry. Use no harsh or abrasive cleaners. Then dry thoroughly with a cleaning cloth.

TEXTURED WALL COVERINGS. Any textured wall covering will have dust and dirt resting in the thousands of little pockets of the design, which will spread out all over when the wall is wet or rubbed. Vacuum walls like these first before wet- or dry-cleaning.

and the joints are taped compound with emulsives—it'll just turn to putty if it's wet. Paint it with two coats of enamel and next time you'll be able to wash it.

What to do about wall spots

When you run into marks and spots on the walls that don't come clean when you wash them, just leave them until you finish. Then come back and try to remove them by rubbing hard with a cleaning cloth and a little solution. Toothpaste, peanut butter or abrasive cleansers will get them, but will also take off the paint or at least kill the sheen on the wall. Don't try to clean spots before you wash down the whole wall—they might come off with the first washing. *Let the solution do the work!*

Most wall marks can be removed by simply finding a cleaning agent with the same base as the spot. On a tar spot, for example, you can scrub and rub with high-powered cleaners, sweat and swear, and not get the spot; a little turpentine or paint thinner will remove it in three seconds and not hurt the wall. Use your head, not your hands—you won't scour off the paint or streak the surfaces.

Cleaning woodwork

You can wash the woodwork or baseboards while doing the walls, but I seldom do, because woodwork is covered with lint, hair, dead gnats, etc., that will get into your sponge and be difficult to get out. Before you start washing the room, use a damp paper towel to wipe the baseboard and pick up all the residue, then just dispose of it. Use a damp cleaning cloth to finish it up, if need be, streak- and lint-free.

How to clean paneling

Remember that raw wood must be coated with a finish so that moisture won't penetrate it. Then you'll be cleaning the finish, not the wood itself—it's faster, and much easier on the wood and you!

Don't be like the homemaker who decided to leave the wood paneling in her new home unfinished. She loved that natural wood look because it looked warm and homey. But then one afternoon, her children got into the Crisco and the crayons, and a generous percentage of the mess ended up on the wood wall. No matter how she scrubbed or what formula she tried, the spots and marks remained visible.

She should have finished the wood with a low-luster varnish or polyurethane. This would have formed a protective shield on the surface of the wood that would keep grease and marks from penetrating into the wood and staining it. A flat or satin resinous or polyurethane finish will dry with a low sheen and preserve the natural look of the wood. (Follow the instructions on the can, remember to stir well, and keep your work area as dust-free as you can.)

On wood paneling with a sealed surface, or vinyl paneling (much "imitation wood" paneling is actually vinyl, or vinyl-coated composition board), use only a mild oil soap or neutral all-purpose cleaner solution, and apply it sparingly with a sponge. (I use an oil soap that I had a chemical company formulate for me; you could also use one of the vegetable oil soaps on the market such as Murphy's.) Then, going with the grain, dry-buff it with a cleaning cloth. If you dry with the grain, occasional streaks will never be noticed. A clean, dry surface on a paneled wall is much better than covering the paneling with "El Gunko" panel polish or cleaners that leave a sticky surface to collect and hold handprints and every passing particle of dirt and dust. The oil soap cleans the wood surface and leaves a nice shine.

Clean ceilings

Ceilings are always tough, even the easier-to-clean types like enamel, with no texture or special finish of any kind. There is good news and bad news for you women who for years have had aching arms and back and neck from working above your head. The bad news first: A physiologist told me that the muscle structure of a woman's torso is built to transfer to her shoulders the weight of a child carried during pregnancy. When a woman works above her head, she pulls against these muscles, so overhead work is much more difficult for her than it is for a man. The good news is: what an excuse to get a man to do the high work (such as ceilings)!

You don't have to wash the ceiling every time you wash the walls (ceiling-washing is hard work, even for experienced experts). Ceilings only need cleaning about one-third as often as walls (unless you have a ceiling heat vent or exhaust fan, and then you can just clean the area around it and feather the cleaning line). Except for fireplace soot and cigarette smoke, ceilings just don't get the abuse that walls do. They don't have the fingerprints, crayon marks and everyday spatters, so they can go several years between cleanings.

For fairly smooth ceilings with washable paint (gloss or semigloss enamel), use the same two-bucket technique described for wall-washing. If the ceiling is greasy or nicotine-coated, use heavy-duty cleaner or degreaser solution rather than neutral all-purpose cleaner.

Most flat-painted ceilings can be cleaned quite well by wiping with a dry sponge. Should a few flyspecks remain, dip a cotton swab in white shoe polish or matching paint to mask them. Flat paints are not very washable, no matter what the label says. You almost always leave streaks and lap lines when washing them. It's usually faster and easier to just roll on another coat of paint, especially if you're faced with heavy smoke or water stains, hanging lamp scars, etc.

When you clean the ceiling, take down any ceiling light fixture diffusers or globes first, pour cleaning solution on them, and let them soak in the sink while you clean the room. This keeps you from cutting your arms on them as you clean the ceiling. After you finish the room, use a cleaning cloth to wipe the loosened film and dirt from the plates. Rinse with hot water, dry, and put them back up immediately.

Textured or acoustical tile ceilings

Builders often leave textured ceilings unpainted in a new home. When five to seven years later the ceiling needs cleaning, it can't be washed because the texture (which is a water-based compound) will dissolve when water touches it. If you rolled one coat of latex paint on when the ceiling was new, it "filled" the texture and left the ceiling looking fantastic. But five years later when you try to wash it, the moisture gets to the compound (which turns brown when wet) and you have a streak. So always paint two coats on an unpainted ceiling and it will be sealed enough to clean.

If you have either "cottage cheese" or those sparkly ceilings, your cleaning choices are limited. You can try vacuuming them with your extra-long hose and soft bristle attachment, or maybe you can dry-sponge them. You should also resolve never to hire any architect or contractor who uses the stuff.

Acoustical ceilings generally won't show dirt until it's too late to clean them. Clean annually with a dry sponge; it will only take a few minutes. A badly dirtied acoustical ceiling can be resprayed with an acoustic finish or cleaned by the bleaching or oxidation process—you could do this yourself with supplies from a janitorial-supply store, but it's safer to have a professional do it for you. If you paint an acoustical ceiling, you'll ruin the looks and the acoustics.

Washing closets

I'd wash the inside of the closets once every twenty years or so; most of them are closed, so they don't get dirty. Closets generally take longer than the whole room, and besides, nobody ever sees them anyway. But when you paint your closets, use a hard-finish, light-colored enamel so they'll be easy to clean whenever you do wash them.

Don't forget the doors

Our doors get much more use than any other part of the house, yet we spend very little time keeping them clean and looking sharp. Doors are so taken for granted we seldom appreciate their contribution to a neat, attractive house.

I once gave my wife a rest and got the house in top shape. When I finished my cleaning marathon, for some reason the house still looked unfinished. When I looked everything over, I found the floor glistening, the walls clean, no dust anywhere—but the *doors* had marks all over them. Marks from hands, scratches from carrying suitcases through, the black marks from kicks, mop and vacuum bumps, etc.

Most of my doors are natural wood with a clear finish. Some are painted. I cleaned the painted doors with a soft nylon scrubbing sponge. If marks and nicks were present or the doors were dull, I simply repainted them. I scrubbed the natural wood with a good ammonia solution and a nylon pad. I cleaned with the grain of the wood and rinsed the cleaner off with a damp cloth. They were now clean, but a little dull. I made sure they were dry and with some extra-fine sandpaper, I again went over the door, lightly, with the grain. The sanding removed lint, dust and hair particles that got in the previous coat of finish. I took a cloth dampened with mineral spirits (paint thinner and tack cloths work, too) and wiped the doors to get off every speck of lint and dust. (By the way, I left the doors on while doing all this and put cardboard under them to protect the rug/floor.)

I applied a coat of low-gloss varnish (you could also use a polyurethane finish) to each door (even on the tops), rolling it on so it was evenly distributed, and then brushing with the grain to prevent runs and misses. Then I let them dry.

You won't believe the difference it will make in your doors' appearance and the ease of keeping them clean! It will take just a few hours and will help protect the doors from future abuse. Pick a day when the house is quiet—signs and warnings about keeping out of varnish aren't heeded. Do those doors on a dry summer day and they'll dry quickly (on a rainy day it can take 50 percent longer). As soon as your bedroom door is dry enough to close, take a rest. You deserve it for all the time and money you have saved.

Remember—where there's a wall, there's a way!

Doorknob dodging:

It took twenty years of professional painting for me to finally learn that loosening the two screws on the doorknob so I could paint around it sure beats trying to mask it or sash it with a brush.

If You Have a Dirty House

and Just a Few Minutes . . .

At my cleaning seminars and conventions, when I speak on time management, I always ask the audience (whose ages range from twenty-five to ninety-five):

"How many of you notice, as you grow older, that you find more time?"

Even in the largest groups, not one hand goes up; not even retired people report that they suddenly have "more time." My parents ran a large ranch almost alone, yet they still seemed to have time when they were younger to go fishing, visit neighbors, etc. After they retired, I couldn't believe how busy they were. I almost needed an appointment to see them. Now my own family is grown, too, but with more than a dozen grandkids and several businesses, I have to beg and pry and hustle to do half the things necessary to live a satisfied life. You know what I mean, it's happened to you. We just don't have the time to get our slice of life and still do justice to our home and its contents.

So I thought you might be interested in a professional strategy for cleaning the whole house . . . in minutes. It's a way out for when you have "the house to clean": the whole house—living room, bedrooms, kids' rooms, kitchen and yes (shudder), even the garage—and there's no time for tooth-clenching or lip-quivering; the gunk has to go. . . .

There are two possible approaches: either the whole house as a unit, or one room at a time. How about a compromise for maximum efficiency?

Trash and police

In these two operations, you do want to hit the whole place at once. Armed with a box or the biggest of all garbage containers, quickly scout the place and dump the trash and garbage—get rid of what's in the wastebaskets as well as what's just lying around (old newspapers, soft drink cans, petrified pizza crusts, etc.).

As for the clothes, cups, pillows, and all those "too-tired-to-put-back-where-they-belong" things—they're left in the nicest homes in the world by the most loving people. But they *are* left. To police the place, I carry a plastic laundry basket with me and toss in all the dropped socks and jackets, all the stray towels and tennis shoes. That way you can pick up the whole place really quickly, and when you get to the laundry room it only takes a couple of minutes to toss the dirty clothes in the hamper and quickly assemble everything else—dishes, books, magazines, mail, earrings, hats, duffel bags, tools, school papers, toys, etc.—together with its kind for later dispersal. Dump any questionable stuff into a box that you designate "Lost and Found."

If you do these two things first, you won't believe how much cleaning is already done when you hit the individual areas. You'll be amazed how fast you did all this—in maybe ten or fifteen minutes, especially if you do both jobs on the run.

Now the individual rooms: Which first?

Bedroom

Why? Psychologically, it's the easiest, and offers the most instant gratification. And it'll be pretty clean to start with now that the litter and clutter is gone. Only a few things remain. With all your equipment in your cleaning caddy and a lambswool duster in hand, start from the right and work to the left.

1. Making the bed. You should have made it when you got out, but if

you didn't, make two trips, one stop on each side. First go to the most restless sleeper's side, straighten out all the layers, and pull them into place (pull everything over about a foot farther than you need to on that side). Then go to the other side, straighten, and, when you pull the missing foot of cover back from the other side it will tighten the covers to perfection. Once you work up some speed, a bed should take between one and two minutes to make. If you follow my recommendation and use a comforter instead of bedspread you're looking at thirty seconds. Do the beds first so stuff won't fall in them as you dust.

2. Dusting. Start with the high dusting; get the cobwebs out of the corners. Don't take time to look and see if there are cobwebs; just take a second to hit those corners. Catch the wall lightly as you go by because dust hangs on the wall and, by keeping it down, you'll keep wall-washing to a minimum. Get the light fixtures, door frames, tops of the doors and drapes. As you move down off the high dusting hit the lamps on the dressers, the tops of mirrors and any furniture. Just dust around any doilies or dresser scarves. Then do the fronts and sides of the furniture and work from right to left around the room. (If you feel brave, step in the closet for a second and hit the dust on the shoulders of your hanging clothes.) Don't forget the front of the TV that's in every master bedroom in America. As you dust down the wall

392

to the floor make sure you remove any buildup from the bottoms of the furniture and the baseboards.

3. Now straighten the headboard, nightstand and dressing table.

4. With a spray bottle of glass cleaner and a cloth hit the mirrors, and then with neutral all-purpose cleaner do any handprints on the walls, door frames and dresser tops (they get pretty grungy from all those set-down coffee cups and pocket residue).

5. Now bring in the Eureka and do the vacuuming—start at the farthest corner of the room and work your way out. In quick routine cleaning like this, hit the traffic lanes and as far under the bed as you can reasonably reach. But keep that thing moving. As you back your way out of the room park the vacuum just outside the door. (And yes, clean the doorknob as you go.)

That was your bedroom, and you should have been able to do it in 7½ to 11 minutes, max. Now on to the guest room, or heaven forbid, the kids' room—but it does have to be done.

Kids' room

1. First remove any potentially damaging stuff (that might spill, grow mushrooms, or injure carpeting, furniture or innocent bystanders).

2. De-junk that thing that's old and worn and ugly and always in the way—they won't miss it.

3. As for litter, you trashed and dumped a lot on the initial run-through, so there'll be surprisingly little left. If you clean their room entirely you'll teach kids that

they're not responsible for their own messes, so sweep and pile the rest in the center and leave a note: "No McDonald's until all this is gone." Brutal, but effective.

4. Dust the available horizontal surfaces and spot-clean the black marks and handprints (the kids will *never* see *them*).

5. Leave the vacuuming for them, too. Vacuum handles fit any size hand, and what kid isn't just itching for a chance to drive something? If they can plug in a Nintendo, a vacuum is a cinch.

The time you spend in the kids' room will depend on how determined a delegator you are. If you get them to do what I've suggested above, you'll be out of there in 5 or 6 minutes. Otherwise, you'll probably spend 10-12 minutes in the junior jungle.

Halls and entryways

Halls are fast and easy; they're kind of the rapids of the home: little accumulates or stays there in the swift current.

1. Dusting is probably the biggest issue in a hall. All those bodies moving through distribute dust onto pictures, door frames and light fixtures. Hit the hallway running with your lambswool duster. The lighting in a hallway isn't always the greatest but you should be able to catch the cobwebs. Dust well. Get those corners, chandeliers, and the tops of wall-hangings and furniture. Don't forget the baseboard.

2. Spot-cleaning. Narrow halls (which means most of them) get fingerprints and bumps, grazes and leans.

Armed with your spray bottle of neutral all-purpose cleaner and cloth, touch them up. Get them as soon as you see them—wait for a month and you'll have a whole wall to wash. Don't forget the light switches.

3. Vacuum the entire hall, not just the traffic areas. Halls are kind of the doormat for the house, so they get it bad. And before you start vacuuming, sweep anything off the edges with a plain old broom.

You should be able to hustle through a hallway in no more than five minutes.

On the other hand, lots of housework originates in the area just inside and outside the door—the entryways to your house.

1. Hit the doors, ceiling, and railings with your lambswool duster.

2. Spot-clean any spills or marks on the walls (people are always going in and out of entryways with their hands full of everything from hero sandwiches to TVs).

3. Floors in entryways also get a beating from all the coming and going. If the entry has a hard floor (tile, ceramic, brick or wood), it probably needs mopping, so mop it at the same time you mop the kitchen. If it's a carpet or a hard floor that just needs sweeping, vacuum or dustmop now. Get up all that grit, gravel and other debris that will otherwise just get pulverized and tracked all over the house.

4. Vacuum your inside (and outside) floor mats (see chapter eight) well, and keep them vacuumed. They're your lifesavers.

Entryways are highly visible parts of a home, and a little extra time spent here—a total of 5-7 minutes—should keep them presentable.

Living room or family room

Avoid the temptation to switch on the TV and collapse a minute. Keep going! Remember the exercise you're getting, the calories you're burning, and all the praise you're going to get from the rest of the household when they notice how nice things look (fat chance, but dreaming always does a lot for our morale).

1. Straighten up everything first—furniture, pictures, books. It'll make you feel good.

2. Then dust everything. Always dust before you vacuum, so the clipped fingernails, bug bodies, and dead leaves will end up where the vacuum will get them. Work from the top down with your lambswool duster, and if there are blinds on the win-

dows be sure to include them. Start with the top of the furniture, too, and work all the way down to the floor on each piece so you don't have to come back to do the low dusting. There's lots of dust within three feet of the floor, on the bottoms of the chairs and legs of the furniture. Work your way around the room this way and then finish off again with the baseboards.

3. Spot-clean the place (the carpet too, especially in the area of the TV and stereo). There are lots of food-to-hand and food-to-floor transfers here. (I call it "Orville Redenbacher residue.")

4. Spot-clean the windows and glass. (Notice I didn't have you clean the windows in the other rooms; best to do that with a squeegee as a whole-house project). But touch up any smudges here with your spray bottle of glass cleaner and a cloth.

5. Vacuum the traffic areas; remember, the edges and under and behind things don't really have to be done more often than once a month or so. Then set the vacuum outside of the room as a signal that the room is finished.

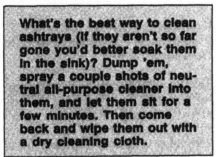

What's the best way to clean ashtrays (if they aren't so far gone you'd better soak them in the sink)? Dump 'em, spray a couple shots of neutral all-purpose cleaner into them, and let them sit for a few minutes. Then come back and wipe them out with a dry cleaning cloth.

It shouldn't take more than ten to fifteen minutes to do a living room. If you have a lot of decorations it may take a little longer. But don't get caught up in knickknack renewal or you'll never get out of there.

Kitchen

I'd save the kitchen until last for several reasons. This is usually the depot for the rest of the house—where we bring things to be cleaned or emptied. The kitchen is the catchall, where we wash out vases and fill spray bottles, rinse mops and collect the garbage. Then, too, the kitchen is where we come for breaks and phone calls; if you clean it first, somebody (maybe even *you!*) is sure to come in there while you're cleaning the rest of the house and dirty it, which is demoralizing. If you get bogged down anywhere it's probably going to be the kitchen. Better to have that happen at the end of your cleaning than at the beginning.

When you do get here:

1. Dust everything from the top down. High dusting is critical in the kitchen because all the steam and vapors of cooking will turn dust into greasecake pretty quickly, and then it'll take a major wash job to get it off. If you keep it dusted this buildup will have less of a chance to develop. Still, it hardens pretty quickly in places such as the range hood and the tops of the cabinets, so for much of the kitchen a cloth dampened with dish detergent solution is unquestionably the best duster. The dish soap will give your wiper enough dissolving ability to remove the oil slick. Buff dry with a cleaning cloth right after you damp-wipe so you don't leave streaks or film.

Damp-wiping is a two-step process: clean with a damp cloth, and buff and shine with a clean, dry cloth. This is especially important in kitchen-cleaning.

2. Hit the light fixtures and the tops of things—even above eye level—with a lambswool duster first and then the window ledges and moldings. Then with your damp cloth hit the handprints on the fridge and stove front, and the handle area of dishwashers, doors and drawers. Remember those smudge-collecting small appliances, being especially sure to polish these dry to remove any residue. If you come across

People often correctly guess that can openers are one of the dirtiest places in the house, yet few ever clean them. If you have an electric one, unplug it, and then spray dish detergent solution onto the cutting and clamping area. Wait four or five minutes. Scrub with a vegetable brush and rinse. That will get the crud and the germs, too!

any hardened sticky spots, wet them down and let them sit a few minutes while you do something else—you should be able to come back and just whisk them away. This wash/wipe dusting is key to kitchen-cleaning. When you do it, save tables and counters for last.

3. Then straighten things in the kitchen area—the countertops, tools and decorations.

4. Do any dishes and pans that are left around, and wipe the tabletop, chair seats and counter. On countertops, start at the back and move canisters and small appliances out of the way. Wipe, then replace them as you go. Don't worry if any crumbs fall on the floor, because next. . . .

5. You do the floor. Sweep or dustmop carefully. On a light day that will be enough. If kids or company have

been around, just toss a shot of neutral all-purpose cleaner into a bucket of water and quickly damp-mop the floor (see page 320 for pro mopping technique). Any soap residue left will cause dullness, so if you have a super-shiny vinyl or ceramic tile floor, you might want to rinse with your mop, too, using a little vinegar solution (half a cup of white vinegar per gallon of water) to neutralize it.

6. While the floor dries, take out the garbage and wash the container.

All done!—in twenty to thirty minutes.

Once you get your system down, this whole-house overhaul can all be done in a couple hours. No, I'm not kidding. Soon you'll be racing the clock instead of watching it. A streamlined system like this may also eventually tempt some of the other household residents who haven't turned much of a hand to help in the past.

(If you live in a house rather than a condo or apartment, you'll want to go on to read the rest of this chapter.)

Stepping outside for a few minutes a week . . .

For my first twenty-five years in the professional cleaning business, we were taught (and believed) that the area right inside the door of a place created the first and overall impression of it, and thus we cleaned lobbies to death. About ten years ago a perceptive building manager pointed out that no, the parking lot and *exterior* entryway were actually the image makers. He was right. We all form a

preconception of the inside of a place by what we see and feel going in.

From then on we cleaned the area directly outside the door as earnestly as the area immediately inside—and with phenomenal results. This is only more true in a home—what do you think when you walk up a sidewalk or onto a porch that resembles an obstacle course of clutter? It sticks in your mind and poisons it even if the whole inside of the house is immaculate.

It only takes a few minutes a week to keep the outside nice enough to complement the inside. A little attention to exterior cleaning can also prevent lots of long-range problems inside. Let's take a quick trip around the outside now.

●Litter

Maybe it wasn't yours to begin with, but it is now. Litter around the front yard and the lawn is often the first declaration of dirt. Wrappers, cigarette butts, cans, wet envelopes and newspapers, animal drag-ins, dead possums—Mother Nature even chips in some in the form of fallen branches and rotting fruits.

Cure: Make it a practice to pick it up as soon as you see it, coming and going, and once or twice a month walk around the place with a little sack or box to police under the bushes and against the fence. If you do it right before you take the garbage to the curb you'll be dressed for it.

●Driveway

We often have one vehicle per person, and they all bleed oil and transmission fluid, shed car interior fallout, and drip mud, snow and road cinders. This not only looks bad on the driveway, it can be tracked in and offend the house after it offends the eye.

Cure: Once the driveway is policed by hand or broom, an oil stain on a concrete driveway can be lifted the

Problem

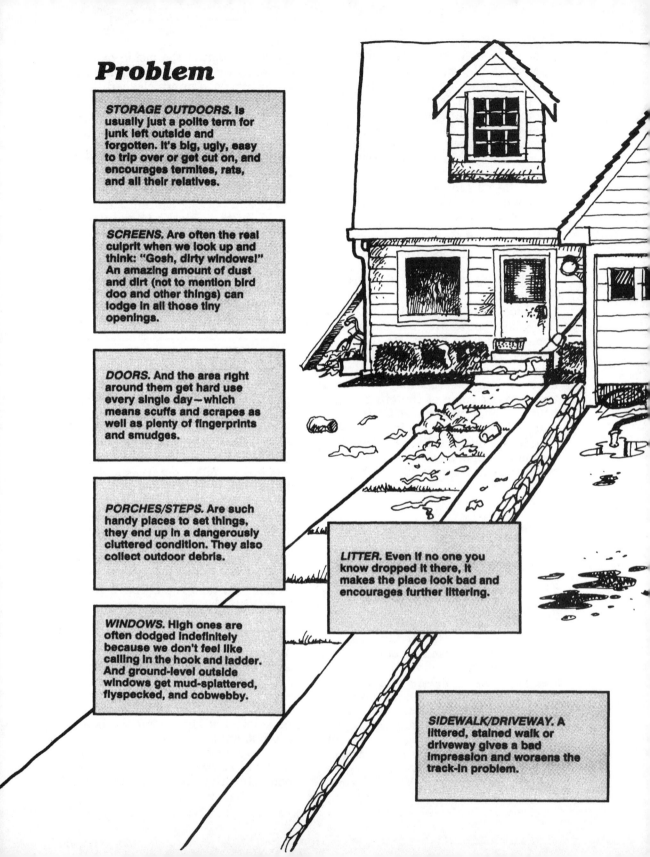

STORAGE OUTDOORS. Is usually just a polite term for junk left outside and forgotten. It's big, ugly, easy to trip over or get cut on, and encourages termites, rats, and all their relatives.

SCREENS. Are often the real culprit when we look up and think: "Gosh, dirty windows!" An amazing amount of dust and dirt (not to mention bird doo and other things) can lodge in all those tiny openings.

DOORS. And the area right around them get hard use every single day—which means scuffs and scrapes as well as plenty of fingerprints and smudges.

PORCHES/STEPS. Are such handy places to set things, they end up in a dangerously cluttered condition. They also collect outdoor debris.

LITTER. Even if no one you know dropped it there, it makes the place look bad and encourages further littering.

WINDOWS. High ones are often dodged indefinitely because we don't feel like calling in the hook and ladder. And ground-level outside windows get mud-splattered, flyspecked, and cobwebby.

SIDEWALK/DRIVEWAY. A littered, stained walk or driveway gives a bad impression and worsens the track-in problem.

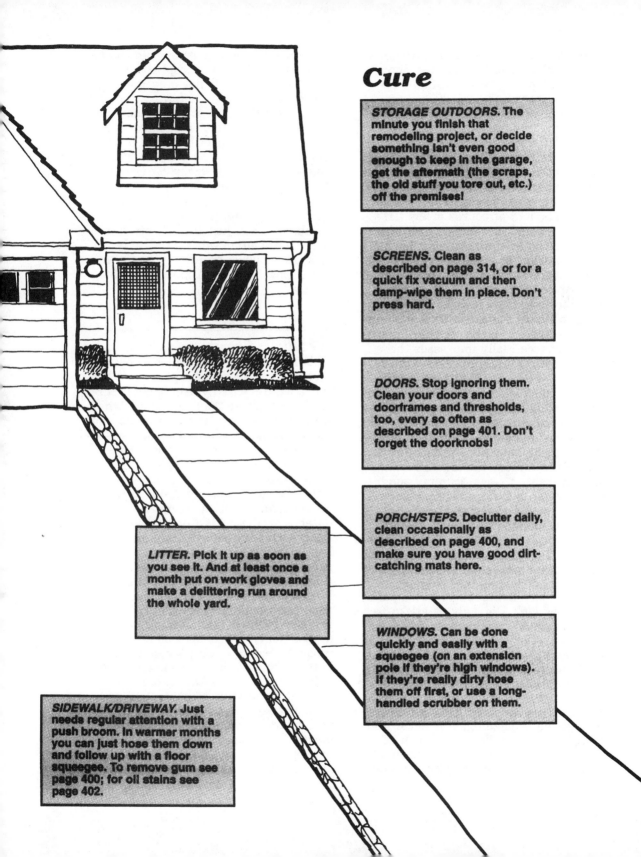

Cure

STORAGE OUTDOORS. The minute you finish that remodeling project, or decide something isn't even good enough to keep in the garage, get the aftermath (the scraps, the old stuff you tore out, etc.) off the premises!

SCREENS. Clean as described on page 314, or for a quick fix vacuum and then damp-wipe them in place. Don't press hard.

DOORS. Stop ignoring them. Clean your doors and doorframes and thresholds, too, every so often as described on page 401. Don't forget the doorknobs!

PORCH/STEPS. Declutter daily, clean occasionally as described on page 400, and make sure you have good dirt-catching mats here.

LITTER. Pick it up as soon as you see it. And at least once a month put on work gloves and make a delittering run around the whole yard.

WINDOWS. Can be done quickly and easily with a squeegee (on an extension pole if they're high windows). If they're really dirty hose them off first, or use a long-handled scrubber on them.

SIDEWALK/DRIVEWAY. Just needs regular attention with a push broom. In warmer months you can just hose them down and follow up with a floor squeegee. To remove gum see page 400; for oil stains see page 402.

same as one on a garage floor (see page 402). Hosing (during the above-freezing months) is a nice finale for the driveway.

Sidewalk

This is the highway to the heart of your house, and all too often it's covered with mud, leaves, twigs, gravel, mashed acorns, leftover ice-melting chemicals, and of course a few flattened blobs of chewing gum. Is this how we want to introduce ourselves?

Cure: Get out a good, sturdy push broom (see Equipment Chart, page 264) and use short strokes to sweep the debris off the sides. Or if it's only lightly littered, in the warmer months you can simply hose it. A clean, newly dried surface really impresses those walking across it. (That's one of the reasons people are so taken with Disneyland, as I discovered snooping about in the undercorridors with the maintenance people. They don't sweep every night, they hose things down.) Then take a floor squeegee and de-water the walk so the low areas won't have a chance to form scummy puddles as they dry. Policing the walk each day as you come and go takes only seconds and keeps sidewalks looking smart! (Pull those weeds in the cracks, too. If they keep coming back, pour in some salt water—not so much that it runs all over.)

Gum on sidewalks and paved parking areas isn't just ugly, it sticks to the bottom of your shoe on a hot day. Go out there when it's cold or at least cool, and you should be able to chip it right off with a chisel or a hoe. Be sure to pick up the pieces the minute they're free or you'll have a worse mess—they'll be tracked everywhere and get on everything. If it never gets chilly where you live, use a can of "gum freeze" from a janitorial-supply store. De-Solv-it or dry-cleaning fluid

will take care of any remaining traces. Don't use solvents on asphalt!

As for moss, it not only gives the walk a five-o'clock shadow—when wet it's slicker than ice! Water alone won't remove it (it'll just make it grow), and bleach won't do it either. Mix a warm solution of neutral all-purpose cleaner and spread it generously on the spot. Let it sit awhile (but not until it evaporates), then scrub and loosen it with a stiff push broom, brush or hand floor scrubber. Then just flush it off with a hose (the solution won't hurt the lawn). If a bit remains, go after it again and get it now, while you have everything handy.

Porch

This is often a permanent outdoor "junk room." Or if it's a prelude to the entrance we actually use, it gets more traffic and abuse than even the kitchen or bathroom, since it has both us and the elements to contend with.

Cure: Stop using the porch as a place to stash stuff you haven't decided what to do with. *Decide*—and either bring it in or get it out of there for good. Move out all the out-of-season outerwear, dry-rotted boots and mildewed tennis shoes. Make sure you have a good floor mat here, too (see pages 294-305)—if you have an enclosed porch you have room for a good long one—and clean it often (just step out the door with the vacuum). Get rid of those cobwebs with a lambswool duster (on an extension handle if necessary). Regular sweeping of a porch is the number one way to keep dirt at a distance; swab it afterward occasionally with a solution of neutral all-purpose cleaner. Then scrub it lightly with a hand floor scrubber (see Equipment Chart, page 264) and rinse. A fresh porch gives a good impression and prevents a lot of inside dirt.

● Door area

Doors and the area around them are about as concentrated an area for dirt collection as they come. We usually carry something with us as we come and go, and as we open and close the door—push, nudge, and lean against it—we usually transfer a little of it to the area, especially coming in from the garden or from fixing the car.

Cure: Most doors—painted or varnished wood, metal or plastic—can be cleaned the same way. Take a spray bottle of neutral all-purpose cleaner, a thick towel, a white nylon scrub sponge and a whisk broom, and visit all your outside doors, including the garage door.

1. Whisk and dust the entire door frame and doorway—the top and sides will have cobwebs, mashed bugs and static-clinging fuzz; the bottom (threshold) will have sand and debris in the crevices.

2. Spray the entire door (especially the area around the knob, and any spots) lightly with the neutral all-purpose cleaner, and while it "simmers" take your soft white nylon sponge and gently hit the black smudges or marks. Keep the surface good and wet while you scrub and don't scrub too hard—remember, the outside surface of the door oxidizes and if you scrub that off, the cleaned spots will be a different color.

3. Wipe the entire surface dry with a towel. Switch sides as it becomes soiled, so you don't transfer any dirt to already-clean areas.

4. The doorknob and area around it will be dirtier than it looks; hit it. Then check the doorbell, mailbox and little message area, if any. The windows and any light fixtures can be cleaned with a spray bottle of glass cleaner. You'll often find tape residue from decorations, messages, deliveries, etc., here—carefully use a little De-Solv-it to remove it chemically, rather than by scrubbing or scraping.

5. Storm doors: Get a lot of hard use and abuse, and most of them are made of two of the toughest materials to clean: aluminum and Plexiglas. Never take any aggressive cleaner or anything sharp to them. Clean them just like the other doors except be sure to dust or rinse any Plexiglas parts first to remove as much as possible of the dust and grit that can so easily scratch it. Unanodized aluminum, of course, will turn your cloth black everywhere you touch it, and you won't notice much difference in its appearance. Oh well, at least you'll *know* you have a clean door.

● Windows

The upper ones are only noticed from the inside, and they're not usually too bad anyway. But the lower windows are often splattered with bird droppings and mud from rain splashes, the sills and frames littered with dead bugs and paint chips. And the window wells are usually full of everything from lost caulk and broken glass to dog bones and deflated basketballs.

Cure: Clean the high windows like you do inside ones, with a squeegee (just add an extension handle). As for the lower ones, hose them off well first before you apply any cleaner with a window-washing wand. If they're really bad, use a long-handled scrubber (see Equipment Chart, page 264) with a white nylon pad to clean them; rinse them well with the hose and squeegee them dry. Then put a bucket down in the window wells and (using a gloved hand) fill it up with all the awful stuff you find there.

Screens

These slowly but surely get plugged up, dirty and damaged, and it ends up saying "sloppy."

Cure: If you don't have time to give them the whole treatment as described on page 314, sweep them lightly with a brush or broom, then damp-wipe them in place (don't push hard or your screens will soon sag!). Replace any that are ripped or bulged.

Outside storage

The worst of outside cleaning is "stored" stuff, especially anything right up against the house or around the entrance or porch. All those broken bicycles, left-behind tools and containers, piles of rotting firewood, scraps and half-finished projects don't exactly project cleanliness and order.

Cure: Don't ever allow anything to be stored against or around the house. Get rid of it right now. It looks tacky, encourages pests, and injures people as well as siding. If it isn't worth storing in a garage, barn or shed, it probably isn't worth keeping. Pile it up by the back fence and cover it with a tarp if you must, but keep loose stuff away from the house—all of it!

Now I put away my cleaning tools, start my somersault of victory and then gasp. There's one spot of horror left—the garage.

Garage

If the car(s) can even get in, it surely has junk fitted in all around it.

1. First and always, de-junk the garage. This is a regular ongoing process, not a once-a-year spring garage sale surge. You go to the garage for some reason almost every day, passing right by all this stuff. So take one or two things with you each trip and keep the junk controlled.

2. Pick up all the scattered tools and sports equipment and hang them up. If you've done this twenty-seven times this month already, it's time to take a break. Go down to K-Mart or somewhere and get some of those Rubbermaid shop organizers, and lick the problem once and for all.

3. Whisk (don't dust) off any horizontal surfaces such as tables, cabinets and shelves with one of those counter or foxtail brushes. You may find it hard to locate the horizontal surfaces—so de-junk more and do it anyway.

4. Treat the shop area the same as the kids' room. Trash the trash, remove anything deadly, and round up the rest. Then pile it neatly in the owner's territory.

5. Put all that broken stuff (the "I'm-going-to-fix-it-someday" junk) in a sturdy box and pray for its delivery.

6. Get out your push broom (if you have a garage you ought to have one!) and sweep the floor. (Sweep *around* the oil drips.)

7. As for the oil drips, sprinkle some sawdust or kitty litter on them, pour a little paint thinner on, and mix well. Then cover the spot or spots with some plastic wrap or a damp rag for a few hours. You've just created what we call a "poultice." It will suck up the oil and after it's done its dirty work you can sweep it away into the trash. If any stain remains it can usually be removed by scrubbing with a stiff brush and a solution of ordinary powdered laundry detergent and water.

Why Not Be a Professional Housecleaner?

Can you picture yourself next Monday morning? It's 9:00. All your housework is done. Your home is organized, and you're leaving it to go clean four other homes . . . for $10 or $20 an hour? No, it isn't a fantasy or a joke.

One of the biggest economic and social realities of the '90s is the two-career family. The effects of an extra job on family and marital relationships can be problematic. But that doesn't eliminate many families' growing need for a second income. Homemakers with

or without children have flocked to the job market in an attempt to meet ever-mounting inflation. To secure employment, many have found it necessary to purchase extra transportation, accept close to minimum-wage jobs, hire expensive child-care services, and spend a lot of money on a business wardrobe. Actual benefits from most homemakers' second jobs would be questionable if both direct and indirect costs were calculated.

Why go through the expense of all that overhead to gain a tiny percent of income when you can double your profit for half the emotional and physical price you're paying? Why not start your own professional housecleaning business? It's not only possible, but it will offer you some great personal and family advantages:

1. Excellent income: $10 to $20 per hour for your time.

2. Tax deductions and depreciation breaks.

3. The potential for family involvement.

4. The ability to work on your own schedule, part time or full time.

5. Rewarding social and educational experiences.

6. Regular physical exercise.

7. Equipment to do all your own housecleaning.

8. The opportunity to pick your own working associates.

9. More control over your time and environment.

Why get a job that makes it impossible to spend any time with your spouse or friends? Why have children you can't enjoy? Why fight traffic and parking and rigid schedules every day? Why answer to "bosses"? Why tolerate excessive deductions from

your check? Why clear just a small amount of money for forty hours of hard work? On your own terms and at your own energy level, in your own selected environment, you could make the same money in half the hours and feel better physically and emotionally.

The market for housework is wide open. There isn't a household in America that doesn't need housework done—and many will hire it. Think of all the two-career families that desperately need help keeping the house clean. The maid business is booming!

Many struggling homemakers can't cope with their own housework, so that leaves the majority of your neighborhood or town needing help. You can provide it! There are lots of cleaning companies, but good professional housecleaning companies are hard to find.

If you are a woman, you have the advantage over a male in landing a professional housecleaning job. Homemakers are extremely particular as to whom they turn loose in their houses to clean, and you, another homemaker, will more easily win their trust.

Though the image of being a "cleaner" and the hard work involved are big concerns to most potential scrubbing entrepreneurs, I assure you that handling the "image" is fun. And hard work will make you twice the person you are now!

The predominant fear most people have about trying their own business is, "Can I get customers?" This will never be a problem if you do high-quality work for an honest price. Even when I first started out, my success rate in getting the jobs that I bid was nine out of ten.

If you just follow the directions in this book, you'll know more about housecleaning than anyone you'll ever work for. Every job will multiply your experience. You'll find that with your skills you can consistently average $8 to $12 per hour. Sometimes you'll get as high as $25 per hour on special jobs.

Regular everyday housework-type services (sweeping, vacuuming, dusting, etc.) are always in demand. But almost anyone can do that kind of housework, at about the same rate of speed, and this holds down the worth of such jobs. Try to specialize in the areas where the average homemaker struggles: floors, walls, window-washing, rugs, etc. Competence in these areas will lead you to other, even more lucrative, jobs.

Getting started

The idea of getting started seems to cause even the most talented to shake in their boots. I know you can do it, and once you start, you'll look back, after the first three jobs, and laugh at yourself for being nervous about it. Visions of arming yourself with a mop bucket and dust cloth and parading up and down the streets beating on doors for business are out. You want to go to work, not jail! The following are some good ways to get started. (And don't be afraid to call people in the business—in other towns—for advice. They'll help you.)

1. Get a name and a slogan
Just think—a chance to name your own company! Avoid personal names like Mabel's Cleaning, Betty's Broom Service, Jones Cleaners. Instead, use names like Century, Belair (like car names)—except relate it to homes. Such names have a ring of authority, and will inspire confidence. (Would you rather be termite-proofed by TermiteMaster or Joe the Bug Stomper?) Just be sure you don't use someone else's name.

2. Print cards or leaflets
Always use a picture or visual symbol on your "advertising" literature of any

kind. A bit of creativity, some rub-on lettering, some help from an artist, or a little free help from the printer will give you an inexpensive but effective tool to attract business. Avoid tacky "clip art" decorations. Be fresh and original. Your materials should be professional-looking and eye-catching.

Shop around for a good local printer and print at least several hundred for the best cost breaks.

3. Check into rules and regulations

Make a call to state, federal and local tax offices and the telephone company and explain to them the scale on which you intend to operate. If you're just going to do an occasional job, with no employees, they'll probably say "no problem." But if you're going to operate on a large scale, hire a couple of neighbors, have a vehicle, etc., it's best to inform the agencies involved. The Yellow Pages, or your local Small Business Administration, will direct you to the right place to find rules and regulations. Explain your intention, and regulatory agencies will generally send you everything you should know, free. They are fair, friendly, and will tell you exactly what's needed to operate a business. Don't get buffaloed by this part. It's easy, and the cost to you generally is little or nothing. "Acting dumb" to see what might happen seldom pays.

Check with your insurance company. The personal liability coverages you have now may also cover you and your little business, but check it out. Insurance companies don't cover workers or workmanship, only liability. If you fall through a window or rip a couch while washing the ceiling, you're covered under the liability section. However, if you break the window or rip the couch while working on it, *you* are responsible. Arm yourself with the necessary insurance, but don't get caught up in morbid fears of what might happen.

House Cleaning / Janitorial Service /
Painting / Rugs & Upholstery

You'll have a few bad experiences, but be careful and conscientious, and your victims will have great compassion.

4. Advertise

A business card pinned up in a laundro-mat or on a supermarket bulletin board

Spring Clean-up Specials

Let Varsity bring spring to you.

- Window Washing
- Floor Stripping
- Wall Washing
- Carpet Shampooing
- One-Time Clean-ups
- Insurance Estimates
- Painting

Don A. Aslett, Owner **(208) 232-8598**
311 S. 5th
P.O. Box 1682
Pocatello, ID 83204

Reminder: Use Varsity for your summer painting needs!

may have some success but usually won't get you the kind of people you want to work for. If they can't afford a washing machine, they generally won't be able to afford you.

Classified ads in the newspaper are always good. Dropping cards off at local businesses gets both owners and clients. But the best advertising for housecleaning is unquestionably the personal referral. People who have their homes cleaned professionally love to brag about it, and if you do a good job, you'll never be able to handle the work that will flow in. A card or two left at a house or a business you clean will quickly find its way into the hands of friends, and you'll find your way into another assignment. If your work is good (even if it's a little expensive), your business will boom and prosper.

5. Start small, and test it out

You'll be surprised what happens. One thing it will do is make your own housework easier and simpler.

6. Some of the best sources for work

(and reliable payment) are:

- Local personal residence cleaning
- Smoke-loss cleaning jobs for insurance companies
- Small medical or professional offices
- Construction cleanup, such as in new housing developments

7. Some accounts to avoid:

- People moving out and away
- Shopping malls and supermarkets (there's often no clear-cut authority to make decisions or payment)
- "Maid" work for finicky folks

8. Hire cautiously

Wrapped up in the thrill and vanity of becoming a "big boss," you may discover a tendency to promise every ambitious or down-and-out friend a job. Be careful. You could end up working for *them*. Once your friends, relatives, or other job-needing associates go on a job with you, you may feel obligated to keep them on every job, even if they turn out to be worthless. You could end up spending your time assigning, supervising and cleaning up after them. Go slow. Start with yourself and a reliable helper, and work up from there.

9. Get your own equipment

You wouldn't be very impressed if a high-class restaurant asked you to bring your own dishes, or if a surgeon asked you to furnish the scalpel. There is power and mystery in "professional equipment and supplies." They are dependable and deductible, as well as usable in your own home.

Don't go over your head on expensive specialty items if your business doesn't justify it. The Equipment Chart on page 264 should give you a good start. Put your name and emblem on all your equipment, for security and advertisement. You don't need a great deal of equipment, and you can store it in the garage and transport it in your car. If your business expands and you need a bigger vehicle, get a van. You don't need a $20,000 fur-lined one. A van three to ten years old is fine because you won't be driving it that much— maybe a couple of miles, and then it's parked for hours while you clean a house. There's no sense carrying the insurance, interest and overhead on an expensive new vehicle, because you'll probably only put 5,000 or fewer miles a year on it, as most of your work will be close to you. Paint your van white or a bright color and letter it; it will be great advertising. Don't let your family use it to go fishing or haul firewood or hot-rod around in. Have a few simple shelves built into it, and install curtains if there are any windows. The curtains will serve two purposes: they make the van look more homey, and they reduce temptation to thieves.

10. Involve the family

These days there aren't enough paper routes or grocery store bagging jobs to go around. Once you get clients who love and trust you, they'll need other services such as painting, grass-cutting and yard work. This is a natural for your children while you clean house. Imagine your spouse cleaning the fireplace or toilet bowl under your strict supervision. (It will probably never happen, but it's a great thought!)

11. Fill your work list and time schedule

Having a small housecleaning business isn't going to give you an ulcer. The fact that you book your own clients leaves you the master. You have the freedom to work just a couple of hours a week — or eighty, if you have the energy. Everyone's family and social obligations are as unique as his or her physical stamina and emotional needs. If your children are in school, you'll have three hours in the morning and three in the afternoon. You could work all week or once a week. Many businesses like their cleaning done from 4:00 to 6:00 a.m.; for a nervous-energy type like me, that's a good time. You're the captain of your own ship; you decide when, where and how. If you can't conform enough to meet a client's particular wishes, then don't; they can get someone else. The reason you got into the business was to run it your way, not to let it run you.

12. Learn to bid your work

Don't work by the hour! Everybody in the world thinks a "cleaning lady" or a "janitor" should get a few bucks an hour. If you quoted $5 an hour to wash someone's windows she'd gasp unbelievingly at your nerve, even if you told her it would only take three hours ($15). However, if you said, as you wrote the price on your card and handed it to the homemaker, "I have looked at your windows carefully and feel that, considering labor, materials and equipment, I can do them for $30," she would nod gratefully. Most customers find that a set price is more acceptable than a per-hour rate. Plus it's a relaxed situation — they know what it's going to cost.

The most-asked question in the industry is, "How do I know how much to bid?" That's easy: Figure how long it will take you and multiply by what you want to make an hour. The better and faster you become, the more you should charge. After a few months, you'll know your actual production time and will be able to estimate closely. You'll over- or underestimate a few times (you might have to work free a few times) — and you'll learn from it. But once you get good, your confidence will "wax" strong, and you'll get almost every job you bid. The following table of average professional costs will give you some guidance in getting started.

Remember, this table is only a guide. You'll be able to plug your own figures in after a little experience. Who you work for, as well as the quality of home and furnishings you work on, will make a lot of difference in the amount of cleaning time required. Much depends on the total area, size of rooms, type of paint on the walls (enamel or flat), density of furnishings, who furnishes the equipment, whether you or they get the area ready, the level of previous maintenance, how far you have to travel, etc. You'll have a few losses, but that will stimulate your desire to be more accurate, and you'll get good!

Always bid work. This is the basic formula for success in your own busi-

Bid Estimate Guide

(These are ball-park averages—your area, location, the state of the economy, and the desperation of the client or the prospective cleaner can affect these prices in either direction.)

Walls and ceilings *Cleaning*	per sq. ft.	small room	medium room	large room
Hall	3–4¢	$ 9	$12	$14
Den	3–4¢	13	18	22
Recreation room	3¢	20	27	32
Living room	5¢	20	28	38
Dining room	5¢	14	18	20
Bedroom	5¢	12	17	23
Entrance	5¢	7	10	15
Bathroom	5¢	7	10	14
Kitchen	5–6¢	16	27	37
Stair landing	6¢	14	16	22
Utility room	6¢	12	14	16

Hard-surfaced floors	lightly soiled	average	filthy
Clean	3¢ (per sq. ft.)	5¢ (per sq. ft.)	7¢ (per sq. ft.)
Clean and wax	8¢ (per sq. ft.)	10¢ (per sq. ft.)	12¢ (per sq. ft.)
Strip and wax	10¢ (per sq. ft.)	12¢ (per sq. ft.)	14¢ (per sq. ft.)

Carpets			
Vacuum and spot clean	1¢ (per sq. ft.)	2¢ (per sq. ft.)	3¢ (per sq. ft.)
Surface clean (spin bonnet)	4¢ (per sq. ft.)	5¢ (per sq. ft.)	9¢ (per sq. ft.)
Shampoo and extract	9¢ (per sq. ft.)	12¢ (per sq. ft.)	14¢ (per sq. ft.)

Windows (per side)			
Small, accessible	4¢ (per sq. ft.)	5¢ (per sq. ft.)	6¢ (per sq. ft.)
Large, accessible	3¢ (per sq. ft.)	4¢ (per sq. ft.)	4¢ (per sq. ft.)
Small, inaccessible	5¢ (per sq. ft.)	6¢ (per sq. ft.)	7¢ (per sq. ft.)
Large, inaccessible	4¢ (per sq. ft.)	5¢ (per sq. ft.)	5¢ (per sq. ft.)

Upholstery			
Small chair	$ 3 (each)	$ 4 (each)	$ 7.50 (each)
Large chair	10 (each)	12 (each)	15.00 (each)
Small couch	20 (each)	25 (each)	35.00 (each)
Large couch	30 (each)	40 (each)	50.00 (each)

Furniture *Clean and polish*			
Small end table	$1.00 (each)	$1.50 (each)	$ 2.00 (each)
Average TV	2.00 (each)	2.50 (each)	3.00 (each)
Piano	4.00 (each)	4.75 (each)	5.25 (each)
Desks, dressers	3.50 (each)	4.00 (each)	5.00 (each)

Contract cleaning	small office 7–10¢ per sq. ft. per month	med office 6–7¢ per sq. ft. per month	large office 5–6¢ per sq. ft. per month

Targeted hourly production rate	light cleaning 3,000 sq. ft.	med cleaning 2,800 sq. ft.	heavy cleaning 2,000 sq. ft.

(When estimating square footage, consider only the areas you will actually clean.)
Other business operation costs:
   Vehicle—charge 25¢ a mile
   Overhead—add 5% to your total bid to cover phone, advertising, etc.
   Daily vacuuming, dusting, watering plants—add $8.50 per hour to the contract amount.

ness. On a bid job, you can earn twice as much money by the hour if you work twice as hard.

But unless the customer demands it, or the job is very small, never give a bid price at the time you go to look at a job. Leave the customer convinced that you're the best-qualified person for the job and that she'll miss out if she doesn't have you do the work. (Brag on yourself a little.) Return home, prepare the bid, and mail it to the customer. Handing the customer a bid and then standing and waiting for a decision creates an unpleasant atmosphere. Especially with large expenditures at stake, the customer likes to study the bid and think it over before making a commitment. A commitment given in haste or under pressure often develops into a bad customer relationship and affects the job and the promptness with which the bill is paid.

The proper conversation while the job is being estimated can make a big difference. If you can see that money is a problem at the moment, and if you know that her credit is good, let a prospective customer know that you're agreeable to arranging suitable terms. (Compensate for this in the bid.) Remember, jobs you consider small or common may be great and expensive decisions for some customers. Take your time, examine the whole job, and add your personal touch to the negotiations. Don't be an estimator who deals only with square footage and not with people. The personal touch can be one of the biggest factors in whether or not you get the job.

Helpful techniques in preparing a bid

When preparing a bid, itemize and describe clearly the service you will provide. Picture words and specifics are much more effective than the bare minimum of information. For example,

here are two ways a job could be described in a bid to paint a floor:

Example A
Painting porch floor, one coat gray enamel: $45.00

Example B
Preparation of complete rear porch floor area including light sanding, renailing protruding nails, removing all dust and foreign material, and applying one coat of Benjamin Moore Floor and Deck Enamel in Dover Gray color. Total cost: $44.50

Almost anyone would accept the second bid rather than the first because it appears to offer more for the money. "Preparation" is simply getting the area ready, and both bids include that. But Example B *tells* the customer about it. "Light sanding" means removing paint blisters or scaly areas, and "renailing protruding nails" may take three or four minutes. "Removing all dust and foreign material" just means sweeping the floor. Example A didn't even bother to tell the customer that the floor would be swept. "Applying" is a professional word; "painting" is Tom Sawyer stuff. Professional-sounding words in your bid will help sell the job.

For large or long-term jobs, submit your bid with a one-page standard contract agreement form. Most office-supply stores have them; your name can be stamped or printed on the blank form. Once a relationship of trust is established with a regular customer, a contract may not be necessary on every job.

Tips of the trade

Here are some of my "Key Management Secrets for Successful Residential Cleaning." These are the small things that help get a job done—and help keep a customer for life.

1. Don't lend or rent out your equipment. Few people know how to care for professional equipment, and a lost or damaged part can cost you a month's profit.

2. When bidding a job, project the idea: "We are professionals who can and will take care of your problems."

3. Be careful about bidding or giving prices by phone. Type of paint, condition, location, accessibility, and the personality of the client can all create a bidding problem if you don't look over a job in person.

4. Show up at the house dressed for the occasion. A clean uniform always makes a good impression.

5. Carry crisp business cards, a new dry sponge, a clean notepad. Everybody likes to be the first one.

6. Tell the customer what will clean and what won't. Don't say "if" or "maybe."

7. Point out any damage or problem subtly, but don't criticize sloppy painting or construction—chances are they or their grandpa did it.

8. With urine stains and smells—dogs, kids or other—advise the customer about permanent damage.

9. Look for more work as you go along. Mention it in a helpful way, without applying pressure. They'll appreciate it and gain confidence in you.

10. Always know beforehand who has the keys, how you'll get in and lock up, and who is authorized to be there.

11. Will there be water? Light? Heat? Don't make any assumptions about utilities—it can cost you all the profit.

12. Volunteer to repair things (touch up nicks, refinish doors, etc.) if you can do so profitably. If they hired you to clean, it's certain they'll need other chores done around the house.

13. Even if the job you're doing is inside, ask about exterior cleanup.

14. Problem items: Some appliances can take longer to clean than a $30 room, yet charges of more than $5 will stagger the customer. Kitchen floors can be much the same problem. Be careful.

15. If you send a crew, always designate one person as "the boss" so the owner only needs to communicate with that person. If about every hour "the boss" makes quick rounds, nodding and grunting a few corrections and/or praises, the homeowner will feel greatly relieved that someone is in command and that he or she will not have to inspect. "The boss" should also sell future jobs while there.

16. Even though the job is done, always list in detail the operations performed; this makes customers feel good and helps get future jobs.

17. Always do some extras at no charge; after you've finished the job, casually point them out. If the owner finds a speck or two after you're gone, he or she will be less likely to call.

18. Always lock the house if you leave and no one is there.

19. Use professional forms for equipment, material and operations.

20. Never, *never* arrive late.

One of the best and most complete books available on starting and running your own cleaning business is *Cleaning Up for a Living*, which I wrote with one of the sharpest minds in the business, Mark Browning. Both this book and a complete cleaning business startup kit (including models for all the forms and contracts you need) are available from The Cleaning Center, P.O. Box 39-H, Pocatello, Idaho 83204.

Your Reward: There *Is* Life After Housework

Well, that's it. We've covered enough aspects of housework to provide a fresher, more realistic view of the subject. And until a robot is developed that can be programmed to do your housework for you, you'll find the methods and equipment outlined in the foregoing chapters to be the next best thing for getting the most work done in the least amount of time.

Don't come unglued if you discover that even after applying all the best methods of housecleaning and home management, you sometimes experience the mundane realities of the profession. Every job has them, and housework is no exception. So brace yourself, and take it with a smile, for you too are vulnerable to slipping vacuum belts, flyspecked windows, plugged drains, sticky floors, ring around the collar, muddy boots, tidal waves of dirty laundry, and five dozen cookies to bake for the Halloween party (on two hours' notice).

But you've made tremendous progress! You've learned how to clean house faster and better. You've also seen the error of the notion that everything to do with cleaning and housework is dull, unglamorous and unrewarding.

I've been exposed to the same image you have of "the cleaner," and am still confronted with it every day. When I started my business while going to college, I received newspaper

write-ups and a lot of publicity, and everyone admired my cleaning activities—as long as they were leading to something else. When I finished my schooling and still remained a cleaner, my social prestige diminished greatly. Several little incidents brought this to my attention.

One time I was doing a special job in a bank, cleaning the vault floors with a buffer. Customers were drifting in and out of the lobby, casting pitying glances, as they usually do, at the "janitor." At the time I had five children and was deeply involved in community affairs—I was a Scout leader and was active in my church, I attended concerts and art shows, and I thought I was riding the tide of social prestige along with the rest of upstanding society. One of the bank's customers was irritably dragging her loud and disobedient child along when suddenly, in disgust, she grabbed the little fellow, shook him violently, and, gesturing toward me, said, "Behave, you little snot, or you'll end up just like him!"

As the years have gone by, I've found that woman's opinion of cleaning people is nearly universal. Whenever I mingle socially and my community work or other accomplishments are described, some newcomer will always ask, "Well, what does he do for a living?" A hesitation and silence follows every time, because nobody wants to say, "He's a cleaning man."

People who meet me on the street and remember me from the early days because of the publicity my housecleaning business received will inevitably ask, "Well, how are you, Don? What are you doing now? Are you still a. . . ." They always hesitate because they can't bring themselves to say "housecleaner."

While she was at college, my daughter Laura skied at the nearby resorts whenever she and her friends got the chance. Since she had the car that could haul the most skis and students, it was generally used as a taxi. After everyone was loaded in and they were off to the mountain, someone in all the chatter would always comment, "This is sure a nice car. What does your dad do for a living?" And Laura always answered cheerfully, "He's a janitor." The interior of the car would go silent for approximately three minutes, no one knowing what to say. Finally, in a politely patronizing voice, someone would say, "That's nice."

One of my managers, right after he was listed in *Who's Who in Technology Today in the U.S.A.*, was registering his wife at the hospital to have a baby. When the clerk asked him his occupation, he answered confidently, "Janitor." She looked up at him and said shyly, "Oh, come now. You don't really want me to put that down, do you?"

I could relate dozens of such stories, all hinging on the questionable status of being a "cleaning person." The image that society associates with cleaning—both in business and in the home—is totally incorrect.

I assure you, voting in a Senate chamber is no more important than cleaning a bed chamber! A glittering five-star restaurant has no more vital things take place in it than your ordinary, everyday kitchen. The home is the most sacred and exciting place on the face of the earth. For anyone to pronounce that caring for a home is a hardship, a drag and a bore is only to admit a lack of imagination. Those who clean and care for a house, whether on a full-time basis or in addition to another career, can get great satisfaction from it.

Remember, though, that a house is to live in, not live for. Cleanliness is very important, but it should never become all-important. There is merit in being meticulous, in adding that extra touch of excellence to your efforts, but there is also room for caution here: Our zeal to achieve superior results can become slavish devotion to meaningless detail.

Homes are more than showcases and status symbols. Your home is the background against which your life is lived, your retreat from the world's buffetings. Why direct all your efforts toward impressing society? There's great fun and satisfaction in giving yourself to your surroundings, and in making your home a pleasing reflection of your personality and interests.

People will enjoy coming to your house, not because of its impressive trappings and expensive adornments, but because so much of *you* is there.

Personal freedom is life's real reward. Housework is an important and worthy endeavor, but the less of your life it requires, the more will be available for other pursuits that add dimension and joy and meaning to living. Housework may have become your responsibility, but it is not your destiny. Your real role in the home goes far beyond housework.

Pulpit, pedestal or poetry cannot enrich the lives of others like a clean, happy, well-organized home life can. Humankind needs examples of order and confidence, and both of these virtues can be superbly exemplified in the home.

Children, and grown-ups too, need order in their lives. A feeling of contentment, comfort and well-being grows out of neatness and order, not clutter and chaos. Self-esteem and achievement germinate in a quality environment, and no environment is more influential than the home. Our home atmosphere has a great influence on all of us—it can affect lives far more than any movie star, president, or professor. The spirit of our home can touch and change not only all those who enter and all who live there, but our own close personal relationships. It can make us irresistible as people — someone not just to be needed, but loved and appreciated.

The home is the power lever of the world, and *you* control it.

Why do we mind the time spent cleaning?

The whole thrust of humankind is to do, build or create something that will last forever—be it a family, a reputation, a building, a poem or a pyramid. We want something that will last, maybe for thousands or tens of thousands of years, to testify to our lives of hard work and inspiration. . . .

And then there is housework—especially cleaning. We spend many (including some of the best) hours of our life making something beautiful and presentable—a glossy floor or sparkling windows, a dust-free curio cabinet or lint-free living room rug—then a few hours or a few days and little appreciation later it's gone, and we're right back where we began. We size it all up, the thirty or forty tasks that we do over and over each day, and think, "I should look forward to doing *this*?"

Yes, and here's why: When it seems you've been unjustly stuck with cleaning up behind someone or some-

thing, think past that dirty pad—launch pad, I mean. There's always cleanup after launching any worthwhile project. As a giant life-enhancing cargo is launched into space to impact the world with scientific excitement and information, we hear and read about this great accomplishment, yet it rarely occurs to us that it left a dirty launchpad behind. Yes, getting that payload raised and up and out left the place blackened, sooted, smoked, scratched and scummy, just like getting a family launched into life. Great meals, great buildings, great novels, bumper crops and crown jewels all create some dust and mess getting the job done. Cleaning it up is not only worthwhile, it's actually part and parcel of the end result. Cleaning affects the quality of life much more than parties, socials, entertainments, vacations, etc., and look at all the effort

and money we pour into them. So just think as you clean up, "This is not the aftermath, but the launch.... I'm preparing for the lift-off of great things."

When you think of the impact, the accomplishments of the "clean" you've created in your life, when you focus on the end result, cleaning feels good and necessary and even noble.

Not for women only . . .

Managing the home usually ends up being a woman's responsibility, not necessarily because she is a woman, but because no one else can or will do it as well. Some men think they can, but they can't.

If mechanics were all that was involved in homemaking, men might be as good at it as women are. But when it comes to bringing out the charm of a room, or adding the beauty and special warmth that make a clean home more than just a clean house . . . well, that transcends the realm of applied science or mechanics, and I'll admit without reservation—that usually takes a woman!

It's not surprising that men were for so long the ones out in the world plowing the fields, sailing the ships, operating the machines, and haggling in the business world. With brawn and a little brains, men can be taught to handle those things.

But the home is where we need the artists—the greatest concentration of intellect and sensitivity, creativity and devotion. It's the home front that needs the natural diplomats and the real multifaceted managers.

It is a delight and a marvel to see what a woman can do with a house. I'm continually in awe of a woman's ability to make things inviting with cheerful decorating ideas, imaginative color schemes, plants and flowers, and

Maybe some day cleaning will be part of male fantasy.

all the special little touches that have such a pleasant and positive influence upon our moods and senses.

In teaching, marriage counseling, and employing thousands of people, I have found that women are special! On speaking assignments, for example, I've faced every size and type of audience imaginable, but every time I face an audience of women, I feel a great deal of warmth and compassion. It is real and it radiates from women in a way that it doesn't from men. Many a philosopher and psychologist has tried to convince me that women are as mean, evil, scheming, and lazy as men, but I'm positive the philosophers and psychologists are wrong. I grew up in a good home, and my sister, mother, aunts, and grandmothers were all beautiful, positive people. I was eighteen before I ever heard a woman swear. The longer I live, the more apt I am to place a woman on a pedestal.

If you are not experiencing exhilaration from your role as a homemaker, it may be because your family has so much emotional and physical clutter that they can't reach each other to give love and appreciation. There is no greater goal or achievement on the face of the earth than the opportunity

to love and in turn be loved. Thrashing around in the clutter of a home too often thwarts the opportunity to achieve this. Skilled, efficient house care will take fewer hours, fewer supplies, fewer repairs, will prevent tension, and will give us more room and a greater capacity to grow into new friendships and experiences. First things first. *Living* is life . . . and we want to have as much of it as possible after housework!

You can save about 75 percent of the time, tools and money you spend on cleaning if you use the methods and materials the professionals do— and if you face the ultimate problem of housework:

Ninety percent of housework is caused by men and children and...

ninety percent of the work is done by women.

If they're old enough to *mess* up, they're old enough to *clean* up. Remember that your resources include your family's ability to pick up after themselves and otherwise help out.

What you used to see as the thankless chores of housework might well be some of your greatest teaching moments. Remember the potential lesson to be taught the next time you (1) spend four hours preparing a lovely family dinner and end up with only a three-foot stack of dirty dishes; (2) spend sixteen hours sewing a satin drill team costume and are rewarded with a whimper about the hemline; (3) proudly present a fat, tidy row of freshly ironed white shirts and he says, "Where's my blue one?"; (4) are on duty around the clock nursing the family through a siege of the flu, yet when it's your turn to collapse into a sickbed, there's not a soul around to nurse you; (5) know the kids are home by the trail of coats and books left in their wake or by the jam and peanut butter and empty glasses covering the counter.

Remember, if you don't teach them, who will?

It's not a woman's job to clean, but tradition takes time to change. Millions of readers have gotten quite a chuckle from chapter four's observations on getting help from husbands and children, and this is probably still the case in the majority of homes across the country—but it's a slowly shrinking majority. There are ever more enlightened men out there who've always liked things clean but wanted an efficient way to accomplish it without making it a full-time job—they've found life after housework and are giving it to their offspring and mates. I give a standing ovation to the rising minority of homes where everyone takes care of him- or herself and is not dependent on Mom to pick up and take care of everything. Cleaning isn't women's work, it's the work of those who created the need for it, and I promise you I won't rest until that truth is taught to all and practiced by most. One day, if you hang in there, you will start hearing "our washer," "our fridge," "our sink," and "my vacuum," instead of the feminine labeling of all cleaning tools so popular for so long now. Help me out; give cleaning books (or a copy of *Who Says It's A Woman's Job to Clean?*) to the groom, the athlete, the son, the engineer, the father. It's slow, but you watch: It will work. I see a change coming.

THERE IS LIFE AFTER HOUSEWORK!

About the Author

Don Aslett isn't just convinced that there is life after housework: He champions the belief that there is life everywhere every minute, and that everyone has a sacred obligation to take full advantage of it. Since his birth in a small town in southern Idaho, Don has pursued every channel of opportunity available to him. Teachers wrote on his grade-school report cards, "He intensely takes over and never runs out of energy." At age fifteen his parents taught and then assigned him to operate eighty acres of the family farm; he still found time to participate enthusiastically in high-school athletics, school government, and church and community projects. Don left the farm for college knowing how to work for the other guy, but found it unchallenging—and so launched his own career in cleaning, organizing a group of college students into a professional house-cleaning and building maintenance company called Varsity Contractors.

But Don's first love, writing, was never dormant. Throughout the years of building a family and a business, he amassed volumes of notes on a unique variety of subject matter. In 1979, at the request of thousands of homemakers who wanted his housecleaning seminar information in writing, he wrote *Is There Life After Housework?*; the first edition alone sold half a million copies in the United States and England and was translated into German, Dutch, French, Swedish and Hebrew. In 1982, Don followed with *Do I Dust or Vacuum First?*, and in 1984, *Clutter's Last Stand*. In the years since, "America's Number One Cleaning Expert" has authored several bestselling books on cleaning and decluttering, from *Who Says It's a Woman's Job to Clean* to *Make Your House Do the Housework* to *How to Handle 1,000 Things at Once.*

Today, Don is chairman of the board of Varsity Contractors, a multimillion-dollar enterprise that now operates in twenty states, and the owner of a maintenance consulting company. Don is a popular youth speaker and leader, devoting much of his time to family, church and scouting. He and his wife Barbara live in the world's first maintenance-free house in Kauai, Hawaii, but they still spend much of the year at the Idaho mountain ranch on which they raised their six children and numerous foster children—who now visit regularly with *their* children.